PC NORTHWEST, INC.
7912 S.E. 13th
P.O. BOX 82175
PORTLAND, OR 97282

Hal Morgan
*and*
Kerry Tucker

A FIRESIDE BOOK
Published by Simon & Schuster
New York London Toronto Sydney Tokyo Singapore

# COMPANIES THAT CARE

The Most Family-Friendly
Companies in America—
What They Offer and How They
Got That Way

Simon & Schuster/Fireside
Simon & Schuster Building
Rockefeller Center
1230 Avenue of the Americas
New York, New York 10020

Designed by Black Angus Design Group.
Manufactured in the United States of America

10  9  8  7  6  5  4  3  2  1
10  9  8  7  6  5  4  3  2  1  PBK

Library of Congress Cataloging in Publication Data
Morgan, Hal.
     Companies that care : the most family-oriented companies in
  America, what they offer, and how they got that way / Hal Morgan and
  Kerry Tucker.
        p.   cm.
     "A Fireside book."
     Includes index.
     1. Employer-supported day care—United States—Directories.
  2. Employee fringe benefits—United States—Directories.
  3. Parental leave—United States—Directories.   4. Work and family—
  United States.   I. Title.
  HF5549.5.D39M67   1991
  331.25—dc20                                              91-6655
                                                              CIP

ISBN 0-671-74101-2
      0-671-73598-5 (pbk)

# Acknowledgments

Although just two names appear on the cover of this book, and the words and opinions expressed are our own, we could not have completed this project without help from many quarters. Greatest thanks are due to the people at the many companies we contacted in the course of our research: to the employees who agreed to be interviewed and whom we have quoted anonymously throughout; to the managers and human-resource executives, both at the companies we included and at those we did not, who took the time to answer our questions and shed light on their organizations' policies; and to the directors and staff of the child-care centers we visited, who took time from their busy schedules to show us around and to talk.

We would like to thank the many experts who guided us in our search for companies, who helped us as we worked to define the issues and our standards of judgment, and who contributed to our historical research. Special thanks are due to Gwen Morgan, Fran Rodgers, and Beth Fredericks, of Work/Family Directions, and Ellen Galinsky and Dana Friedman, of the Families and Work Institute, for their insights throughout the project and for their critical review of parts of the text, and to Dr. Andrew Scharlach, Dianne Piktialis at Work/Family Elder Directions, and Milt Hansen at the Institute for Creative Aging for sharing their knowledge of elder-care matters. Many of the companies included in the book were brought to our attention by child-care and work-and-family consultants throughout the country, and while it would take up too much room to credit everyone who contributed, we would like to extend thanks to Margie Curry at Child Care Resources in Birmingham, Alabama; Kathleen Martin at Corporate Child Care Consultants, also in Birmingham; Glenda Bean in the Governor's Office in Arkansas; Patty Seigal at the California Child Care Resource and Referral Network; Ron Garner at Child, Youth & Family Services in Los Angeles; Judy David at One Small Step in San Francisco; Karen Hill-Scott at Crystal Stairs in Los Angeles; Liza Lidke at National Employee Benefit Consultants in Denver; Dianne Warner at the Connecticut Department of Education; Phoebe Carpenter at 4C for Central Florida, and Couny Madison, formerly at that agency; Ruth Anne Foote at Child Care Solutions in Atlanta; Barbara Morgan at PATCH in Honolulu; Cass Wolfe at the Day Care Action

Council of Illinois; Mary Kay McGuire at Jane Addams Hull House in Chicago; Karen King at the Polk County Child Care Resource Center in Des Moines, Iowa; Elizabeth Grever at Community Coordinated Child Care in Louisville, Kentucky; Dianne Stetson at the Office of Child Care Coordinator, State of Maine; Jaqueline Townes at Child Care in the Workplace, Montgomery County, Maryland; Chris Dillon in the Executive Office for Economic Affairs, Commonwealth of Massachusetts; Linda Mills of Mills & Pardee; Jean Holbrook at Child Care Connection in Worcester, Massachusetts; Leslie de Pietro at the Michigan 4C Association in Lansing; Cora Visscher at Ottawa County 4C; Michigan State Representative Lyn Bankes; Constance C. Bell at the Greater Minneapolis Day Care Association; David Allen at Resources for Child Caring in St. Paul, Minnesota; Sue Vartuli at the University of Missouri at Kansas City; Donald Checkett at the Child Day Care Association in St. Louis; Helen Wilson at Child and Family Services of New Hampshire; Kathleen Ross at Children's Services, Morris County, New Jersey; Marlene Weinstein at Resources for Child Care Management; Nancy Kolben at Child Care Inc. in New York City; Louise Stoney at the New York State Day Care Coordinating Council; Patricia Fisher at the Greater Syracuse Chamber of Commerce; Marjorie Warlick at Child Care Resources, Inc., in Charlotte, North Carolina; Stephanie Fanjul at Workplace Options in Raleigh, North Carolina; Lynda Staycer at the Center for Human Services in Cleveland; Mary Kerrigan at the Akron YMCA; Beth Sliwowski in the Ohio Governor's Office; Elisabeth Bryenton at Child Care Insights—Elder Care Insights in Cleveland; Leslie Faught at Northwest Family Network in Portland, Oregon; Janis Elliot in the Oregon Department of Human Resources; Elizabeth Werthan at CHOICE in Philadelphia; Martha Isler at Employers and Child Care in Pittsburgh; Gail Johnson at Options for Working Parents in Providence, Rhode Island; Dr. Jean James at Greenville's Child in Greenville, South Carolina; Susan Kruk at Initiatives for Children in Houston, Texas; Michael Rush at Austin Families; Roberta Bergman at Child Care Dallas; Andrea Van Hoven at the Child Care Resource and Referral Center in Burlington, Vermont; Therese Keegan at the Employer Child Care Council in Arlington, Virginia; Deborah Robbins at Child and Family Resource and Referral in Seattle; John Briehl at the Department of Human Development, City of Tacoma; Marsha Holand at the Business Assistance Center, State of Washington; Lori Ohmes at 4C of Milwaukee County, Milwaukee, Wisconsin; and Patricia Mapp at the Children's Audit Project, University of Wisconsin/Extension.

# Contents

# Introduction

Ellen, an engineer at IBM, has had four children over the past ten years and for the birth of each has taken a yearlong leave. She is happy with her career progress, and when she returns from her current leave will come back to the same job she left several months ago, supervising a team of engineers.

Tina, a software developer at SAS Institute in Cary, North Carolina, brings her daughter to work with her every day and leaves her at the company's 350-child day-care center. She pays only for her daughter's lunches; the care is provided as a completely free benefit to employees. When pressed for time, she sometimes purchases inexpensive take-home dinners from the company's subsidized cafeteria.

George, a senior bond trader at NCNB Corporation, in Charlotte, North Carolina, took a one-month paternity leave when his first child was born, to fill in between his wife's return to work and the arrival of an *au pair*. He was pleased with the leave, his managers are pleased with his work performance, and when his next child arrives he plans to take an even longer leave, this time taking advantage of the company's new paid paternity leave policy.

Susan, a marketing analyst at S. C. Johnson & Son, in Racine, Wisconsin, has two children who have outgrown the company's near-site child-care center. When the younger one entered school, she shifted to a part-time schedule and now leaves work in time to pick them up from school every day. Even with her reduced schedule, she still receives high-level assignments and recently turned down an offer for a full-time management position.

Tom, a manager at Fel-Pro, in Skokie, Illinois, lives with his elderly mother. Several months ago she fell and broke her arm, and suddenly required full-time care. He called the company's emergency care-giver service, which sent someone to his home during the day while he worked, until his mother's arm had recovered enough that she could stay by herself. The company paid three-quarters of the service's fee. Tom has since hired the same care giver himself, so that he could take his first weekend away from home in seven years.

Although these stories may sound too good to be true, like fantasies of how companies should treat their employees, they are all real examples. All are people we spoke with during our research for this book, and they are just a small sampling of the positive stories we encountered. They are also part of a dramatically growing trend in American business. If your company isn't doing much to support the working parents on its staff, or its employees who have elder-care responsibilities, chances are it is thinking about doing something soon. It is probably aware that competing companies are reacting to the changing realities of the workplace, and that in order to attract and keep the best workers, it too will have to become more responsive to the family needs of its workers.

The once-typical American family, with a father at the office and a mother at home with the children, has become the exception rather than the rule. Just one family in ten fits that profile today. Two-income couples have become the norm, and single-parent households have become far more common. More than half of all mothers now return to work before their children are a year old, and almost three out of four mothers of school-age children are in the work force. Farsighted companies understand the importance of those sweeping societal changes and are responding with greater flexibility and helpful support programs. Given the breadth of the changes, it is surprising that so many companies have *not* reacted.

Companies with rigid managers, unbending scheduling policies, no leave allowances, and no child-care or elder-care support programs, while the norm through the 1980s, may soon find it increasingly difficult to attract and keep good workers. One company explained to us that it offers only the minimum maternity leave required by law in its state, for fear of losing "competitive advantage" with the decreased productivity and efficiency caused by long absences. This company and others that cling to that argument may soon be outnumbered by companies that find a competitive edge by offering more progressive policies that attract and retain talented and loyal employees. More and more companies are realizing that by offering flexibility, understanding, and help with key family issues they can strengthen their organizations and increase profits.

Family-sensitive policies can help companies attract quality people, both men and women; support systems can help those workers focus on their jobs; and corporate cultures that value people with family responsibilities and understand their needs are rewarded by reduced turnover and tremendous savings in recruitment and training. All over the country, businesses are discovering that it pays to create family-friendly work environments.

In the course of our research we talked to executives and

employees at more than three hundred companies recommended to us by child-care and other work-and-family experts in every state in the country. In order to get a sense of the problems the progressive companies are addressing, we also sought out employees who have had difficult experiences with work-and-family conflicts at less responsive companies. We heard hundreds of positive stories, and found scores of companies meeting the challenges of the modern work force in a variety of ways. We also heard plenty of horror stories.

The examples given above of the policies and programs at IBM, SAS Institute, NCNB, S. C. Johnson & Son, and Fel-Pro are among the shining examples we found. Others include:

- Stride Rite, in Cambridge, Massachusetts, which has offered on-site child care to its workers since 1971, and in 1990 added an elder day-care wing at one center, with a common area for intergenerational activities.
- Merck & Co., which has had an eighteen-month parental leave policy since the 1960s, has supported a parent-run child-care center near its Rahway, New Jersey, headquarters since 1980, and has recently extended support to additional centers in West Point, Pennsylvania, and Reddington, New Jersey, and to a program that pays for the care of employees' mildly ill children.
- Joy Cone, in Hermitage, Pennsylvania, which has offered split shifts and flexible shift assignments at its factory for more than twenty years.
- Arthur Andersen & Co., the only big-eight accounting firm to pride itself on the number of part-time professionals on its staff, and the only one to offer Saturday child care during the tax season.
- United States Hosiery Corporation, in Lincolnton, North Carolina, which answered the critical need for quality child care in its area by spearheading a model consortium center, complete with a sick room for mildly ill children, and hours that accommodate both first- and second-shift workers.
- Lotus Development Corp., in Cambridge, Massachusetts, which offers a month of paid parenting leave to mothers, fathers, and adoptive parents—even grandparents in some circumstances.
- Johnson & Johnson, which has launched an effort to reshape its corporate culture to be more responsive to employees' family needs, capped by the construction of a $5.8 million child-care center at headquarters, and the revision of the "corporate credo," an important expression of the company's

basic beliefs—it now includes the statement, "We must be mindful of ways to help our employees fulfill their family obligations."

*Work-and-family benefits: the trend of the 1990s*
As a result of our personal observations of work-and-family conflict among our friends, and our occasional reading of newspaper and magazine articles about companies that have responded with child-care supports and other initiatives, we decided to compile a directory of the most family-supportive employers around the country. In our selection process we looked at what the companies are doing with child-care and elder-care benefits, with leave policies, with flexible work options such as part-time work and flexible work hours, and with methods of making managers more sensitive to family needs. We have only included those businesses that are committed to comprehensive programs of flexibility and support.

We found companies of every size, in every region of the country, and in almost every industry moving forward to meet the challenges posed by the work force of the 1990s. We also found that these businesses are a part of a growing trend. Of the one hundred twenty-four companies cited in this book, at least thirty would not have been included had we compiled the list three years ago. Had we written the book five years ago, we would have been hard-pressed to come up with fifty names. The fact is that the American workplace is in the early stages of a fundamental revolution, brought on by the steady increase in the numbers of women workers over the past several decades.

Most companies are well aware of this trend toward answering the needs of the new work force. While still in its early stages, the movement shows signs of explosive growth. In 1970, for example, just fewer than two hundred employers around the country offered any sort of child-care benefit, and most of these were hospitals with their own on-site centers. By 1990, with a much wider array of child-care benefits to choose from, the number had climbed into the thousands. That figure is still insubstantial when measured against the total number of employers in the country—approximately six million—but those in charge of personnel policies at most companies have taken note of the trend. A survey of Wisconsin employers in 1989 showed that only one in ten offered child-care benefits, but more than half had child-care plans on the table.

Employees have been a little slower to catch on to this trend. Just as people have learned to investigate vacation policies, insurance benefits, and opportunities for advancement before accepting a job, so must they learn to look for family-care benefits.

And just as workers at companies have strived for better wages and standard benefits such as pensions, they must also learn to ask for better work-and-family policies.

## Work-and-family conflict: a problem for employers and employees

Advisers on work-and-family conflict have traditionally focused on how parents can alter their behavior or reset their own goals to accommodate conflicting demands. They have focused on stress-reduction techniques, on ways to manage family matters with greater efficiency, and on the idea that it may be impossible to have it all at the same time—a full-time, hard-driving career and a satisfying family life. That advice certainly has merit, and most of us can certainly benefit from rethinking our goals and managing our time more efficiently. But that approach tends to overlook a key player in the game: the employer. If a manager refuses to give us time off when our children are sick, how can we continue to feel like good parents? And how can we contribute effectively at work, knowing that our children are alone and sick at home? If a parenting expert recommends that we take at least four months off after the birth of a child in order to establish a strong and trusting relationship with a new infant, yet our company allows just six weeks of leave, how are we to achieve that balance between work and family? How are we to feel good about our dual roles as parents and employees? And if we are threatened with losing our jobs when we take time off from work to make necessary arrangements for an ailing parent, how are we to act as responsible family members while maintaining our loyalty to our employers and our enthusiasm for our jobs?

In the course of our research we interviewed dozens of people who had left jobs because of work-and-family conflicts. Some had left when the stress of the conflicts or the guilt of ignoring their children became too great; some left after seeing how the company treated others. And, contrary to popular assumptions, not all were women. We interviewed a number of men who had changed jobs in order to have more time for family and personal pursuits.

A few examples will give some sense of the conflicts that the more progressive companies are trying to address with their work-and-family programs.

Susan D., a financial analyst for ten years with a major oil company, finally left her job when she decided the company and her managers would never treat her fairly as both a parent and an employee:

*Eight years ago, my husband and I adopted our first child. We found out that she was coming about six weeks before she arrived, and as soon as we got the news, I went right in to my manager and said, "We're going to get this baby. I want to take some time off." They thought about it for more than five weeks, and finally told me the day before she arrived that I would be allowed to take two weeks off without pay. That was very hard, and to this day I regret having accepted it. She was an older child. She had spent eight months with her biological mother and five months in an orphanage. She needed a parent at home longer than two weeks. To this day I regret my decision to go back so soon.*

*Over the years, through the adoption of another son, and through one family emergency and another, the company has remained very rigid and inflexible. Last summer, for example, we had a storm with a fantastic amount of rain. It created floods all over the area. My children were at camp that morning, and I knew they had nowhere to get inside, just an overhead canopy. As I drove in to work, I saw that the water had come up to the bridge over the river, and I realized that if I didn't go get them and they closed the camp, I wouldn't be able to get to them. Now my daughter had suffered fairly severe psychological trauma as a result of early childhood experiences, and I did not want her to be troubled and fearful of what was going to happen next. So I turned around and went back and picked them up. By the time I'd got them and tried to come back to town, we could not get through. The roads were flooded. We went into a grocery store, which closed while I was there, and I called my supervisor to tell him what had happened. He told me that I was lying, that the roads were indeed open, and that I was using this as an excuse. That made me kind of angry. I'd been working at the company for ten years, and I'm not the kind of person to slough off an accusation like that.*

*After about two hours the waters receded enough that we could get through, and I brought the children into the office with me. When we got there my supervisor told me I had no business bringing the kids to the office, and that I had no business coming in late. And it came out in my review this year. I can remember it word for word. "If you continue to place your family ahead of the company, we will consider that you take your job less than seriously, and your professional career will stop."*

*I finally put a stop to that career myself, by taking a*

*job at another company, but I still look back with frustra-
tion at my ten years there. I loved my work—I was involved
in it and did enjoy it—but my children will always come
first. My children have to come first.*

Lauren S., an executive at a software company, broke ground
by becoming the first female manager at her company to have
a child, but after seven years she finally gave up the struggle and
left for a more accommodating employer:

> *There was really nothing antifamily about the com-
> pany. In fact, the formal policies were pretty good. But there
> was a cultural attitude that kept families out of the picture.
> We had to pretend that our families didn't exist. For ex-
> ample, I can remember not bringing pictures of my son to
> the office when he was a baby, and not volunteering any
> information about him. I noticed very quickly that it was
> the secretaries, and never the other managers, who wanted
> to see pictures and know how he was doing. It was an
> attitude thing: if you cared about your baby then you
> couldn't be serious about your job.*
>
> *On one level my career was not at all hurt by my having
> a child. Before I went on maternity leave I was given an
> important promotion, and after I came back I was made
> division manager. So it wasn't that being a mother was
> overtly discouraged, it was just that in no way was it en-
> couraged, nor was there any sensitivity to it at all. Every-
> body said, "Yes, we value our employees," but when it
> came down to what they did to value us, they did nothing.
> The personnel department said that they had a list of child-
> care facilities near the workplace. But when someone who
> worked with me inquired about it, she found out that they
> had a list of six. Two were closed and the other four were
> full. So although they said, "Yes, we do this," they weren't
> helpful at all.*
>
> *Then people would call after-hours meetings. At three
> o'clock they'd say, "We'll all meet together on this at five."
> And that put me in the very difficult position of making
> an issue of the fact that I had to leave because of my child-
> care arrangements, of saying, "I cannot stay." Nobody ever
> did that at my company. Sometimes my husband could
> leave early and cover for me, and sometimes we were able
> to make special arrangements with the care giver. She
> would sometimes keep our son until ten at night.*
>
> *Though it was very difficult all along, I didn't end up
> leaving the job until my son was in school. Having a child*

*in school complicates things—it doesn't make them easier. You need a care giver in addition to school because of the short hours. You need transportation in the middle of the day. You find out on Monday that there's a teacher conference on Wednesday. The school closes when it snows. Our school closed one day because a skunk had walked into the cafeteria. You have to go through this entire system of having a baby-sitter, a backup baby-sitter, and a backup for the backup. You find yourself scurrying around making endless phone calls, all of which takes time away from work. But we handled all of those problems. I just didn't realize until after I left how exhausting it had all been.*

Employees often leave after watching how the company treats other people, and one supervisor's response to a situation may have far-reaching effects. One woman, who now works for a publishing company, left her former job largely because of its treatment of other workers. She is now in a position to decide whether to award business to her former employer:

*Before I came here I worked at an insurance agency in town, with about thirty-five people, most of them women. At the time I didn't have children, so I didn't have to confront those issues. But a lot of the other workers there did have families, and we tried to get the agency to allow flextime and job sharing. And they were totally unresponsive. Several women ended up quitting, particularly after they had a second child, because the company just couldn't accommodate any kind of modification to their schedules. I think the managers felt like they had their pick of employees, and that we should all be grateful to them for our jobs. It's sad, because initially I had a very good attitude about working there. But that just deteriorated as I watched how they handled their relations with their employees. I'm now in kind of a sweet position here, because that agency is soliciting our business, and I'm handling this company's insurance. They want to get in here in the worst possible way. It's kind of gratifying to be on the other side.*

Achieving a balance between work and family is almost always a difficult proposition, but it can be made close to impossible by an unresponsive employer. In order for it to succeed, workers have to find businesses and managers who are willing to act as partners in the effort.

The employee must do what he can to ensure that family

needs do not necessarily infringe on work. He must be sure that all care-giving alternatives are explored, that time is managed efficiently, and that other family members are doing what they can to meet family needs. But the employer and manager also have roles: to be flexible, to be accommodating and understanding when family needs do require time away from work, and to offer appropriate support for those who need help finding or paying for dependent care. Too often, companies and managers ignore their responsibilities to parents and care givers, retreating into the adage that family and work are distinct realms that should never overlap or interfere with each other. And too often, workers accept that outdated excuse and try to shoulder the entire burden themselves.

*Employer support systems: building on old ideas*
Many people assume that employer involvement in family issues is a recent concept, and that companies that offer flexibility and family support programs are ahead of their time. In fact, while some of the family benefits offered by employers today—such as elder-care referral services and pretax spending accounts—are inventions of the past decade, employer interest in aiding working mothers and their children is almost as old as the industrial revolution.

It was with the creation of the first factories and mills in the late eighteenth century that women began to work outside the home in any large numbers and that extended-family networks found in farming communities and in villages of family-run shops began to break down. With that change came some of the first ideas in the long debate over work-and-family issues—specifically over the role of women and children in the new society created by mass production. Alexander Hamilton, in a 1791 report to Congress on the need for large-scale industries, argued that "women and children are rendered more useful . . . by manufacturing establishments than they would otherwise be. . . ." The industrial revolution also brought the first company-sponsored child-care centers, and many ideas and models established almost two hundred years ago look remarkably like those surfacing as "innovative" concepts today.

Robert Owen, an English businessman, created what was probably the first employer-supported child-care center in this country at an industrial and farming community in New Harmony, Indiana, in 1825. Not much is known about that school, but a great deal of information survives about Owen's earlier child-care initiatives in Scotland.

In 1800, Owen took charge of a cotton-mill complex in New Lanark, Scotland, and over the next several years reorganized it into a social model for other industries. He reduced work hours, restricted child labor to those over ten years old, and, in 1816, created a company school open to all children over age one. No system of public education existed in Great Britain at the time, and Owen's school served not only the children of the factory community, but those who lived in a nearby village, some of whom had no connection at all to the mill. The school offered classes every evening for older children who worked in the mills, and for any adults who cared to attend. During its first year, more than 750 students enrolled.

The fact that Owen created a company-supported school and preschool for mill workers in 1816 is remarkable in itself. More astounding is the educational philosophy on which the school operated. "The children were not to be annoyed with books," Owen wrote of the younger classroom, "but were to be taught . . . by familiar conversation when [their] curiosity was excited so as to induce them to ask questions." Pictures of animals, maps, and objects collected in the woods and fields nearby helped to stimulate the children's curiosity and provide a starting point for lessons. Instructors were never to use harsh words with the younger children, and never to use artificial rewards and punishments with children of any age, but instead to rely on the natural pleasure of learning for incentive.

The school certainly provided the mill with educated and obedient workers, but it also helped the working mothers there. A visitor in 1818 noted that, "this baby school is of great consequence to the establishment, for it enables the mothers to shut up their houses in security, and to attend to their duties in the factory, without concern for their families." The emphasis on educational goals, and on reducing stress and worry so that parents could concentrate on their work, are key elements in most of today's child-care proposals, often brought up as if the ideas were new to the 1990s. Owen's goal of creating a widely followed model at New Lanark was not realized as fully as he might have liked, but his efforts were widely influential. Between 1816 and 1825, he received visitors at a rate of almost 30 a day—some 20,000 in all—among them businessmen and kings.

Owen moved on to create a similar industrial community and school in Indiana, in 1825. The New Lanark school served children at the Scottish factory until 1875, when Scotland created a comprehensive system of public schools, and much of the need for the classrooms disappeared.

The nineteenth century also saw the start of the kindergarten movement in Germany—begun as a system of educational preschools for the children of factory workers—and its spread to other countries, including the United States. In France, a corresponding system of preschools, called *crèches*, was created for young children of working mothers. Although the first of them, opened near Paris in 1844, was not associated with a specific business, a number of French industries sponsored crèches over the next few decades so that mothers could continue to nurse their babies while they worked. A "Miss Biddle" visited a crèche during a trip to Paris, and created a similar center for the children of working parents in Philadelphia during the Civil War. By the 1890s, settlement houses and charitable groups operated kindergartens (which were full-day centers, open to children as young as two) and day nurseries in a number of cities, many of them supported by business groups. The Ewa Sugar Company, for example, opened a free preschool for its plantation workers in Honolulu, Hawaii, in 1897, staffed by teachers trained in Friedrich Froebel's educational theories and in the newer ideas of John Dewey. The company established the school "with the understanding that all expenses connected with it should be paid, like other necessary plantation expenses, by the Plantation Company."

While charitable efforts in the nineteenth century concentrated on helping the poor to help themselves through work, that focus began to shift around 1900 to initiatives that encouraged mothers to stay home with their children, and that change has had a profound effect on child-care and other work-and-family efforts ever since. President Theodore Roosevelt, speaking in 1909 at the White House Conference on the Care of Dependent Children, gave clear voice to the new attitude: "Home life is the highest and finest product of civilization. It is the great molding force of mind and character. Children should not be deprived of it except for urgent and compelling reasons."

Jane Addams had founded a day nursery at the Hull House Settlement in Chicago in the 1890s to aid mothers who were, as she described it, "bent under the double burden of earning the money which supports them and giving their children the tender care which alone keeps them alive." But she began to question the good of her efforts in the early years of this century as she observed women struggling with the dual role of parent and breadwinner, and she joined in the political effort to convince government to pay mothers to stay home with their children. By 1910, her writings began to reflect that new approach, as she wondered whether it was right to "tempt" mothers to "attempt the impossible. . . . With all the efforts made by modern society to nurture and educate the young, how stupid it is to permit mothers of young children to spend themselves in the coarser work of the world! It is curiously inconsistent with the emphasis which this generation has placed upon the mother and upon the prolongation of infancy, that we constantly allow the waste of this most precious material." Another day nursery in Boston closed that same year, according to one critic of the nursery system, "because its promoters became convinced that it was doing more harm than good."

In the face of this growing societal ambivalence toward working mothers, the idealistic notions that had driven the child-care initiatives of the nineteenth century came to be viewed in a critical light. Along with measures outlawing child labor, the years around World War I also saw the introduction of "mothers' pensions"—state-funded welfare systems to support single mothers and mothers married to imprisoned, ill, or handicapped husbands. Those same years also saw the rise of social work as a profession, and with that professionalization came the strong influence of Freudian theories. One of the roles the new social workers played was to screen access to the day nurseries, to admit children of only the neediest mothers, since a mother's desire to work was now viewed as a pathology to be cured.

In spite of the negative attitudes shown toward them, mothers continued to work in growing numbers. The pension money was not universally available, and even when paid was often inadequate to support a family. And many mothers preferred work to a subsistence-level subsidy. In the years after World War I, women also began to enter the professions at an ever-increasing rate.

Probably because of the prevailing attitudes of the time, employer supports for child care and other family measures in this period were not recorded in any systematic way, and went largely unnoticed by the press. But some companies did respond. The Kellogg Company, in Battle Creek, Michigan, for example, opened a child-care center in 1924, because founder W. K. Kellogg thought that it would be "a service for working mothers." Open to children from one to six years old, it provided both first- and second-shift care (from 7:00 A.M. to 11:00 P.M.), medical and dental checkups, and an isolation room for children who were ill. All care and services were entirely free to the company's workers. The company changed to six-hour shifts in the early months of the Depression, and perhaps in response to that change, perhaps to other changes in the work force, enrollment declined and the center closed in 1932.

World War II saw another surge of employer interest in family concerns, and an intriguing lapse in the popular disapproval of working mothers. Because men were pulled from industry for military service, and because the war effort required increased output, businesses actively recruited women workers. Among the new laborers were hundreds of thousands of mothers with

young children. The new women workers were hailed in prop-
aganda newsreels, and touted as the answer to the labor shortage
on the home front. But they brought with them a fair share of
problems for American industry. One Michigan defense plant
found that 15 percent of the mothers on its payroll missed work
because of child-care problems, the Douglas Aircraft Corporation
in Los Angeles complained of high absenteeism during school
vacations, and newspapers regularly turned up shocking stories
of children left in parked cars or locked rooms while their mothers worked on the production lines.

The federal government provided some money to help communities expand child-care services during the war, but some of
the most effective and innovative efforts came from the industries themselves. Among the businesses that created child-care
centers in the war years were a tent and uniform factory in
Cleveland, Ohio, a tank plant in Peoria, Illinois, and the Curtiss-
Wright Corporation in Buffalo.

Kaiser Industries created child-care centers at two of its ship-
building plants in Oregon, and though they have been closed for
almost fifty years now, they remain among the best examples
of business support for parents and children. At their peak, in
1944, the two centers provided twenty-four-hour care for more
than 1,000 children. They focused on quality care and education
by hiring skilled teachers and paying them well; but they also
tried, perhaps more than any corporate child-care centers since,
to help parents concentrate both on their work and on their
families. Not only did the centers offer a comprehensive child-
care program—including afterschool and vacation care for older
children, infirmaries for the care of mildly ill children, flexibility
for parents who needed to alter their work hours, and a strong
educational program—they offered a long list of support services
for parents. The centers' kitchens prepared take-home meals, a
mending service patched and repaired clothes while parents
worked, a staff shopper did errands for parents, and an appointment service arranged for and took children to dental and medical checkups. No corporate child-care center, before or since,
has offered such a supportive program for working parents, and
Kaiser was probably only able to do it because, in the exigencies
of wartime, the expenses could be built into manufacturing costs
billed to the government.

After the war, many women left their industrial jobs, federal
support for child care was cut off, and the war-industry child-
care centers closed. Popular disapproval of working mothers re-
sumed as well, as voiced by Dr. Benjamin Spock in his 1945 book
*The Common Sense Book of Baby and Child Care* (a passage
reprinted in editions through the 1950s): ". . . useful, well-

adjusted citizens are the most valuable possessions a country has, and good mother care during early childhood is the surest way to produce them. It doesn't make sense to let mothers go to work making dresses in factories or tapping typewriters in offices, and have them pay other people to do a poorer job of bringing up their children." But, contrary to popular notions, women did not abandon the labor force in wholesale numbers as men returned from the war. Two-thirds of the women who worked during the war had been working before, and more than three-quarters continued to work after the war's end. When the United Auto Workers surveyed its female members in 1944 it found that 85 percent of them wanted to keep their jobs after the war.

Evidence of continued employer interest in child care through the 1940s and 1950s can be found in a few centers that have survived from this period, among them one at Riverside Hospital in Toledo, Ohio, which has been caring for the children of hospital employees since 1942. Other companies, like IBM— which has a long history of race- and sex-blind employment practices—responded to the needs of working parents with generous leave policies.

The 1960s saw a renewed public interest in child-care programs as a part of the antipoverty efforts of the Great Society, its most successful and visible result being Project Head Start, launched in 1965 with goals very similar to those propounded by Robert Owen 150 years earlier—to break the cycle of poverty by educating young children in order to help them realize their full potential. Many of the company-supported child-care initiatives of the period reflected the antipoverty sentiments of the time. KLH, a stereo-equipment manufacturer in Cambridge, Massachusetts, opened an educational child-care center in 1968 to serve a largely immigrant and minority employee population. Stride Rite, the Cambridge-based children's shoe manufacturer, started its center in 1971 as a charitable effort to aid children in the poor and largely black community near its Roxbury, Massachusetts, plant; only after it was opened did it begin to consider the center as an employee benefit as well. And Polaroid Corp., also in Cambridge, introduced a child-care subsidy program in 1971 which reimbursed workers for a portion of their child-care expenses, the greatest funding concentrated on lower-income employees.

Nineteen seventy-one also saw President Nixon's veto of the Comprehensive Child Development Act, the first major piece of federal legislation since 1946 to propose public funding to help both low- and moderate-income parents pay for child care, and to help expand the supply of educational preschool programs.

Congress failed to override the veto, and with George Bush's veto of the Family and Medical Leave Act in 1990, the United States remains the only industrialized country in the world with no national child-care support system, and with no guarantees of time off from work for the birth of a child or for serious family illness. Without federal support systems, working parents in the United States must rely on scattered state mandates and programs, and on the policies of individual employers. The importance of employer policies can be seen in the fact that just fifteen states had any family-leave laws on their books in 1990, and several of those applied only to state workers.

During the 1970s and 1980s, the trickle of employer efforts to help working parents grew into a small stream, and in the 1990s it seems about to swell into a flood. The number of companies offering child-care assistance to their employees, for example, grew from fewer than two hundred in 1971 to more than 5,000 in 1990. Today, as in World War II, more and more companies are trying to attract and keep women workers because they need them. But today, unlike fifty years ago, companies are responding with long-term initiatives, with the understanding that women workers are here to stay. And today, unlike in the 1940s, employers are responding to the needs of men as well as women with their family-care measures, and to a broader set of employee demands. Workers today want greater flexibility; they want help with both child care and elder care; and they want management to recognize that family demands often take priority over the demands of work.

*Today's work-and-family crisis: why business is responding*
Companies in the 1990s are taking great leaps forward in providing flexibility, longer leaves, and greater child-care and elder-care supports. The business decision-makers we spoke to offered four basic reasons:

1. *The composition of the work force has changed, and along with that change has come a shift in employees' attitudes toward work.* The old stereotype of the male worker, devoted to the company for life, with a nonworking wife at home to take care of the children and other family, has become an anachronism. The decades-long trend toward greater numbers of women in the work force has finally reached a sort of critical point, where many companies feel they *have* to respond. At Warner Lambert, to give just one example, the percentage of women workers rose from 29 to 45 percent in the six years between 1984 and 1990.

That massive shift has brought other, equally dramatic, changes to the work force. As more and more women accept work as a normal part of their lives, more and more men have had to adjust to family life with working wives. When couples have children, men are often forced to play a greater role in child rearing and other household tasks because their wives no longer have the time to do it all. And many men today *want* to play a greater role in child rearing. The same movement toward toppling sexual stereotypes that has brought women into the work force has freed men to play a greater role in the home. A 1990 poll by Robert Half International, an executive recruiting firm, showed that more than half of the men surveyed would be willing to cut their salaries as much as 25 percent to have more family or personal time. Almost as many said they would turn down a promotion if it meant spending less time with their families.

In the 1980s, companies also began to recognize elder care as a widespread concern of employees. One advocacy group estimates that the average woman will spend seventeen years caring for children and another eighteen caring for elderly relatives. Company surveys repeatedly turn up remarkably high percentages of employees who have responsibility for the care of elderly relatives. The Travelers surveyed its employees in 1987 and found that one in four was responsible for the care of a child under the age of thirteen, and one in five for the care of an elderly relative.

2. *Demographic projections show that most companies will face a labor shortage in the 1990s, and that, unless action is taken, many potential employees will not be able to work because of shortages of child-care and elder-care services.* Colleges across the country felt the bite of declining enrollment in the fall of 1990, one of the more visible signs of a population dip that will soon show up in a shortage of available young workers. Farsighted companies already recognize that that shortage can only be made up by hiring the people who have created the growth in the labor force through the 1980s: women, minorities, and immigrants. As a manager at IBM told us, "Twenty years ago some employers might tell a woman 'Look, if you can't solve your child-care problem you'd better consider staying home.' Now they've got to say, 'We need you to come to work. We'd better help you solve this problem.' " The same demographic projections show an increasing demand for child care, and a greatly increasing need for elder care.

3. *Companies that don't change in response to changes in the work force are being punished with high (and costly) turnover rates, recruiting difficulties, and drops in productivity.* A 1987 study at Corning, Inc., showed that women and minorities

were leaving the company at twice the rate of white men, and the company has responded with an all-out assault on its corporate culture, including a training program for all of its managers and professionals on race and gender issues in the workplace. A 1988 survey at Du Pont showed that 25 percent of male employees and 50 percent of females had considered leaving the company for a firm that offered more flexibility. The business has responded with a full-scale management-training program, and with a revised set of work-and-family policies. And those are two progressive companies, bold enough to release their survey results and shrewd enough to act. In the next decade, companies too blind to ask those questions and too set in their ways to make changes may find their businesses increasingly troubled by high turnover rates, recruitment difficulties, and possibly worker shortages.

Studies have shown again and again that companies that do respond—with longer leave allowances, greater flexibility, or child- and elder-care supports—have been rewarded with lower turnover, better-quality recruits, improved morale, and increased productivity.

4. *The future of American business, and of our society, rests on our children. If we ignore their education and upbringing, and allow them to be placed in poor-quality care, our future as a country will be threatened.* This argument lies behind some of the most positive initiatives we saw in our research—including some of the best corporate-supported child-care centers, some of the most innovative corporate contributions to community efforts, and some of the moves to allow workers greater flexibility and more time away from work. Managers at United States Hosiery Corporation and the other businesses that supported the creation of a consortium center in Lincolnton, North Carolina, did so to create an educational and nurturing environment for children who would otherwise be left to some of the worst child care in the country. IBM, in its massive initiative to increase the supply of community-based child care around key employment sites, has stipulated that the funding only go to centers and care givers that meet the standards of the National Association for the Education of Young Children, citing numerous studies that show the positive effects of good child care, and the harmful effects of substandard care. NCNB Corporation instituted a policy in 1990 that allows its employees paid time off to participate in school activities, citing studies that show parental involvement as an important determinant of quality education. In fact, all research on school success has found that parent-teacher collaboration is essential. Companies that do not

permit parents to attend meetings with teachers are contributing to the failure of our schools.

*What employees can do*
Just as employers are finding it to be in their best interest to respond to the family needs of their employees, employees are also realizing the importance of family benefits to their own career success. Now that two-earner couples are the norm, now that most women return to work while their children are infants, and now that fathers have become more involved in the day-to-day tasks of child rearing, it is more important than ever that employees begin their careers with their eyes open and an understanding of how their employers will respond to their changing needs over the course of their careers.

But many prospective employees are reluctant to inquire about parental benefits like child-care support and parental-leave policies because they are afraid that they will be considered too demanding or not committed to their work. Workers at companies that don't yet offer such benefits have the same concerns. They want to broach the subject with their managers, but they fear that by making an issue of their family needs they may be dubbed "family first" rather than "career first," and put their hopes for advancement in jeopardy.

Although no one can predict with certainty how particular employers will respond to such inquiries, there are ways of framing questions at interviews and of advocating change within a company that are better than others. What employees and prospective employees who are looking to employers for support with work-and-family issues absolutely must do is clearly convey to the employer that they need such benefits because they want to remain productive, loyal, long-term employees.

Just as it is generally advisable not to ask questions about sick leave and vacation time at a first interview, job applicants should stay away from questions about family leave early in the interviewing process. After all, any successful job applicant must concentrate on projecting confidence, competence, and commitment at the outset. But if you really are committed to making a career at a company, it makes sense to find out what sort of culture you are getting into before you accept a job. You can take advantage of the multistep interviewing and job-acceptance process that many employers offer by timing your inquiries at strategic points, and leave certain questions unasked until the prospective employer has made clear that it is interested in you.

Here are some rough guidelines that will provide you with a framework within which to time your questions:

*Step 1. Do some research.*
- Look at the lists in this book, and at the lists published in magazines such as *Working Mother.* The best companies are getting media attention for their efforts.
- Look for articles about the company in magazines and in books at the library. Read the annual reports; it is a good sign if they mention employee policies there, a great one if they boast about family benefits.

*Step 2. Ask some safe questions at the first interview, to show your interest in a career and to get an initial sense of the business's attitude toward its employees.*
- If you are a woman, ask how have women progressed at the company, who the highest-level women executives are, and what paths their careers have taken.
- Ask about "safer" benefits. Find out what you'll pay for family health insurance and what coverage you'll receive. Ask if employees have access to a fitness center, and if the employer contributes to a savings plan.
- Ask about the review process. Workers should be reviewed regularly and fairly, so they know where they stand.
- Find out about the company's involvement in the community. Where does it apply its charitable efforts? Does it encourage employees to become involved in community activities? Has it ever given money to local child-care facilities?
- If you are *only* looking for part-time work, or *must* work restricted hours because of family responsibilities, make that clear at the outset, and make a good case for how you can contribute to the organization on those terms. You'll quickly weed out those employers who won't make scheduling concessions, and who would be harrowing to work for anyway.

*Step 3. At later interviews, after the company has offered you a job or shown a strong interest in you, ask some tougher questions.*
- Ask if you can see an employee handbook. These are passed out as a matter of course to new hires, and they are the best source of information on employee policies, such as family support programs, leaves, sick time, vacations, and insurance benefits.
- You are planning on being with the company for a long time, and, thinking realistically, your circumstances and needs are likely to change over time. What sort of retirement benefits

does the company offer, and what sort of support systems does it offer for people with family responsibilities?
- Does the company offer help in finding child care? Is quality child care available in the area?
- How often are people relocated at the company? Can you expect to be relocated in the course of your career, and are moves necessary to real career progression? If you are moved, will the company pay for house-hunting trips? Will it help your spouse find a job? Will it help you find child care?
- On the rare days when you have to stay home with a sick child, will you take unpaid time, vacation time, or can you use your own or specially designated paid sick days?
- Can you ever take work home? Are people ever furnished with computer hookups at their homes?
- Are you allowed to call home from work? How would you receive an emergency call from home?

*Step 4. Before accepting a job, ask to talk with other employees. This will give you a sense of who your co-workers will be, and a feel for prevailing attitudes and culture. Some questions for potential co-workers include:*
- What sort of work hours can be expected of those on an upward career track?
- In your reviews, which is more important, the number of hours worked, or whether you get the job done and how well you do it?
- Are meetings often scheduled before or after conventional work hours? How much notice is given, as a rule?
- Look around the office. It can be a good sign if children's pictures are displayed in people's offices; a very good one if you see them in the offices of women managers.

Those who already have good jobs, but at companies that have yet to offer much flexibility or support, are bound to wonder how changes are made, what role they can play in making the company more family responsive, and that is a tougher nut to crack. Companies vary tremendously in their attitudes toward their employees, so we would be reckless to suggest a single approach to take, but some general rules do apply:

- Present your proposal, whether it be for parental leave, paid time off to care for a sick family member, or even for an on-site child-care center, with consideration for the needs of the employer. Before making demands of the company, be sure you have exhausted all of your own alternatives. On the simplest level, a worker who says to a supervisor, "I need to take tomorrow afternoon off to take my child to the doctor," is likely to get a very different reaction from the employee who says, "My child has a doctor's appointment tomorrow afternoon. My wife is out of town, and her parents both have important business meetings, so I'm the only one available to take him. I've arranged with Jane to cover my calls, and I'll finish the report tonight so that you can check it over while I'm out." It seems like a simple concept, but many people seem to ignore it. That same consideration for the manager's need to get the work done, and the business's need to make a profit, should underlie any request for more important changes.

- Consider your value to the company. Are you a key employee? Or are you easily replaced? Obviously, valued employees are in a much stronger position to ask for scheduling and other concessions than those who are expendable. They are also able to act with the confidence that they could as easily apply their skills at another company. If you feel lucky to have your job at all, think carefully before making tough demands.

- Consider the timing. A company in shaky financial condition, one in the midst of layoffs and cutbacks, is not a likely candidate for expensive new work-and-family benefits such as on-site child care. Less costly benefits, such as greater scheduling flexibility or a dependent-care referral service, might be attractive to a company in a short-term slump. These options are valuable to employees and come with a far lower price tag than enhanced health insurance benefits.

- Make the business case. Find out what the competition is doing. Cite the bottom-line return in lower turnover and recruitment costs, improved morale, and increased productivity. We've tried, in the profiles in this book, to show why the companies have taken the steps they have, and insights of those decision-makers should be helpful in making your own case. If you're proposing something expensive, such as a child-care center or an emergency care-giver service, hire an expert to evaluate the need and recommend the best options. A little money spent on advice up front can save time and money down the road.

- Know the options. Many employers equate family benefits with child-care centers. The range of options is actually far more extensive. Scores of examples are given throughout this book, and in the final chapter "Family-Friendly Options." See what companies of similar size and with a similar employee population are doing. Present only the options that make the most business sense, and that fit the corporate culture.

- Make sure the issue is understood broadly. Family care is not just an issue for women with young children but for fathers and for middle-aged employees with elderly relatives. A 1989 study of flexible work practices at over 500 major corporations showed that more than 40 percent of the employees who work from home were men, and that almost 90 percent were managers.

In case after case, we've seen the results of personal employee input on company decisions. In a few instances, organized employee initiatives have led to important company responses. Too often, employees conceal their family-care responsibilities, thinking that they will interfere with career advancement. In some cases this fear is well founded. One employee we spoke with had sought out a sympathetic manager to broach the subject of maternity leave and was told, "You got yourself pregnant. It's up to you to prove you deserve more than the state-mandated leave." Another employee called in to say her child was sick and was told that she would have to decide which was more important, her family or her job. But that fear may be a self-fulfilling prophecy. If you don't ask, if managers at the company aren't made aware that employees have family responsibilities, then they are unlikely ever to respond. In general, even an initially rigid response eventually gives way to some flexibility, and often managers are far from resistant. An employee at Hanna Andersson, in Portland, Oregon, went to her boss to ask for a four-month maternity leave and was encouraged to take at least six months off. A manager at Unum Life Insurance finally gathered the courage to confront her boss about early-morning meetings that were difficult to attend because of child-care hours. He asked her why she hadn't mentioned it sooner, and the practice was stopped. On a larger scale, AT&T began to move toward its broad family-care benefit package after a group of employees from all over the company sent a letter to the vice chairman detailing the business reasons why the company should support child-care and other family-related initiatives.

Ask with confidence, frame your request in terms of your long-range plans for employment at the company, consider the needs of the business, and most people will be pleasantly surprised at the results. If that doesn't work, if your company is simply intractible, your manager completely unresponsive, for your own good and the good of your family, you should seriously consider another job.

This is a high-stakes game. Poor-quality child care can threaten your children's well-being and their futures. Your own lack of time to attend to their needs, or to the needs of elderly relatives, may be just as damaging. As one mother told us, "I feel as though women of our generation got the shaft, in a way. We've been given a choice that no one should have to make. Because to work and to feel fulfilled and to have a career we often have to sacrifice other people." Your career is also bound to suffer if your company refuses to help or to bend, or if it relegates you to a permanent "mommy track."

The farsighted companies listed in this book are trying to ensure that their employees don't have to make those impossible choices. Many are working to make affordable, high-quality child care available to their employees and do help them find the elder-care services their families need. Most are allowing employees adequate time away from work to deal with family emergencies, to bond with new babies, and to participate in children's schooling. Many are rethinking traditional work schedules to allow more flexibility. To ensure that part-timers and employees who work unusual hours aren't unfairly held back in their careers, some are moving away from evaluations based on number of hours worked, and adopting assessments based on contribution. A few are training individual managers to be responsive to the needs of employees with family responsibilities. If you can't convince your company to join their ranks, perhaps you should think about working for a company that has.

# THE MEDALISTS

In-depth profiles of sixteen companies that have taken leadership stands on work-and-family issues

# AT&T

550 Madison Avenue
New York, NY 10022                              212-605-5500

**Nature of business:** Telephone service; manufacturer of
computer and telecommunications equipment.
**Number of employees:** 260,000.
**Female employees:** 47 percent (36 percent of officials and
managers, 8 percent of officers).
**Child care:** Nationwide resource-and-referral service; significant support for efforts to expand the community supply
of quality child care; pretax salary set-aside (DCAP).
**Elder care:** Nationwide consultation-and-referral service;
significant support for efforts to expand the community
supply of quality elder care; pretax salary set-aside (DCAP).
**Family leave:** Six weeks paid maternity leave, plus up to a
year unpaid parental leave; up to a year unpaid leave for
care of ill family members; one paid personal day may be
used, in two-hour increments, for personal and family emergencies.
**Flexible work options:** Flextime possible in some positions
and in some divisions; some part-time work; pilot work-at-
home programs in Los Angeles and Phoenix.
**Other benefits:** Employee-assistance program; adoption aid
up to $2,000; profit-sharing plan; preretirement planning.


A large-company response to changing demographics.

*"Providing benefits that are responsive to the needs of
employees and their families is a tradition at AT&T. The
Work and Family Program not only continues that tradition, but also recognizes the changes in American families
that are affecting our lives. The way we address the family
concerns of AT&T's people is an important issue for all of
us—a competitive issue. . . . These initiatives will help us
attract and keep the talented work force we need to win
in the marketplace. And they will help all of us maintain
a healthy balance between our work and families, so we*

*can concentrate on giving our customers the best we have
to offer."*

ROBERT E. ALLEN
Chairman of the Board
(From a December 1989 letter to employees)

A T&T has long had a reputation for being a company that
pays well and provides excellent benefits. One of its divisions, Bell Labs, is among the premier research-and-develop-
ment organizations in the world, a prime job target for the best
scientific minds coming out of graduate schools. Another division, American Transtech, has earned a reputation as a place
where women have received unusually fair treatment in promotions and upward mobility. But in terms of family issues,
through the mid-1980s, the company lagged behind such leaders
as IBM and Merck & Co. AT&T offered a six-month parental
leave even before the 1983 breakup, which was among the most
generous written policies in American business. But by 1985 it
was still doing nothing to help employees deal with child-care
issues, and flexible work hours remained as concessions granted
by scattered individual managers based on the needs of the business.

AT&T had opened two experimental child-care centers in
the early 1970s, in Dayton and Columbus, Ohio, but these were
deemed failures after short trials. Attendance at the centers had
remained low, possibly because they were at some distance from
the work sites, and not on workers' commuting routes. AT&T
managers who remembered them generally thought of them as
examples of why the company should not get involved with child
care again.

A consent decree, signed in 1973, forced the company to pay
closer attention to the hiring and promotion of women and minorities. One result of that was the formation of affirmative-
action committees throughout the organization charged with
finding underlying sources of discrimination and proposing solutions to eliminate them. Through the late 1970s and early
1980s, many of these committees began to look at family issues
as part of their mission, and some began to do surveys of the
employee need for family supports at specific sites, and to send
proposals to management calling for policy changes or new initiatives.

Many of AT&T's workers belong to two unions, the Communications Workers of America and the International Broth-
erhood of Electrical Workers, and in contract negotiations in
1980, 1983, and 1986, the two unions brought child-care pro-

posals to the table. Each time management brushed them aside in the early discussions, as the union-management teams concentrated on issues of wages, job protection, and retirement and insurance benefits. Union pressure did lead to a movement within the company toward participatory management, with greater worker involvement in decision-making at the job level, which gradually gave individual workers a greater voice within the company and may have indirectly led to some later changes. But neither management nor the union seemed ready, even by 1986, to consider family issues as fundamental concerns for employees or for the business.

> *I have worked part-time since my daughter was born three years ago. We looked at centers in this area, but couldn't find any openings. One center had my name on a waiting list for two years before they finally called. We looked at family day care, and during a visit to one of those, the woman's little girl, who was about three, came up and kicked my daughter, who wasn't even crawling yet. It just struck me that I wasn't prepared to put her through that. So I worked out an arrangement to return to work part-time, and so did my husband. Together we provided all of her care until she was two. At the time the company had no policy for part-timers, and it wasn't clear whether my manager would allow it, but he eventually did. Now that the company has a policy, I feel I stand on firmer ground. For example, I know that I'm entitled to full benefit coverage if I work twenty-five hours.*
>
> *Over the three years I have been able to get some very challenging part-time assignments. I'm now in the process of looking for another position in the Labs, because my venture is winding down, and I have a lot of opportunities to choose from—real jobs and challenging opportunities. None of the managers I've spoken with has told me that I can't have a job because I'm a part-timer.*

Individual workers and ad-hoc groups also began to lobby for a response from management to their family concerns in the early 1980s. In Naperville, Illinois, for example, a small group of employees in the Bell Labs office started to examine the company's role in work-and-family conflicts in 1984. They put together a proposal asking the department's affirmative-action council for support in surveying the department, which had about 150 employees, to find out what the needs and concerns were. Employees volunteered their time to distribute the questionnaire and tabulate the results. The group then obtained permission from the affirmative-action committee for the entire Indian Hill campus, which included several AT&T organizations, to distribute the survey to all of the 4,000 employees who worked there.

The numbers showed that the site had a high percentage of single parents, a very high percentage of workers with young children, and, most dramatically, that about 5 percent of the employees were pregnant. A number of productivity-related questions also showed that AT&T was losing a great deal of work time to family concerns. With those results in hand, the group addressed management groups on the need for flexibility and family policies, and began work on proposals for a corporate response. They eventually settled on an arrangement with a local YWCA, which had established a child-care resource-and-referral agency. Like similar agencies in other areas, this one helped educate parents about child-care options, referred them to openings for care, provided support to existing child-care providers, and worked to improve the quality and availability of care by recruiting and training care givers. The group received approval for a two-year contract with the agency from the site management in Indian Hill late in 1985, but before the arrangement could be made final, corporate headquarters asked that the project be put on hold while it reviewed a growing number of work-and-family proposals then being put on the table and formulated a company-wide policy.

> *I'm in management, and I just recently came back from maternity leave. I called the resource-and-referral service when I first had the baby, and through them found a family day-care person I was happy with. I visited with her during the leave. Then, a week before I was ready to go back to work, the whole thing fell apart. When I first talked to her she had told me she had two adults there to care for four infants, which I thought was great. Then, just as I was getting ready to go back to work, I found out that she had five babies—all under nine months—with just one adult. I knew from the information I'd received through the referral service that the ratio must be too high. And when I called back to question the referral service about it, they went through the roof. They told me it was not legal. They checked into it and told the woman she could not represent the infant care in her house as licensed. She had another licensed facility for older children in another building, which is how the service had her name at all, and it turned out that the infant care was not being done legally.*
>
> *So there I was without any child care. I was on vacation*

*in Florida when all this happened, and was planning on coming back to a new job in a few days. The resource-and-referral service told me not to consider sending my son to the first place, and they gave me three more family day-care providers. One of them turned out to be right around the corner from where I live. She's a wonderful woman and he's the only infant there. She just has him with her own kids.*

Among those other proposals was one from Kansas City, Missouri, to create a near-site child-care center in a then-vacant downtown building; and one from Murray Hill, New Jersey, to help fund the expansion of a chain of high-quality nonprofit centers already in operation, in return for priority access for AT&T employees. The New Jersey proposal grew out of the work of two groups at Bell Labs, one in the research area and the other at the development organization. Ken Lyons, a researcher at Bell Labs, spearheaded part of the effort. "I chaired the research area's affirmative-action committee in 1985," he explains, "and was a member of a subgroup that decided that work-and-family issues were something we really wanted to try to do something about. We surveyed the research-area employees and took the results, which showed a clear need for some sort of response from the company, to Arno Penzias, our vice president for research."

The group wanted Penzias to push the matter up the chain of command. He declined, not because he was unsympathetic, but because he thought the group's strategy was wrong. "He explained that there was really only one person in the organization who could say yes to corporate involvement in anything related to child care, and that was Charles Marshall" (at the time the company's vice chairman, the second in command at AT&T, and the person ultimately responsible for all personnel and benefit policies). "In between him and Charles Marshall were any number of people who could say no. So he advised us to use our questionnaire results as the basis for an approach directly to Charles Marshall, and to try to involve people from other entities outside of Bell Labs."

That same week, Lyons's group found out that the affirmative-action committee for the development organization at Murray Hill had conducted a very similar survey and was analyzing the results. The two groups put their survey results together, and began a process of employee networking to find other groups and individuals at AT&T who shared their interest. They arranged to attend a meeting in Basking Ridge, New Jersey, at which a group of vice presidents reviewed the proposal for a near-site center in Kansas City. At that meeting the Murray Hill group met or found out about several other groups, and had a chance to see a high-level reaction to a sophisticated child-care proposal. The vice presidents were not impressed with the idea.

Some members of the Murray Hill team went back to work to find sensible options for a corporate response at the site. They eventually came up with an innovative proposal to support the expansion of an organization called Summit Child Care Centers, a nonprofit company that operated five child-care centers in the area, three of which were in former school buildings. The centers had empty classrooms available for expansion, but no money to hire new teachers. The Murray Hill proposal was for AT&T to guarantee a new teacher's salary every time a new classroom opened up, until the class had filled to the point that parent fees could cover the teacher's cost. In return for that small contribution, and until the centers had filled all the rooms available, AT&T employees would have a ready supply of care.

Lyons, meanwhile, moved forward with the approach to Charles Marshall. He wrote a letter asking Marshall to consider the formulation of, as he put it, "a corporate policy regarding child care and other issues relating to conflict between the demands of family and careers." He pointed out the demographic trends, and emphasized that changes in the work force, without a response from the company, were having adverse effects on work performance, "including effects such as absenteeism, shortened hours, and unproductive time at work due to parental concerns. Many of those problems," he wrote, "are related to the lack of available high-quality child care." He mentioned the growing number of questions he, as a Ph.D. recruiter, was hearing about the availability of child care and about the company's child-care benefits. He asked for a policy statement making it clear that AT&T recognized child care as a valid corporate concern. He mentioned the wide range of possible responses, from on-site child care to resource-and-referral services. And he wrapped it up by saying that the child-care issue presented an opportunity for AT&T "to make a powerful statement about fundamental concerns and issues which affect employees."

He circulated the letter for review by and the signatures of the many other individuals who shared his concerns. When it was finally mailed to Marshall, the letter had been signed by about thirty people from different AT&T organizations across the country, among them a director of one of AT&T's business units and various lower-level employees who had become involved in grass-roots efforts through working-parent clubs or affirmative-action committees. Along with the letter, Lyons sent a copy of a book, *Child Care and Corporate Productivity*, by John Fernandez, which cites statistical evidence of the adverse effects of child-care problems on business productivity.

"We sent the letter toward the end of January 1986," remembers Lyons. "About two months later Charles Marshall called me directly. He said that the company hadn't really thought of child care as a productivity issue before, and that he wanted AT&T to look into it." A task force was formed, composed of people from human resources in various AT&T organizations, as well as representatives from public relations and labor relations. Since the unions had put forward child-care demands in previous bargaining sessions, labor relations saw this as a bargainable issue, one that would eventually have to involve the unions, and they wanted their own representatives in on the discussions from the beginning.

The first step the task force took was to put the Indian Hill resource-and-referral initiative on hold, and to consider it, along with the proposals from Kansas City and Murray Hill, as a potential pilot program. The three groups made presentations at the first formal meeting of the task force, and all three received initial approval, with labor relations registering a "no" vote on the Kansas City center. The proposals then moved up the executive chain of command, and in the fall the company decided to go ahead with two—Murray Hill and Indian Hill—as two-year pilots, and not to act on the near-site center in Kansas City. The Kansas City proposal had also included a resource-and-referral service and a program of lunchtime seminars, and AT&T chose to implement only those parts of the package in the pilot there.

The task force continued to meet, and over the next year added a resource-and-referral service in New Jersey to the test program. It also put two work-and-family questions on an employee-input survey conducted in 1988.

The labor relations people worked with the task force on all of this, looked closely at the use of the pilot programs, analyzed the survey results, watched what other companies like IBM and Johnson & Johnson were doing, and began to formulate a package of measures to bring to the table in the 1989 bargaining session.

Robert McNiff, a member of AT&T's national bargaining team at that session, described those preparations to us. "From our research, we decided that we had to have some response to the family. While we started out thinking in terms of child care, we pretty quickly began to include elder care in our plans as well, and to consider them together as family care. That then led us to look at adoption supports, leaves of absence, and flexible work schedules. Ray Williams, our vice president of labor relations, asked the benefit people to give him a package that they thought they could afford, and after some discussions back and forth they came back with one that included national resource-and-referral services for child care and elder care, extended leaves of absence, and a number of other measures. He said, 'I like the plan, but what happens if the whole industry changes in the middle of our contract and we are sitting there with a resource-and-referral program and everybody else is doing something new and novel. We have to have the ability to turn the ship in another direction. Why don't we put some money in a fund?'" A pool of money was added to the plan, to be used to take advantage of local opportunities, to address areas of particular need, and to respond to new concepts in family care that might develop before the next bargaining session in 1992.

> *I have been at AT&T since 1973, and have taken three maternity leaves in that time. I took off six months the first time; I was out four and a half months the second time; and five months the third. In each case I came back to the same job. The first time they hired someone to fill in for me, and during the others they just split my work between my co-workers.*
>
> *It's very reassuring to know you have the leave time. I know people who work at other companies who have had to string together vacations and sick time, and have had no other leave time. It's just nice to know that you can take some time and come back to a job. At six weeks, which is all that many companies offer, you've hardly gotten to know the baby yet.*

The unions, too, had been doing their research. Child-care proposals had been brushed aside by the company in earlier bargaining sessions, but this time they knew things would be different. They were aware of the pilot programs, aware that the task force had been meeting, and they knew that AT&T was aware that some other large companies had already adopted family-care support systems. "It was just something whose time had come," says Louise Cadell, the negotiator on family issues for the CWA in 1989. "From the demographic trends and the research studies, it was clearly in AT&T's best interest to do something with family benefits. It might cost them some money up front, but all the studies showed that they'd end up with a net gain from increased productivity. The question became: What to ask for? Well, we decided to ask for everything. We decided to let them know we were serious about this, and to bargain for the future."

Cadell gave a three-hour presentation at one of the early bargaining meetings, citing demographic projections, productivity studies, and the experiences of other companies. She asked for on-site child care at sites large enough to support them, she asked for support for before- and after-school programs, for elder-care services, for dependent-care subsidies for lower-income workers, for national resource-and-referral services, for longer family-care leaves, and for greater flexibility. "Our thinking was that there was no telling what we'd get this year, but that these things would be on the table for the future. This would be a benchmark and we could work on it and add to it as we have traditionally done with health care, pensions, and other benefits."

"They had very specific proposals," says McNiff, "very well thought out, very well researched. And I said to them, early on, that we would be responsive." Over the course of two weeks of talks, AT&T's negotiators came out with one piece after another of the family-care package they had discussed internally: national child-care and elder-care resource-and-referral services, a pretax salary set-aside plan, adoption assistance, an extension of the leave-of-absence policy (with reemployment guarantee) from six months to a year, and increased management support for flexible scheduling practices. The final piece was the family-care development fund, a pool of $10 million to be administered jointly by the company and the union to enable the company to respond with additional community-based initiatives, and to be spent over a three-year period.

> I adopted three children last year, from Costa Rica, and AT&T's adoption assistance program was a big help. It didn't cover everything I spent, but it sure made a big dent in it. I made two trips to Costa Rica, plus I lived down there for twenty-eight days. I'd say I spent between sixteen and twenty thousand dollars, and the company reimbursed me for six thousand dollars—two thousand for each child. My wife works full-time too. She took two months off when the kids first got here. When they get sick now, we take turns staying home with them. And my managers have been very good about that.

The unions agreed to those proposals, the labor contracts were signed in May of 1989, and the various programs were put in place over the following year, the last being the elder-care referral service, launched in January 1991. The first grants from the family-care development fund were announced in the summer of 1990; among them contributions to the expansion of existing centers in New Jersey and North Carolina; funding for training programs and resource rooms for family day-care providers in Missouri, Utah, and Virginia; and some start-up money for an after-school program in New Jersey.

The three pilot programs that began AT&T's initiative showed the importance of being able to respond to local opportunities, and of being able to take advantage of the efforts of interested and motivated employees. The Murray Hill child-care venture, for example, was a relatively inexpensive response to an existing initiative. If the company hadn't responded when it did, it might have missed that chance forever. The development fund gives the company a mechanism for responding to local opportunities, of contributing to joint efforts with other businesses and acting when a small contribution can do a great deal of good.

The fund also gives the company a chance to respond to and encourage the grass-roots groups that have been so important in the creation of its family-care benefit package. Far from disappearing with the adoption of the expanded benefit package in 1989, most have continued their work, and new groups continue to spring up. Many have now joined together to form the Working Parents Support Network, with more than twenty chapters around the country. Most of the development-fund grants have been in response to proposals from grass-roots groups such as those that created the earlier initiatives in Kansas City, Indian Hill, and Murray Hill.

"Our grass-roots organization didn't die," says Diana Nolte, a member of the group at Indian Hill. "We rested for about a year after the resource-and-referral went in as a pilot, but we've since become as active as ever. We recently submitted a grant proposal from the site. The largest school district in our county has decided to consider a before- and after-school program, so we put together a proposal to provide ten thousand dollars in start-up funds for that, and another ten thousand dollars to fund an advocate to push for similar programs at other school districts in the county."

Ken Lyons is still sometimes awed by the changes that have taken place. "What is startling to me is that it is possible that the formation of the task force, which eventually led to the agreement with the unions, might have been the result of our approach to Charles Marshall. It wouldn't have gone anywhere if he hadn't responded, of course, and the task force might not have done much if there hadn't been so much activity within AT&T and at other companies, but that letter seems to have been the catalyst."

Such rapid changes will take time to work their way into

AT&T's corporate culture, and while the company has made some moves toward greater flexibility, it is too soon to pronounce the company completely responsive to its workers' family needs. Yet it has come a long way. AT&T now has one of the most liberal parental- and family-leave policies in the country, allowing up to a year off with full benefit coverage for the first six months. (Many of the other telecommunications companies scrambled to match it after it was announced.) As we went to press, only IBM had created a comparable funding initiative to address local child-care needs.

Management training and greater scheduling flexibility are AT&T's next frontiers. In 1990, the company had policies in place for part-time workers, and had begun to encourage managers to accept more part-timers, but had not really begun a push for greater flexibility for full-time workers. Since policies regarding leaves and flexibility are really determined by individual managers—the written policies always leave much to the discretion of supervisors—the company is looking hard at the possibility of a formal management training program to ensure that the full effect of the company's policies are actually felt by its employees.

# Alley's General Store

State Road
West Tisbury, MA 02575                           508-693-0088

*Nature of business:* General store and food-service business.
*Number of employees:* 20 to 50 (varies with season).
*Female employees:* Approximately 75 percent (in 1990, all three operations managers were women).
*Child care:* No formal policy, but company provided complete subsidy for care of three children at near-site center in 1989 and 1990.
*Elder care:* No formal program.
*Family leave:* Unpaid leaves negotiated to fit the needs of the individuals and the business.
*Flexible work options:* No formal policy, but the business accommodates the needs of its workers.
*Other benefits:* Health insurance with employee contribution during the first year; paid vacations and sick leave.

Near-site child care—a small-business model

*"I see it as a moral obligation, because I really do think it's important that young women, particularly single mothers, have a chance to be in the work force."*

HOWARD ULFELDER
Owner

W hen the doors open at Alley's General Store at 8:00 A.M., an hour-long flow of coffee meetings begins. Customers—most of them on this cold morning in the island's tourist off-season workers clad in boots, jeans, and flannel shirts—stomp in along the long front porch, pour themselves coffee at the table near the front door, hunt around for any odds and ends they might need that day, and cluster into groups to shoot the breeze.

With its worn plank floors, heavy wooden support posts, and utilitarian inventory—the shelves hold everything from work gloves and hammers to doughnuts, eggbeaters, and cough drops—the scene could be taken from a Norman Rockwell painting. The boxes of the town post office line a section of the back wall. A big shelf of canning supplies tops the doorway to the hardware section. Bins of cranberries, unshelled peanuts, apples, and potatoes stand just inside the entrance.

A holdout from another era, Alley's seems an unlikely place to look for progressive action on a pressing social issue. But since 1988, Howard Ulfelder, the store's owner, has provided child care as a fully paid benefit to three of his employees, and has worked out a schedule to keep the store fully staffed while allowing the parents on his payroll the time they need to care for their children.

Alley's General Store has been operating in West Tisbury, a community on the south side of Martha's Vineyard, since 1853, and it remains the only store in the village center. Its extensive hardware selection combined with the sweeping range of its other stock draws in customers looking for snacks, last-minute additions to a menu, or hard-to-find household items. A scan of the shelves turns up egg slicers, replacement mop sponges, Bag Balm, disposable diapers, pie tins in several sizes, flag-pole mounts, cooking pots, toys, and guitar strings. Many customers count Alley's among the island's unique attractions, and the store's T-shirts have been seen in such far-off spots as Paris and the Great Wall of China.

Howard Ulfelder bought the store in 1986 as part of a plan to ease into retirement after a career as a corporate executive and a stint in the retail liquor business. For two years, Ulfelder, his wife, Susie, and store manager Dianne Wall ran the store much as it had been run for decades. The Ulfelders added an upscale food-service business, Back Alley's, in an adjacent building, but otherwise left the store's successful formula alone.

Then, in early 1988, the new owners were confronted with a series of pregnancies, both among their workers and among women they wanted to hire. In quick succession Alley's had three future mothers on the payroll. Two were single women who were pregnant when they applied for work that spring. The third was Dianne Wall, who announced that she was expecting a child the next winter and that she planned to continue working after a short maternity leave.

The three pregnancies presented Ulfelder with a host of considerations. Would the two new women stay if he hired them as full-time year-round employees? How were all three going to cope with the dual responsibilities of working and parenting? What could he do to lessen some of the parenting worries so that the women could better devote themselves to their work? And what were his responsibilities here, both as a businessman and as a person with some power to affect the lives of all three women?

In the end he decided to hire both of the applicants as full-time employees, and committed to help all three women find and pay for suitable day care once the children were ready. "I see it as a moral obligation," he says, "because I really do think it's important that young women, particularly single mothers, have a chance to be in the work force. I view day care as a fringe benefit just like health care and vacation time. I think the business decision followed—it appeared to be a wise business decision after I had made the decision to do it anyway. I just thought it was something that had to be done to be fair to a segment of the community."

> I didn't get married, so I had to do this all by myself, and it's been difficult for me. When it became clear to me that my baby couldn't come to work with me forever, that I'd need to find some child-care arrangement, I shopped around and found that there is no child care here that I can afford. I called community services, and they told me there was nothing they could do for me. There is a program that provides child-care subsidies to low-income working mothers. But in order to get on that program you have to lose your job, go on welfare, and then apply for it and get another job. You can't get in the program to prevent your-

*self from going on welfare. But I earn nine dollars an hour, I pay five hundred dollars in rent (there really isn't anything cheaper here), and I just can't pay four dollars an hour for day care. I couldn't live. If it weren't for Howard I would have had to go on welfare.*

While Ulfelder and Wall looked into day-care possibilities, the solution for infant care, as Ulfelder put it, "just happened": the women brought their babies into the store. The first returned to work in late September when her son was five weeks old, and the second came to work with her son soon after. Wall's daughter was born in January. "She had the baby on a Saturday morning," recalls Ulfelder with pleasure, "and Sunday she appeared here with the baby." She came back to work after about a month.

Everyone who was there seems to remember that fall and winter with fondness. "It was a nice change for everyone to suddenly have children in the store," says one of the mothers. "People came to Alley's just to see the babies. The customers thought it was the greatest thing, especially the older people. And I think it was good for my son. I think he learned a lot from it. He saw a lot of faces and got real familiar with people. And people loved him."

"We had a wonderful atmosphere here last winter when these babies were small," says Ulfelder. "It was really one of the most pleasurable parts of this whole thing."

That fall and winter Ulfelder and Wall looked at more formal day-care arrangements and at ways to balance schedules to accommodate the parenting needs of the three women. One idea that attracted the two at first was a plan to start a day-care cooperative, with the mothers as the providers. The five-day work schedules would be cut back to four, and each woman would spend a full day as care giver for all three children. For a variety of reasons, Ulfelder didn't pursue the idea. First, there was no place for it at Alley's and no room at any of the women's homes. An apartment over the store looked like a possibility, but state regulations require day-care centers to be on the first floor. (An exception is made for family or in-home care, but in order to qualify the care giver has to live in the space.) "And real estate prices being what they are on Martha's Vineyard," says Ulfelder, "it's not a practical idea to go looking to buy a place to do this, or even rent a place. It would not be cost effective." The second obstacle was that one of the women was reluctant to participate, feeling that the necessarily close relationships at work would be strained by the added child-care responsibilities.

The two then looked into family or in-home day care with

another provider. A friend of one of the workers, who had a child of her own, heard about Alley's child-care search and offered to take care of the children at her house. State licensing requirements presented an obstacle here too. While day-care centers in Massachusetts must have at least one provider for every three children under two (or two adults for every seven babies), family day-care regulations require one provider for every two infants (as part of a larger group of up to six children). To care for all three babies, Alley's would need to pay two family providers. Again, cost ruled out this option. It was cheaper to send the children to an established center.

By late winter, it became clear that something had to be done. "Having the children in the store got to be too much after a while," says one of the mothers. "My son started walking at nine months and he's an active child. It got to the point where either I had to watch him or someone else did." Another of the women took the step that precipitated Ulfelder's action. "I happened to get a big tax return," she explained, "so I decided to put my baby in a nearby day-care center and pay for it myself for a couple of months. Nothing was really decided at Alley's, so I didn't know what I would do after that. Day care is very expensive here—the cheapest is about a hundred forty dollars a week—and I knew I couldn't afford it for long. But I had to do something."

Ulfelder then made an arrangement to place all three children in the center she had chosen, and to pay for the major portion of their care. A fourth employee, hired during the winter, had a four-year-old daughter at the same center, her bill mostly paid by the state under a return-to-work program. Ulfelder and the four mothers worked out an overlapping schedule to provide full staffing for the business through the week, with days off staggered in a such a way that only three of the children needed care at the center on any given day. The women with family help available—husbands, mothers, or siblings—shared the weekend work, since the center is open only during the week. None of the mothers had to pay anything for the weekday care, and with the overlapping schedules, Ulfelder was effectively buying care for three children for the price of two. The state picked up the cost of the fourth.

*Sometimes I feel bad because I wish I could stay home with him all the time. You see, I work a lot. Sometimes I work nights after I'm here. But I just cherish that one hour before he goes to bed. When it's bedtime now, he wants to go up onto my bed and he grabs a book and makes me read to him. He sits there and he laughs and he tells me what*

> *things are. It's a long day here. We're here at seven-thirty*
> *in the morning and I'm here until five o'clock. Then two*
> *nights a week I teach a class and he goes to my mom's.*
> *It's a long day. I'm tired when I get home.*

All of the mothers were openly appreciative of the financial support—even to the point of feeling guilty that so much was being done for them. And all seemed comfortable with their schedules, even if they sometimes wished they could spend more time with the children. "The scheduling flexibility is really a key part of this," says Ulfelder. "We can do it because we're small. And because the employees help work things out. They share some. When somebody really has a problem one will take another's baby."

While the day-care arrangement seemed to fit everyone's needs at the time of our visit, nobody at Alley's considered it the ultimate solution. In fact, Alley's experience is a good example of the constantly changing environment faced by small business managers and the flexibility with which they must adapt their policies on family issues. Dianne Wall had a second child in the fall of 1990 and decided to leave the business. At about the same time, one of the other mothers decided to leave as well. Alley's continued to subsidize the care of the two remaining children, but Ulfelder and the two employees were still exploring other options. One possibility was a revival of the family day-care solution, with Wall offering her services as a provider in her home.

"It's hard not to look at the cost of this, because it's very expensive," says Ulfelder. "But I keep trying to tell myself that it's just part of the cost of doing business. It isn't entirely, because you do have the option of hiring people who don't require it. But I was aware of the need, and, after all, this was not a faceless situation. These were people whom I knew and knew were good workers. It's a whole lot easier to think about providing a benefit for people you know than it is in the abstract.

"I'm hoping that if enough employers provide day care there will be a push for it. I'm a very small voice in an even smaller wilderness. But if enough people provide it, maybe it will become an expected, negotiable policy. An applicant will go to a company and say, 'What's your vacation policy, what's your health policy, and what's your day-care policy?' on roughly equal terms."

# BE&K, Inc.

2000 International Park Drive
Birmingham, AL                              205-969-3600

*Nature of business:* Industrial construction; among the twenty largest contractors in the United States.
*Number of employees:* 11,000 to 13,000.
*Female employees:* 47 percent in corporate office, 9 percent in construction.
*Child care:* Modular near-site center in Port Wentworth, Georgia, for 65 children, aged six weeks to ten years, the building designed to be moved at the end of the construction project; on-site center planned at headquarters site.
*Elder care:* No formal program.
*Family leave:* Paid disability leave for childbirth; additional unpaid leave negotiable.
*Flexible work options:* Limited flexibility in construction jobs; flexible work hours arranged individually in office positions; some part-time office work.
*Other benefits:* Training program; employee-assistance program; retirement plans for hourly and salaried workers; resort condominiums open to all employees.

Bringing women into the construction industry: child-care and training programs as part of a new employment strategy.

*"We work odd hours in the construction industry, and that puts us off cycle with most day-care centers. You can't walk into a community and say, 'I wonder if you can adjust your schedule to ours.' So I began to wonder what prevented us from having our own day-care center."*

TED C. KENNEDY
Chairman and Chief Executive Officer

The child-care center on South Coastal Highway in Port Wentworth, Georgia, doesn't look like anything special. It has a spacious, grassy playground with separate fenced areas for toddlers and older children. It has a tricycle track, a sandbox, swings, slides, and climbing structures. The building itself would win no awards for architectural style—laid out in a square with seventy-foot sides and painted plain white, it has no dramatic lines or floor-to-ceiling windows.

But at the end of the day, when mothers and fathers in hard hats and steel-toed boots show up to retrieve their children, the visitor is reminded that this center, the BEKare Child Development Center, is, in many ways, a revolutionary facility. These parents are building a paper mill a mile away, and this center is among the first to serve a population of construction workers. It is *the* first to be built at a remote construction site with the idea that it will be broken down when the project is finished, and reassembled at another site. The center's long and irregular hours—matching those of the construction workers it serves—are yet another break with child-care traditions. Most of these parents work ten-hour days, then stay at the site for free training classes to improve their construction skills. When rain shuts down construction on a Tuesday, they work an extra day at the end of the week. When weather-sensitive work is being done, such as pouring concrete, their ten-hour days sometimes stretch to twelve or fourteen. And the child-care center is always there when they and their children need it.

For women who have been in construction for years, such as Shirley Johnson, a general foreman at the Port Wentworth site, the child-care center is an affirmation that the company thinks their contributions are important. "When I first started, I always had to worry about who was taking care of my kids," she says. She sometimes wonders how much farther she might have risen in the business if the center had been built fifteen years earlier. For younger women, like nineteen-year-old Valerie Grocaw, the center and BE&K's training sessions mean a sense of a future for her and her two-year-old son. As a secretary, a waitress, or in another of the jobs traditionally reserved for women in this country, she could look forward to a bare subsistence living. In construction she can earn a decent wage, save for her son's education, perhaps even buy a house.

> *This is my first construction job, and I don't think I could have taken it if they hadn't had the child-care center. My boy, who's three, is in there now. I worked in restaurants before, but I never could keep the jobs for very long. The longest I ever kept one was seven weeks, because I'd have problems with my baby-sitters. They wouldn't want to watch my son anymore. Or I'd miss a day when a babysitter had to go do something and I'd lose my job.*
>
> *The pay of this job is better than at other jobs I've had, too. And there's a chance to move up here. You're always progressing. The longer you stay the more you progress. I'm in the training program. I'm going to take Supervision 1*

*and 2 next. I'm going to stick with it here and try to get as far as I can.*

*The child-care center means a future for both of us, me and my son. My little boy is my life. I'm doing everything for him. And this has made a world of difference for us. If the day care moves, I'm following the day care. I've been to California and to Mississippi, I don't really care where we end up so long as we can keep going with this.*

BE&K, Inc., took the first steps toward this child-care center soon after the company's founding in 1972. Around 1975, it started to offer the first training sessions at its construction sites, conducted after-hours and designed both to improve the skills of the company's workers and to bring more women and minorities into the profession. Ted Kennedy, now chairman and chief executive officer at BE&K, has been an advocate of training from the beginning. He recognized, earlier than most in the industry, that the construction labor force is changing and that in the next few years, all construction companies will need to hire more women and minorities in order to have enough workers to build. During the 1990s, analysts project that women and minorities will represent two-thirds of the new entrants to the labor force; construction, long a male bastion, will feel its share of that shift.

"By 1980 we were into training in a big way," says Kennedy. "We were really pushing it. And we never stopped training, all through the downturn in the construction industry in the 1980s. When we were all hunting for work it was hard to maintain the faith, but our belief was that it was coming back, that we were going to need all the trained people we could get. We've been proven right on that. We push training throughout the organization, it's not just an after-hours add-on. We expect our supervisors to get involved in training. We expect them to teach classes at night. And we judge them for promotions and salary raises by their involvement in training, by their encouragement and their success in getting people into the training program."

While women hold just 2 percent of all construction jobs nationally, at BE&K the figure is close to 10 percent and growing quickly. The training program accounts for part of that difference; it has allowed unskilled women an entry into the profession and helped them raise their value as workers. But the company also has an unusually liberal policy about hiring pairs and teams from the same family. Antinepotism rules, many of them holdovers from the Depression years when employers tried to ensure that scarce jobs weren't concentrated in a few families, have kept many businesses from hiring husband-wife teams. At

BE&K, such teams are encouraged, as are parent-child teams. The only antinepotism rule here is that people can't work directly for their relatives. A husband and wife can work alongside each other as welders, but one cannot be the other's foreman.

"The construction industry used to be composed of a lot of families that went from site to site," explains Kennedy. "There were whole families who got to be known, who worked together, who stayed together. And they were very good workers. We decided that hiring family members was a good idea as opposed to a bad idea. When you start encouraging family teams, you immediately start talking about husband-and-wife teams too. It hasn't been common in construction, but it should be more of a natural thing. When you move around from location to location—and in industrial construction some of the sites are pretty remote—a husband is going to be a more satisfied employee if his wife is with him, if he doesn't have to drive home five or six hours on Friday night and all night Sunday to get back. So we encourage the idea that they stay together, and that has often meant bringing the wives onto the payroll."

As the company hired more women, it had to overcome the attitudes of many male workers that construction work could only be done by men, that women weren't strong enough for the heavy lifting required. "We had to start thinking in different terms," says Kennedy. "We started asking how many men can do that heavy lifting, and questioning how much of it was really necessary. We've mechanized construction work so thoroughly that we've moved away from manual labor on most jobs. And you put strong people on the jobs that require real strength. You don't put a one-hundred-pound male on a job that requires lifting five hundred pounds, nor do you put on a one-hundred-pound female. And we found that women are actually better at some jobs, like welding, that require particularly dexterous handwork." In fact, the company's welding training program is popular with women. Once they've become competent they can move directly into skilled jobs paying $12–15 per hour.

> *I was in the Army before I came to BE&K, and I got out because they wanted me to go to Korea for a year. They would not work with me in any way, either to let me take my son or to reassign me. And I wasn't going to leave a four-month-old baby for a year. The day care was one of the things that drew me to BE&K; they told me that they were building the center when I came for my job interview.*
>
> *I had him in a home day care before this center opened, but I wasn't really happy with it. They didn't do much with him, they didn't pay much attention to him. Here*

*they're teaching him. They have trained teachers here and it's quality care.*

*He's so important to me, and it's really nice to know that I can go to work and feel confident that he's getting good-quality care. I've never had that before. It means peace of mind for me. And when I work late I just call up, or my supervisor calls, and they stay open, at no extra charge to me. It doesn't cost me five dollars for every five minutes the way some places do.*

Through the 1980s, the company found more and more women on its payroll, more husband-and-wife teams, and more single mothers attracted by wages that were high enough to support a family. With that trend came an awareness by some managers at BE&K of the difficulties employees must face in finding child care that accommodates the time demands of construction work. BE&K's construction employees work four ten-hour days. That alone shuts parents out of many child-care centers that offer more limited hours. But the company also varies the starting time with the season in order to take advantage of as much daylight as possible. The normal starting time of 7:00 A.M. is shifted back during the early spring and fall to as early as 6:00 A.M. If it rains on one of the four work days, they make it up on the Friday, or even the Saturday, so the employees can get a full work week. If they are pouring concrete and the weather calls for rain the next day, they may keep working until 9:00 P.M.

"Those schedules create a problem with child care," says Kennedy. "We can't just walk into a community and say, 'I wonder if you can adjust your schedule to ours.' They'd ask us what our schedule is and we'd have to say, 'Well, we're not quite sure.' We'd thought about child care from time to time and dismissed it. We had decided the problem was just something we'd have to live with. But the more we thought about it, the more it didn't seem right. We'd found a way to train at every site, and to fit our training programs to the changing work schedules. We might start classes at five-thirty one night, at seven o'clock the next, then skip a night and start again on Friday. And I figured if we could be that adaptable there, we should be able to find some way to adapt child care to our schedules. If we could pull it off it would be a tremendous help to the single parent, male or female. It would help those parents who would like to work on Saturday but who can't find care. And it might help bring in those people—mothers in particular—who would like to work with us but can't find child care to match our hours."

Kathleen Martin, a child-care consultant in Birmingham, had

written a letter to the company offering her expertise in assessing the business's child-care needs. She had in mind a survey of BE&K's headquarters population and perhaps, if the numbers warranted it, advice and help in setting up programs to meet those needs. (Martin also acted as a consultant in the creation of the day-care center at St. Vincent's Hospital. See separate description.) "I got a call from them shortly afterward," Martin remembers. "At our first appointment they asked me to survey their home-office site about the need for on-site child care. But at the same meeting they asked me if I could build a day-care center that moved around. So I said I thought I could, that I'd have to look into it, that no one had ever asked me to do that before. And they said, 'We don't want to hear the problems, we just want to hear that you can do it.' "

Martin did look into it, and found that a number of child-care centers had been built with modular construction, using long, trailerlike units that can be combined into all sorts of configurations. Some builders had opted for modular construction because of severe time restraints, others when the technique had proved less expensive than conventional construction. None of the centers had been built to be movable, but Martin figured that the basic units could be combined into a child-care center for two or three years, then separated back into single units to be moved. She talked with modular-construction companies that had some experience with child-care centers, educated herself on the possibilities and the pitfalls, and drew up some specifications for BE&K.

For a year they talked informally about the idea, and she worked on the survey of the headquarters population. Then, in August 1989, the company decided to go ahead with the mobile child-care center and to build it at the Port Wentworth, Georgia, site. Says Kennedy, "I decided we were going to bite the bullet. We decided on the location in Georgia for two main reasons. It was a long-term project that we knew was going to have some odd hours. And we knew there would be other construction projects in the area and that we would be competing for people. We were going to need an edge."

To work with Martin and to oversee the project for the company, Kennedy chose a sixty-five-year-old veteran of the construction business, Irving Pearl. Pearl had worked on dozens of large-scale industrial projects, managing the construction of automobile manufacturing plants, cement plants, food-processing plants, and paper mills. Kennedy remembers the reaction he got when he assigned Pearl to the task. "He looked at me and said, 'Why me?' "

"I've been in industrial construction for forty years," says

Pearl. "When we first talked about it I was really concerned about the liability of taking on children of construction workers. And when they told me the age range, that they would take kids from zero to ten, I was appalled. It took a little doing to get myself acclimated to that thinking, though I wasn't really involved in that end of it. My primary duty was to select the site."

After careful consideration, BE&K leased land for the center about a mile from the construction site, close enough to be convenient but not so close that the children might be exposed to industrial hazards. The lot is well off the route taken by trucks bringing material to and from the job and has the added advantage of being a short walk from the town's elementary school, a tremendous asset for the center's before- and after-school program.

Martin and Pearl supervised the assembly of five 14 × 70–foot modular units into a square 70 × 70–foot building. They oversaw the installation of plumbing, electricity, and a complete fire-sprinkler system. They planned and supervised construction of the playground. Martin worked on the staffing and the program planning. And the entire facility was completed less than five months after the decision was made to build it. It opened on January 8, 1990, while the construction project was still in its early phases. By June, when the project was in full swing, it was caring for its full quota of sixty-five children. All of the mothers with children enrolled were taking advantage of the training program, and to accommodate their schedules the center stayed open ninety hours each week.

> I'm a subcontractor to BE&K, and they allow us to use the child-care center at the same rate as regular employees. My wife had to take care of some pressing family matters— her grandmother needs to be moved from a retirement community into a nursing home—so I'm keeping my son on the road for about a month and a half.
>
> Without the center this would have been very difficult. We come into an area to do a job and we don't know anyone, and there's not really time to meet the local people and find day care. To find care to match these hours might have been impossible, and who knows what our chances would be of finding good-quality care. It would have just been potluck. My boy is enjoying it here. He's taken to it like a duck to water.

Inside the building, little evidence remains of the modular sections from which it was built. While some of the early publicity described it as an assemblage of "trailers," the term is not quite accurate, and the open spaces inside bear little relation to the fourteen-foot widths of the sections. The rooms feel spacious, and with the children's paintings on the walls, the shelves stacked with blocks and toys, and the obligatory classroom pets, it feels much like any other child-care center.

The care here is actually quite a bit better than the standard in the community. While Georgia state regulations allow ratios of up to seven infants for every teacher, and up to ten toddlers, BEKare holds to the much stricter standards established by the National Association for the Education of Young Children. BE&K spent $750,000 building the center, a cost that might have been reduced substantially if the company had not demanded such a high level of quality. "I've always had the view that you should do things right if you're going to do them at all," says Kennedy. "That has guided our decisions about everything from the design of our offices to our company picnic. And when we came to planning the child-care center that was doubly important. It wasn't just a matter of how comfortable we were in our offices. The well-being of those children was at stake, and the peace of mind of their parents. I'm not about to face some mother who is irate because we don't have first-class facilities and first-class teachers. Because I know how I would have felt about that if they were my children when they were young. I know how irate I would have been. So it was either going to be a quality center or we weren't going to do it. And while we may have spent some extra money to do that, those expenses get amortized over the next five years, and we won't miss them. I always find that if I do it right the first time I don't miss the money."

The modest little center probably earned back a healthy chunk of that investment by generating a wave of free publicity. During the spring of 1990, it was featured in *The New York Times*, on NBC's "Sunday Today," on the CNN "News Hour," and on ESPN's "Nation's Business Today."

BE&K came back to Kathleen Martin in the summer of 1990 with yet another child-care project. Her 1988 survey of the home-office population in Birmingham had showed no great need for on-site care. Employees were generally satisfied with the quality and cost of the care they had. Some relied on relatives and weren't interested in care outside the family. But after seeing the success of the center in Port Wentworth, Ted Kennedy decided that even the low numbers of interested parents were enough to warrant the company's attention to the matter. He decided to go ahead and build a center next to the main offices, to open in 1991. "I guess I am going on my gut reaction," he says. "My feeling is that people don't give surveys much thought. I have five grown children of my own, and I know that if I had had the opportunity to bring them to work with me, and to drop them off at a center with the highest possible quality of care, I would have taken advantage of it. My feeling is that once it's there, and people see how good it is and how convenient, they will want to use it. I'm confident that it will become an asset to us."

Irving Pearl, the manager who oversaw the construction of the Port Wentworth center, is looking forward to the day when that building is moved. "I think we'll get about a year and a half out of this location," he says, "and then we'll take it to the next one. I'm anxious to see just how well we can amortize the investment in the facility. We'll lose the money we put into the landscaping, of course, and the underground utility work, and much of the fire-sprinkler system. But we should be able to move the building two or three times before it gets so worn that repairs would make another move impractical. It will be interesting to see how well we can keep the relocation costs down.

"But for now," he adds, "I think we have some happy children out there and some pleased parents."

# Dunning, Forman, Kirrane & Terry

Box 560, Route 28
Mashpee, MA 02649                                        508-477-6500

*Nature of business:* Law firm.
*Number of employees:* 22 (10 attorneys).
*Female employees:* 14 (2 of 5 partners).
*Child care:* On-site center for 57 children, aged two years nine months to five years; child-care subsidy program.
*Elder care:* No formal program.
*Family leave:* Job-protected leave of twelve weeks at half pay with option to extend without pay.
*Flexible work options:* Flexible work schedules and part-time work available for partners and support staff.
*Other benefits:* Annual length-of-service bonuses; attendance bonuses; flexible benefit plan.

Where accommodation is a policy.

*"Lawyers who work here who've worked other places say it's totally different here from any place else they've been.*

*Not in terms of the strict benefits, like health insurance, but just in the added benefits, or things that they didn't expect.*

*"Every man in this office is very, very involved with his family, and it's refreshing to see—especially the ones who come in in the morning with their little kids. You know, the fathers are walking in the door and they've got a teddy bear hanging from one hand and a lunch box in the other, and they look very masculine to me."*

PAM TERRY
Partner

*"We have two-wage-earner families now, and we need to service our employees and get a competitive edge in the marketplace. This is reality."*

ROBERT TERRY
Former Partner,
now Associate Justice,
Barnstable District Court

Clients who visit the Cape Cod law firm of Dunning, Forman, Kirrane & Terry on Halloween day are likely to have a surprise. Children from the child-care center located in the same building as the law offices parade through the firm in costume, just as they do at Christmas, Easter, and on the center's very own holiday—"Musical Hat Day." Do the clients object to the brief, lighthearted intrusion into their legal matters?

"No, they don't," says a senior partner. "The clients like to see the parades, they really do. You know, so often they're here because they have a problem. It helps lighten things up for a minute."

The firm began in 1974 with three attorneys. Since then, it has tripled in size. Two of the five partners are women; one associate is a woman; and, until recently, when founding partner Bob Terry left the partnership to become a judge, the roster of attorneys included two married couples, who, like other attorneys at the firm, have raised or are raising children while practicing law.

In 1980, managing partner Bob Terry initiated a program of directly subsidizing employee child-care costs. He says that the subsidy arrangement met an "obvious need" given the age profile of the firm; at the time the oldest employee was forty. In 1985, he decided that it was time to meet the child-care needs of attorneys and staff at the firm in a more direct way. Although he and his wife, Pam Terry, also a partner at the firm, already had satisfactory child-care arrangements of their own, they began to look at the possibility of on-site care.

Terry initially explored the idea of renovating existing space in the building in which the firm was located, but the plan appeared prohibitively expensive. A man not easily daunted, Terry persevered. By chance, his investigation of on-site care coincided with the independent decision of several partners to build, as a personal venture, a small office complex that would house the firm and several other tenants. With Terry at the helm, the firm decided to plan the space to include a child-care center.

Using no particular employer-supported center as a model, Terry devised an innovative financial structure for the center. He persuaded Paula Martin, a family child-care provider in a nearby town, to be the center's director and owner. Together, Terry and Martin planned and oversaw the development of the center—Terry concentrating on supervising the building of the center so that it met Massachusetts legal requirements, and Martin hiring staff, purchasing equipment, and developing the educational program.

The firm leased the space to the center at no cost for a start-up period and guaranteed that it would fill and subsidize a specific number of places with children of Dunning, Forman, Kirrane & Terry employees. In exchange, Martin agreed to give preferred status on the waiting list to children of firm employees.

Bob Terry attributes much of the success of the firm's child-care program to the fact that only two people, Paula Martin and he—with the firm's support—were directly involved in the project, and invites a contrast to the approach a large metropolitan firm might take: "They'd set up a committee of ten, fifteen, maybe twenty people and start talking about hundreds of thousands of dollars and come up with fifteen reasons why they couldn't do it. Then it becomes overwhelming and impossible to keep pushing the plan forward. It's better to do it from the bottom up instead of the top down."

The all-day child-care program the children of firm employees attend is made possible by the center's half-day nursery school program. Forty-seven children from the ages of two years nine months to five years attend its morning preschool program only; ten additional children, four of whom are children of the law firm's employees, attend the preschool program plus an extended-day program that lasts until 5:00 P.M.

Aside from the obvious benefit of reduced commuting time, Paula Martin sees a special advantage for the children whose parents work in the same building as the center: "The most important thing is that the center is like an extension of the family. You can keep consistency between family and center going. You really know the child, because you know the family."

> *I have two children, a daughter in the center, and a baby in family day care, and I've arranged a part-time work schedule for myself. I work five days, but I leave at 3:00 P.M. I usually go down and visit my daughter in the morning. Eventually, I think, when I can get the baby here, too, I'll feel comfortable going back to full time. I could go down and spend ten minutes twice a day with them. Those little visits make a big difference to me—maybe even more than to the children.*

Parents at the firm who have children in the center feel free to visit them during the day and often have lunch with them. Before he left the firm, Bob Terry, who had no children of his own at the center, often visited for snack time and joined in at coloring sessions. The children reciprocate by visiting upstairs, not just for parades, but for spur-of-the-moment field trips to the photocopy center and the mailroom.

The firm continually struggles with efforts to provide care for infants as well as preschoolers. Although it is located in an area with abundant family child care for infants, it would like to provide on-site care for infants of employees. So far, the firm says, the expense of meeting the staff and physical requirements for licensed infant care is prohibitive, given the little and sporadic demand it feels for such care.

> *When my daughter first started, I'd go down there every hour. Now I go down there, if I'm not at court, maybe at 10:00 or 10:30 A.M. Sometimes she says, "Hi, Daddy, go back to work." I'll go down at lunchtime some days, and again at 3:30.*

Several large law firms have created emergency child-care systems—some of them on-site—to provide temporary help for parents whose usual child-care providers are sick or unavailable for other reasons, or to provide additional care to allow parents to work on weekends or holidays. Bob Terry is not especially impressed with this response to child-care needs. "It's a start," he says, "but there's no reason why they can't move along into a regular program."

By the summer of 1990, Dunning, Forman, Kirrane & Terry was the only American law firm we could discover that provides regular on-site care for employees' children during ordinary working hours. The firm also continues to subsidize employee child-care costs, not only for parents who use the on-site center, but also for parents who choose other child-care options.

The firm's pro-family attitude shows in other ways as well: part-time and flexible schedules are available as a matter of course to working parents, both attorneys and support staff; and weekend work is not expected routinely, but only, as one partner put it, "when the work demands it"—for example, when a trial is imminent or under way, or a deal is about to close. A partner who concentrates in real estate work and has two small children leaves at 3:00 P.M. each day; Pam Terry has worked a four-day week for her entire career with the firm.

Parents may take three months off at half pay for the birth or adoption of a baby, and may extend the time with additional unpaid leave. One employee took six months off; the firm says it has not yet received a request for a longer leave.

In a time when the legal profession is generally making greater and greater demands on the time of its workers—many metropolitan law firms routinely expect attorneys to work late into the evening, on weekends, and holidays—Dunning, Forman, Kirrane & Terry remains committed to allowing its employees time to be with their families and to be involved in their communities. The partnership says that, unlike many firms, it evaluates employee performance not so much on the number of hours billed to clients as on the quality of the work performed. And while many law firms divide benefits on "class" lines, offering more flexibility and greater support to attorneys, while providing staff with a reduced benefit package, Dunning, Forman, Kirrane & Terry extends the same family-friendly benefits to all of its employees.

Dunning, Forman, Kirrane & Terry may be a small firm, but its size belies its potential as a model for other firms. For the few fortunate enough to work there, it offers a haven for working parents in the legal profession.

# Fel-Pro Incorporated

7450 N. McCormick Boulevard
Skokie, IL 60076                                708-674-7700

**Nature of business:** Manufacturer of engine gaskets and chemical products.
**Number of employees:** 2,100.

**Female employees:** 40 percent (10 percent of officials and managers).

**Child care:** On-site center for 45 children, aged two to six years; summer day camp for 300 children, aged six to fifteen; subsidized in-home care-giving service for temporary care emergencies and for care of mildly ill children; informal information-and-referral service through child-care center.

**Elder care:** Subsidized emergency home care; consultation-and-referral service through employee-assistance program.

**Family leave:** Paid disability leave for childbirth, plus up to two months unpaid family-care leave.

**Flexible work options:** Flexible work hours arranged individually; some part-time work.

**Other benefits:** Tutoring service for children with learning problems; college scholarships for employees' children; $100 gifts to newlyweds and to employees' children on graduation from high school; $1,000 gift to new babies; $1,500 adoption aid; subsidized cafeteria; tuition reimbursement; 200-acre recreation park; on-site fitness center; employee-assistance program; legal information service; tax preparation service.

Helping employees by helping their families.

*"Someone once asked me what would happen if every company did what we do, whether we would lose our competitive advantage. Well, I think that would be wonderful. It would be wonderful if our children weren't used as bargaining chips. We really would have an educated work force if every company thought a little more about what they could do for their employees' children. And I'll tell you, we do have tough competition out there—in Germany and Japan. All of us in this country should be doing a little more to educate the next generation of workers."*

ELLIOT LEHMAN
Former Co-Chairperson

It is seven-thirty on a summer morning outside Fel-Pro's manufacturing plant and headquarters in Skokie, Illinois. Drivers speeding through this industrial part of town might not notice the low brick factory building, similar to many others in the blocks nearby; but they can't help noticing the six yellow school buses lined up in front, and the hundreds of children climbing aboard and yelling good-byes to their parents. This is not a special family day at Fel-Pro, not an annual company picnic in the country. This massing of children and buses is a part of the daily routine. Every morning during the summer months, more than three hundred children ride to work with their parents and board the buses for a day of summer camp at the company's 200-acre park in Cary, Illinois.

By 8:00 A.M. the buses are gone and the stamping, pressing, vulcanizing, and coating work is well under way inside the gasket factory. But not all the children have left. At the far side of the company's parking lot, another forty-five children, too young for summer camp, are beginning their day at the company's child-care center.

With its own summer camp and child-care center, Fel-Pro has long been a leader in the trend toward corporate support for parents and children. But the company's support programs don't end there. Somewhere in the city of Chicago, children of other Fel-Pro employees may be sitting down to tutoring sessions to overcome problems they have encountered during the school year. Other Fel-Pro offspring hold summer jobs at the plant, on break from college educations funded, in part, by Fel-Pro scholarships. A younger child who feels a little sick this morning may be staying home with an experienced care giver sent out by the company's emergency child-care service. An elderly parent recovering from a broken arm may be attended by an aid from the same service.

No other American company offers such a comprehensive array of supports for working family members; and while other companies newer to this game boast loudly of their efforts, Fel-Pro goes quietly about its business, and seems almost embarrassed by the attention it has received. Managers at Fel-Pro don't see their efforts as remarkable, but wonder instead why so few companies have followed their lead.

*My daughter has been in the day care since she was two, and she will go to school in the fall. That's going to be a difficult transition for her, because every single child in that class is going to a different school. But you know what she is looking forward to? The summer day camp. She knows that she's going to be separated from these kids that she's been with for four years. They're her family. But she knows that she'll see them next summer at the day camp. She says, "I went to day care, Mommy, and I'm going to day camp. Then I'm going to work in the summer at Fel-Pro. Then I'm going to work at Fel-Pro." She's a Fel-Pro kid.*

"We didn't sit down and decide to help the family," explains Elliot Lehman, who shared control of the company during the years when many of these programs took shape. "These things just evolved over time from our efforts to listen to our people and to help out where we can."

The company has a tradition of listening to its employees and of responding. Its Employee Forum has met monthly since 1952, attended by top officers and managers and by employee representatives from each work area in the business. Employees listen to financial reports, sales and production goals, manufacturing plans, and other management concerns, then get a chance to ask the head of the company whatever questions are on their minds.

At those meetings, and in the day-to-day contacts of business, managers at Fel-Pro try to get a sense of their employees' needs and concerns. Sometimes these come out in the form of point-blank questions and requests, which can range from basic issues like wages to the lighting in an area of the plant. Now that people realize the possibilities, employees sometimes ask about expanded child-care services, such as infant care or evening care. But just as often, Fel-Pro's managers have come up with the ideas themselves by listening to employees' personal worries, projecting from their own concerns as parents, or by noticing patterns of absenteeism and trying to figure out the causes.

> *There are a lot of ethnic groups here and they all work as a family. We're all different people, of course, but when you're in Fel-Pro you're all the same. There are no big I's and little you's. The presidents and vice presidents eat what we eat. They drive in the weather that we drive in. There are no limousines or chauffeurs or anything like that. We're all people and we need to be treated as people, and at Fel-Pro that's understood. The company has systems for listening to everybody. They have monthly meetings where you can voice your opinion—the Employee Forum. Two years ago I was a representative—now someone else in my group is—and it was very enlightening. People would talk about all kinds of things. And they listened. That's the key. They do listen. And you do get results.*

In the late 1960s, the company's owners realized that many employees lived in the city and had few options for recreation during the summer. Lake Michigan's beaches are generally crowded during the summer, and the area has a limited supply of public parks. Employees' recreational choices were further complicated by racial issues. The company has long been committed to building a diverse work force, and many of its black, Hispanic, and Asian-American workers felt threatened and unwelcome at some parks outside of the city. Fel-Pro responded by buying a 200-acre parcel of land in Cary, Illinois, and opening it as an employee park—the Triple R Ranch.

"The Triple R Ranch didn't start out as a pristine resort," explains Robert O'Keefe, vice president of industrial relations. "In fact, I would describe it as a dump when we bought it. It had two spring-fed ponds, and we could see the possibilities in them, but they were filled with old tires. I remember seeing two washing machines in one of them. There were also two motorcycle gangs who thought of the property as their own for the first few months, and some neighbors who were afraid of the kind of population we'd be bringing out there. Someone tried to burn down the first pavilion we built. But when we showed that we were determined to improve the property, that we would call the police whenever we needed them, and when the neighbors had a chance to see that our employees could enjoy the property without bothering them, everything settled down nicely. We felt accepted after the first summer." The ponds were cleaned out in that first season, and since then the company has built an Olympic-sized swimming pool, an adjacent wading pool for children, a baseball diamond, and cross-country ski trails.

After a year of operating the park, Fel-Pro noticed that it wasn't used much during the week. Managers also began to pick up on worries some parents had about leaving their children with older siblings or overburdened relatives during summer vacations, or even alone to play on the streets. The answer: a summer camp at Triple R, launched in 1973. "There were forty-five children at the camp that first summer," recalls O'Keefe. "Five of them were mine. We could have handled more, but many people don't jump right into new programs. They want to wait and see how they turn out. The second year we had about seventy children; after five years it was up to a hundred and fifty; today we send over three hundred every day during the summer. If you tally up the number of children who've gone to the camp since it opened, you can see that we are reaching a major part of our population."

> I have two girls at the day camp, one eleven and the other eight. They go to the day camp each year. My oldest daughter also went to the day care when it started, back in 1983. She was one of the first ones in there. Both of them love the day camp. They learn a lot of new things there and they always look forward to going. And we know that Fel-Pro provides the best of care for them. We don't have

*to worry that they're in someone else's hands. They're not just in someone else's hands. They're in Fel-Pro's hands.*

Fel-Pro investigated the possibility of a year-round child-care center for younger children in the mid-1970s, but decided it would be too expensive, too difficult, and that the company could not afford to sacrifice any of its factory space. Then, during the early 1980s, federal budget cuts and reductions in social-service programs, including cuts in funding for child-care programs, prompted the company to take another look at the subject. "We felt a social responsibility to respond," says O'Keefe. But the lack of space almost derailed the plan again. The owners felt that the center should be on the premises in order to be of full value to employees, so that parents could visit easily during breaks from work. Yet the plant simply didn't have room to give up. Fortunately, a warehouse building adjoining Fel-Pro's lot, across the main parking lot from the factory, came on the market at about that time, and the company had a convenient answer. "If that land hadn't become available," says O'Keefe, "it might not have happened. But with that building it became a natural thing. It made perfect sense."

The company hired Scott Mies, who had been teaching courses in early-childhood education at a nearby college, to create and direct the program. He worked with the company's architect to renovate the building for its new purpose, and with the company's owners to establish the basic form of the program. One of the first decisions he made was to limit the center to children two or older who were already toilet-trained. This was partly because of space restrictions—to give up room for infants and toddlers would have eliminated play space for older children—but also because of the extra staff required for infant care, and the additional expenses of operating such a program. "It was sort of a decision to walk before we ran," explains O'Keefe.

The child-care center has since expanded to include an all-day kindergarten program; an effort to meet the needs of parents who faced care and scheduling difficulties with the half-day programs offered at most public schools. But, while Mies helps parents find other care for younger children, Fel-Pro has still not taken on the challenge of providing infant and toddler care.

The center opened in 1983 with about twenty children. It now serves more than twice that number, and the warehouse has been almost completely converted to classrooms. A large open space at one end of the building has been set aside for indoor play when the weather is bad. Mats cover the floors here, around a cluster of tunnels and climbing structures. Two large skylights overhead let in natural light on even the stormiest days. The outdoor playground has the usual tricycle tracks and climbing towers, and, at one end, a real caboose, donated by a Fel-Pro owner with a special interest in trains.

> *I have worked for this company for nineteen years, and if I didn't have the day care here, I wouldn't have continued working. It has made that big a difference to me. Coming from my culture—I'm Mexican—my thinking has always been that the mother stays at home once the children come. For the first two years after my daughter was born, my mother took care of her. But she was taking care of my mother-in-law at the same time, who had cancer, and it got to be bad. It was just too much for my mother.*
>
> *I decided that I would either have to leave work or find a day-care facility. Well, I didn't care for the day-care facilities I looked at. They would have all the infants' play-pens in the center of the room, and the older children were touching the infants. And I just didn't like that. I thought that something could happen to my daughter. I got scared. You know how it is. Toddlers two and three years old don't know what they're doing. They could throw a toy in the playpen.*
>
> *I had to make a decision at that point about whether to leave work. Somebody suggested I go in and talk to Bob O'Keefe. I told him what was going on in my personal life, and he said he would talk to the people at the day-care center. The next day my daughter was in the center. That's how quickly Fel-Pro acted. Because they understood my need. And having her over there gives me a peace of mind that I can't describe to you.*

Another piece of Fel-Pro's family-support system actually predates both the summer camp and the child-care center. The company has offered college scholarships for employees' children since the 1960s. Many companies offer a limited number of scholarships to children selected as National Merit scholars, or to a few children from low-income families. Fel-Pro has chosen to create a scholarship program that benefits a broader spectrum of employees. "We chose not to base the program on financial need," explains O'Keefe, "because that sort of selection process sometimes belittles people. And we chose not to limit it to great scholars, because those people are likely to get scholarships anyway. In our program, all the kids have to do is attend an accredited school and meet the academic requirements to stay there. They don't have to get A's."

Fel-Pro pays up to $2,800 a year for four years, to help cover the costs of tuition, books, and supplies. The school must be an accredited institution, it must require a high school diploma to attend, and students must apply for the funding at least a month before school starts. Beyond that, the company places virtually no restrictions on the scholarships. While some large companies give out a handful of scholarships, Fel-Pro awards more than one hundred every year, and over the course of the program has helped almost 1,000 students earn their degrees. A good number take summer jobs at the company, and many come aboard as full-time employees after graduation. "It was never intended as a benefit for us in this way," says O'Keefe, "but an incredible number are working with us today."

The company has recently expanded its college aid with a service that helps high school students decide which college is right for them. "They have this service at most high schools," says O'Keefe, "but it's poorly done. We decided to offer a personalized service that gives them one-on-one consultations with real experts in the field, Saturday seminars, and weekend visits to area campuses."

Two other services were created to plug gaps in the family-support system. One of the owners noticed that the scholarship program was providing a tremendous help to those children who graduated from high school and went on to college, but that other children were missing out—children who encountered difficulties in school, started to lag behind, and eventually dropped out or gave up their educations after high school. The owners discussed the concept of offering help to troubled students, then came across a service that offered just that, called One-to-One Tutoring. Since 1984, Fel-Pro employees have been able to call on the service for free consultation, and, if deemed appropriate, to proceed with diagnostic testing and in-home tutoring, the fees largely subsidized by Fel-Pro.

An emergency-care service was added to the benefit package in 1987. "We found out that having a day-care center doesn't answer all the care-giving problems of our employees," says O'Keefe. "Many of our employees weren't interested in the day care at all. It was more convenient for them to bring the children to a grandparent or a neighbor. But when a child is sick, or when that care giver is sick, parents run into problems, particularly when they are involved with something at work that makes it difficult for them to take time off. The day-care center couldn't help with those problems. We realized that an emergency care-giver service could take care of this other link."

Trained providers are sent out by Family Care Services of Metropolitan Chicago, a one-hundred-year-old social-service agency. The service costs $8 per hour, of which the company pays $6 and the employees $2. Though it was designed as a child-care service, Fel-Pro soon discovered that it could be just as valuable an aid to workers with elder-care emergencies. In fact, some of the most dramatic and successful stories of its use have come from employees whose elderly parents have needed short-term assistance.

> *My mother, who's eighty-nine years old, lives with me. She's not a sickly person. But two months ago she fell and broke her arm. And she could not be left alone. And I had a problem. I have a major responsibility here, and it's im-portant that I be here every day. There was no way I'd be able to work at all unless I had someone stay with my mom. You can get people to stay on your own, of course, but it's very costly. Well, we have this care-giver program, and I'd heard it worked well with the kids, so I called them. They immediately made arrangements to send someone to our house for those two weeks. I was there the first morning, and I met the care giver. She was wonderful. She was mar-velous. My mother loved her. My mother would have loved to keep her forever, just to be with her.*
>
> *The same service offers a respite program. If I need to get away for an evening or a weekend day, they can send someone to our home. I haven't used it yet, but I'm plan-ning on trying it this summer. My mom's been with me for seven years, and I haven't been away at all. I haven't had any vacation. Up until this person came to stay with her, she would never agree to have anyone come in. I would say, "I'll get someone to come in while I go away for the weekend," and she would say, "No, I don't want anyone to come in." Now she's open to it. So the broken arm was a good thing in a way. Because now she's aware that this place will furnish us with someone who's wonderful. And I'm really looking forward to a weekend away.*

Because of its long history of support for employees' family needs, and because for many years it stood out as one of the few companies responding to those needs at all, Fel-Pro has for many years served as a model for what employers can do. Visitors regularly make pilgrimages to the plant, the day-care center, and the summer camp. And business executives continually ask what the bottom-line results have been, whether the company is earning a return on its investment in family benefits.

"We are a for-profit corporation," explains Elliot Lehman, "and if our profits can contribute to the well-being of the people who are associated with us, we are delighted. And it does work

out that way. We also think that this is good for our business."
Lehman and O'Keefe point to the company's low turnover rate
as one key benefit for the business—more than a third of Fel-
Pro's workers have been with the company ten years or more,
and 60 percent have been there for more than five years—and
to the tremendous sense of loyalty among Fel-Pro's workers.
Both know individual workers who would have left the company
if the day-care center had not been available, who would have
missed weeks of work without the emergency care-giving service, and both talk about the tremendous commitment Fel-Pro's
workers feel to the company.

Explaining why the company does so much for employees'
children, O'Keefe says, "As a parent, your greatest concern will
always be your children. If an employer really wants to turn on
a parent, it should do something for the children. And I'm telling
you, we get loyal people by doing that, people who will go to
the wall for us." O'Keefe can recall terminations at which "the
employees were furious at their immediate supervisors but
walked out the door thinking that Fel-Pro was the greatest company in the world," so strong was their loyalty to the company.

Lehman tells of the day he needed a ride home, and started
talking with the worker assigned to drive him. "I asked him
where he was from, and he said Puerto Rico. Then I asked him
if he wouldn't like to go back there, now that the weather was
getting lousy in Chicago. He said, 'I know who you are. What
I'm going to tell you you may think I'm telling you because of
who you are. I want to die at Fel-Pro. I waited three years to get
a job here, and now that I'm here I never want to leave. I want
my family to stay here.' "

Lehman also talks of the importance of educated workers to
the company's future. "Why do we give out scholarships? Why
do we subsidize this tutoring program? Why do we run a summer
camp and a day-care center? Because 37 percent of the kids who
graduate from high school are illiterate. We have to have workers. There's not a job in this place that doesn't require some
education. We're not a high-tech company, but everybody has
to read. To monitor quality you have to know simple arithmetic;
you have to be able to read a micrometer. And by doing what
we do, we're saying, 'This is what society needs and we are a
part of that society.' And if we are in competition with other
companies for the employees of the future, we have an advantage
by growing our own. Sure, we're doing it for the kids and because
we think it's right. But we're also doing it for ourselves."

*I've worked for good bosses at other companies, and I
was loyal to them, but I've never had the loyalty to the*

*company that I have here at Fel-Pro. A lot of that has to do with the feeling I get that they care. They care about me. They care about my family. They want to do whatever they can to accommodate me and give me the tools to work with so I can take care of my family and have some peace of mind when I walk in here. I've been with companies that give me big raises. And that impressed me. But this impresses me much more.*

*I'd never heard of Fel-Pro before I came here. When a headhunter called about this job, he said, "You just won't believe the benefits." I never thought that benefits could be like that. I always just said, "What's the pay?" But after I went in and talked I thought I just had to get a job here. There is a lot of involvement here. I didn't apply anywhere else. I actually took the job because of the work I would be doing. I am a systems analyst and the job was to put a new system in. But the benefits are why I tell everyone they should come here. And they're why I hope never to leave.*

Fel-Pro defines its self-interest in broader terms than most businesses. "Someone once asked me what would happen if every company did what we do," says Lehman, "whether we would lose our competitive advantage. Well, I think that would be wonderful. It would be wonderful if our children weren't used as bargaining chips. We really would have an educated work force if every company thought a little more about what they could do for their employees' children. And I'll tell you, we *do* have tough competition out there—in Germany and Japan. All of us in this country should be doing a little more to educate the next generation of workers."

Lehman has traveled the country speaking to business groups on the importance of addressing family issues. He has served on task forces and committees, all with the goal of raising awareness in the business community to the need for greater support for child care and education. But he has always been frustrated by the lack of proof that efforts like those at Fel-Pro pay off in dollars and cents. "How do you put a value on trust and loyalty?" he asks. "How much does a company gain from a healthy and educated work force?"

Fel-Pro is satisfied that it is succeeding in creating a supportive work environment for people with family responsibilities—few companies come close to the breadth of its support programs—but it is less happy with its success as a role model. To strengthen its case, Fel-Pro decided in 1990 to find out what the bottom-line results of its policies are. It commissioned a study by the University of Chicago, to be conducted as a joint effort by both the Graduate School of Business and the School of Social Service Administration. "Their job is not to prove that enlightened employee benefits contribute to profits," says Lehman, "but to determine whether they do. We know for ourselves that it works for us. We have enough anecdotal information that comes back to us and says this works, that our people want it."

Though Fel-Pro remains frustrated at being a leader with few followers, the company's owners and managers are pleased with their successes. They are proud of the loyalty that Fel-Pro has earned from its workers. They are proud of a work force that includes younger workers who have attended the company's summer camp, gone to college with the help of its scholarships, and on graduation have wanted jobs at their parents' company. And they know that some day soon they will have graduates of Fel-Pro's day-care center on the payroll.

# Grieco Bros., Inc.

50 Island Street
Lawrence, MA 01840                                    508-686-3833

*Nature of business:* Manufacturer of fine men's suits sold under the Southwick label.
*Number of employees:* 750.
*Female employees:* 59 percent (4 of 11 foremen; 7 of 12 department heads).
*Child care:* On-site center for 85 children aged fifteen months to six years, income-based subsidies, pretax salary set-aside (DCAP).
*Elder care:* Pretax salary set-aside (DCAP).
*Family leave:* Paid disability leave for childbirth, plus unpaid family-care leave to total of six months.
*Flexible work options:* Limited flextime; some part-time work.
*Other benefits:* English classes on company time; 401(k) plan with employer contribution; family health insurance for all employees including doctor and dentist visits.

On-site child care—finding answers in partnership

> *"We didn't realize how much of a partnership it really was until it started to come together in the late part of that summer of 1985. When we got everybody in the room together at the dedication of the center, and we started to check off who had done what, we finally convinced ourselves that it had in fact been a partnership effort."*
>
> ANTHONY R. SAPIENZA
> Vice President, Manufacturing

Approaching the Grieco Bros. factory in Lawrence, Massachusetts, is like driving backward in time. From the wide lanes of Interstate 93 an exit ramp arcs alongside a canal into a cluster of massive brick mill buildings that stir up images of another era. The largest, just across the Merrimack River, supports a Victorian clock tower that soars eight stories above the current. That building, and the one beside it, lie vacant, waiting for some new wave of enterprise to take the place of the textile businesses that once thrived here.

A side street takes the visitor to the Grieco Bros. factory, a five-story expanse of brick with the year "1916" carved in stone over the doorway. At first glance the mill looks like its silent counterparts across the river—a historical artifact ready to be turned into a museum or condominium development. But a closer look shows that work has been done here and continues to be done. The multipaned windows of the old mills have been replaced with picture windows, the parking lot is full of cars, and through the mill's windows the lights and activity of a working factory can be seen. And just to the side of the main entrance is a fenced-in playground with slides, swings, and a sandbox.

The hum of work that sets the mill apart from its empty neighbors marks Grieco Bros. as a tenacious survivor in a city where most of the old businesses have failed or moved to where labor is cheaper. The sounds from the playground, and from the day-care center just inside, mark the company as a pioneer in answering the needs of its largely female work force.

"We simply saw it as a necessity," recalls Anthony R. Sapienza, manufacturing vice president, of the decision to provide on-site employee child care.

Nicholas and Vito Grieco, brothers from a mountain village near Naples, Italy, came to the United States in 1904 and for two decades plied their tailor's trade in New York City. From a suit-pressing business in Brooklyn, they advanced to a tailor shop on Manhattan's Fifth Avenue, and, in 1929, to their own suit-making business, which they dubbed Grieco Bros., in Lawrence, Massachusetts. Over the years, the business has carved itself a reliable niche in the manufacture of fine-quality men's sack suits—suits whose classic lines aren't greatly affected by gyrating fashion trends. Today the firm's customers include such dignified dressers as George Bush.

From the start, Grieco Bros. drew its workers from Lawrence's close-knit Italian community. In these first-generation immigrants, and later in their children, the company found a ready supply of skilled and dependable craftspeople—men and women trained in the cloth trades, many of whom had left poverty to build new lives in America. The cultural cohesiveness of the community carried over to the factory. Owners, foremen, and workers generally lived in the same neighborhoods, shopped at the same stores, went to the same church, and spoke the same language. Those bonds fostered a family atmosphere at work and helped to keep people at their jobs, often for decades. As a result, workers often knew their jobs better than their supervisors did. And—critical in a piecework factory making fine-quality suits—they understood where the balance lay between production speed and quality.

> *My mother worked here. She retired here after fifty-one years. My father retired after forty-two. There are still quite a few people from when my parents worked here. They keep in touch. My father plays cards with them on Friday night. I started working part-time when I was still in high school. Then I went on to full time. I liked it. I like the people. And I think that's a lot when you like the people you work for. And I like my job.*

"That work force was the blood and guts of this company," recalls Sapienza. But, as the company aged, so did its workers. Vito Grieco retired from the business in 1962, and Nicholas died in 1979 at the age of eighty-two, leaving the business in the hands of his son Richard. Sapienza assumed his own role of vice president in charge of production when his father Angelo retired from the post in 1981.

In the late 1970s and early 1980s, up and down the production line, workers began retiring. Some amazement still enters Sapienza's voice when he remembers the turnover problems in his first years on the job. "We started to have incredible numbers of retirees—thirty, thirty-five, forty people a year, people with twenty-five to fifty years experience with Grieco Bros." And that retirement wave collided head-on with a growth in sales and a need for increased production.

To cope with its growing labor shortage the company explored several options at once. It opened a factory closer to Boston, hoping to draw experienced workers sloughed off by cutbacks at other businesses in a bigger population center. But the company was unable to attract the semiskilled workers that it needed there—workers willing to accept low wages during a long training period while they gained the speed necessary for good piecework pay.

With the taste of that relocation disaster in their mouths, the new managers redoubled efforts to find workers in Lawrence. In the early 1980s the company actively recruited in countries as distant as Turkey, trying to find skilled hand-stitchers willing to immigrate to the United States. Sapienza's background in social work—from 1971 to 1973 he had worked at a settlement house and had run a job-matching and delinquency-prevention program for the city of Cambridge—led him naturally into the network of government-sponsored employment programs. He hired some ex-offenders through a state work-release program. He took some graduates of the regional vocational school. And he picked up workers through Supported Work, a poverty-agency program run by the Greater Lawrence Community Action Council. This last program brought in a new, stable group of workers— welfare mothers who had been out of the labor force because of child-care responsibilities. The company provided a full-time training program, set up in a separate part of the factory, and the state chipped in with some support for the parents' child-care costs.

That Grieco Bros. did manage to find new workers to replace its retirees was due as much to a fortuitous change in Lawrence's population as to Sapienza's diligence. Just as a wave of Italian immigration had provided Grieco Bros. with its first workers, new waves of immigration from Central and South America, the West Indies, and Southeast Asia provided their successors. The result of the company's drive for fresh hands was a dramatic change in the work force.

One obvious difference was in language. Where supervisors had once been able to talk to employees as easily in Italian as in English, Spanish now took over as the dominant language on the factory floor. To help minimize the language barrier, says Sapienza, "We began to do things differently, whether it was hiring a personnel clerk who spoke Spanish, or a payroll clerk who was Hispanic, or a mechanic, or a stitching examiner. Whenever we could we would hire Hispanics."

Just as fundamental was a shift in the nature of employees' links to the company. The old cultural and community bond between owner, supervisor, and worker was now more tenuous when all came from such different backgrounds. Management worried that without the old cultural cement to bind them to the factory, these new employees would not last as long, and might not earn back for the company their high training costs.

Finally, the new workers were much younger than those they replaced; many were mothers of young children; and many of those seemed to be surviving without the support of the extended family that had so often helped young families of the previous generation. While the typical Italian worker of the 1950s had lived in a triple-decker with grandparents upstairs and uncles and cousins next door, many of these young mothers were raising children alone.

This last work-force change was not as hidden as it might seem. In the early 1980s the Grieco Bros. factory sometimes looked like a nursery school as children arrived after school, or when day-care arrangements broke down, and either sat by their mothers' machines (against company orders) or played in the conference rooms and offices on the fifth floor. Personnel manager Gerry DeFrancesco remembers afternoons when five or six children played with coloring books on the floor of her office. Although the company had always liked to think of itself as a family, this somehow wasn't part of that vision.

> *I have a three-year-old son in the day-care center. My mother took care of him when he was a baby, but now he's gotten more active, and I figured he'd be happier with other kids his own age. And he loves it. He's learned to speak Spanish. My mother just had him by himself, so he was kind of confined, just at her house. Some mornings I'll say to him, "Would you rather go to Nanny's?" And he'll say, "No. I want to go to school." And he used to love to go to my mother's. And he's doing real good. They evaluate them, and they say he's really smart, he's the first one to answer in English and in Spanish.*

"I remember the conversation with the few American-born women that we had," says Sapienza, "women we'd attracted through the employment training program—because everybody wasn't Hispanic—saying that they were going to leave because they were going to have babies or they just couldn't find appropriate care for their kids. And we had a meeting one day and said we really should think about a day-care center. This was in October or November 1984.

"I had a sense that it would not only help us recruit, but, more importantly, would help us build some linkage to this new population. Because when people are on piecework if they don't care about this company they're going to butcher the work. I felt very strongly that we could, with a child-care center and with other programs, start to develop this quality consciousness, this positive reinforcement if you will, for what we stood for as a company and for the kind of product that we make.

"So I went to my cousin, Richard Grieco, and said, 'Look, I think we can put a day-care center together that will really help solve my recruiting problems.' He said, 'What's it going to cost?' I said, 'I think I can do it for about fifty thousand dollars.' And he said, 'Hey, that's cheaper than some of the other things you've been suggesting that we do around here. Let's do it.' "

> *The day-care center opened when my oldest daughter was four. The baby-sitter I had before had three children of her own, watched three of mine, two of another lady's, and one more. She had six baby-sitting and three of her own. It was all I could get. I used to pay seventy-five dollars—twenty-five dollars a week for each kid. And I used to bring my own food, diapers, and milk. I didn't even know when she used to give them medicine. There were so many, she didn't keep track.*
>
> *And she had to do things of her own sometimes, because she had three kids, and when she did I couldn't go to work that day. If I couldn't find anybody to baby-sit at the last minute I couldn't come in. Or I had to come in late. I lost a lot of time, believe me. That whole year before the day care opened I used to be late, or I used to be out. I never finished a whole week. And the supervisors used to get mad at me. I used to have to explain to them that it wasn't my fault. But I can't leave my kids on the street. What could I do? They gave me hell sometimes. I had to go to the office a couple of times because of it. And I had to explain. If my baby-sitter cannot take care of my kids, what am I going to do?*
>
> *My work performance improved as soon as I started bringing the kids to the day care here. If they're really sick, I've still got to take them to the doctor. But before, it was more. Because it was up to her too. She had her own kids, and they got sick too. If one of them had the chicken pox, I couldn't take my kids over there. And Saturdays, I couldn't ever work Saturdays when we were open here. She wouldn't baby-sit on the weekend.*

Sapienza's wife had done volunteer work at the Child Care Resource Center in Cambridge—one of the country's oldest day-care resource-and-referral agencies—and his first step was to ask her to find out who the child-care experts were in the Lawrence area. The Center suggested Sheila Balboni, executive director of Community Day Care of Lawrence, an agency that ran four day-care centers.

"I remember that first call," says Balboni. "People had brought in some toys; they thought there was some space in the factory; they'd heard there were some unemployed teachers in the area; and they thought we could settle the whole thing on the telephone."

Instead, Balboni set up a meeting with Sapienza and person-nel manager DeFrancesco, and brought along Marie Sweeney, a former day-care center director who'd just begun her own child-care consulting business. The two suggested that the managers start out by doing a needs assessment—a survey that would give the company a clearer picture of its employee population and its real child-care needs.

Over the next few weeks, the company distributed written surveys in English, Italian, and Spanish; and conducted small group interviews in other languages. Posters in the elevator areas and at the main entrance emphasized the importance of the survey. Almost 80 percent of the work force responded.

Sapienza remembers the results of the survey clearly. "The statistics told us what I had already guessed: that my older Ital-ians didn't need any service; that my work force was increasingly Hispanic; and that every single one of them had a serious child-care problem. They were spending reasonable amounts of money—fifty to sixty dollars a week—for sitters or for sisters-in-law to take care of their kids. And the appraisal told us that the need was going to grow, because most of the people we surveyed thought they would be having more children. And in the course of doing the study, before we'd seen the results, we'd hired another fifty people and they were almost all young His-panics."

The survey also pointed out a need for financial assistance with child care. Parents of young children were much more likely to be on the low end of the company's pay scale: 79 percent of the parents with preschool children earned less than $20,000, as opposed to just 29 percent of the parents with school-age children.

Parents were piecing together whatever child care they could with the meager resources available. Relatives and family day-care providers were by far the most common care givers—fewer than 10 percent of the children went to centers—and most par-ents were paying less than $100 per month for the care of each child. Asked about problems with their current day-care arrange-ments, most parents expressed concern about quality. And the problem was not limited to parents. To the question, "During the past year has your work been made more difficult because of other employees' day-care problems?" 20 percent of all respondents answered "yes."

*I have a little girl in the day-care center now. She's four and a half years old and she started there last year. Different people used to watch her. In one year I had to change five times. It was hard for her to get used to the new person and it was hard for me too, because every time I had to bring her to a different house I felt sorry for her. She was crying and all that. So I really felt uncomfortable changing her so much. It's hard on them and the parents too.*

*There was always some reason that they couldn't take care of her anymore. One was an older lady, and it just got to be too many kids for her. She was watching five. Even though I brought everything to her, everything that my daughter was going to eat during the day. I brought the soup, the rice, whatever I had cooked for my daughter. I used to get up at five-thirty and cook everything up. It was hard. Now I'm resting a lot with the day care here.*

*And then there was always that inconvenience. One lady was a diabetic, so she used to go see the doctor once or twice a month. And I would have to leave work early. Things like that were always happening. And I would lose pay for those hours. These ladies would say, "I can't take care of your daughter tomorrow." Then that night I had to go out and look for somebody. I was lucky that I usually found somebody to watch her. But it was exhausting, and it made me very anxious. Because I knew for sure she'd cry when I left her at a strange place.*

*I was ready to leave my job. I said to my husband, "If I don't find a person to take care of my daughter, I'm just going to quit work. Because she comes first. She's the most important thing." But now it's so easy. I don't have to wake up early now to make her meal. I just bring her in here and everything is taken care of. I bring her in at five minutes of eight. If I have to work half an hour more I call them and they will say okay, as long as I say something to them a couple of hours before.*

*She likes it there. The first day it was like always, she didn't know how it was going to be. But the second day she didn't even want to leave with me at the end of the day. "Can you wait a minute? I have these things I have to cut out." They have a lot of activities, which I didn't*

find with the other baby-sitters. The other ones didn't have
a big space where they could play. They didn't have activities for them. So this is good. She's learning at the same
time.

The survey confirmed the company's sense that its workers
needed help with child care, but before committing to an on-
site center, Sapienza asked Balboni and Sweeney to find out if
arrangements could be made with existing centers. Perhaps the
$50,000 could be used to reserve spaces for the children of Grieco
Bros. employees, or to provide tuition subsidies to bring center
rates down to an affordable level. It didn't take long to find out
that the openings weren't available; at least not in the numbers
the company would require.

So the team returned to Sapienza's original idea of an on-site
center. With the employee data in hand, and with the consultants' practical expertise, the group was able to refine its plans.
While Sapienza had envisioned a company-owned center, Balboni and Sweeney made the case for one that was owned by the
parents or by some outside agency. "What will happen when
your needs change?" they asked. "Do you really want to own
this thing? It's going to be yours for life." If the young mothers
Grieco Bros. had hired really did stay for years, as the company
hoped, then their children would outgrow the center and other
children from the community could eventually take their places.
As the company's use of the center shrank, community or parent
ownership would seem more and more sensible.

Following that line of thought a little farther, and looking at
the employee-survey data, the consultants realized that since
the parents to be served by the center were predominantly Hispanic, a parent-owned center could be classified as a minority
business enterprise. "The idea of a parent-owned center seemed
a perfect philosophical blend of the family-oriented goals of the
company and the needs of its workers," recalls Balboni. "And
pragmatically it gained us access to state-funded slots." Massachusetts' Department of Social Services pays the child-care
bills of qualifying working mothers through the use of fully
funded "slots" at day-care centers. At the time, DSS was expanding this program and had allocated a number of the new
slots to minority-owned businesses. By helping a parent group
set up the center, the company could help guarantee its success,
because the DSS slots would provide a secure paid enrollment.
In July 1985, Merrimack River Community Child Care was incorporated as a minority-managed not-for-profit enterprise, its
board of directors drawn from parents, company managers, and
some outside experts.

> *At the day care it's better than where my kids were before. They take naps. They play. They learn things. When my daughter was ready to go to first grade, she was smart. She learned a lot of things that usually they don't know. As a matter of fact all of my nephews have been to the day care. Our whole family. I've got two sisters working here, and both put their kids in the day-care center. So they grew up down there.*

The next problem Balboni and Sweeney tackled was money. A careful look at the space that had been set aside for the center turned up some expensive problems. The brick walls were covered with lead paint, and heating pipes were wrapped in asbestos insulation. The cleanup alone would take the company's $50,000. Another $100,000 would be needed to install equipment, hire staff, and get the center running. "That was the only bad piece of news Sheila and Marie gave me," says Sapienza.

"At that point business started to flatten out and our financial vice president began to get cold feet—he was always a little cool to the idea. I said, 'I'll raise the rest of the money somehow.' And Sheila and Marie and I sat down and figured out how we were going to get another hundred thousand dollars."

In a way, the future center would be strengthened by Grieco Bros.' unwillingness to foot the entire bill, because other players would be drawn in with a stake in its success. But for Sapienza, the idea of company-supported child care had just turned from a simple excursion into a complicated expedition. In April 1985, he, Balboni, and Sweeney applied to about forty private foundations for grants, hoping to raise the balance needed for the center from charitable sources. They also applied to the Lawrence City Council for community development money, but were rejected in favor of a new fire truck. The same month, they approached neighboring Polo Clothing Co., a company with about 250 employees that manufactures for the Ralph Lauren label, and convinced management there to contribute $10,000 for five reserved spaces in the center.

In May, Sapienza began prenegotiation talks with the union for a new labor contract. Grieco Bros. and Polo Clothing had just broken away from their national trade association and decided to negotiate separately, fearing a national strike action because of poor business conditions in the South. In a series of informal meetings with Edward Clark, International Vice President of the Amalgamated Clothing and Textile Workers Union (ACTWU), the suggestion arose that the union make a contribution to the start-up cost of the center. In the plan that evolved from those talks, each worker at the two factories would contribute a penny an hour for a year, which added up to about $21 per worker.

"We thought there would be some resistance from workers who wouldn't benefit directly," Clark remembers. "But that was not the case. When we held the ratification meeting on the contract, several hundred attended, and lots of the older workers stood up and spoke out in support of the center. They felt that though they hadn't had help with child care when they were young, the union had helped them in other ways. They saw that times had changed and that this was what the young workers needed now. In the end only three or four voted against the contract."

As a symbolic gesture, the union contribution was invaluable. It showed that the center was really being built as a joint effort—as a partnership. Grieco Bros. had started things moving, and now both Polo Clothing and the Amalgamated had made substantial commitments. As a practical contribution, a penny an hour from a thousand workers for a year added up to $21,000.

Sapienza now returned to the Lawrence City Council, which had spurned his proposal earlier. But this time he could show that Polo and the union had signed on. And this time the City Council came up with $10,000 to build the center's playground.

As momentum began to build—the funding pool was now up to $100,000—Grieco Bros. tried to get other area businesses to join in. Sapienza addressed the Chamber of Commerce luncheon. But the moment must not have been right. In the end, Lawrence General Hospital alone offered $2,000 for one reserved spot. A local nursing home made a charitable contribution of $500. The banks were scared off by the problem of equity for workers at other branches. And plants and offices of such companies as Honeywell, New Balance, and AT&T didn't have the power to act locally.

Though a more comprehensive business consortium never came together, other small pieces fell into place. Two family foundations responded to the proposals, submitted back in April, with outright grants: the Stevens Foundation gave $15,000 and the Webster Foundation gave $5,000. ("That was the good news," says Sapienza. "The bad news was that thirty-eight other foundations gave us nothing.")

Then the center lined up a groundbreaking loan from the Massachusetts Industrial Finance Agency. MIFA was originally created as a source of low-interest and interest-free loans to industries for capital improvements—mostly plant and equipment—with the goal of creating new jobs. Brian Carty, the new executive director, was looking that summer at ways to expand the agency's reach into support for employer-sponsored child care. "It had become clear to us," Carty says, "that providing adequate child care could be just as important to the growth of a company as providing bricks and mortar. In fact, the lack of child care was preventing some companies from expanding. They had the market, the equipment was modernized, but they just couldn't get enough people."

Sapienza approached MIFA for a loan of the balance needed to complete the center, and Carty took the request to his board. "We asked them to make a policy decision as to whether we should be in this business. And not only did the board agree we should be, they capitalized a child-care loan fund with a million and a half dollars.

"We were the right guys in the right place," says Sapienza. "We already had one hundred twenty thousand dollars for the center. The walls were halfway up. The sandblasting had all been done. The bathrooms were built. It was just that we needed another thirty-five thousand dollars to finish the job. And Grieco Bros. was willing to co-sign the note. So MIFA knew they had a win that they could show off for this type of program. They loaned us the thirty-five thousand dollars in early September. And we finished the renovations in the course of the fall and we opened in January 1986."

> *I don't think I'll leave this job. I know everybody here. And when you have problems, they give you time out. You tell them you have a personal problem and they don't ask questions. If you need time out, they'll give it to you. And not a lot of places do that. Sometimes they even help you. If you need money, they'll lend it to you and take it out of your paycheck weekly. And not a lot of places do that. If people don't have money, you can't just go to a bank and ask for a loan. You know they're not going to give it to you. At least you know you have this. They help you sometimes. I think they care about the employees.*

At a dedication ceremony in February, all of the key contributors came together, and it was then that Sapienza realized how much of a cooperative effort it really had been to get the center going. "When we got everybody in the room together," he remembers, "and we started to check off who had done what, we finally convinced ourselves that it had in fact been a partnership effort. We didn't feel it as much when we were doing it, but when we got everybody together—the Stevens people were there, the Webster people, the people from the city, Evelyn Murphy, Michael Dukakis, the DSS people, the union people—when we got everybody together it really did seem like a partnership.

Because without any one of those pieces we would never have put the center together."

Sheila Balboni was impressed by the gathering too. It led her to tick off in her mind all of the different state agencies that the group had dealt with in bringing the center that far. She came up with forty.

One persistent worry during the planning stages was that when the center opened no children would come. In the end that was taken care of by the state's most important contribution. The DSS awarded the center twenty-six contracted slots. With a capacity of just forty children, the center was practically filled before it opened. The fourteen other spaces were quickly grabbed by parents who didn't qualify for the DSS funding, but even their tuition was heavily subsidized by their employers. In its first year of operation, the center didn't have a single full-paying child.

Today the center has room for ninety-four children after a series of expansions, the latest of which, a new toddler room, opened in May 1990. Children from fifteen months to six years start to arrive every morning at seven, some carried by their parents, some holding a grown-up's hand, and some dashing ahead, ready to get on with the activities of the day.

The space itself is remarkable, nestled on the first floor of the turn-of-the-century factory, with brick walls and huge wooden support posts running from the floor to the massively beamed ceiling. At seven-thirty, when the work begins upstairs, the rhythmic sound of the sewing and pressing machines above fills the rooms with a gentle rumble.

Parents we spoke with said the children love the center, often asking in the morning, "Are we going working?" or "Are we working today?" The parents also appreciate the convenience of having their children right downstairs. They can come down and visit during lunch, or bring a child up to the employee cafeteria. They can easily attend special holiday festivities at the center. And if a child comes down with a mild fever during the day, they can walk down and give a dose of Tylenol. (Care givers are prevented by law from giving nonprescription drugs to the children.) If the fever improves and the child seems happy the parent can continue with the day's work. Since workers aren't paid for the hours they miss when they're home with a sick child, that flexibility makes a difference.

While the center is a key element in the mix that makes Grieco Bros. an attractive place to work, our talks with parents showed that it's not the only thing that keeps them there. Many said that they had come to work at the factory because they'd heard it was "like one big, happy family" or that "people care about you here." And they did not seem disappointed by reality. Supervisors, on the whole, seemed to understand and accommodate the special needs of individuals. One single mother comes in at eight, rather than seven-thirty, because of her daughter's school hours. "If my supervisor weren't flexible about my schedule," she told us, "I couldn't work here. At another company I might have lost my job." Though down time due to sick children can cause minor havoc in a factory like this—more than one hundred people apply their skills to the many pieces of a suit before it's done, and each depends on the station just upstream for a steady flow of work—most supervisors seem to take family interruptions in stride.

While the garment industry has a reputation for contentious labor-management relations, Grieco Bros. has never had a local strike, and relations between the owners and the union seem genuinely friendly. Each side hands out plenty of compliments about the other on the strides taken together to make the workplace more humane. The union negotiated a parental-leave policy into the company's labor contract twenty years ago. And in the last five years the company and the union have worked together to expand the health-insurance package, add a 401 (k) retirement-savings plan, and establish a Dependent Care Assistance Program that pays for child and elder care with pretax payroll deductions.

The union and Grieco Bros. have also joined forces to establish a program of English classes at the factory in which workers can participate on company time. In its way this has turned out to be as important a benefit as the child-care center. Graduates of the program can communicate with their co-workers and supervisors and can become more involved with the community outside of work. Through the classes, the company has also been able to identify workers with education and skills that might enable them to perform higher-paying jobs.

> *I'm expecting another baby, and I already signed up for day care, because I know there's a waiting list. I don't know yet what I'll do when the baby is small. I was saying to them, "You should have something for the little ones too." I'm planning to take three months off, but who knows? If I don't find somebody to take care of the baby then I may change my plans. I said to my husband, I can always find a second-shift job, because the children are the primary thing. Money is not always the primary thing. The kids are. You work for them. You live for them. I think it's very important that they're comfortable, that they're well taken care of. If I got a second-shift job, I could take care of them*

> *during the day and my husband could watch them in the afternoon, like it or not. I would like to have the same hours as my husband so we can see each other in the afternoon. But if you have to do something for your kids you do it.*

Despite the big changes that Grieco Bros. has made in the past few years, the company still entertains new possibilities. The child-care center is exploring the idea of creating a network of family day-care providers—a sort of satellite system— to provide for additional children, particularly the infants and toddlers under fifteen months that the center does not accept. A 200-child waiting list shows that even in the age range that it does serve, the center is not large enough to satisfy all of the community's needs. (Since Grieco Bros. employees have priority access, only a few on that list are children of workers upstairs.)

The evolution of the company's programs is mirrored, in a way, by the change in attitude of Robert Nelson, financial vice president of the company. In 1985 he was cool to the idea of on-site day care. Today he sits on the center's board alongside the working parents who use the center. And according to center director Marianne Zeller, he's become an invaluable source of help and advice.

# International Business Machines Corporation (IBM)

Armonk, NY 10504                      914-765-1900

**Nature of business:** The world's largest manufacturer of computers and office equipment.

**Number of U.S. employees:** 210,000.

**Female employees:** 30 percent (20 percent of managers, 11 of top 250 executives).

**Child care:** Nationwide resource-and-referral service; significant support for efforts to expand the community supply of quality child care; reimbursement for uninsured expenses connected with raising an emotionally or physically disabled child, to lifetime cap of $50,000 per child.

**Elder care:** Nationwide consultation-and-referral service; significant support for efforts to expand the community supply of care; long-term care insurance at group rates.

*Family leave:* Fully paid disability leave for childbirth; three-year unpaid personal leave with full benefits available to new parents (including adoptive parents), employees with elderly relatives requiring care, and others (employees must be available for part-time work after the first year); preretirement leave program offers certain employees a trial run at retirement or a new career, with job guarantee if the employee wants to return.

*Flexible work options:* Flextime an option in most positions; part-time work limited to those in second and third years of personal leave; pilot work-at-home program; home-terminal program used by 20,000 managers and professionals for temporary, specific business needs.

*Other benefits:* Mandatory training program to sensitize managers to family issues; lunchtime seminars on family issues; relocation with spouse-placement assistance; employee-assistance program; family video library; health courses in weight control, exercise, smoking control, etc.; Community Service Assignments pay full IBM salary to employees on loan in public service; Community Service Career Program and Technical Academic Career Program pay two-year salary supplement to employees who retire from IBM for jobs with nonprofit community agencies or to teach college-level math and science; Faculty Loan Program pays full IBM salary to employees on loan to education.

Making the first move—a referral service as part of a comprehensive work/family program.

*"The challenge to business is to provide employees the flexibility they need to pursue and advance their careers while minimizing the impact on their personal lives. IBM continues to respond significantly to this challenge."*

JOHN AKERS
Chairman

*"If you have a problem with an elderly relative or a child that's a care-giving problem, no matter what your commitment to work is, that problem will be your priority. It will present you with a distraction in the workplace. And we ought to be trying to respond to your problems so that we can eliminate your distractions. It's not altruistic."*

TED CHILDS
Manager, Work/Life Programs

The story of IBM's eight-decade transformation from a lit-
tle-known business-machine manufacturer to the largest
computer company in the world is nearly lengendary. Many consider the company the paradigm of successful business practice;
its name synonymous with competence, quality, and leadership;
its sales force and customer-support systems universally recognized as exemplary. Another facet of IBM is not so well known.
Over the past decade the company has, without fanfare, established itself as a trailblazer in the corporate effort to ease employee conflicts between work and family.

The degree of IBM's commitment to that effort is reflected
in its current dependent-care initiative. In November 1989, IBM
announced a five-year, $25 million program to expand the supply
of child care and elder care in selected communities nationwide.
With data from its child-care and elder-care referral services, the
company knew which of its employees' communities had the
most serious supply shortages, and it had a good idea of the types
of services needed. The company targeted $22 million to increase
the supply and improve the quality of child care, aiming the bulk
of the money at communities with high concentrations of employees. IBM placed the remaining $3 million into a fund to
support and initiate elder-care projects. That IBM launched such
a massive program near the end of a poor business year (just two
weeks after the announcement of a restructuring plan that would
trim 10,000 employees from its payroll) shows how seriously
the company treats work-and-family issues.

"We're talking about a business expense, not a charitable
contribution," says Ted Childs, manager of IBM's Work/Life Programs, "and that's important. This is not altruistic. This is an
investment in the long-term economic and competitive health
of the company. Our senior management understands the im-
plications of the demographic changes we are seeing, the importance of focusing on education in America, the importance
of launching these children with quality care, and the importance of minimizing the distractions of our employees in the
workplace.

"We have a need that is born of the demographic shifts that
are taking place in the country, in terms of women moving into
the work force. We know that about 70 percent of women with
children between six and seventeen are now in the work force.
We know that more than 50 percent of women with children
under one are in the work force. That's a major shift—people
coming back to work while their children are that young. If we
project IBM data from 1965 out to the year 2000, our male population declines by 25 percent while our female population tri-
ples. Thirteen percent women in 1965, 30 percent women today,

38 to 40 percent women projected in the year 2000. They bring with them another set of issues that's important for us to respond to. If our work force is shifting that much, we can't ignore that population. We need employees and we're going to be competing harder for them. Twenty years ago some employers might tell a woman, 'Look, if you can't solve your child-care problem you'd better consider staying home.' Now they've got to say, 'We need you to come to work. We'll help you solve this problem.' "

And IBM is helping, perhaps more effectively and on a larger scale than any other company in the country. Its innovative programs have consistently set a path for other employers to follow, and, because it has worked to establish and strengthen community-based systems to help its own employees, its efforts have had far-reaching, positive effects on the population at large.

> *Two years ago my father had a heart attack and I called in and said I'd really like to go see him in the hospital. And it was no problem. "Stay as long as you feel you need to." I guess IBM's attitude is their workers are important to them, and if they want to keep them they need to respect their rights as individuals, respect their wishes. Keep them happy and they'll be better workers. I see that put into practice.*

IBM has a long history of leadership and fairness in employment issues. In 1935, then-chairman Thomas J. Watson, Sr., told the *New York Sun* that a group of women professionals hired to start the company's new systems service department would have "neither handicap nor advantage over the young men," and that men and women doing the same work would receive the same pay. In 1953, long before the enactment of Title VII, Thomas J. Watson, Jr., formalized a company policy forbidding racial or religious discrimination, a policy later expanded to prevent discrimination based on gender or national origin as well. The company makes genuine efforts to reward people for the quality of their work, and it has a reputation for fairness in moving people up the corporate ladder.

The pay has always been good at IBM, and the benefits exceptional. A full-employment tradition started during the Depression essentially guarantees jobs for life (with work-force reductions accomplished through incentives and early retirement). But perhaps more important to the quality of work life at IBM is the company's long-held respect for individual workers. Watson, Sr., boiled the IBM philosophy down to some simple beliefs, "the most important [of which is] our respect for the individual. This is a simple concept, but in IBM it occupies a major portion of management time." In the 1930s he eliminated the position of foreman and renamed all supervisors "managers," with a corresponding change of role. According to Peter Drucker, who described the move in a 1983 *Esquire* article, an IBM manager's job was "to assist workers, make sure that workers had the tools and information they needed, and to help them when they found themselves in trouble. Responsibility for the job itself was placed firmly in the work group." The company still strives to empower individual workers, and to challenge them to take greater responsibility in their work.

Early signs of IBM's interest in family issues can be seen in the company's Special Care for Children Plan, adopted in 1966, and its Adoption Assistance Plan, started in 1972. Through the Special Care Plan, the company provides financial assistance to parents of children with special needs, up to a current lifetime cap of $50,000 per child. The adoption program, one of the first such plans in the country, helps parents with the costs of adoption.

In 1982, partly in response to soaring health-insurance costs, the company decided to look into other ways to help employees with personal problems, particularly those problems that were cutting into business profits. Steve Marcus, then manager of employee-assistance planning, was assigned to develop an employee-assistance program, with the initial goal of establishing a counseling service to deal with alcohol and drug abuse. As he and his team dove into their task, they discussed a host of other possible services that might be included in the program, including help in dealing with emotional and mental distress, marital difficulties, and problems with children. While those issues might not have a direct impact on health insurance costs, they certainly take their toll on profits in terms of hours lost on the job. The personnel staff had also been thinking for some time about ways to help employees with child care, and this, too, was added as a possible service of the new program. IBM had no specific data on the need for child care among its workers, but Marcus and his team were well aware of national trends—the growing number of couples in which both partners worked, of families headed by single parents, and of women going back to work while their children were young—and assumed that the IBM work force shared characteristics of the general population. They knew that the old model of husband at work and wife at home with the children was no longer the dominant reality, and that the parents on the IBM payroll—men and women—must be losing time to the task of finding child care, sometimes over and over again.

As the group continued its research, explored what other companies were doing, and talked to the individuals and agencies who might provide the services, it quickly encountered a logistical roadblock to the expanded scope of its plans. The people who could offer counseling in addiction, stress, and marital problems had little experience with child care, and the pople who knew how to find child care would not be much help with psychological counseling. So the team decided to split the initiative into two parts and look toward separate counseling systems for child care and the rest of the assistance plan.

> *Even before they had this new program in place my managers were always very flexible. There have always been flexible hours. I could come in at nine and work until six, or take an hour or two out of the middle of the day and make it up at either end. The normal working hours are eight to four-thirty, and I very rarely work those hours. Because of child care, just getting the kids out in the morning. Often I'll take off in the middle of the day to go watch a school play. Things like that. Working slightly different hours has never been a problem, as long as I'm there during certain core hours of the day and am there when problems arise. I'm there to guide the team when I need to be.*

From the start, IBM had two basic criteria for its employee-assistance plan: it had to be both equitable and flexible. If the company was to offer any new benefit, it wanted to offer the same benefit to all of its employees. "We couldn't offer one level of service in Westchester," says Marcus, "or in some of our other high-employment areas, and another to the people who worked in other areas of the country. We wanted to offer the same thing across the board to everyone." And the company wanted to create a system that could not only respond to the wide range of employee needs, but could also change as those needs changed. These criteria defined the path of the initial child-care research, just as they would set the course for the final programs.

The team discussed the idea of building child-care centers, but, as Marcus recalls, "bricks and mortar didn't offer us the flexibility we needed. It was too rigid a solution. Our needs were likely to change as the company expanded or contracted in different regions, and as the demographics of the work force shifted. And we wanted to be able to meet the varying needs of individual employees with some flexibility. Not everyone would want their children in centers. Some parents prefer small family day-care groups or providers who can come to their homes. Some parents want care close to work; others want care close to their homes. We wanted to give parents as many options as possible." Subsidies, another possibility, "didn't solve the problem of finding care."

Child-care resource-and-referral services, which help parents find care and offer assistance and support to providers, came a little closer to the team's initial concept of child-care counseling. Marcus visited a number of these organizations in 1982 and 1983. Child Care Resources, Inc., an agency in Charlotte, North Carolina, particularly impressed him. It was structured as a public-private partnership—its budget shared equally by the county and the local United Way—to provide four basic services. It offered child-care information to the general public and helped parents find child care; it trained and provided technical assistance to child-care providers; it consulted with businesses about employer options in meeting child-care needs of employees; and it administered government subsidies to assist low-income working parents with the cost of child care.

Marcus visited Child Care Resources, and was impressed with the scope of the agency's services, but recognized it as a local solution. How could IBM offer the same service nationwide to its 200,000 employees? Fewer than a hundred such agencies existed in the country at the time, and only a handful of those offered such a comprehensive program. Marjorie Warlick, the agency's executive director, referred him to Gwen Morgan at Wheelock College in Boston.

Marcus had heard the name before. "We had visited a number of resource-and-referral agencies," he says, "and talked with day-care experts and with other business people who'd dealt with the issue. And Gwen Morgan's name kept coming up." Morgan had been a leader in the field of child care for more than twenty years. She had started one of the country's early employer-sponsored day-care centers (at KLH, in Cambridge, Massachusetts, in 1967); she had served as the child-care planner for the state of Massachusetts; she had participated in a federal program that had created local child-care coordinating bodies all across the country; she had been teaching management to day-care directors for several years; and she had recently conducted a national study of child-care resource-and-referral services.

So Marcus and Bill Stopper, then director of employee services, made a trip to Boston, in June 1983, to discuss IBM's vision for a national child-care referral service. Morgan invited Fran

Rodgers to join the discussion. Rodgers was, at the time, a consultant to businesses on child care and other matters relating to work-family conflicts. She had set up child-care centers for Procter & Gamble and other businesses, and, more to IBM's point, had just finished a study for Westchester County, New York, that recommended the establishment of an agency similar to the one Marcus had just seen in Charlotte.

In the course of the discussion, Marcus and Stopper outlined their ideas for a child-care resource-and-referral service, one that would help IBM employees find all kinds of care, one that would be available in the same form to all of IBM's employees, and one that would be set up outside of IBM, that would build on community resources. They wanted to know, first, if such a plan seemed possible, and, if so, whether Morgan and Rodgers could help make it a reality.

"It was a real meeting of the minds," remembers Rodgers. "IBM's requirements were really the formula for a national child-care resource-and-referral network, which is something we'd been thinking about as well. We actually sat down at lunch and sketched out—I think on a napkin—how we might structure a national program."

By the end of the day the two women had agreed to do a feasibility study. Over the next few months they worked with IBM to define exactly what the service would be, and contacted child-care people all over the country to find out how existing services could be adapted to meet IBM's needs. "We talked children to IBM and business to the child-care world," says Rodgers. "We educated them in both directions."

By November, Morgan and Rodgers were able to report back with their analysis of what could be done, how much money it would require, and how long it would take to put the system in place. And what had they found? "There were some resource-and-referral services already," says Morgan. "None of them met all of IBM's standards, but all of them met some. And where there were no referral agencies there were day-care experts. We knew in any city who they were or how to find them. If IBM committed to the project, we knew we could put the service in place wherever they had employees."

> *I've been off for a year now with my last child and I'm going back in July. I really enjoyed the project I was working on before I left. It's long term, and when I come back I'll take charge of the same project again. My manager found another person to fill in for me for the year I was gone. I have a home terminal and he sends me notes just to keep me up-to-date. I can choose to read them or not*

> *read them. And he invites me to all the functions. It's very flexible.*
>
> *I could choose to return and work part-time for two years, but I've decided not to do that. I feel I'm ready to go back to work full-time. I've found a good baby-sitter to come into the house. I haven't really done any work while I've been off, but I've been keeping pretty much up-to-date with what's going on, either by phone or by talking on the terminal. But that's just my own choice. I could have worked part-time. My manager is pretty flexible, it was just "whatever you want to do."*

The plan and the results of the feasibility study were presented to IBM's Policy Committee that month. On the morning of the presentation, one of the committee members got on an elevator with a harried-looking administrative assistant. The assistant revealed that she was late for work because her daycare arrangement had fallen through. "If we had wanted to plant someone," says Marcus, "we couldn't have done a better job."

Approval came through on December 1 for both the child-care referral service and the employee-assistance program. Both were given start-up dates of July 2, 1984. IBM gave the contract for organizing the child-care service to Morgan and Rodgers, who launched their venture as Work/Family Directions, with IBM as their first client. Over the next six months, the new business negotiated contracts with more than 250 local agencies, many of them formed that spring. "In communities where there was no resource-and-referral," explains Rodgers, "we had to work with people to build the services from the ground up." All had to agree to adhere to certain standards in order to guarantee uniform service to IBM employees. They had to maintain files on all kinds of care, from in-home providers to day-care centers; they had to provide current information on vacancies; they had to teach employees how to evaluate care options and advise them on the type of care that best fit their needs; they had to make follow-up calls to find out if care had been found and to obtain employee evaluations of the service; they had to make quarterly reports detailing employee use of the service; and they had to recruit and train new care givers so that IBM's employee demands did not overload existing community facilities.

Work/Family Directions also put together a parent handbook that became an integral part of the child-care resource service. This, too, broke new ground. The handbook explained, in clear language, what research showed were the elements of quality in child care. It was accompanied by a booklet explaining licensing standards, produced in different editions for each state and local jurisdiction. ("That was a hard job," says Morgan. "The licensing information had never been collected before.") IBM parents could see from the booklets which elements of quality their states' laws required and which they would have to look for on their own.

IBM contributed computer hardware and software to the local agencies so that they could maintain up-to-date files on child-care openings, keep close track of employee requests, and make timely reports back to Work/Family Directions. The software, Carefinder, was created specifically for the initiative.

To reduce the risk of liability to all parties, the local agencies agreed to refer to but not to recommend providers, and to set up written complaint policies with a prescribed set of actions to be taken if parents found dangerous or unhealthy situations in their search for care. Parents, and not the referral service, were to make the child-care decision. This emphasis on parent decision was not just a legal device to avoid liability; it was basic to the philosophy of the service. Both IBM and Work/Family Directions believed in strengthening parents' roles in the care of their children.

As the launch date neared, IBM and Work/Family Directions sponsored a meeting of the local resource-and-referral agencies, to bring them together and introduce them to IBM. From all accounts it was an exciting gathering. "It was a wonderful experience when we all came together," remembers Marjorie Warlick. "We'd all been working in relative isolation in our local communities, and it was exciting to find other people who were sharing the same kinds of problems and were at the same stage of development." Steve Marcus didn't arrive until late on the first day of the meeting. "I explained in my talk to the group that I had devoted myself to this initiative for two years, but that my daughter had been working hard on something for six years and that I felt I had to attend her graduation from elementary school. That's why I'd come late. It's the only time I've ever received a standing ovation. And I think it came from the heart. It was a wonderful group of people. And I think my coming when I did told them something about IBM."

By July 2, 1984, everything was in place. IBM had announced both the Employee Assistance Plan and the Child Care Referral Service to its employees with a mailing to their homes, backed up by pre-announcement preparation for managers and video presentations for all employees explaining how the services would work. "The launch date was one of the most exciting days of my life," remembers Marcus. "Because we really didn't know what would happen, how it would work out. For a lot of reasons we had decided not to go with a pilot on either program. We felt the needs were real enough that we should go ahead and offer them to everyone all at once. And we just didn't know what the response would be and whether the system we'd set up could handle it. With all of IBM's employees, spouses, and retirees we could have had five hundred thousand calls that first day. Or none. But it went off without a hitch. I can't remember a single problem."

Eight thousand parents called the Child Care Referral Service in its first year, seeking care for 9,000 children. By its fifth anniversary in 1989, the service had helped 36,000 families find care for 41,000 children.

> *My husband and I moved here from the East Coast recently, and we knew no one out here when our son was born. We have no family here. I didn't know where to go to find someone I could trust to care for my child, so the referral service was a great help. It gave me a list of very qualified people, enough that I could go interview and have a choice, and it directed me to people who met my specific standards. I was looking for in-home care, but someone who limited herself to a smaller group of children than allowed by law in this state. You can have six children here, plus your own, and I felt that to be too many for an infant. Through the referral service we found an older woman who only takes in three babies, including our son. We're very happy with her, and I felt comfortable going back to work after my leave knowing he was there.*

But the numbers and the personal accounts tell only part of the story. "The service has certainly been a direct benefit to our employees," says Marcus. "And that's why we created it. But when we started it, we also set something larger in motion. We created a model for other companies to follow. When they saw what we had done, many began to put their own plans into action. I think on July 2, 1984, we really helped change the face of child care in America." Indeed, more than one hundred companies now offer national child-care resource-and-referral services to their employees, most of them tapping into the network that IBM helped to create.

Morgan sees an impact from the program on the nature of the country's child-care delivery system. "I happen to believe that it would be better to have a diverse, varied child-care system and a lot of parent choice than a centralized system such as one concentrated in the schools. I just think it's hard to achieve quality in large institutions and much easier in smaller ones responsive to parents. But in order to have a diverse system, there needs to be some kind of infrastructure support. And we didn't have the infrastructure until we had a national network of resource-and-referral services. Now, just with the IBM contracts, and more recently with AT&T—two of the biggest employers in the country—we have a real national infrastructure, places that are providing training and advice to day-care providers, helping new centers get started, recruiting family day care, and helping parents find their way around the system. The consumer information is critical in a system with a diverse array of small programs. The small-scale providers aren't as visible as a single institution would be. With the resource-and-referral network we also have a way for money to get to the programs from a variety of sources."

The IBM program can also take some credit for about 70,000 new family day-care homes and 4,000 centers, started during the first five years of the program in part through the recruitment efforts of the local agencies. "All of the agencies in our network are required to identify the types of care that are in short supply in their areas and take steps to help improve the situation," says Rodgers. "In one community, that might mean working with the local zoning board to make family day-care homes acceptable. In another it might be helping someone through the maze of licensing procedures to open a new day-care center." In Boca Raton, Florida, for example, just one family day-care home existed in 1984. By 1989, that number was up to 43.

> *When we had our first child we had some difficulty finding day care that we were comfortable with. My wife and I visited a number of homes and centers, but we didn't find one that we really liked. We thought we had exhausted all resources, and had just about settled on a center we had found, but we had some reservations because it was almost twenty miles away. Then I tried the referral service, which had just started at that time. The counselor gave me the names of a few more homes and centers, and I decided to give it another try. One turned out to be an excellent family day-care home which has been just wonderful for our daughter. And it's only three miles from my lab, just off my normal route to work.*

IBM has refused to rest on its laurels since the start of the Child Care Referral Service. Within a year, the company began to think about offering the same sort of service to employees who need help with the care of elderly relatives. No national network of elder-care agencies existed at the time, but a 1986 feasibility study showed a fairly comprehensive infrastructure, thanks in part to government support through the Older Americans Act of 1965.

The study also pointed out some fundamental differences between child-care and elder-care counseling. While parents seeking child care need information about three or four kinds of care, an elder-care counselor would have to advise on dozens of different services, from housekeeping and cooking help to transportation to full-care nursing homes. Estate planning might be as important as information on care options, or an employee might need counseling for emotional distress. And while children who need day care almost always live with their parents, an elderly relative might live hundreds of miles away from the employee calling about care.

This time the company had some data on employee need. A 1986 survey showed that 30 percent of IBM's employees had some responsibility for elderly relatives, 8 percent had elderly dependents, and 4 percent had elderly dependents living in their homes. Combined with national demographic data showing increased longevity, and information from other studies showing how much time and money such care-giving duties demand (a study a year earlier by The Travelers Companies showed that 8 percent of its employees spent more than thirty-five hours a week on elder care), IBM realized that this was a serious issue for its work force, and one that would only grow in importance.

In the summer of 1987 IBM's Management Committee authorized funding for the Elder Care Referral Program. Once again the company went to Work/Family Directions, who set up a new company, Work/Family Elder Directions, to manage the project. Contracts were drawn up with local agencies, handbooks were prepared, the service was announced with a home mailing to employees, and the program was launched in February, 1988.

"In the beginning there was very heavy usage," says Muriel Morgan, who supervised the planning for IBM, "a lot of pent-up demand, which we had anticipated. But it went extremely smoothly. The people were very appreciative. And there have been some wonderful stories of people who've been helped, and such diversity of situations."

The stories and the statistics from the first year of the program illustrate just how complex the problems can get, and how helpful experienced advisers can be to employees. Over eight thousand employees, spouses, and retirees, who needed everything from legal advice to information about health insurance to referrals for care, used the service in its first eleven months. Fifty-two percent of the callers lived more than a hundred miles from the relative needing care, and 22 percent lived more than a thousand miles away.

Follow-up calls by the agencies routinely yield praise for the service and comments like, "I had no one else to turn to." And because the condition of an elderly relative can change, many of the callers have come back with entirely new sets of questions or problems.

"I think we did it at a good time," says Muriel Morgan. "Problems with elder care certainly are there, but perhaps not as much as they will be in the future. As the population ages, more of our employees will be facing questions about and difficulties with the care of elderly relatives."

> *I live in Vermont and my parents live in Florida. My father is really pretty helpless, and my mother takes care of him when she is able to. Well, a year ago, she ended up in the hospital with a heart condition. I flew down. I knew they were going to need help at home. And I called the elder-care referral service. They gave me the names of agencies, and suggested different things that I could do. They gave me names of services that did shopping for people. It was just so much help. I had to make my own arrangements, of course, but it gave me a place to start. My mother came home from the hospital and I went back to Vermont.*
>
> *Ten days later, they both ended up in the hospital with heart problems. Then we decided to move them up to my sister's home in Massachusetts. She had a little apartment off her house. But my sister works all day, so we needed more help. And the elder-care referral service helped us out again. I must have called them twenty different times. They helped us find different services we would need in Massachusetts. They even gave us names of heart specialists because they needed continuing medical care. Then my sister's husband died. So we needed different kinds of help for Mother and Dad, to take over the things that he had been doing for them.*
>
> *The referral service was a lifesaver, because with each new crisis I didn't know what to do. I didn't know who to call. And just by calling them I got names. I'm just grateful for that help, because I had no idea what to do or where to turn. And they were very empathetic. They just made me feel that I wasn't alone. They encouraged me to call back any time. And whenever I called they came through.*

As innovative as its child-care and elder-care programs are, "We never lose sight of the fact that we have a menu of offerings," says Childs. "The issue is not child care or elder care. The issue is the balance between work and family, and our offerings try to cover the entire field." IBM offers flextime with a two-hour window at the beginning and end of the day, with some schedule restrictions based on customer or company needs. In pilot programs it is testing an additional midday flextime window and the possibility of an expanded work-at-home program. When IBM employees are transferred, the company provides relocation assistance and helps spouses find jobs. And while the company was once known for its frequent employee transfers (the joke among employees was that the initials "IBM" stood for "I've Been Moved"), it now limits these moves to about 3 percent of the work force each year, about half the rate of a decade ago. The Employee Assistance Program helps workers deal with such difficulties as mental or emotional distress, relocation adjustments, alcohol or substance abuse, depression, marital problems, and problems with children. Work-and-family seminars offer information to parents on such subjects as safety, health, parent-child communications, and adolescent issues. Preretirement seminars help workers prepare for leaving the company. A one-year preretirement leave program provides certain employees with a chance to try either retirement or a complete change of career, with a job guarantee if they want to come back.

> *I've been an engineer at IBM for twelve years. Right now I'm essentially a project leader. I'm in charge of a particular project and have five or six technicians and engineers working with me. I also have four children, aged ten, eight, five, and eleven months. I've had them all since I've been at IBM, and the older ones came long before this new three-year leave policy went into effect. With my first three the policy was a year leave of absence, no part-time. But I was able to take a yearlong leave of absence ten years ago. That was company policy. It was pretty much at the discretion of your management, whether they could spare you for a year. But I haven't heard of very many cases where they wouldn't. I've gone through a lot of managers—with each pregnancy I've had a different manager—and I've never had one say that my work was more important, that I couldn't take that time off.*

Infant care is a particularly troubling problem for businesses and for working parents. Good care is both expensive and difficult to find; and research suggests that the nature and quality of the care can have a profound effect on a child's development and on the emotional bonds between parent and child. IBM has come up with an important part of the answer in the form of a three-year personal leave policy, in place since 1988. (The one-year leave policy it replaced had been in effect since the 1960s.) Employees with new children, children requiring special care, or elderly dependents requiring care can apply for the leave on a yearly basis. Eligibility is determined both by the needs of the employee and the needs of the business. The leave is unpaid, but company-paid benefits remain intact, and a job is assured on return. Employees may work part-time during the first year of leave, and they must be available to work part-time during the second and third years—both to give IBM the benefit of their skills, and to keep those skills up-to-date. At any given time, about 2,500 employees are out on leave, a little more than 1 percent of the work force (up from about 2,000 in 1987, when the leave was limited to one year).

At this writing, no other American business offers such a long leave as a formal policy, and the flexibility it offers does make a difference to IBM parents. Pamela Paffett, a child-care-referral counselor in St. Louis, notices the difference when the employees call. "Many families are struggling with the customary six-week parental leave, and it makes such a critical difference when the family has the time to plan for care when it is right for both the parents and the child. It is evident, even in our brief consultations, that IBM parents are more confident, relaxed, and 'together' than many of the parents facing the six-week wall."

The success of the policy for employees, of course, depends on the front-line managers who make the decisions about who is eligible and for how long. The wording of the policy gives tremendous discretionary power to low- and mid-level managers. IBM recognizes this, and it is working to see that the company policies are understood all the way down the line. "The first-line managers write your family policy," says Childs. "It really doesn't matter what your family policies are—it's how they get implemented. And that's the team that has to confront the employee's problem and make the decision about how to respond."

Between June 1989 and June 1990, IBM put all of its 25,000 managers through a training program to sensitize them to the concerns of working parents, and to explain to them the business reasons for responding to changes in the work force. In a video prepared for the sessions, Terry Lauhtenbach, senior vice president in charge of U.S. operations, detailed the importance of the manager's role in the company's strategic moves, pointing out that if employees are labeled "not serious" for taking advantage of IBM's work-family progams, then the programs will fail. A series of statistics and study results drove home the message that the company must respond to the new realities of dual-income couples and working parents; that in order to attract and retain the best workers, the company needs managers who are aware of the issues and flexible enough to deal with them. In discussions afterward the managers were confronted with a number of hypothetical situations and asked to respond. "Management training in 1990 on the subject of work and family," says Childs, "is comparable to management training on the subject of equal opportunity in 1965. We have a cultural upheaval taking place and we need the management team to be prepared for the changes that are going on in the workplace."

IBM reconfirmed its commitment to work-and-family issues with its $25 million funding initiative, announced in November 1989, aimed at increasing the community supply of child care and elder care. The referral services had made an effort all along to increase the supply of care, and in some areas had made great strides. But the company could see that many of its employees still faced problems. While 95 percent of the employees who used them were satisfied with the referral services, 5 percent were not, and most of these dissatisfied employees had had problems with child care. Some had not been able to find care at all, or had not found care of the quality they expected. And those unhappy employees were a vocal minority. "When you're having a problem finding child care," says Muriel Morgan, "you don't care about numbers showing how many people have been helped."

Not only was it hearing some complaints, but IBM was concerned that after five years the luster was wearing off the referral service. "This is a 'What have you done for me lately?' kind of field," says Childs, "and with other companies now offering resource-and-referral services, or on-site centers, or coming up with innovative ways to subsidize their employees' child care, we felt we should take the next step so that we could still say with some comfort that we were a leader.

"We started looking at how much money we should make available for this. And it was evolutionary. We started talking about two, three, five, ten million dollars, and we decided that we needed a five-year program. If we were going to get into this, we were going to have to get into it with a long-term view that would give us time to implement quality programs, and time for those programs to yield results." The bulk of the money was allocated to child care, with $3 million set aside for elder care.

"That's not a reflection of a dim view on our part of the importance of elder care," explains Childs. "It's just that child care hasn't got the legislative framework that elder care has, through the Older Americans Act of 1965. And we're hearing more from our employees about problems with child care."

The child-care money will go to support such community initiatives as new and expanded child-care centers, new family day care, expanded and new school-age programs, expanded and new programs for the care of mildly ill children, help with accreditation of centers and licensing of family day care, and provider training. (As part of its emphasis on quality care, IBM has stipulated that centers must meet a set of standards established by the National Association for the Education of Young Children in order to receive funding.)

The elder-care money will go to support an even wider variety of programs, including transportation services, programs to recruit and train in-home care givers, and initiatives to create additional adult day-care centers.

> *I'm glad they have these policies, because it's worked out well for me. I'm not just a full-time stay-at-home mother. And I know that at other companies women have had to make that choice, whether to keep working just as before and sacrifice their families in a way, or quit. I feel that I've had enough flexibility that I could keep working.*

In coming to grips with personal matters like child care and elder care as business issues, IBM has learned some valuable lessons. "When you start off in this field," says Childs, "one of the issues you confront is equity, that it's important to have programs that treat everyone the same way. I think that in working through this we are redefining equity. We now see that equity is not treating everyone the same way. Equity is responding to people's needs when they have them. That means that I may do something different for you than I do for your fellow employees in the same department. But you've got a different problem. And I'm trying to build partnerships with all my employees and respond to all of their needs. You're single, and you've got a problem with an elderly relative. He's a single parent. She's got children and elderly relatives. And all three of you are trying to balance your commitment to work and your commitment to those relatives." The company now looks at benefit use over its employees' entire careers, and tries to offer a package that is fair to employees at all stages of their lives.

IBM is sometimes dismissed as an example by other employers because of its size. With more than 200,000 employees, it is one of the biggest companies in the country, and its earnings have consistently been among the largest in the world.

Steve Marcus understands, but is somewhat disturbed by such talk. "Some people look at what we have done and say, 'But you're a huge company with vast resources. You probably put an army of people to work on your child-care referral service. We could never do that.' I think one of the best things about what we did was how we did it—we had six people working on it at the company. The rest were outside vendors."

Ted Childs echoes the sentiment. "I was speaking on a panel and a lady asked, 'Your programs are great, but everybody doesn't have two hundred thousand employees, or even five thousand employees, or your money. What about the company that only has a hundred people?' It seems to me that no matter how many employees you have, if you're an employer, your common denominator is that your employees are your greatest asset. And to the degree that they have distractions and are not focusing on you, your company is suffering. Whether you're a two-hundred-thousand-employee IBM and you can spend the money to develop programs for yourself, or you're a small employer and you have to go to the local resource-and-referral agency or develop contacts with other companies that are willing to come together with you to address your common issues, they're issues that require addressing or your company's going to suffer. I don't think it matters how many employees you have. If your work force can't focus on your business—and it could be frying chicken or building computers—if you don't have the people to fry the chicken or you don't have the people to build the computers, in either case your product will not be ready for your customer and you'll have a problem."

# Johnson & Johnson

One Johnson & Johnson Plaza
New Brunswick, NJ 08933                    201-524-0400

**Nature of business:** Manufacturer of health-care products.
**Number of U.S. employees:** 33,000.
**Female employees:** 51 percent (6.4 percent of top executives).
**Child care:** On-site center in New Brunswick for 200 children, aged six weeks to six years, with room for care of

mildly ill children; income-based subsidies applied to parent fees at center; on-site center in Raritan, New Jersey, also for 200 children, to open in 1991; nationwide resource-and-referral service; pretax salary set-aside (DCAP).
**Elder care:** Nationwide consultation-and-referral service; pretax salary set-aside (DCAP).
**Family leave:** Paid disability leave for childbirth, plus up to a year unpaid parental leave.
**Flexible work options:** High-level support for expanded use of flexible work hours and part-time work.
**Other benefits:** Company-wide training program to sensitize managers to family issues; on-site fitness centers at almost fifty sites; adoption aid up to $2,000; 401(k) plan with employer contribution.

Shaping a corporate culture.

*"We must be mindful of ways to help our employees fulfill their family responsibilities."*
From "Our Credo"

*"I've talked a lot about the importance of quality and the need to be more competitive if we expect to be as successful over the next decade as we have been for more than a century. Those two principles—quality and competitiveness—and others near and dear to Johnson & Johnson, such as our credo commitment to employees and their families, are reflected in this [child-care] center. By recognizing and supporting the child-care responsibilities of our employees, we are investing in our own future."*
RALPH S. LARSEN
Chairman

On a May morning in 1990, Johnson & Johnson's chairman, Ralph Larsen, spoke before a crowd of several hundred at the opening of a new building at the corporation's headquarters complex in New Brunswick, New Jersey. His remarks touched on issues of competitiveness and the future health of the business. The building he stood in front of, designed by I. M. Pei & Associates, looked much like the other finely styled buildings at the site, with its cream-colored metallic skin and dark windows. But this was not just another office building. It was a child-care center. Built at a cost of more than $5 million, the Johnson & Johnson Child Development Center is one of the finest such facilities in the country, and the most visible sign of the company's commitment to becoming a premier employer for working parents. It also marks a dramatic step in what may be a fundamental change in Johnson & Johnson's culture.

The company has long had a reputation for treating its employees well, with above-average pay, a solid benefit package, and systems for listening to employees' concerns. But through the mid-1980s, Johnson & Johnson had not addressed the concerns of working parents and those with elder-care responsibilities in any comprehensive way. In part, the company's attitude and its policies simply reflected the times. Few large companies responded to family needs in the early 1980s, and the groundbreakers were only just beginning to show what could be done.

Johnson & Johnson may also have been held back by its relatively formal atmosphere, which is revealed immediately to visitors in the appearance of the company's New Brunswick headquarters. Nestled in the center of the city, its formidably beautiful cream-colored tower rises above carefully manicured grounds. A low stone wall presents the only barrier between company and city, but people rarely sit on the company's perfect lawns. Rutgers University, just a block away, offers a casual contrast to the site.

Until recently, Johnson & Johnson's surface orderliness was matched by a tendency toward rigidity among some managers toward family concerns. Like most companies, Johnson & Johnson through the early 1980s treated such ordinary family concerns as child care and elder care as personal issues to be dealt with by individual employees on their own time. And, like many other companies, it had its share of managers who stepped outside of official policies to grant individuals an extra measure of flexibility. But unlike many companies, Johnson & Johnson has always had good mechanisms for listening to employees' concerns, and the company lives by a set of beliefs that places the well-being of employees high on its list of priorities.

A visitor to a Johnson & Johnson facility anywhere in the world is likely to see a copy of a statement called "Our Credo" hanging prominently in a hallway or on the wall of a manager's office. Managers are required not only to read it, but to believe in it and follow its tenets.

It is a remarkable document. Written in 1943 by then-chairman Robert Wood Johnson, and revised only slightly since, it spells out the company's commitments and priorities in plain language. And it places them in an unusual order, detailing the company's responsibilities to its customers first, then its employees, then the communities in which it operates, and, finally, to its stockholders. "When we operate according to these principles," it ends, "the stockholders should realize a fair return."

Because Johnson & Johnson is a highly decentralized corporation, with 175 companies around the world, the credo provides a valuable cohesive influence. The corporation does not impose many policies on its companies but expects them to abide by the credo, and the document tends to unify the business as powerfully as more tangible organizational structures. In the 1970s, then-president James E. Burke initiated a series of "Credo Challenge" meetings, to ask managers throughout Johnson & Johnson whether the document still had meaning thirty years after it had been written, or whether it should be abandoned. The result was an affirmation of the credo, and a renewed sense of commitment to its philosophy.

To ensure that the credo is followed throughout the corporation today, Johnson & Johnson conducts regular "credo surveys." These give employees a chance to evaluate the company's and their managers' adherence to the letter of the document, and the results give staff at corporate headquarters a sense of where managers are straying from the corporate philosophy. Since the credo states that "employees must feel free to make suggestions and complaints," the surveys also give workers a chance to air their grievances and offer new ideas.

In the early and mid-1980s, Johnson & Johnson began hearing more about work-and-family conflicts on the credo surveys. The questionnaires came back with spontaneous comments about child care, and with requests for greater flexibility. Reinforcing that trend toward greater family concerns as revealed by the surveys, outside demographic data showed that the working population was changing throughout the country, with more women in the work force, more parents of young children, more employees with working spouses, and more single parents.

> *I have one child who's almost a year old. My boss offered to allow me to work at home for three months after my paid leave ended. They moved a PC home for me. I was able to tie into the mainframe and work from home. I did that for three months, then I continued to work at home three days and came in two days for another three months until the center opened. My husband rearranged his schedule to be home with her those two days.*
>
> *I was a little apprehensive about bringing her in here. Everybody was telling me how great it was and how wonderful it would be, but she'd been home with me or my husband her whole life, and I couldn't imagine it being*

*that good. I still wanted to stay home, but I couldn't afford to do it. I was worried about leaving her for eight hours a day. It just sounded so cold to me. But now that she's there, and the teachers have turned out to be so warm and loving, I'm perfectly comfortable with it. And she's happy, so that's helped me adjust. I don't worry about her during the day. And I can still go over to visit her any time.*

*I see her out the window sometimes. The teachers push them in these little six-seaters. It's really nice to see children around. Not just her. You have this corporate atmosphere, with people in their business suits, then you see babies and teachers in their shorts.*

In 1986 Johnson & Johnson decided to look at the issue of work-and-family conflict in some depth, to find out how it was affecting employees, and how the company could respond. It did a small-scale survey on the issue to get an initial sense of employee needs, and conducted a series of focus groups. John Heldrich, corporate vice president of administration, recalls the general sense that came back from those explorations: "Our employees, particularly our women employees, were saying to us that Johnson & Johnson was a wonderful corporation, that we had excellent employee relations, but that we weren't as sensitive to family needs as we thought we were."

Heldrich established a formal task force to look into the matter, and he seems to have charged it with a sense of urgency. By appointing his corporate vice president of human resources, John S. Brown, and other senior human-resource executives from the many Johnson & Johnson companies, he also insured the task force a powerful voice. "We decided to pull the stops on this," he says, "to call for a complete audit of all of our human-resource policies. I wanted to know what should be abandoned, what should be modified, and what new policies should be added."

The task force commissioned a more detailed survey of all 13,000 workers in New Jersey, which came back with more detailed figures on child-care and elder-care needs, on the desire for more employee control over work hours, and on the productivity effects of work-and-family conflicts. It also confirmed that many employees thought the corporate environment, its managers, and its policies could become more sensitive to family needs.

Over the next year, the task force worked on a response, and in 1989 and 1990 the company put its recommendations into action in a sweeping series of measures that propelled the com-

### OUR CREDO

We believe our first responsibility is to the doctors, nurses and patients, to mothers *and fathers* and all others who use our products and services. In meeting their needs everything we do must be of high quality. We must constantly strive to reduce our costs in order to maintain reasonable prices. Customers' orders must be serviced promptly and accurately. Our suppliers and distributors must have an opportunity to make a fair profit.

We are responsible to our employees, the men and women who work with us throughout the world. Everyone must be considered as an individual. We must respect their dignity and recognize their merit. They must have a sense of security in their jobs. Compensation must be fair and adequate, and working conditions clean, orderly and safe. *We must be mindful of ways to help our employees fulfill their family responsibilities.* Employees must feel free to make suggestions and complaints. There must be equal opportunity for employment, development and advancement for those qualified. We must provide competent management, and their actions must be just and ethical.

We are responsible to the communities in which we work and to the world community as well. We must be good citizens—support good works and charities and bear our fair share of taxes. We must encourage civic improvements and better health and education. We must maintain in good order the property we are privileged to use, protecting the environment and natural resources.

Our final responsibility is to our stockholders. Business must make a sound profit. We must experiment with new ideas. Research must be carried on, innovative programs developed and mistakes paid for. New equipment must be purchased, new facilities provided and new products launched. Reserves must be created to provide for adverse times. When we operate according to these principles, the stockholders should realize a fair return.

(Italics indicate 1989 additions.)

pany into a leadership role on work-and-family issues and transformed it into one of the country's brightest prospects for working parents.

In February 1989 John Heldrich announced the first of those changes: an amendment to "Our Credo" to add fathers to the list of important customers, and to add the statement, "We must be mindful of ways to help our employees fulfill their family responsibilities."

"That was a very significant change," says Heldrich. "We don't just change the credo for any little reason. These are very important issues for us, and we wanted to institutionalize this as part of our value system. And because we're highly decentralized, that was one way to reach the whole organization. The credo is a very important thread that ties us all together as a corporation. We're constantly measuring ourselves against it."

To reinforce the credo change, the company began a mandatory management and supervisor training program, designed with help from the Families and Work Institute in New York. In 1989 and 1990, all of Johnson & Johnson's managers, from entry-level supervisors to senior vice presidents, participated in the program. Other companies have run similar management training programs, but the sessions are generally added as a final phase of a work-and-family plan. "We're doing the right things first," says Michael Carey, chairman of the task force and vice president of human resources at Johnson & Johnson's Personal Products Company. "By changing the basic document that guides our decision-making process—"Our Credo"—and by putting our management supervisors through an awareness and sensitivity training program, we're helping to insure that the rest of the program really works. We think we always had a number of enlightened supervisors who bootlegged and did things under the table. Now we're empowering them to do it legitimately. And now we're telling everybody to do it."

With those pieces of the plan in place, Johnson & Johnson rolled out an array of new work-and-family policies and programs. It lengthened the leave-of-absence limit to a year, and extended it to include time off for child care, elder care, and other pressing family needs. It introduced nationwide resource-and-referral services for both child care and elder care. It established as company policy that management would accept and look for ways to encourage alternative work arrangements, such as flexible work schedules and flexible workplaces. It enhanced the relocation-assistance program to include job-hunting help for spouses and help in locating schools for children. It also added an adoption-assistance benefit, which reimburses employees for up to $2,000 of their adoption expenses.

> *I have a copy of the credo on the wall right in front of me. There have been big changes since they changed that wording; you can just feel it around here. With the new programs and with flextime, a lot of tension has disap-*

> *peared. I've run into conflicts a lot because I'm divorced
> and I don't have anybody to help me. My son has asthma,
> and I'd get to work some days and the school nurse would
> call, and I'd have to run and go get him. I don't have family
> nearby, so that was always on my shoulders. And even
> though my boss has always been good about that, it just
> makes me feel more comfortable now that it's in writing.*

At the time the credo change was announced, the company also unveiled plans for a child-care center at its headquarters campus. The facility opened in the spring of 1990, the cornerstone of a year of tremendous change for Johnson & Johnson. Carefully designed as part of the corporate environment, the center could easily be mistaken for an office building from the front. But inside, it opens into spaces that have clearly been designed with the best interests of children in mind. Pyramid-shaped skylights, an attractive architectural detail from the outside, allow natural light into the upper-floor rooms and down through a two-story atrium to a huge open play space on the lower floor. On days when the sun is too bright, or at times when the rooms need to be dark, shades can be pulled across the roof openings at the touch of a switch. The rooms for younger children include separate sleep areas, and changing tables with built-in sinks and motion-activated faucets. Special nooks have been built into the older children's rooms for multilevel play structures. The common play space on the lower floor, which stretches over an area about 30 × 100 feet, offers plenty of room for activities on days when the weather doesn't allow use of the outdoor playground. Just off it are three special rooms for use by all the center's children in small groups: a computer room, a music room, and a "messy room" (built with a tiled floor and drainage so that it can be hosed down for quick cleanup). Two "get well" rooms for mildly ill children give parents the option of bringing their children in when work must get done and the children are suffering from low-grade fevers and certain noncontagious diseases.

The program at the center has also been designed to offer the best possible care for the children. The company has contracted with Resources for Child Care Management to run the facility, an organization with a reputation for operating quality centers. Under the terms of the arrangement, both the company and the parents have a voice in the direction of their program. The center is staffed with trained and experienced teachers, maintains low child/teacher ratios, and offers a program that encourages warmth, spontaneity, and learning. The total effect is of a center that should serve as a model for other corporate child-care efforts for years to come.

It is already serving as a model within Johnson & Johnson. As an organization of many companies, Johnson & Johnson is encouraging independent initiatives in work-and-family programs, and as we went to press an additional child-care center was in the works. Ground was broken for a second center in Raritan, New Jersey, in the summer of 1990. When it opens in 1991, it will serve approximately 200 children of employees who work at Ortho Pharmaceuticals and other Johnson & Johnson companies in the area. The company is also examining the options for child care at two other sites.

"We didn't build the center in New Brunswick because we wanted to have a child-care center," Michael Carey explains. "We built it because the demand for child care far exceeded the supply in this geographic area, and because we have a high concentration of employees here. We're building the second center for the same reasons, and those are the right solutions for those two areas. But they may not be the right solutions at other sites. A consortium center, built in cooperation with other companies, might be more appropriate for some of our other companies in Illinois, or Texas, or California. We're simply encouraging all of our companies to look into this. We're doing the same thing with flexibility, and many of the companies have come up with wonderful programs—telecommuting, part-time work, job sharing, major levels of flextime use. But we don't mandate those programs. The solutions have got to fit the environment."

> *I actually feel more comfortable with my son in the center when he's a little bit sick. They have a pediatric nurse, and a doctor nearby. We lost our first son to crib death, and our baby is on a monitor. And I feel very comfortable with him over there. Everyone at the center knows him. They all were trained in the monitor. They had a representative from the company come down and show them the monitor, which I was very impressed with. I know they take extra-special care because of the monitor. They call me all the time to say he's okay. I feel very comfortable and confident having him there. Plus the baby's happy. He's smiling all day. I don't know what I would have done if the center wasn't here. I don't think I could have left him in someone else's home. I might have left my job.*

The New Brunswick center stands as a powerful symbol of Johnson & Johnson's commitment to the family needs of its employees. "It would have been less costly to put the center somewhere else," says Heldrich. "If we had built it out of sight of the campus, it wouldn't have had to be designed to blend with the existing structures. If we had built it outside of the city, the site preparation wouldn't have been so difficult. But we are in the business of babies and families and health. We have an emphasis on families in our product line. To put the center off away from our headquarters would have sent the wrong signal. It would have said to our employees that we have to do this, but we don't want the kids next door. By building it here we are saying that they are important."

As a part of the headquarters complex, the center may also be having a softening effect on the corporate culture. The company had become used to the sight of runners on the paths around the campus, but eyebrows were raised the first time a string of children trooped out of the center and over the carefully manicured lawns around the office buildings. The children have now become as common a sight as the runners, and employees seem to enjoy their presence. "The teachers have these carts that hold six babies," says Heldrich, "and we can look out the window and see them walking around the building. Every day someone comments on them. It's added a special touch to the work environment. It creates a different ambience."

As the children become an ordinary part of the environment at Johnson & Johnson, not just in New Brunswick, but at other sites around the country; as the effects of the credo change and the management training programs begin to work their way into the company's culture; and as more employees try out a variety of flexible work arrangements the company should become one of the country's outstanding employers for those with family responsibilities. "Five years ago," says Carey, "while we had some managers who were responding, who were being flexible, the overt management commitment wasn't there. The recognition was beginning, but there were still many people who questioned whether this was a legitimate business issue. And I think we've made that leap. We have support for these programs from the highest level of the company, and we're working on communicating their importance all the way down the line."

# S. C. Johnson & Son, Inc.

1525 Howe Street
Racine, WI 53403-5011                    414-631-2676

**Nature of Business:** Manufacturer and marketer of home, personal care, and insect-control products—including Johnson floor and car waxes, Raid insecticide, and Agree shampoo.
**Number of U.S. employees:** 3,400 (15,000 worldwide).
**Female employees:** 29 percent (13 percent of managers).
**Child care:** Near-site center for 200 children aged six weeks to twelve years; summer day camp; pretax salary set-aside (DCAP); subsidy for care of sick children an option in flexible benefit package.
**Elder care:** Pretax salary set-aside (DCAP).
**Family leave:** Paid disability leave for childbirth, plus up to three months unpaid personal leave; paid time off for short-term care of ill dependents.
**Flexible work options:** Flextime in most areas; some job sharing; some part-time work.
**Other benefits:** On-site medical center; employee-assistance program; on-site and near-site fitness centers; recreation center in Racine; resort facilities with priority access for lower-level employees; full reimbursement for job-related courses or degree programs; scholarships for employee children; adoption assistance to maximum of $500; cash and deferred profit sharing; 401(k) plan with employer contribution, pension plan.

A tradition of listening and of looking out for employees' interests.

*"If you can take care of some of your employees' basic human concerns and needs, and not throw a lot of extra ones in their way, then your people are going to be able to do their jobs in a much more creative way. By taking away some worries you free their minds up. We've always been a leader when it comes to important employee benefits. And that comes out of an attitude that says our employees are very important to us. Because our employees are our company. So it was very natural for us to look favorably on child care when the issue was brought to our attention."*

RAYMOND F. FARLEY
Former President and
Chief Operating Officer

Few companies present such a striking blend of tradition and innovation as S. C. Johnson & Son, Inc., and few have such long histories of leadership when it comes to doing well by their employees.

The stories here reach back to the 1880s, when founder Samuel Curtis Johnson took over the parquet-floor business for which he had worked as a salesman and added floor wax to the company's line of products after mixing up a batch in his bathtub. In 1900 the company became a leader in American corporate benefits when Johnson began to offer his employees paid vacations.

As the company has grown from a small manufacturer of flooring and paste wax to one of the world's largest makers of aerosol products and household cleaners, and as the reins have passed from son to grandson to great-grandson, its founder's commitment to leadership in the area of employee benefits has been followed as if an inviolable command. As H. F. Johnson, Samuel Curtis Johnson's son and president of the company from 1919 to 1928, said in a 1927 speech to the employees to mark the occasion of the company's tenth profit-sharing celebration, "The goodwill of the people is the only enduring thing in any business. It is the sole substance. The rest is shadow."

The company initiated one of the country's first profit-sharing plans in 1917, launched a pension plan in 1934, and offered hospitalization insurance in 1939. In 1951 it opened a resort facility in northern Wisconsin for employees and retirees. (During the busy season, access is determined through a system that turns position and seniority upside down—lowest-ranking employees have priority on the reservation sheet, and in the case of conflict between two employees of the same rank, the junior worker gets the spot.) In 1957 the company created a park for employees on the outskirts of Racine, which has developed over the years into an amazing recreation facility, with a massive indoor gym, squash courts, exercise rooms, an expansive indoor pool, running trails, baseball diamonds, fishing ponds, playgrounds, even a miniature golf course. The company has offered financial assistance for adoptive parents since 1971, dental care as part of a comprehensive medical insurance package since 1975, and has supported a near-site child-care center since 1985.

In 1976, 200 delegates from the company met to draft the company's philosophy in document form. Titled "This We Believe," it has become a handbook for managers and employees throughout the company, and offers as its first premise: "We believe that the fundamental vitality and strength of our worldwide company lies in our people."

The founder's legacy of charitable giving also endures to the present day. His substantial gifts to and involvement with the local YMCA and YWCA, an industrial school for black children in Mississippi, and a society for the care of blind and crippled children have been followed, through the years, by strong company support for the United Way, for other local charities, and for the revitalization of downtown Racine.

> *I've worked here for twelve years. There were a number of things that attracted me to the company initially. As a child I had to move a lot, so I wanted to find a company that had its offices in one place, one that wouldn't want me to move around. And I wanted to find a company that was very responsive to employees. So I read S. C. Johnson's material and was impressed enough to schedule an interview. They sent me the company philosophy statement, "This We Believe." And I thought, "A lot of other companies say these things, that employees and the community are very important to them, but these folks really have a cohesive story here." It wasn't just S. C. Johnson saying this about themselves. They had articles from other people saying this about them. It seemed like more than just chest thumping.*
>
> *Then, when I came to interview, they took me to the cafeteria downtown for lunch, and we sat down, and not ten minutes later in came Sam Johnson. He got his lunch and sat down just a few tables away from us. I was impressed by that. In a lot of companies officers have their own dining rooms.*
>
> *I also got a chance to drive around Racine a little bit the night before, and ask people around town what they thought of the company. And their answers impressed me too. The people in the community thought a lot of this company.*

S. C. Johnson & Son has created a number of avenues for keeping top management in touch with employee concerns, and most of the recent benefit innovations at the company can be traced to concerns and ideas voiced through those channels.

The "Just Ask" program offers employees a chance to submit written questions to management on any subject. Signed queries get personal responses. Anonymous submissions receive posted answers if the question concerns only a small area of the company, or responses in the weekly newsletter if the subject is of general interest.

About every two years, top management holds a series of meetings with people throughout the company to review and discuss the company's long-range business plans. At these forums, the president and other company leaders present their strategies and objectives, then field questions and listen to suggestions. Those who for any reason do not wish to voice their questions can submit the queries in writing. We spoke with several people who have attended the sessions, and all commented on how impressed they were with the openness of the forum, and with the tough questions asked and answered.

The most detailed information about employee concerns comes to management through employee-opinion surveys, conducted every three or four years. The polls ask for comments on everything from the food in the cafeteria to the performance of supervisors. Since 1949, when the company drew up the first of these surveys, the answers and comments have led to a series of important changes at the company, and employees have come to see their answers as a real chance to influence company policy. Though the answers are anonymous, they are identified by area, and analysis of the results regularly leads to management changes—both shifting of people and training to make individual managers more responsive to employee concerns. The polls have also led to a number of additions to the benefit package, among them the swimming pool at the company's recreation center.

> We have the opinion survey every three years and there have always been major changes in the company after the results are in. If you write down what you want on there, and it's felt by the majority, that's what happens.
>
> Even before we had our child-care center the company always put a lot of emphasis on children. The parties they have for these kids are just incredible—the Christmas party, the Easter party, the Halloween party, a fishing derby. And the company picnic is really centered around children—they bring all these rides in. And they have swimming lessons and tumbling lessons at the recreation center. This company has always had that orientation. One of the things that attracted me to come work here was the emphasis on family. We don't miss their children's programs for anything. My husband and I set up our schedules around those parties because they're great. We live in Milwaukee. My husband works at a company up there that gives a lot of children's parties too, but we just blow those off and come down here.

On the 1984 employee-opinion survey, a significant number of people responded to the questions about benefits with write-in comments on the need for help with child care. Some offered specific suggestions—that the company should set up a referral service to help them find care, or that it should offer classes in how to look for quality care—while others just wrote that they were having trouble and would like to see the company respond somehow.

Since the comments came back spontaneously, rather than in response to specific questions, and since so many people wrote about the need for child-care assistance, the company decided to look into the matter. Raymond Farley, then president and chief operating officer at the company, appointed a task force of people from different parts of the company to do some research and come up with suggestions for a response.

The team began meeting in October 1984, and over the next three months conducted an additional employee survey to get a clearer picture of the need for child care. JoAnne Brandes, an attorney at the company and a member of the task force, remembers the results that came back. "We were surprised at the answers we got from our employees. First, we found that they wanted a child-care center. No matter how you ran the numbers, their need was for reliable, quality child care. They weren't so concerned about cost, and maybe that's because our employees are pretty well paid, but they wanted a quality environment for their children, and one that they had some control over."

The task force also surveyed community resources to obtain an understanding of the available child-care supply. Brandes and Bob Inslee, director of human resources at the time, visited a number of child-care centers in the area. "We found that there wasn't much nearby," says Brandes, "and that what was available wasn't anywhere near the quality that we sensed our employees expected, and that we felt they should expect. We were really appalled at what many considered to be quality child care. I didn't go into many centers at that time that I would consider sending my child to. We saw teacher-child ratios at the maximum allowed by the state. We saw care givers without any early-childhood education backgrounds. We saw facilities without enough space. We saw care givers being paid minimum wage. And all those things really bothered us."

*The company says that the reason we have a day-care center is for our employees. The last day care I took my children to was not like that at all. I think the woman who ran it had an underlying belief that women should really stay home with their kids. Sometimes they would just close* the center arbitrarily. If they wanted to take Good Friday off—and they knew that 80 percent of the kids' parents worked on Good Friday—they'd close. And that caused me a lot of problems. My parents live twenty miles away, but it's twenty miles in the opposite direction. So to take our son there meant getting up at five, packing him up, driving all the way there, dropping him off, and driving all the way back again. Now that he's at the company center my life is so much easier, because they only close when we close. And they only have a snow day if we have a snow day.

The last day care used to call all the time. One day they called and said, "Your son has run out of diapers." I said, "Well, why don't you borrow from Kenny? His mom will understand. I'll drop more off for her tonight." And they said, "No. You have to leave work and bring diapers." The day care was twenty miles from here. They said, "If you don't bring more diapers, we're going to leave him in these dirty ones all day." That's kind of indicative of their attitude toward working parents. And I wasn't too happy with the way they treated the kids either. One two-year-old bit another child and they made him eat a bar of soap. They had a really negative approach.

My son also got quite sick at the last day care, and it could have been avoided. I still regret that I didn't have my eyes open a little bit more. I dropped him off one morning, and there was a sign on the door saying one of the children had meningitis. I knew that there are two kinds of meningitis, one very contagious and one not. So I asked the teacher if she knew what type it was. And she said, "I don't know. I'll check into it and when you come tonight I'll let you know." When I came that night she told me not to worry. I should not have accepted that, but I did. She led me to believe she'd checked it out during the day, and I trusted her. Well, it turned out to be a strain of bacterial meningitis, and my son caught it and almost died. He was near death in the intensive-care area of the hospital. He was in the hospital for eight days.

I think there's a lot out there that people are not aware of. I finally took my boys out when the woman's husband was caught for indecent exposure with the three-year-olds. Those are the horror stories that make me an absolute believer in what we have in the Johnson Wax child-care center. You don't have to worry about any of that with Johnson's. It's a very safe environment. To me it's a gold mine.

Brandes and Inslee felt that the employee survey and their community research indicated a need for the company to sponsor its own high-quality child-care center, one that would not only provide a convenient service, but that would relieve parents of their worries about inadequate care. And they decided that instead of presenting this concept as the task force finding they should take the idea a step farther and develop a model for such a center.

The two looked first at how such a center would be operated. "As an attorney, my number one concern was liability," says Brandes. "But as I studied the law, I realized that our goal of providing a quality center was our best answer to the problem of liability. In any liability issue you try to minimize the risk. And if we could provide a high-quality center we would minimize the risk tremendously. If we could contract with another company or agency to run the center and make sure that they had adequate insurance coverage, then our risk would be insignificant."

They looked at several operating models, including having the company run the center itself as a new department within the corporation. Aside from the issue of liability, they decided that the company lacked the expertise and needed to create a partnership with an organization that had child-care experience. They also ruled out a contract with a for-profit center. "We didn't think you could make a profit in child care and run the center in the way our employees wanted," explains Brandes. "And with a for-profit center we wouldn't have the quality control we were after." They finally settled on Catholic Social Services to run the center, a nonprofit, nondenominational agency with a fifty-year history of counseling families and children.

The two then found space for the center in a church building, midway between the headquarters building and the production plant, which was used for Sunday school but remained empty during the week. They projected enrollment from the employee survey results, drafted a budget for the center, and brought the whole package before the executive committee.

"We kept hearing from other companies how difficult it was to convince top management to get behind child care," says Brandes. "So we went in, made our presentation on the need for child care, including how difficult it is for employees to cope with child-care problems on their own, how nicely a center would fit in with our family philosophy and our wellness program, and how valuable it would be as an employee recruitment and retention tool, and ended with a yes or no proposal. I said, 'If you give us the go-ahead, we'll open at the end of the summer. We'll start the marketing tomorrow. All we have to do is sign the lease, sign the contract with the agency, and put some money down.' I remember they chuckled a little bit. And within fifteen minutes they said yes. And that was it."

Raymond Farley, president of the company at the time and chairman of the executive committee, had talked with the two beforehand, and supported their idea. "If you can take care of some of your employees' basic human concerns and needs," he explains, "and not throw a lot of extra ones in their way, then your people are going to be able to do their jobs in a much more creative way. By taking away some worries you free their minds up. We've always been a leader when it comes to important employee benefits. And that comes out of an attitude that says our employees are very important to us. Because our employees are our company. So it was very natural for us to look favorably on child care when the issue was brought to our attention.

"We were also aware, perhaps a little earlier than some companies, that there is going to be a shortage of qualified, skilled employees in the 1990s. Quite frankly, every business will have to have a program like this in order to sign up and keep good people. And when we discussed the idea we didn't see any real downside risk. Near the end of their presentation they asked us if we were willing to take the risk. Well, I asked myself, 'What's the risk?' There are some costs involved, but that's a known thing, and you can measure that against the benefits, which also seemed clear.

"Finally, we just felt that it was the right thing to do. So in the last analysis we were looking for ways to make the program work. We wanted to be sure that it was a good, high-quality program and that the cost didn't put it out of reach of our regular employees."

*I guess the thing that I like most about the center is the quality of the staff. I feel very comfortable leaving my children there. And the children enjoy going. You know when you come to pick them up and they say, "Oh, Dad, can't you come back later?" that they like to be there. The teachers are really involved. They'll be as involved with your child as you want them to be, in terms of addressing certain behavior. Our son, for example, has had some problems with listening, and in addition to our regular ongoing meetings with the teacher, we've had a couple of separate meetings where we've discussed that. He's going into the first grade next year and we've talked with his teachers and with the director about what we should do, what we should look for, how we make the decision about whether he goes to first grade or stays in kindergarten. And they have been very helpful. They put us in touch with the psychologist for the school that we've selected, and he has talked with us about our concerns and is going to try to help us get the right teacher for our son's needs.*

The Johnson Wax Child Care Center opened in September 1985, with a capacity for eighty children aged two to twelve. The executive committee granted a generous subsidy with the understanding that it be used to keep rates at about the standard for the community while providing service that was of much higher quality. Samuel Johnson, great-grandson of the company's founder, suggested the donation of a new van to provide transportation to and from area schools for the before- and after-school program.

While many centers open with low enrollment at first, as some parents wait to see what a center looks like in operation before they sign their children on, the Johnson Wax center opened with seventy-eight children. "I think our employees really trusted us," says Brandes. "They think that if S. C. Johnson is going to do something it's going to be quality. We don't come out with a product unless it's the best quality product at that time. And it's the same with our benefits. We just do things right."

And the center is a quality center. In 1988 it received accreditation from the National Association for the Education of Young Children, an organization which sponsors a review process that remains one of the only comparative judgments of quality that parents can rely on in determining center quality. At the time it was one of only four accredited centers in the state.

When we visited in the summer of 1990, the center was still housed in the church building where it began. The facility itself was fairly ordinary—with boxlike rooms off a long hallway, and a small playground—but it was spacious and the encouraging educational approach clearly made it a place the children liked to be in. Teachers were plentiful—in each room a child could sit in an adult's lap for a story while others received help and supervision with other projects.

The school-age program expanded a year after the center opened when the company started a summer camp on the grounds of its recreational park. The camp has grown steadily, and took care of about two hundred employee children during the summer of 1990.

Although no formal "family-friendly" agenda exists at S. C. Johnson, the company has accompanied its move into child-care assistance with a growing acceptance of flexible and alternative schedules. Most office jobs have been on flexible schedules for a number of years, with starting times that vary from seven-thirty to nine o'clock, but more and more employees are also working out part-time schedules with their managers, or negotiating job-sharing arrangements. The company has had salaried part-timers since 1985, and in 1990 allowed the first managerial job-sharing team. Furthermore, part-timers and job-sharers here have support from the top of the company. When staff changes put them under new managers who aren't as accepting of their schedules, pressure from above helps to smooth out the conflicts.

*I've been with the company for ten years, and about four years ago, pretty soon after my second child got to school, I decided to cut back to part-time. I had felt the pressure all along. It was just a question of when was I able to do something about it. I was a single parent for a while when the kids were young. Then I remarried and full-time work became less of a financial necessity. But rather than leave entirely I looked at alternatives. And what I did was propose to handle a full-time job on a part-time schedule, one that would allow me to pick my children up at school.*

*I think the breakthrough came for me when I took my oldest son to Cub Scouts at the young age of eight. It's the first kind of public thing you do with your kids. And the Cub Master got up and said, "By the time you get to Cub Scouts, half of your time with your kids, or your influence with your kids, is already done." And I thought, "It can't be. We're just getting started." It was a very disturbing thought to me. I could suddenly imagine them being seventeen years old and not around anymore. It was probably a fear of being fifty or sixty years old and having my kids call, and saying, "I wish I'd spent more time with you when you were here," that drove me to part-time as much as anything else.*

*About six months ago a job at my level opened up. And the woman who was leaving the position got together with the woman who'd been hired to replace her—they both had young children—and they decided to propose the job as a job share. And they got approval. Some of that had happened in more clerical jobs, but these women were really breaking ground by doing it in an executive position. When that happens and it is okayed by the company, I think it creates a better atmosphere for everyone. It was my boss who spearheaded it. They came to him and said this was what they wanted to do. And he sold it up the ladder. It's nice to work for somebody like that. There are a lot of reasons why he might not understand that. He's young. He's single. He doesn't have kids. Yet he respects a lot of the people around here who do. Like me. I keep weird hours sometimes. My wife works too, so I take the kids to day care, and I can't get here at eight. I just can't. Normally I'll work later than most of the people here do. But he's real good about that flexibility.*

*I think it's a two-way street. When people are treated professionally like that, they tend to act professionally. That's a style of management that ends up making people more productive. As long as you're treated with respect and with the dignity you deserve, you're certainly going to treat the company that you work for the same way. I know I do.*

The company has reaffirmed its commitment to child care and to answering the needs of working parents in many ways over the years—with baby-sitting facilities at Saturday exercise class, with nudges from above to managers who resist part-time arrangements, with college scholarships for the children of S. C. Johnson employees, and with a continued subsidy for the child-care center—but twice since the child-care center opened it has made that commitment particularly clear.

When the center had been in operation for two years, and most of the start-up expenses had been absorbed, JoAnne Brandes drew up a budget for the center that included a smaller contribution from the company. The center was at capacity, at its peak operating efficiency, and had come much closer to being self-sufficient. She still remembers with some surprise the reaction her budget drew from Raymond Farley. "He said to me, 'We get so much publicity out of this. We're in newspapers. We've been on TV. It's doing a lot for morale here. I don't want our parents to pay for our publicity. We ought to pay for that. I want you to come back with a budget that reflects more of that value to us.' " She added an aide in every classroom, raised the salaries for the teachers, and added money for new equipment. The committee approved the new budget.

In 1989 the company decided to build its own child-care facility next to the fitness center at the company's recreational park. The need for infant care had grown even clearer since the center first opened, and waiting lists for children of all ages pointed out the need for expansion. Because the company is privately held, precise figures aren't released, but the 20,000-square-foot child-care center will obviously be a major expense. "This is not a paternalistic move," explains Farley. "Starting a child-care center was a good business decision. And I think a facility with infant care is going to be an outstanding business asset. It's just plain good business."

It should also be good child care. When it opens in the spring of 1991, the center will provide care for 200 children, aged six weeks to twelve years. A short pathway will lead to the gym and to the spectacular indoor pool, with its separate wading area for toddlers and younger children. In nice weather the children will be able to venture out onto the fields and playgrounds at the 146-acre park. And the site is just a fifteen-minute drive from both the production plant and the headquarters building. "The child-care program has grown to the point where it's a part of our company," says Brandes. "And the decision to build it at Armstrong Park shows the company's commitment to leadership in its support for quality child care."

S. C. Johnson's long history of employee support has led it confidently into the age of working mothers, single fathers, and dual-career families. The child-care center is a natural outgrowth of benefits and policies that have been in place for decades. As more flexible work policies prove themselves and spread through the workplace, this should become an even better company for working parents. We find it telling that when JoAnne Brandes presented the child-care proposal to the company's executive committee, she did not include turnover and absenteeism among her list of reasons for going ahead with the project. "Turnover is not really a problem with us," she explains. "People don't leave."

"Some outsiders see us as a generous company," says Brandes, "but they don't understand that there are sound business reasons underlying everything we do. And it works. We've been around for over one hundred years with this philosophy, and I think that's one of the reasons we're successful. Because of the way we treat our people."

# Joy Cone Co.

3435 Lamor Road
Hermitage, PA 16148                    412-962-5747

**Nature of business:** Manufacturer of ice-cream cones.
**Number of permanent employees:** 250 to 400 (seasonal).
**Female employees:** 64 percent (62 percent of production managers).

**Child care:** No formal program.
**Elder care:** No formal program.
**Family leave:** Up to eighteen months unpaid leave with same or similar job on return; no paid disability leave for childbirth.
**Flexible work options:** Flextime in certain positions; part-time production jobs common; rotating shift assignments with allowance for individual requests.

Flexibility in production jobs.

*"Our style is to be close to these people—to be demanding, to ask a lot of them, to constantly ask them for more—but not to use them like numbers. They're human beings. They deserve respect. They deserve consideration. And to say, 'No matter what your personal needs, these are the days you'll work and this is the shift you'll work,' that's just not how you treat human beings."*

JOE GEORGE
Chairman

The Joy Cone factory has grown up in a residential neighborhood of Hermitage, Pennsylvania, and sits surrounded by single-family homes on grassy lots. The sound of a motor starting up beside the plant might as easily be the next-door neighbor's lawnmower as a semitrailer truck setting out with a load of cones. One old house has practically been surrounded by the plant—the home where co-owner Joe George raised his family during his early years with the company. As the business grew, the factory expanded onto the back lawn and finally edged right up against the house, which now serves as adjunct office space.

What began, in 1918, as a small bakery to make ice-cream cones for local shops and restaurants has become the country's largest ice-cream-cone factory. The company sells to Hardee's, Dairy Queen, Swenson's, Baskin-Robbins, McDonald's, and Nabisco. Its own Joy Cone packages are a common sight on grocery store shelves throughout the East and the Midwest, and they are starting to appear in West Coast stores.

Inside the plant, huge vats of batter feed through a network of overhead tubes into cone-cooking machines that the company created to meet its own special needs. In the cake-cone department, these are huge circular contraptions, in which dozens of individual cone molds orbit past gas flames, the whole machine covered with a flying-saucer-like hood. Jets of batter squirt in at one end; completed cones feed out the other. A single packer mans the machine, watches for any breakdowns or backups, and puts the never-ending stream of finished cones into bags and boxes. In the sugar-cone area, the cones must be cooled before packing, and here the baking machines feed onto overhead conveyor belts. Hundreds of little brown cones snake through the air before descending to the teams of packers.

> *I train people on all the different machines, and I move around myself, so there's some variety. It's interesting. I like it. Sometimes I'll add up in my head what I'm packing. I go through six cases an hour. Do you know how many cones that is? And if you think about four hours on a machine, that's a lot of cones. And you're in charge of your machine. You're responsible. You have to know how to keep it running right, when to get hold of your foreman if there's a problem.*
>
> *If Joy Cone wasn't here, I'd probably have to work full-time somewhere. I'm working a half shift here so I can spend more time with my daughter, and avoid day-care problems. And Joy Cone pays better than other part-time work around here. So I really wouldn't know where to start if they weren't here.*

In our talks with employers across the country, one qualifying statement rang like a chorus in our ears whenever we talked about flexible scheduling: "But the policies don't apply to workers in our production facilities." Over and over, companies would describe flextime arrangements, or policies for integrating part-timers and job-sharers into the work force, then admit that production workers remain on rigid full-time schedules. What's more, in plants that operate around the clock, younger workers—who tend to be the ones with young children—are often stuck for years on the afternoon and night shifts, waiting to accumulate enough seniority to qualify for a move to the more popular day shift. When we consider the problems of office workers who must rely on day-care providers with inflexible schedules, we often forget the far more difficult child-care problems faced by parents who work night shifts.

The Joy Cone Company looks like a typical old-style manufacturing plant, one where fixed shifts give workers a choice of full-time work or nothing, one where young parents put in their years on the night shift waiting for openings on the day turn. As a business with an annual cycle that requires many more workers in the spring and early summer than in the fall, the company also looks like one that must take on and slough off a sacrificial batch of workers every year. But the reality here is a pleasant surprise. Joy Cone is one of very few manufacturing plants that considers personal need before seniority in shift assignments, and that allows production employees to work less than eight-hour shifts. Its annual cycle allows it to give parents of school-age children the time off they want during the late summer, fall, and winter.

> *I'm part-time, and what shift I work all depends on my husband's shift. They give me the opposite of what he works. So every week when the request sheet comes out, I just write on it what I need, and they give me that turn. I don't have a sitter, so I couldn't work if they didn't give it to me. I have three children—seven, five, and twenty months. The oldest is in first grade, the next is in preschool, and the baby is at home.*
>
> *When I'm on day turn and he's on afternoon he gets them up and gets them ready for school, takes them to school, and picks them up. Then, when I get home, I get his dinner ready for him and he goes to work. And then vice versa. He does his share. He has to. I have three boys, so there's a lot going on. When I'm not there he takes them and when he's not there I take them. It has to work that way. My oldest has T-ball practice twice a week and then there's games. When he's on days I go on evenings, and he does their homework with them, he bathes them, he gives them their snack, and he puts them to bed.*

This business has grown up with flexibility and responsiveness to employee needs as two of its basic tenets. In 1964, when Joe and Fred George took over the business their father had started almost fifty years before, they managed to squeeze out just $25,000 in sales. Four years later the figure reached $300,000. That year, as the company finally began to work its way out of the slump into which it had settled in the 1950s, Joy Cone began to employ part-time production workers.

"We had two married women who worked full-time during the busy season," remembers Joe George. "When we slowed down in mid-August they came to us and said, 'Look, instead of laying one of us off, why don't we split a shift between us?' And I said fine. Then when we started getting busy again they said, 'We don't want to go back to full-time. We'd like to continue splitting the shift. With this schedule we can take care of our kids and our houses and still get out and earn an extra paycheck.' " He assented again, and began an employment practice that has since grown common throughout the factory.

"When I approved that first split-shift arrangement, this was a small operation," says George. "I knew the two women pretty well and understood their needs. And I think we were open to new ideas. We already had women foremen back then, which was unheard of in this business. We were just willing to try things. We've come to see that the split shifts offer advantages both ways. Sure, the scheduling is a little more complicated, and we have to keep track of more people to keep the factory staffed at the same level, but it's a tremendous retention tool for us, it gives *us* some flexibility in scheduling, and it gives the workers who use it a great deal of security. Our employees know that—within reason, and not at the snap of a finger—they can move back and forth between full- and part-time. If a woman's husband gets laid off and she needs the extra income, she knows that come our busy season she can go to full-time. And she knows that if her husband then gets called back to work, she can go back to part-time to spend more time with her kids. She's not locked in one way or the other. And that gives her a real sense of security."

A schedule-request sheet has also been a fixture at Joy Cone since the 1960s. As the business grew, and a second shift was added, then a third, the Georges tried to work out weekly schedules that met all their workers' needs. Days off were scheduled around doctors' appointments, weddings, and graduations, and shifts rotated with allowances for special circumstances. Parents who needed to work opposite shifts, for example, so that one was always home with the children, could explain that on the request sheet, and the schedule would be drawn up around their needs.

"We don't assign shifts by seniority," says George. "We don't do that because we'd end up with all the kids and all the new people on either afternoon or midnight. That's one rule that we won't budge on. Everybody has to be ready to rotate. Now as a practical matter we manage to give people what they need. If someone asks for steady afternoon or midnight, they get it, but we can't give steady day turn. The request sheet allows people to let us know their particular needs each week."

> For almost five years, up until this year, I worked part-time, steady, 7:00 to 11:00 P.M., so I could be home most of the day and be with my husband a little bit. My husband would get them to bed after I left. And then I came to full-time last month. They have really good benefits here, and I sort of need it for my family. When you're working part-

*time you get the same benefits, but you don't get the health insurance for your family. When you have small children you really need good insurance. And my husband's was really bad. We had to pay a lot for it.*

*We start at 7:00 A.M. for day turn, and get out at 3:00, so I'm there for my son when he gets off the bus. I'm home for him in the evening this way, and I can help him with his schoolwork and be there for that. When I'm on afternoon I only see him for an hour in the morning when I bring him around for school, just one hour a day, and I can't deal with that. That's why I prefer to switch between day and midnight. I don't work a steady rotation. I tend to request certain shifts to meet my needs at home, and they're usually pretty good about meeting that for me. I sometimes have to ask for special shifts, rather than just the regular rotation, because of day care. In fact, I did for next week. It just depends on doctors' appointments and everything.*

In the early days, Joe George kept track of the requests in his head. As the business grew, he pinned up a request sheet and worked all the penciled notes into a weekly schedule that kept everybody happy and every machine manned. When the company had just twenty or thirty workers, the schedule was a puzzle, but not a time-consuming one. With four hundred workers, it has become a far more complex task. The sign-up sheet has a space next to each name, and by the end of the day on Wednesday, when the sheet comes down, most lines have some sort of note. Some are easy to fit in: "Need Tuesday off, bowling tournament," or "Saturday off for wedding." Some are a bit more complicated: "Need 7:00 to 11:00 A.M., ride with Sadie Smith." "Afternoon, please, husband on days this week." Or, "If not on midnight would like Thursday off." With the ride shares, the couples who want to work opposite shifts, the company's effort to give people two days off together and to rotate them fairly from shift to shift, the scheduler's task is a tough one.

Glenn Miller had the job when we visited. He explained that he normally took the request sheet home on Wednesday night, worked on the schedule late into the night, and had it up for review by lunch the next day. That left time for adjustment if he'd made any mistakes or if anybody complained. He also told us that his was a high-turnover job. Since Joe George had passed the torch along, four people had tried their hand at it. The first was now production manager, the second had moved into sales, the third drove a truck, and Miller, fifteen months into the job, had outlasted them all.

Hermitage is in steel country, and many of Joy Cone's employment practices have grown up in reaction to, or perhaps to complement, scheduling practices at the mills. Sharon, Pennsylvania, is the next town to the west; Youngstown, Ohio, lies within commuting distance across the border; and Pittsburgh is just an hour's drive to the south. Many Joy Cone employees are married to mill workers, and the rigid shift rotations at the mills not only provide a foil that makes the cone company more attractive to prospective employees, they also offer a fixed schedule for couples to work around. Those without children can try to match the Joy Cone schedule to that of the partner at the mill. Those with children can try to set up opposite schedules so that one adult will always be home with the children.

"We could do our schedules like the mills do," says Miller. "Either set it up on seniority or do straight rotations. That way people would have the convenience of knowing six or eight weeks ahead of time which shift and what days they were going to work. But they wouldn't have the convenience of saying, 'Well, I didn't want to work that shift,' or, 'I wanted a different day off.' We could set the schedule up on a computer and it would save me twenty hours of work every week. But if we did that, if we got rid of the request sheet, I think we might lose as much as half of our work force. We've got a lot of people, parents and people with other responsibilities, who *need* to have a schedule that bends a little."

> *The scheduling, the way they listen to my needs, those are big factors keeping me here. Because I couldn't work if they didn't do that. I don't have a sitter. One time I ran into a problem where I needed the 7:00 to 11:00 P.M. turn when my husband was on day turn, and someone with more seniority had got it. So I went up and talked to Joe George. I told him I had to work that turn. There was no other way. I told him that I will not hire someone from an ad to watch my children. I just don't trust anyone. And he understood. We worked it out. My sister was on that turn. She was working it steady. So the one week that I needed it, we came up with the solution that she would bring her son to my house and I would watch him, and she would switch the turn with me for the week.*

When business starts to fall off in the late summer, Joy Cone is faced with another scheduling problem—how to cut back to its off-season production level with the least personal hardship.

As a first step, beginning in the middle of July, people are encouraged to take their summer vacations. By mid-August, more drastic measures are needed: the company lays off students who've been hired for the summer and starts a process of voluntary layoffs. "We have a lot of women here," says Joe George. "And by the end of the summer, if they've worked through the season, many of them are happy to have a week or two, or maybe even a month or two of layoff. One person might want the month of September to get the kids ready for school. Somebody else might want the month of December. So we just let them roll through the layoffs. In general, people with at least two years of seniority don't have to worry about involuntary layoffs during the winter." Production then resumes at the spring pace around January, though strong orders have, on occasion, required callbacks in December, when many people leave for vacations around the holidays. "We do that by reverse seniority," says George. "People with the least seniority get called back first."

Newer workers, those subject to involuntary layoffs, probably have a hard time with the income loss during the fall. But for most workers, the fall layoffs seem to be a welcome break. Some of the workers we talked to pointed to them as one of the reasons they continue to work at Joy Cone.

> *You get laid off from time to time during the off season and I look forward to it. That's one of the reasons I like working here, because I know, come fall, I have that time to spend with my kids and I can collect unemployment while I'm off. The layoffs can be a couple of weeks at a time, or they can be from September to January. I was laid off last year October 1, and I worked two weeks from October to January. It all depends on their orders and how they're running. But I look forward to it. That's the time of the year that I get to spend more time with the kids and we're a normal family.*

The split shifts and the request sheets have been around so long at Joy Cone that people hardly think about them anymore. Workers accept the practices as a matter of course, and some probably assume that most factories have much the same policies. But such practices are still rare in American business.

It would have been very easy for Joe George to deny that first request for a split shift in the busy season—the company had just a dozen workers at the time and could have used the extra hands—or to eliminate the request sheet when the business got so big that he could no longer keep track of the requests in his head. "We would never do that," he says. "First of all, neither my brother nor I feel comfortable being hard-nosed managers, saying, 'This is the way it is. Take it or leave it.' Our style is to be close to these people—to be demanding, to ask a lot of them, to constantly ask them for more—but not to use them like numbers. They're human beings. They deserve respect. They deserve consideration. And to say, 'No matter what your personal needs, these are the days you'll work and this is the shift you'll work,' that's just not how you treat human beings.

"And in the long run, not only is it better for my morale, my ego, and my conscience, but I think our operation will beat a plant that's run without consideration for the employees. In the long run I think ours is more efficient. We could get workers without these flexible policies, but we wouldn't get their loyalty. We wouldn't be able to run like we do, with thirty people and not a single white hat, not a single person walking around checking on others. Every person in our plant is working.

"I think this is the efficient, cost-effective way to run the business. In each of the last four years we've raised our wages, yet unit production costs went down. We're getting more efficient. Something is working when we can pay our workers more and it costs us less."

Joy Cone could perhaps do more to become a truly "family-friendly" workplace. The company offers no help with child care, for example, and some of the parents we spoke with told of the difficulty they faced finding care that matched their changing schedules. We heard how hard it can be, for example, to find providers who will take in children before the start of the day shift at 7:00 A.M. And while the company offers a generous leave policy—up to eighteen months of unpaid leave—it provides no disability insurance to cover the work time lost to childbirth. Still, for a company with a large contingent of production workers, Joy Cone offers an exceptional amount of flexibility. Employee surveys at other companies have consistently shown that flexibility is the most important family benefit that companies can offer. The parents we spoke with at Joy Cone told us again and again that the company's scheduling practices gave them the chance to earn a living while fulfilling their family obligations. In some cases they told us they could not work if the company did not make allowances for their individual scheduling needs.

As an example of how flexible scheduling practices can help both employers and employees, Joy Cone has much to offer other companies as well. While many managers dismiss flexibility as an impossibility in production settings, the Georges have proved that it is not. To them, part-time workers, schedule requests, and voluntary layoffs are the cornerstones of a thriving business.

# The Little Tikes Company

2180 Barlow Road
Hudson, OH 44236                                                216-650-3000

**Nature of Business:** Toy manufacturer.
**Number of employees:** 1,450.
**Female employees:** 36 percent (26 percent of managers).
**Child care:** On-site center for 35 children, aged three to six years, subsidized and run as a department of the company.
**Elder care:** No formal program.
**Family leave:** Paid disability leave for childbirth, plus up to thirty days unpaid parental leave.
**Flexible work options:** Some part-time work and job sharing.
**Other benefits:** Employee-assistance program with on-site counselor; on-site physician; tuition reimbursement; on-site toy store with employee discount; profit-sharing plan.

An ear-to-the-employee approach.

*"I know that other companies look at the figures in black and white and say that they can't afford to support a child-care center. What they don't realize is that they can't afford not to do it. If you're going to run a first-rate company, you can't afford not to do things like this. When you show that you really do care about your people in your total approach to the business—and that is reflected not just in child-care centers but in your day-to-day association with your employees—the intangible benefits to the company are monumental."*

TOM MURDOUGH
Founder and former President

*"The child-care center is certainly a very effective way of testing toys. So there's a clear dollars-and-cents value there. But more than that, the center sets the right tone for the*

*company. It shows that Little Tikes is a quality company, genuinely concerned about employees and genuinely concerned about children, about their safety, about their education. It's just the right thing to do."*

GARY BAUGHMAN
President

It is Thursday afternoon at the Little Tikes factory in Hudson, Ohio. President Gary Baughman sits in a meeting room off the plant floor, flanked by the company's vice president of manufacturing, the human resources vice president, and other key managers. Their audience, the assembled factory staff, has just listened to the executives' presentation and proceeds to bombard them with tough questions.

A bad-news gathering to announce cutbacks? A meeting to crack the whip on product quality? Not at Little Tikes. Sales have been growing at a rate of 40 percent a year for several years, and the company is known for the quality and appeal of its brightly colored plastic toys. No, this is just another monthly meeting, a regular exchange of information and ideas to keep managers in touch with employee needs and employees up-to-date on the status of the business. The company feels that employees will do better work and will feel more involved with their jobs if they know how their particular tasks fit in with the larger goals of the company. And through long experience, the company has learned that great progress can be made by listening to all its people—that newly hired packers often have ideas as helpful as those of seasoned product managers.

*Each shift has its own meeting every month. The president will get up first and give a talk, then the vice president; they go right down the line. They give financial reports, sales projections, and all that stuff. Then they'll answer questions. There are written questions if you don't want to raise your hand. People ask about safety, about new products. They'll raise production ideas. Wages always come up.*

*At the last plant meeting Pat was down to say that there are some openings in the child-care center. And I raised my hand and said, "When are they going to get infant care?" They do need it with so many young people here.*

Little Tikes' monthly meetings have been a part of the company's operating schedule since 1970, when the business began making plastic toys in a barn in nearby Aurora, Ohio. The company has also had an open-door policy since the start. When the company opened for business with nine employees, founder Thomas Murdough found it natural to be accessible to every worker. As the business grew he worked to maintain that openness, as has his successor, Gary Baughman, who picked up the company's reins in January 1990. Both men have realized that daily communication and a feeling among employees that they can approach management at any time with a question or suggestion are important to building an organization with a deep-rooted attitude that employees really do matter.

In the early days, the whole company could sit in one room for the monthly meetings. The business eventually had to divide the sessions and hold meetings for each shift, then separate office and plant meetings. But through the tenures of both presidents, the meetings have remained an important part of the company's operation. "At a company like Little Tikes," says Baughman, "where the production is as much an art as it is a science, the success of the company depends heavily on the motivation of our employees, on their willingness and desire to do it right. And for them to be highly motivated, they have to know what the stakes are. They need to know how we're doing, how they're doing, where we need to improve. We also have to let them know that their concerns are being heard and that their ideas are being used." A profit-sharing plan that distributes substantial year-end bonuses to all employees provides one form of motivation, and a powerful one; the monthly meetings and the company's effort to involve workers in decision-making provides another.

At a typical meeting the executives will read complaints and praise from customers' letters, review any business news, and report on sales and general financial results. Whenever a major new toy nears introduction, the managers will set up a prototype at the meetings and invite comments. "We have very open discussions about our new products," says Baughman, "and very often employees will come up with important new ideas that will change the product."

Questions also come up about such things as the choice of radio stations played in the plant, construction progress on a new warehouse, food selection in the lunchroom, lighting in the parking lots, positioning of the company's products in stores, the need for fans at a particular work station, the length of breaks, and how wages at the company compare with those at competing businesses. "They ask point-blank questions," says Baughman, "and I have to stand there and answer them. I've told them that I'll be there every month—I haven't missed a meeting yet—and that I'll answer anything. I'm there to be accountable."

At some point in the early 1980s, the issue of child care started to come up at the meetings. "It was something that built up gradually," Murdough remembers. "We started getting more and more questions about it. And at first we really couldn't respond. We would have loved to have child care in our old plant, but we just didn't have the space. It wasn't until we moved here in 1985 that we finally had the room to do something."

There had been a toy-testing facility in the old plant, where the company's toy designers watched children react to new designs. When planning the new plant, the company decided to combine the toy-testing program with full-time child care.

> It's a secure thing, having the center right here. It's like you're home. If something were to happen to my daughter, I can be right there. I'm divorced, but my ex-wife still works here, so the center makes a nice bond for my daughter. And it makes it so we can both see more of her. If I don't bring her in in the morning—if she comes in with my ex-wife—I'll stop in right before work and say hi. If I'm not taking her home, I always make sure I stop by and say good-bye. And I have lunch with her every day. So I see her at least three times a day. It's so uplifting to me, and I know it is to her.

"We had a number of employees with children," says Murdough. "We'd fielded a lot of questions about child care at our meetings. And we knew that if we could do it there would be tremendous advantages both ways—for the employees and for the company. We knew that child care was a big financial burden to many of our workers, that many parents worked here because they didn't have the money to stay home with their children. We knew that we had some great employees who might leave if they couldn't get some help with child care. And we could justify it very simply if we incorporated it into our product-testing operation. But it was never designed with product-testing as its main focus. We wanted it to be the best child-care center in the area, one with love and warmth, one where the kids would really grow and learn. We wanted the Little Tikes child-care center to become a really meaningful part of the children's and the parents' lives, something that they would look back on with warmth and satisfaction.

"We were determined to have child care at the company. I

know that other companies look at the figures in black and white and say that they can't afford to support a child-care center. What they don't realize is that they can't afford not to do it. If you're going to run a first-rate company, you can't afford not to do things like this. When you show that you really do care about your people in your total approach to the business—and that is reflected not just in child-care centers but in your day-to-day association with your employees—the intangible benefits to the company are monumental."

The company designed its new plant with a large room for child care in a central spot along the hallway between the offices and the plant. Murdough then hired a child-care expert—Pat Belby, who had been teaching at nearby Kent State University— to create the child-care program.

Because the structure had been built before she was hired, Belby started work with a fundamental limitation. She had to figure out how many children, and of what ages, could be served within that defined space. And since it had been built as an open room that didn't lend itself to division, she had to make a decision about how to create the program in a single space. A needs survey of employees showed the greatest desire was for preschool care—for a facility to take in three- to six-year-olds. Some demand was seen for infant and toddler care, but because of the space, a decision had to be made to serve one age group or the other. "You can't turn people out," explains Belby. "If we had set up the center for babies, we would have had to send the children away when they turned three. The more logical approach was to start with this age group and move down when we got an opportunity to expand."

The center was created as a department within the company, with Belby and the other teachers hired on the Little Tikes payroll. A small observation room with a one-way mirror, built with a separate entrance, allows product designers to watch the children unobserved. (It serves the same purpose for parents, who can peer through the mirror to get reassuring glimpses of their children at play.) Inside and on the playground, the center is well equipped with freshly minted Little Tikes products.

> *My daughter gets so excited if my husband is able to come up. He has a forty-five-minute lunch because he works twelve hours. I have a fifteen-minute lunch and sometimes I don't eat with the people I work with but come up here instead. It just thrills her that we're right here. Sometimes in the morning she'll say, "Mommy, can we leave early and go through the plant?" In my last position I started really early and we had to come in through*

> *the plant, and she loved that. She likes seeing where we work.*
>
> *My son loves the equipment and the kids here. And I can come at any time during the day and say hi to him. We have dates twice a month for lunch, but I can also stop in during the morning at any time. And I can go in the observation room and see how the teachers interact with him. That's something you can't do at a regular day care. The other difference that I see here is that this center has some gifted teachers. I used another day care as a backup, when I was using a sitter, and those women were nice, but they were there for the money and to make sure your child didn't get hurt. And there were so many kids at that other center. This place is so different. The teachers here love my child. The teachers here are always hugging and touching. The people at the other day care didn't do that, and that's important for these little kids.*

Today the long hallway in front of the center, which connects the offices to the plant, continues to serve as a laboratory for tests of riding toys. Children from the center are periodically invited to try out new prototypes or improvements to the company's standard models, while engineers and designers note traits like cornering capability, maximum velocity, and how much fun the toys deliver.

Inside the center, although Little Tikes toys abound, children can also choose from a range of other entertainments. A play barn made from a huge appliance box took up a central spot the day we visited (made after a field trip to a farm), and children played with crayons and finger paints, dolls, wooden blocks, puppets, and puzzles. The center cares for a total of thirty-five children, but no more than twenty attend at once, so the two full-time teachers and two part-time aides are able to give the children plenty of individual attention.

The center opens at 6:45 A.M. and closes at 5:00 P.M., a span that covers the factory day shift and the office hours with some flexibility at either end of the day. Night-shift workers can bring their children in for the day while they go home to sleep, and in emergencies the company will rearrange shift assignments to help solve an individual employee's child-care problem.

The center not only offers convenient hours and a quality program, but its rates are a bargain, too. Each year the director surveys other centers to determine the going rate for child care in the area, then subtracts 30 percent to arrive at the Little Tikes fee.

> *You can't find child care around here with this quality, unless maybe you were to hire a private baby-sitter, and certainly not at the price they charge. They have really positive people working at the day care. I like and trust the teachers. And it makes such a difference when you're at work not to have to worry about your child. I don't worry about my daughter when she's here.*

The toy-testing aspect of the Little Tikes child-care program causes some outsiders to dismiss it as an example of a corporate response to employees' child-care needs. "The child-care center is certainly a very effective way of testing toys," Baughman admits. "So there's a clear dollars-and-cents value there. But more than that, the center sets the right tone for the company. It shows that Little Tikes is a quality company, genuinely concerned about employees and genuinely concerned about children, about their safety, about their education. It's just the right thing to do."

As Pat Belby points out, "There are much cheaper ways of testing toys." Little Tikes could have continued to bring children in as needed for toy testing, rather than subsidize an admittedly expensive full-time facility. When he envisioned the child-care center, Tom Murdough wanted a high-quality program that would ease some of the daily worries working parents face and would help strengthen his employees' ties to the company. Toy testing was a secondary concern for him, merely a plus in selling the idea to other executives who might resist the plan on the basis of cost. Baughman echoed that thinking in his conversation with us and added his hope that other companies would follow Little Tikes' lead.

But while toy testing might be a secondary function of the center, we were surprised in our talks with Little Tikes parents to find out how important the testing process is to them. At many companies, parenthood can be a strike against an employee. Children are often looked upon as distractions from the important concerns of business, or as "problems" to be solved. Because of the toy-testing process at Little Tikes, children here are an integral part of the business, and parents who participate in the tests become involved in one of the company's most exciting functions: product development. Parents know that their children play a key part in the screening process that hones every new toy introduction. Occasionally prototype toys are sent home with the children, and parents are asked to take notes on how often their children play with the toys, and how the toys are used. Far from looking on this task as an inconvenience, parents consider it a special mission, one that can involve lower-level factory workers with crucial company decisions. The pride that a worker feels when a toy his child tested in prototype form finally reaches the market cannot be measured on any objective scale.

In other ways, too, Little Tikes makes parents feel involved with the business. All of the children pictured in the company's catalog, on its packages, and in its other promotions are the children of employees. Studio sessions are announced throughout the company, and any employee can bring a child to be photographed. It seems like a simple idea, and it actually saves the company money in model fees, but it pays off tremendously in loyalty when workers see their children, or the children of co-workers, beaming from packages in stores across the country.

*What I like about Little Tikes is that it's a company that cares about what we think. They'll ask our opinions on toys. Every once in a while they'll pick out a child, give them one of the newer toys, and say, "Will you please take this home, observe them, and fill out a questionnaire?" My daughter brought home the ark—Noah's Ark—when they were developing that, and they told me to make sure she took it into the tub with her. She loved it. She could have stayed in the tub all night.*

*The other day when I came to pick her up, she and another boy were down the hallway in two of the new red cars. The cars still had all the marks on them, the dimensions and everything. They were driving and the toy developers were seeing how the cars moved and turned. So they were actually helping to improve the toy.*

*At least once a year, and sometimes twice, they'll take pictures. And eventually, if you're lucky, they'll use your child's picture on one of the toys, on a carton. But whether they use it or not, you still get the picture to keep, and it's nice for the child. To me, if my daughter were to get on a carton, and I went into a store and saw a stack of cartons with her picture, it would flip me out. I'd probably buy them all.*

*My daughter was on the TV news when they introduced the Little Tikes Place. It's made her feel involved and it made me feel involved with the company as a whole. I'm a little more aware of some of the new things coming out. They're just coming out with a vanity and I know my daughter had a lot to do with the testing of that. With the Little Tikes Place they asked me, as a parent, my opinion of it and what I thought it should go for on the market. And before it was ever in the factory they were in here with a coffee maker and a microwave. They asked her what she thought of them and watched her to see which one she went for first. I happened to be up here that day and they asked me what I thought of it. It's fun. And it's helped my attitude toward my job.*

The basic employee-oriented, listening attitude of the company is also particularly attuned to the ideas and concerns of employees with children. Any worker might have money-saving production ideas, but parents are this company's market, and their comments on new product proposals, on product colors, even on packaging and marketing strategies carry special weight here.

As Gary Baughman translates Tom Murdough's ear-to-the-employee approach into a comparable management style of his own, and as the company continues and possibly expands its support for on-site child care, Little Tikes looks like a great prospect for working parents through the 1990s.

# Lost Arrow Corp./Patagonia, Inc.

259 W. Santa Clara Street
Ventura, CA 93001                           805-643-8616

**Nature of business:** Manufacturer of clothing and outdoor gear, sold through the Patagonia mail-order catalog, Great Pacific Iron Works stores, and other selected retail outlets.
**Number of employees:** 520.
**Female employees:** 66 percent (54 percent of managers).
**Child care:** On-site center for 92 children aged eight weeks to fourteen years; satellite network of family day-care homes; income-based subsidies.
**Elder care:** Consultation-and-referral service for employees in Ventura.
**Family leave:** Two-month paid parental leave for mothers, fathers, and adoptive parents; additional unpaid leave negotiable; paid sick time may be used for care of ill family members; vacation time and sick time may be used in one-hour increments.

*Flexible work options:* Flextime with three-hour window; some part-time work; some job sharing.
*Other benefits:* Tuition reimbursement; generous health-insurance package includes dental and eye care; reciprocal discounts from other manufacturers of outdoor gear.

Putting the pieces together: flexibility, on-site child care, and a responsive corporate culture.

*"We've broken all sorts of rules. That's what we like to do. When this day-care center opened in 1984 it was one of just one hundred and fifty corporate day-care centers in the country, and most of the others were at hospitals. So we were breaking the rules. And there are certain advantages to that."*

YVON CHOUINARD
Founder and Chairman

While we were at Patagonia, an employee we were talking with was called downstairs by the child-care center because her three-year-old son had awakened from his nap a little unhappy. She sped down, hugged him back to cheerfulness, and was back with us in a few minutes. When we asked Anita Garaway, the director of the child-care center, to talk about some of her accomplishments there, she proudly told us of an employee she had convinced to take an additional year of parental leave because her baby was not adapting well to the stimulation of the center's environment. And when we called back after our visit, with a new question for the business's co-owners, Yvon and Malinda Chouinard, we found that they had left the country for a year and would not be available, even by telephone, until mid-1991. Clearly, this is a company that doesn't do things by the books. It is also one that has grown, in the decade of the 1980s, from a relatively obscure climbing-equipment supplier into a major player in the outdoor- and leisure-clothing market, with sales of close to $100 million a year.

Many businesses talk about flexibility. The people at Patagonia live and breathe it. Time off for outside pursuits is almost a requirement here. Yvon Chouinard complains that he can't get enough people to skip out of work with him when the surf is good; his wife, Malinda, talks about strategies for keeping parents out on leave until they've had sufficient time to bond with their babies. Many businesses get involved with child care in order to keep employees at their desks for a few more hours or days each year. While that may be a concern here, it must rank near the bottom of the list of priorities. When Patagonia started thinking about child care, the goal was to provide the best conditions possible for nursing mothers. Many businesses talk about techniques to get employees motivated. The people we spoke with at Patagonia were among the most dedicated and involved we have seen anywhere, the environment one of calm commitment.

*I had come down here before and visited the offices, and had walked around, through the store and all. And just looking at everything you know it's very laid back. People have stress with their jobs, but it's a good overall feeling that you get each day you come in to work. And I got that when I came in to visit. It just felt right. And when I came in to interview that first time, I knew that if I didn't get a job soon that I would just need to work on it and wait until something opened up. It was just perfect for me. The day care was part of it, but I would have applied for the job without it.*

*The day care is just an incredible benefit to have. We pay for it, but it's so good. Just there, that they called me and said he woke up a little teary-eyed. And I can be down there in a minute. If he falls down I can be there in a minute, literally a minute, and I can comfort him and love him. I don't know what I would do without them, without their support and their help.*

*I can't imagine working for a company that didn't have good day care like this. My life would have been completely different. With three kids, I might not have even worked. When the children were younger it was very important to me to continue to nurse them. And that was easy with the center downstairs. They'd just call and say your baby's hungry, and you'd go down and nurse. But the center is not the only thing. I think what keeps me here is that it feels like a big family. I'm very close to a lot of the people who work here. When you're at work you feel that you're sort of home. It's very familial. I've been here a long time and I can't think of any instances of the usual back-biting and clawing over one another to get to the top. You don't see that here. I saw a lot of it when I worked in New York. And I'm completely behind this company's philosophy. It's just good people doing good things. And of course I enjoy what I do.*

Patagonia's mission-style offices are sandwiched between two oil-drilling-supply firms in an industrial section of Ventura, California. The sound of traffic from a six-lane highway behind the lot provides a steady accompaniment to conversations on the patios and at picnic tables set in shady spots around the buildings. It seems an unlikely location for a company oriented to wilderness and outdoor pursuits—until the visitor finds the underpass that leads to the beach and Surfer Point just a few blocks away. As you stand on the sand, watching the surfers slide in with the waves on their brightly colored boards, the office site begins to make sense.

Yvon Chouinard began rock-climbing in the mid-1950s as an adjunct to his interest in falconry: he learned to climb in order to get to the falcons' nests. And as he learned more about climbing, he began to have ideas for improvements to the available climbing equipment. The standard pitons of the day—the spikes that climbers hammer into cracks in the rock to guard against falls—were made in Europe of malleable metal. They fit nicely into cracks, but they also bent easily and had to be thrown away after just a couple of uses. On a long climb, such as those pioneered at the time up faces like El Capitan in Yosemite, a climber had to bring dozens of pitons along to ensure that some were still straight for the final pitches. Chouinard had the idea of making pitons out of hardened steel alloys. He found a book on smithing, borrowed money from his parents for a forge, and in 1957 started hammering out his own, which he dubbed Lost Arrows.

From the start, Chouinard viewed his smithing as a means to an end—to be out in the wilderness climbing, falconing, or fishing. He worked half the year, then loaded his stockpile of pitons in the trunk of his car and headed for the climbing routes—Yosemite or Ship Rock or the Shawangunks—where he climbed and peddled his wares. Climbing in those years was a sport for the dedicated few, and since climbers tended to cluster at the rock faces on nice weekends, word of Chouinard's pitons quickly spread through the community. He soon found himself supplementing his trunk sales with orders that came in by mail. He also began adding to his inventory of equipment improvements. By the early 1960s he was making his own carabiners and climbing hammers and selling them by mail.

Chouinard spent two years in the Army, which interrupted the business briefly, but in 1965 he set up the blacksmith shop again, in partnership with climber and engineer Tom Frost. The two moved the forges and dies out of Chouinard's parents' backyard and into a rented shack behind a slaughterhouse in Ventura—next door to Lost Arrow's current office. Through the late

1960s and early 1970s, Chouinard and Frost conducted a systematic reappraisal of all the basic climbing tools. They brought out improved crampons and introduced what is now the standard curved-blade ice ax. In 1971, noticing the toll that repeated use of their own pitons was taking on the popular climbing routes— hundreds of hammerings in and out had visibly worn down the rock and widened cracks—they launched a crusade to replace the spikes with a new array of wedges and nuts that could be fit lightly into rock crevices to provide the same protection from falls. The system of "clean climbing" the Chouinard company advocated in its catalogs changed the nature of climbing within a few years, and Chouinard's wedges and nuts became the climber's tools of choice.

At about the same time, Chouinard began to add some tough and practical clothes for climbers to the equipment catalog. While on a climbing trip in England he noticed a rugby shirt made of tightly woven cotton and brought some back to sell as climbing shirts. In 1972 he started making shorts of his own design out of heavy-duty canvas. Over the next few years, this soft-goods section of the catalog began to grow as the company introduced pile jackets, polypropylene and capilene long underwear, and other innovative wear for outdoor sports—all sold under the name Patagonia. By 1980, the soft goods had outstripped the equipment line as an income generator, and Tom Frost had left the company, disagreeing with the direction the business was taking. That year sales reached about $2 million. A decade later, with an expanded mail-order catalog, stores in ten cities, and a line of clothes that appealed as much to urban business people as wilderness trekkers, they would close in on $100 million. Throughout those years of explosive growth, Chouinard diligently held to his practice of leaving the business for at least six months of every year to take to the wilds.

> *I was attracted to Patagonia because of the philosophy of the company. Everyone's geared to sports. It's very sports oriented. Whether it's climbing or skiing or whatever, everybody's active. And I really like that. I'm an active person. And it's a nice environment here for that. Everyone either goes for a run at lunch hour or goes cycling. You can sit in some offices and people are really sedentary. I go to Los Angeles to meet some of our brokers, and they can't imagine ever going for a bike ride or a run at lunch hour.*
>
> *The center is definitely a bonus. I'd still work for the company without it, but this is just icing on the cake. If I ever get stressed or feel like I have to leave my desk for a few minutes, I come down here. And I'll bring my daughter*

*back with me. I had her at my desk at lunch today. She was banging on my keyboard. It's nice to sort of bring her into the work group. Everyone who has kids here has photos and toys on their desk. It's quite important. They're part of the family.*

At the head of this growing empire sit an unfazed Yvon and Malinda Chouinard—still the company's sole stockholders— who continue to rely on the tenets that propelled the business in the early 1960s. "Being blacksmiths and machinists," Yvon wrote in an early catalog, "we approached the problem of designing clothes from a functional basis. We were not at all concerned about how they would look because we knew from designing tools that when the design is right, the aesthetics would be there." He has spoken of his belief that if a company does all the little things right, the profits will follow. And he explained to us that his unbending commitment to getting away for several months every year has led directly to the company's flexible and supportive employment practices, including the on-site child-care center. "I can only get off because I have good employees here. So the policies and practices have evolved mostly from selfish motives. I never wanted to be a businessman. I just kind of got stuck in this position. And I figured that since I was going to be a businessman—it seemed as though, for better or for worse, I was doomed to do this—that I had to do it on my own terms. And those terms were not to get tied down. I wanted to be able to take a year off. And when I'm gone I don't call in every two days or even every month. I don't call in to keep my thumb on people. When I'm here I do a lot of the planning, setting the long-term general direction of the company. But when I'm gone the company has to run without me, and for that to happen we need responsible people and good communication. I found that in the beginning the best way to achieve that, the quick fix, was to hire a lot of women, because they communicate better than men do, and they're more willing to work as a team. They're less apt to run solo and sort of ace the other person out on the way up the corporate ladder, that sort of thing. You don't need that stuff. So that's why I initially hired a lot of women. And, of course, if you're going to hire a lot of women you've got to make sure they're around after they get pregnant and have kids."

The Chouinards have two children of their own, born in 1975 and 1980, and they, along with a few other parents at the company, managed to balance work and parenting when the children were young by bringing them into the office. "Our children started in the box method," explains Malinda Chouinard. "We all kept our babies under our desks—in cardboard boxes with blankets in them—or on our backs. There weren't very many of us, but we all did it that way and we had no trouble at all. Sometimes we had to overcome resistance from fellow employees, but that was the only real difficulty. And then we got an employee who had a screaming baby."

Jennifer Ridgeway, the photograph editor for the catalog, was the employee, and Carissa, her daughter, the screaming baby. "I took her in to see everybody one day," remembers Ridgeway. "The typical proud mother. And she just screamed. I had her upstairs in the old building and the receptionist downstairs couldn't answer the phone she was so loud."

"We all felt so bad about it," says Chouinard. "We tried to move a trailer into the front yard so she could work out there and the rest of us could talk on the phone. But it was a logistical nightmare. Her mother ended up sitting in a car in front of the building for a few days so she could work. And that was just totally untenable. But none of us knew what to do about it because the rest of us had our babies in the building. But Carissa was simply too loud."

Pam Murphy, then a newly hired assistant in data processing who had two young children of her own, was given the task of resolving the complicated situation. "Malinda handed me a little manila envelope," Murphy remembers, "and said 'Just figure it out.'" The company was breaking ground for the new headquarters building, and Murphy spent the next year working with the architects, with state regulators, and with a child-care consultant to set up a small day-care center in a corner room on the first floor. "The best advice I can give to anyone looking into building a child-care center is to hire a consultant," she says. "Otherwise you'll fumble around and make mistakes that can be costly and that can set you back a long way. Even doing that we certainly had a rough start, determining our corporate philosophy toward the center, our age groups, and our rates. We decided very early to subsidize the operational expense of the center, so that we could have a high-quality program, but we also decided to make our rates comparable to those at centers in the area. We discussed the idea of giving this away as a free service, but Yvon came down very strongly against that. He felt that it would be more valuable to people if they had to commit to it financially in some way." Over the years, that policy has been modified in one small way with the addition of income-based subsidies—based on a formula that balances family income against the number of children—to help out parents with particular financial needs.

"We got a lot of resistance at first from employees who didn't have any children and who thought they never were going to have kids," says Yvon Chouinard. "They didn't want to see the profits of the company going out supporting a special-interest group." "There was nothing but resistance," echoes his wife. "There was no one who was for this idea. There was no group decision. Everyone was against it. But there was nobody who could stand to hear Carissa scream."

> *It's fantastic having the day care this close. It makes it much easier in the morning. All we do is drop her off and we're both in our respective offices or desks in two or three minutes. And should there be any urgent call we can be down here in a couple of minutes.*
>
> *I come down during the day, maybe too often. But it's our first child and we're really proud of her. Here they promote that. They want parents to go down as often as they can. They're not trying to scoot you out of there.*
>
> *I have a drawer full of toys in my desk for my son to play with, and for any other kids that come up. Crayons and books and puppets. And other kids do come up. We don't make a habit of it every day. But I think it's great that he does come up here, that he realizes what I do. He knows where I am during those hours when he doesn't see me.*

The center finally opened in January 1984 with an enrollment of six children. Though it was planned to meet the needs of nursing mothers, and in particular the needs of Jennifer and Carissa Ridgeway, the center was licensed and furnished to accommodate children of all ages—no restrictions were set at either end of the age range. The expanded scope came largely through Pam Murphy's direction. "I set the program up to suit my needs as a single parent," she admits. "And one of my needs was to have my daughter picked up at school. She was in kindergarten at the time, and for me to leave my job, go to school, and take her somewhere was very cumbersome. The company allowed me to do it, but that still didn't make it easy. So we created a driving service and an after-school program as part of the center."

Even with such a broad program, not all of Patagonia's parents enrolled their children in the program. The Chouinards' children turned out to be too set in their ways to adapt. "Neither of them would ever go to the day care," says Malinda. "They refused. They were used to running around the building and have continued to do that. They take advantage of the bus for the after-school program to come here. But they hang out in the cafeteria or run around outside rather than stay in the center."

The company also found that its policy of allowing children of any age into the center had one negative side effect. "We've had enormous problems getting people to take their maternity leaves," explains Malinda. "When we started the center it was open to children from birth to whatever age they wanted to stay, but we couldn't get mothers to take maternity leave. They came back to work with their stitches still in. We were preventing bonding. So we moved it up to eight weeks to force them to take their leaves." "It's a problem in family-run companies," says Yvon. "Some people have no life outside of work. You have to kind of force them to go home."

Gradually, as other parents saw the center in operation and saw what a high-quality program it was—with low teacher-child ratios and an individualized nurturing philosophy—more and more children began to come aboard from outside child-care arrangements. And with the company's growth, from 150 employees in 1984 to 520 in 1990, the center has expanded to house the new population of employees' children.

> *The whole evolution of the day-care program has been fascinating to watch. Initially it was just a very small group of kids. And I knew all their parents well and there was a real comradery between us. You could trace all their children's development. And now there are eighty-two kids. It's really grown and it's wonderful. You get so close to the parents whose children are with yours.*
>
> *My second daughter started at four months and has been here her whole life. The kids that she's in the pre-K program with now, they've all been together since they were two to four months old. And they're so close. They're like siblings. And they have probably spent more time together than with their actual siblings. They're really a tight little group of kids.*

By the time of our visit in 1990, Patagonia had filled its main office building and had established two satellite employment centers: a warehouse and fulfillment facility a couple of miles away, and a mail-order department in Bozeman, Montana. The child-care center had long outgrown the space originally allotted for it and had taken over one of the outbuildings in the compound. An additional infant-care center had been built at the warehouse, so that mothers there could continue to nurse their babies, and plans were in the works for satellite family day-care networks in both Ventura and Bozeman.

At no other company we visited did child care seem so intertwined with business. Children were the first people we saw when we walked up to the main entrance; the playground is adjacent to the front walk, and the infant room holds a prominent spot just inside the building. Throughout the day, parents drifted in and out of the center, and during breaks children played at desks in the office. Telephones in the older children's rooms allow them to call their parents whenever they feel the need. Even the decor of the center echoes that of the office. Patagonia's own woodshop created furnishings for both. Low cherry tables and solid cherry climbing structures add an elegant counterpoint to environments filled with some of the messier pleasures of childhood—dismantled radios and turntables in the after-school room, an assortment of pets, and displays of multicolor art projects.

Perhaps because both the center and the business take their direction from the same source—the Chouinards—they seem here like parts of a single entity, rather than distinct operations. And because the Chouinards have always encouraged parents both to bring their children into the office and to spend time with them in the center, the walls between child care and business are thin.

Just as Yvon Chouinard encourages people to take time off to be outdoors, Anita Garaway, the center's director, encourages parents to take the time to do what's best for their children. "I encourage mothers when they're coming back from maternity leave to start at thirty hours a week and gradually build up to forty when they feel comfortable and when their babies feel comfortable with it. It's human resources' job to do what human resources needs to do. It's my job to look out for the child's best interest and to make sure the parents have all the information they need to make educated, informed choices about how to fit their work schedules to their babies' needs. And some infants are just not suited to group child care at a young age. They don't have the sensory screening mechanisms to be able to thrive in an environment like our infant program. I have talked a few parents into staying out longer when their babies weren't doing well here. They just needed somebody they trusted to say that it was okay for them to stay home with their babies. And they ended up staying out a little longer. One came back when the child was eighteen months old, and the child did fine. The other one has been out for over a year. It's important that all the parents trust me to protect their children."

The center's teachers do home visits before a child is accepted into the program. "Part of the reason for that is that we need to gather information about people's parenting styles," Garaway explains. "But more important, we need to establish a trusting relationship. The home visit tells the parent right up front that we are willing to go out of our way to make contact with them."

That focus on both parent and child makes the center stand out from others we have seen, and the caring atmosphere is not lost on Patagonia parents. The calls from teachers to parents about the small problems of childhood may take a few minutes here and there from the workday, but the payoff comes in the confidence employees have in the center. All of the parents we spoke with talked about the peace of mind they have when their children are downstairs.

> *I have a four-year-old in the center. He started when he was a year old. That's when I started at Patagonia. He took his first steps here. All those things that you don't want to miss. And I was able to share all that with him. When he took his first steps I had just been down playing with him, I'd been back at my desk for five minutes and they called me and said, "Come back down." I just came back and spent a half an hour with him. And having them with me to share it made it that much better. Being a single parent I don't have that.*

> *The difference between the center here and others that we looked at is more in feeling than anything else. There's a feeling when you put her somewhere else that it's fifty-fifty whether it's going to be good or bad, and at Patagonia it's 100 percent. At Patagonia they really work with the kids from the minute they get into the child care. And I don't see that other places. They're worked with as a dollar, and not as an individual. Here there's a little bit more concern that the children develop properly and that they're cared for, and that every concern of the parents and the children is taken into consideration. Not just the parent and not just the child. There's a nice mutual agreement. Any development that she's made or that she needs work on they communicate to you here. And I don't really see that in other places, unless it's a disciplinary problem like a child that bites or something. You're not informed outside.*

That caring atmosphere and the quality of the program come at a price. The center's teacher-child ratios are among the lowest in the country. ("Now that we've outgrown our space we face the problem of putting children on a waiting list," explains Malinda Chouinard. "But we refuse to just pile kids in with too high a ratio. It might be a legal ratio, but it's not our ratio.") And in order to attract and keep top-notch teachers, Patagonia pays about a third more than the going rate for child-care workers in the area, offers shorter shifts and more time off, and gives teachers the company's full benefit package.

Since labor is the largest single item in any center's budget, and since this center charges fees comparable to centers with higher ratios and lower salaries, it comes as no surprise that Patagonia supports it with a healthy subsidy—close to $200,000 a year.

"We have to subsidize it quite a bit," admits Yvon Chouinard. "But I don't look at that as a real cost. I look at the child care more as a profit center, really, in what it saves us. It costs thousands of dollars to replace an employee—I've heard fifty thousand dollars—in headhunter fees, in training, in lost efficiency and productivity. So if we can save just a few of those over the year, we're making money. And that doesn't even factor in lost time due to distractions from child-care problems, improved morale, and lots of other things. We get suppliers who come into the cafeteria and see mothers eating lunch with their kids. And it has a great effect on them. They trust a company that does that. In fact most of them want to come work here. It's good advertising, that's for sure. And it's just plain good business."

*I started here two months ago. I apparently was one of the first people to be put on a waiting list—always the trendsetter—but my daughter is finally going into the child-care center next week. She's fourteen months old and we're on her seventh provider. We've had a lot of very, very bad experiences. In the first home we found that the lady was propping the bottle in her mouth with towels or pillows so she didn't have to be there when she was eating, which is quite dangerous. A baby can choke on the milk. So we put her into the house of a neighbor we knew really well. We thought it would be perfect, because our daughter had known the woman for her entire life and really liked her. But in the second week she got a case of bronchitis, and we asked that she be watched extra carefully, that she be kept out of smoking environments. Well, we came home to find her sitting between two smokers on the couch. She was choking and couldn't breathe. And yesterday she went to the beach. She has a cold, and I asked the baby-sitter to be really careful about her outdoor activities until she's feeling a little better. They took her to the beach for six hours and she came home not only sick, but with a tomato-red face.*

*Experiences like that have a direct effect on your work, I can tell you. From noon until four-fifteen yesterday I probably accomplished ten minutes' worth of work. I paced a* lot. *I tried to call about every fifteen minutes. It's a really panicky situation, not to know where your child is.*

*She's been here to Patagonia a couple of times, on days when I just didn't have a baby-sitter. And each of those times she's just walked in there like she's been there all her life, with a great attitude. She takes me and shows me all the kids and all the things. And she doesn't want to go home. So now I feel really good that she's starting in next week. When she's here I don't have any stress during the day. I don't feel the need to go over there three or four times a day to check on her and find out how she's doing. I know she's okay and that if there was a problem they would call me.*

Larger companies, such as IBM and NCNB, have accompanied new family-care policies with extensive management training to ensure that the companies' intentions are understood and implemented by managers. While Patagonia's family policies are not new—there have been babies in the office here for fifteen years—the Chouinards also find themselves fighting pockets of management resistance. The company has deliberately decided not to open a child-care center for its Bozeman, Montana, employees. Instead it has chosen to help create a support system that will train and work with family day-care providers in the area. "They still have a community there," explains Yvon Chouinard. "They still have neighborhoods. They still have people living next door to their grandparents. They have a tightly knit, supportive society. Whereas in California, that's gone."

"We don't want to take California to Bozeman," adds Malinda. "We don't want to take the kids away from the lady next door, or take the grandkids away from the grandparents." But local family day care does not answer the need of nursing mothers to be near their babies, so the Chouinards also encourage employees there—as in Ventura— to bring their babies into the office. And they have found that some managers are not as open to babies at work as they would like. "I continually, throughout the company, have trouble with my management," says Malinda Chouinard. "Yvon can't get managers to let people go out and surf and I can't get them to let mothers bring their babies in. We fight it. Every time we see it we stomp it out. But it's like wildfires. The problem keeps cropping up again."

Some readers will undoubtedly look at Patagonia's experiences and say that the company has been able to be so generous with child care and so flexible with its employees because it has been so successful. And that may be true. But it is also true that the company has become so successful while allowing employees the flexibility to take time away from work, and while it built and subsidized an on-site child-care center. Yvon Chouinard has always spent at least six months away from the business each year, and every year the company has grown. In 1984, when the company started its child-care center, it had sales of $20 million. Six years later that figure had more than quadrupled, while the company continued to support a high-quality child-care program.

"I've given talks at Yale, Harvard, UCLA, Wharton, a bunch of different business schools," says Yvon Chouinard. "And I talk to them about creativity in business, about breaking the rules. I've read a lot of business books, but it's like reading a recipe book. I like to read recipe books and then close them and do my own thing. I can't stand to follow a recipe line by line. It drives me crazy. And I approach business books the same way. They should give you the seeds of ideas, but then you need to be creative. You need to break the rules. We've broken all sorts of rules. That's what we like to do. When this day-care center opened in 1984 it was one of just one hundred and fifty corporate day-care centers in the country, and most of the others were at hospitals. So we were breaking the rules. And there are certain advantages to that."

The Chouinards can measure those advantages in their profits, in the support they've been able to give to environmental causes (10 percent of the business's pretax profits are donated to environmental organizations), and in the satisfaction that comes from nurturing a successful business—one in which employees are generally happy with and devoted to their jobs. For employees the advantages are just as real: access to one of the best child-care centers in the country, the flexibility to focus on both careers and outside interests such as families and mountaineering, and the feeling of participation in a renegade enterprise that has carved its own niche in the world of American business.

# NCNB Corporation

NCNB Plaza
Charlotte, NC 28255                    704-374-5000

**Nature of business:** One of the ten largest banking institutions in the United States, with branches in seven Southern states.

**Number of employees:** 25,000.

**Female employees:** 75 percent (48 percent of managers, 11 percent of senior vice presidents).

**Child care:** Region-wide resource-and-referral service; income-based subsidy program; pretax salary set-aside (DCAP); plans for near-site center at headquarters; low-interest loans to help start community-based centers in South Carolina.

**Elder care:** Pretax salary set-aside (DCAP).

**Family leave:** Paid disability leave for childbirth and paid parental leave for fathers and adoptive parents (pay related to years of service), plus job-protected unpaid leave to a total of six months; phase-in option allows part-time return with full benefits during the six-month leave period; paid time off for school involvement.

**Flexible work options:** Flextime in many departments; part-time and alternative work schedules for people with dependent-care responsibilities (the Select Time program); some job sharing.

**Other benefits:** Employee-assistance program; wellness program; tuition reimbursement; matching gifts to school systems.

Keeping part-time workers on track.

*"Each of us needs to focus our vision on an environment where both work and family responsibilities are assigned sincere value, where these dual responsibilities enhance each other, and where each individual solution designed to meet these responsibilities is respected. Then we need to focus our energies on making that vision a reality."*

HUGH L. MCCOLL, JR.
Chairman and Chief Executive Officer

From its glass-and-steel skyscrapers in Charlotte, Dallas, and Tampa, to its 850 branch offices with the distinctive red logo out front, NCNB maintains a high profile in the Southern banking world. The company operates full-service banks in seven Southern states. It is the largest banking company in the South, and the seventh largest in the country.

The business traces its roots to a small retail bank formed in Charlotte, North Carolina, in 1874. The modern corporation, however, started in 1960, when the descendant of that bank merged with an important competitor to form the North Carolina National Bank. NCNB Corporation was formed in 1968 as a holding company to link the business's growing network of branches throughout the state.

By its actions, NCNB has shown itself to be an aggressive and innovative institution. In 1982 it became one of the nation's first multistate banks when it expanded operations into Florida, taking advantage of a grandfather clause in the state's banking regulations and the fact that it owned a small trust company in Orlando. Five years later NCNB National Bank of Florida was the fourth-largest bank in the state, with $9.9 billion in assets. The start of reciprocal interstate banking in 1986 opened the door for expansion into South Carolina, Virginia, Georgia, and Maryland. In 1988, NCNB reached beyond its southeastern boundaries when the FDIC chose it to manage the restructured subsidiary banks of First RepublicBank Corp. NCNB exercised an option to purchase the Texas bank a year later, a move that prompted Salomon Brothers to dub the company "the first of the super regionals."

NCNB has clearly shown itself to be a pioneer in interstate banking. It was also the first U.S. bank to open a branch in London, the first to list its stock on the Tokyo Exchange, the first to operate a full-service securities business, and the first in North Carolina to install automated teller machines.

In the past few years, NCNB has also set out to establish itself as a leader in the corporate response to the family concerns of employees.

> *Our chairman, Hugh McColl, practices something we call management by walking around. If he sees two managers in an office he might just wander in and ask what they're talking about. He did that when another manager and I were sitting in a conference room, and we were actually talking about our children. So we told him that. And I think that says something about him and about NCNB, that it was okay to say that. And he turned to me and said, "How old is your little boy now, about a year?" And he was one week off. Then he stood there and talked about his children. And one of his comments was, "You never stop worrying about them." His kids are twenty-five, twenty-three, and twenty-one.*

Hugh McColl, chairman and chief executive officer at NCNB, likes to say that he values the opinion he hears, not the platform it comes from—he tries to recognize a good idea whether it comes from a part-time teller or a senior vice president. That attitude, and McColl's wandering, listening style of management seems to have spread through the top ranks of the company to make this an unusually responsive, people-oriented company. So when McColl and then-president Buddy Kemp began, around 1985, to hear senior women talk about the strain of balancing jobs with young children, or about their fear that having children might mean the end of their careers at the bank, the two officers decided to explore the matter and see if the bank should respond in any way.

Kemp set up a task force to look into work-and-family issues—to find out if this really was a problem for the company or just an isolated worry of the few people they were hearing, and to examine what the bank could do to keep these people from leaving and taking with them their years of professional expertise. "We want the very best and brightest people in our organization," said McColl, in an address to a conference of work-and-family matters. "We spend huge amounts of time and money in recruiting them, hiring them, and training them. Good business principles dictate that such investments should be for the long haul. Simply stated, we want and *need* the people we hire to stay with NCNB to build careers with the company."

The task force, made up of a broad mix of employees—men and women, junior and senior, childless and with children, from headquarters and from outside offices—met for several months without much measurable progress. Karen Geiger, director of management training at the time and a member of the task force, recalls those meetings with a little frustration. "We talked out of our heads, without really studying the needs of the employee population, and we just got nowhere." The logjam broke when several members of the group attended a Conference Board conference in New York and met Fran Rodgers, a consultant to business on work-and-family issues. "They came back saying she really knew what she was doing," says Geiger, "that Rodgers and Associates, her company, could help us survey our needs, which seemed to make more sense than what we had been doing, just sitting around guessing. So we asked her to come in and help."

Rodgers and Associates settled on a two-pronged approach. They would find out what the needs and concerns were among employees, and what the attitudes toward these issues were among the top managers at the company. The consulting firm helped NCNB prepare an employee survey that went out to a random sample of the entire corporate population, and it conducted employee focus groups to bring out some of the concerns in more detail. At the same time, Rodgers interviewed the top twenty-five executives at the company, from McColl on down, asking such questions as, "What if NCNB were to allow part-time work for professionals and managers, as part of an effort to keep women with children on the payroll? What would you think of people who signed on as part-timers? Would it stop their careers?"

"We got a 72 percent response rate to the survey," remembers Geiger, "which is incredibly high. I think part of the reason is that it was a hot issue. Also, we don't generally survey our people. This was something unusual. And it came with a cover letter from Buddy Kemp urging people to do it at work. So it got a lot of attention."

Not only did the survey generate a surprisingly big response, it also revealed that family issues were important to large numbers of workers. It showed that 50 percent of NCNB's employees either had children or were planning to start a family, that 90 percent of those with children had them in nonspouse care while they worked, and that many felt anxious about the quality of that care. "They were saying that they didn't know what questions to ask about child care," says Geiger, "that they didn't know how to find it, and that they just felt lost about it. And there was an affordability issue. People in the bigger cities had a much worse time finding child care than people in the smaller cities." The response also showed that the company's four-month maternity leave, while appreciated, could be lengthened and made a little more flexible.

"The survey results showed that our culture was generally flexible," says Geiger, "but that this was the result of individual supervisors rather than an overall policy. And it depended on whom they worked for. If the manager was flexible they were happy, and if the manager wasn't they weren't. The numbers showed that about 70 percent of our managers were flexible, but that the good managers felt that they had to keep quiet about it, because they weren't sure that flexibility was really valued."

The executive interviews came back with mixed results as well. Some worried that if the company tried to be more flexible—if, for example, it loosened its control on hours—then staff might not be there when customers called. Others thought that the company should bend a little more, pointing out that even regular full-time employees are often unavailable while out of the office making sales calls. "We had a lot of good debate," says Geiger, "and that was one of the purposes of those interviews."

*When my oldest child was born, a nurse practitioner told me that when they're smaller they don't have personal demands, their physical needs are the primary thing. But when they get to be in, say, the third grade, they start having activities outside and then they are aware that you're not there. They're not able to do things because you're not available. And they resent your working. At that time I had a baby and knew that she needed me, and I didn't understand what the woman was saying. But as my children have gotten older, I've come to see what she was warning me about. With my schedule here, I'm able to be there for them in the afternoons. For instance, they take piano, and most piano teachers like to hold their lessons between three o'clock and six o'clock. My children are able to do that. They're on a swim team, and that's a three-to-six activity. So it really doesn't bother them that I work. They don't resent it. And it's comforting to me that I'm not hurting them.*

In June 1986, the results were presented to executive management, which decided that some response was warranted. McColl voiced the opinion of the company's leaders in a 1988 speech. "If rigid policies and inflexible procedures force these people to make an either/or choice between family and career, a lot of them will—at some point and to some degree—opt for family. My concern on this issue is not purely altruistic. Our resources are finite. If my associates are forced to choose between work and family, and family wins out, NCNB is robbed of one of its most vital resources: experienced people. So, as chief executive, one of my responsibilities to my company is to develop and encourage policies that protect the company from wasting its greatest resource." The committee allocated money for and agreed to support a work-family coordinator who would recommend and oversee changes to make the company more responsive to family needs.

Karen Geiger was snared for the job as she was waiting for an elevator one day. Pregnant with her second child, she had just proposed a shift in her job from management training to career development, which she planned to take on as a part-time task after coming back from maternity leave. "We'd grown from a small state bank to a huge regional corporation," she says, "and we could see we didn't have a way to move people around. As I thought about it, this new family response seemed like a natural addition to career development. If someone is going to be here for a long time and build a career at NCNB, the opportunities for part-time work, the policies and attitudes regarding leaves, and the company's response to child care might be a part of their career planning." That linkage of family issues to career planning has remained an important part of NCNB's response and has guided the policies and benefits that have emerged.

> When our son was born I took a paternity leave. We had planned it out quite early—I think from when my wife was two months pregnant. Because of the demands of both of our jobs—I'm a manager on the bond-trading floor here, and she's an associate at a big accounting firm—we needed full-time day care. We chose to get a nanny, and that created a timing problem, because the nannies didn't start until June and the baby was due in February. So my wife arranged to stay out on leave until the end of April, and we had to figure out how to care for the baby until the nanny arrived. We put together a kind of patchwork. My parents came up for a couple of weeks, her mother did a couple of weeks, her sister-in-law did a week, and one of my nieces did a couple of weeks.
>
> But I took the first shift, the first two weeks after she was back. And the reason I did that was because she knew, even from the time she was three and four months pregnant, that she was not going to want to leave that baby at the end of her leave, that it was going to be a very difficult thing to go back. I think the only way she could go back, psychologically, was to know that I was there taking care of things. I was fairly sure that once she was there and working and a little time had gone by that everything would be all right. But that first week or two was going to be really tough for her. And it turned out to be that way. The first couple of days were very hard. But she felt comfortable calling me. She could be silly about it in a way you couldn't be with a day-care person. And she could come home at night and I would tell her everything he did that day. So she didn't feel she missed anything.
>
> I was only there for two weeks. I would have loved to take longer. And I think on the next one I might. I might take a good deal longer. My problem right now is that my job is so demanding. In ten years I had never taken two weeks at once away from the job. After one week I come back and am completely lost. So two weeks away for me was a big deal. But I enjoyed it immensely. It was a terribly rewarding experience.

Geiger acted quickly in her new role, immediately extending the maternity leave to six months and adding a phase-in option which allowed those on leave to come back part-time at any point during the six months. Those on leave, whether working part-time or not, received full benefits for the entire six months. "There was some resistance from managers," says Geiger, "but nothing like I had expected. And that was partly because people came back to work earlier with the phase-in option. When a full-time return had been the only choice, they waited as long as they could. But when they could come back three days a week or half days, most were happy to get back to work sooner."

The company then tested a child-care referral service in three cities—Charlotte, North Carolina; Tampa, Florida; and Columbia, South Carolina. These were all major employment centers, and areas where, according to the survey results, workers were having the most trouble finding care. The pilot lasted a year, worked out to everyone's satisfaction, and was expanded to the entire corporate population in 1988.

Geiger also set up a pilot program for professionals who wanted to work part-time, and here she ran into more snags. Compensation was the first twist that needed straightening. The payroll department insisted on time cards for these formerly salaried employees, and the system just didn't work well. "I was one of the people who got a time card," says Geiger. "And we all got really mad right away. I traveled quite a bit in my job, and I couldn't figure out how to deal with the time card. Should I clock in before I got on the plane, or when I got to Denver? It was ridiculous. I was working more than forty hours a week on my part-time schedule because of travel." It took a few months, but Geiger was finally able to clear up the major problems with the part-time program.

> *I've been at NCNB for thirty years—I work as a liaison between the programmers and the users of our computer systems—and I cut back to a four-day week to help my mother, who lives by herself. She's anemic and has to go for blood tests every three weeks. And then once a month she has to go to Chapel Hill for observation. When these medical trips started I realized that I was going to run out of vacation days just taking her to Chapel Hill. And then on the days she gives blood I'd miss part of another day. So I just went to my management and asked if I could take one day a week to look after her. As far as the job and the job title, all that has remained the same. And I really feel that I do my job just as well in four days as I used to in five. I'm more efficient now, because I know my work schedule is limited, and I have to look at how I manage my time.*
>
> *It's nice to be able to do what I'm doing without having*

> *to worry about how I'm going to work it into my schedule.
> And my time with her has made a big difference for my
> mother. I feel as long as we can keep her at her own home,
> and she feels good about being there, that's good. I think
> once they lose that independence and control they go
> downhill. It's like the beginning of the end.*

In 1988, after those first family programs had been in place
for about a year, the company took a hard look at the results
and did some fine-tuning. The maternity leave was renamed
parental leave, and was extended in the same form to fathers
and adoptive parents. All could take six months off with the
opportunity to phase in part-time. "That was a little controver-
sial," remembers Geiger, "and it was a fun debate. Someone
would say, 'Let's give the fathers two weeks.' And I'd say, 'Wait
a minute. Let's look at what that's saying. You're saying we
can't spare a man for two weeks but we can let a woman go for
half a year.' So we ended up treating everybody just the same
way. And now we're putting in paternity pay—one week of pay
for every year of service, up to six weeks. Just like a woman gets
for medical disability. And adoptive parents get the same thing."

The part-time program needed even more adjustment, starting with its name, which had turned out to be a problem. "Some
people felt that if you were part-time you were just not there.
Now I'm one of those people that no matter how many days I
work I'm very dedicated. I'm thinking about my job at night. I
work on weekends. I'm still NCNB's person, but I'm taking more
time to be with my kids. So we changed the name to Select
Time." Although it was an apparently cosmetic change, the effects seem to be positive and real. Partly because of the name,
and partly because the program has been launched with such
care and attention, the Select Time participants seem to be
viewed as an elite group. Geiger watches them closely to see
that they are living up to the program's goals, and to see that
they are not unfairly held back in their career progression.

The company also expanded the parameters of the Select
Time program to take in people who wanted to spend time with
older children, or who needed extra time to care for elderly dependents. The pilot participants had primarily been mothers of
infants and young children, and Geiger wanted to be sure the
program was not stuck with that image. To ensure its success,
the company also added some restrictions to the program, lim-
iting it to employees who have been at the bank for a year and
who are at an expected level of performance. "That's a contro-
versial rule," explains Geiger, "and we added it to protect managers who were getting frightened of the program as it expanded.

I understand that fear, because this is an inconvenience. But it's a rule meant to be broken. Any time a manager wants to make an exception, we think it's wonderful. The rule is there for those who are worried and are just not sure. We're oriented toward making it work. We won't say no unless I think no, the manager thinks no, and the employee thinks no. We'll do anything we can to try to think of a plan. I think we've only turned one person down—a woman who wanted to transfer to another city and her job just wasn't there."

> *I think that because this Select Time option is available to me I'm happier. My husband has said that even if I didn't make any money, it's been worth my coming back just for my outlook. I just have an awful lot of education not to be using it. And it's not just my outlook, it's that I'm happier, and because I'm happier my children are happier—how Mommy goes, so goes the family. At the same time I feel a commitment to NCNB. Because they offer this to me. So they have a more dedicated employee.*

To deal with managers who resisted these moves toward flexibility and responsiveness to employees' family needs—the 30 percent uncovered by the survey—Geiger held management-training sessions in which she presented the programs as a business issue. She talked about the changing demographics of the work force, and about NCNB's bid to get and keep the best workers with its awareness of family needs. To make sure people listened, Hugh McColl would make it known that this was an issue he cared about, either on a visit to the site in the days or weeks before Geiger arrived or in some other way.

In his 1988 speech, McColl stated his commitment in no uncertain terms. "Certainly, NCNB's liberalized programs are a challenge to our managers. But challenge is nothing new to them. What is important is that, rather than focusing on the near-term uncertainties or short-term disruptions, we take a longer view. As chief executive I must lead the way. If I do not firmly believe, actively support, and loudly endorse what is taking place, others will not accept or embrace these programs. Let me add this on a personal note: I *will not tolerate* anything short of *complete commitment* to this issue at the executive level. And I expect that total commitment to extend to each and every supervisor in the corporation."

"McColl's backing was critical," says Geiger, "at least for the most rigid managers. If he couldn't speak to them directly he'd find a way to let them know. He just walks around saying it, so before I'd arrive, people would know this was something he wanted."

The company is now in the process of expanding those training sessions with help from Work/Family Directions, of Boston—another Fran Rodgers enterprise. Geiger hopes to use a case-study and discussion format to reach all of the company's managers, from the top down, and get them to think through and understand the issues behind the company's family programs.

> *I went on the Select Time program to spend more time with my seven-year-old son. My wife and I moved from California to western North Carolina—to Asheville—a little more than five years ago to improve the quality of our family life. It's beautiful country around Asheville and the values of the community appealed to us. But I come from an information-systems background, and I simply couldn't find work in the area that paid what I should be earning with my background. After a year of looking I finally went searching beyond the immediate area, and ended up at NCNB in Charlotte. I was grateful for the opportunity to apply my energies and experience in information systems again, but I was working five days a week in Charlotte, and then driving home to be a weekend father. We'd moved to North Carolina for a better family life, and here I was barely a part of it. And my son suffered as a result of the loss of time with me during the week. He just went a little haywire. Now I have a grown daughter, and I lost another grown son, so it meant a lot to me to be a good father this time around.*
>
> *When Select Time first started up, one of the employees I managed went on it, so I was familiar with the program. When I found out it was going to become a regular benefit I did a lot of soul searching and had some long discussions with my wife, and finally signed myself on. I still work forty hours a week, but I do it in four days. I'm off on Mondays. Now I'm able to take my boy to school, pick him up after school, occasionally get involved in baseball or soccer practice, work with him on his homework, roughhouse with him in the evening, put him to bed, and then drive back down here to Charlotte on Monday evening. It cuts my time away down to three nights, and it's really worked very well for him. Looking back, I think that if this program hadn't come along, there's a good chance that I wouldn't be here at NCNB.*

Child-care subsidies are another key piece of NCNB's family benefit package. Geiger and others were concerned that the company was directing all of its efforts toward managers and professionals, without addressing the needs of the company's lower-paid workers. The Select Time program was simply not an option for those who couldn't afford to take a cut in pay. The referral service was not much help to employees who could not afford quality child care. And the six-month leave was really only available to people who could afford to take time without pay. "We have a lot of lower-paid people," explains Geiger, "and some of our programs just don't help them much. I proposed the subsidy program on that basis, saying that we were missing a certain part of our population. I felt we were creating a potential problem, especially with the media attention we were getting. If people read about how great NCNB is for working parents and they can't afford to take advantage of what we offer, then we're going to build a lot of resentment. And I don't want that to happen."

The company knew, from its 1986 survey, that the cost of child care was a major concern for many employees. The fact that it did not address the problem sooner was largely a function of cost. Geiger began pushing for a subsidy program in early 1988, but ran up against the argument of equity—of justifying the program to those who weren't eligible. There was no question that child-care subsidies would direct a large amount of money to a small pool of employees, and it was hard for some at the company to accept that apparent unfairness. Geiger was asked repeatedly to run numbers in different combinations and variations, and the results always came out much the same way. "We're not used to spending big money on small numbers of people," she says. "We're used to doing things for big numbers of people. I understood what their concerns were. But finally I said, 'I'm not going to run the numbers again. No matter how we cut it it's going to be a lot of money for a few people. But we've got to focus our dollars and our time on these needs.' "

The plan was approved in 1989 and went into effect in January 1990 with $1 million set aside for the first year's funding. In the final plan, which was worked out with help from and is administered by Work/Family Directions, NCNB pays half of an employee's child-care costs up to $35 a week per child. In order to target employees with the greatest need, the program is restricted to those with family incomes of less than $24,000. It also puts some restrictions on the care to be subsidized. The subsidy is only for the care of children aged six and under, and the full $35 a week is paid only if parents use licensed or registered providers. A lower rate of $15 a week is paid if parents use legally operating providers who are not subject to licensing requirements. Checks are mailed monthly, in advance, to employees' homes, payable to the child-care providers. Parents and providers must then fill out monthly statements verifying that the other half of the costs were paid by the parents.

NCNB added an additional piece to its family-care package in the summer of 1990, allowing employees two hours of paid time off each week for regular involvement in school activities. In doing this, the company is recognizing the many studies that have shown parent involvement to be a key determinant of school success, and is making an effort to help its workers play a larger role in their children's educations. To back up that effort, the company will match employees' gifts and contributions to their children's school systems.

> *I can't help but feel that I'm losing some ground by being on Select Time. There have been several times that my instinct has been to go for it, when I'm here. It's been really frustrating. Sometimes I want to stay here and work. And when I see other people take on big projects that I can't handle on my schedule, it's hard for me. I was a hard charger before, even with the two. That's one reason I quit after my second child was born. I knew what I would demand of myself here, and I knew what I would demand of myself at home, and I knew that I couldn't do both. So maybe there's some maturity in coming back in that I'm going to set these restraints on myself. But it's not easy.*
>
> *I think the hardest thing is that I could go flat out if I wanted to. That I set the restraints. The person who took my job when I left is now a senior vice president. But you make choices. And I think that's the thing you have to get comfortable with. Sometimes you have to sit back, just like two weeks ago when I was unsure about it and frustrated. And then I went home and felt, "This is exactly what I'm supposed to be doing."*

With its leave policy, the child-care referral service, the Select Time program, child-care subsidies, and management training, NCNB has taken some big strides over the past few years toward making the company a place where parents can continue in their careers while giving their families the attention they deserve. A child-care center, planned for construction near headquarters in Charlotte, will help many NCNB parents even more. And an independent initiative by NCNB South Carolina has made low-interest loan funds available to new child-care centers throughout that state, a community-based effort that should indirectly affect company employees there.

While NCNB's programs cover a great deal of ground, what stands out the most here is the company's recognition that career-oriented employees with family responsibilities don't want an all-or-nothing choice—that many would like to continue in their careers, but with the opportunity to step back for a while and devote more time to their families. In a company as dynamic as NCNB, that understanding has not come easily to every manager. McColl himself expressed the dilemma in his 1988 speech. "Our company is a meritocracy. People who accept responsibility, handle it, and ask for more are rewarded and promoted. The typical NCNB employee is high-energy, competitive, and self-motivated. Any corporate culture is the sum total of the people in the company. For us—a company made up of driven and dedicated people—it is difficult accepting a teammate who has cut back a work schedule—for any reason. I have wrestled with this conflict myself. I wholeheartedly believe in the importance and value of trying to solve this conflict. But when the heat is on, I want to know my good people are *there.* What I have come to realize is *there* doesn't have to mean the office next door. It may mean telephone conferencing or at-home computer tie-ins. We are, after all, in the twentieth century, and there is no reason technology can't help us cope with the logistics of innovative programs."

In our talks with the Select Time employees, we were impressed not only with their self-confidence in embarking on a program that might, realistically, delay their career progression, but also with what seemed to be their barely restrained ambitions. Many of these people, without families, would be charging their way to the top of the company. But because of family responsibility—and largely by choice rather than necessity— they had decided to slow down a little and shift the priorities in their lives a bit more toward their children, their elderly parents, or other family members who needed their attention. If those we spoke with are representative of the group, then NCNB is serving itself well in keeping these people on board. When this stage of their lives is past, most assume, as does the company, that they will be back on the fast track again. The company conducted a study of ambition and family responsibility, which showed no long-term difference in ambition between people with and people without child-care responsibilities. The company has consciously chosen not to relegate part-time workers— men and women—to the so-called "mommy track," where parents who choose to cut back work hours while they are raising children are required to sacrifice their aspirations for advancement. Instead, it provides the opportunity for Select Timers to continue to advance within the company at a different pace if that is what they want to do.

Whether the Select Time participants move up in the company, and whether employees can easily move into Select Time and back to full-time, will depend on the attitudes of peers and managers, and the company seems to be working hard on re-forming those attitudes to be in keeping with the realities of a working world where dual-career couples are the norm. "I watch the Select Timers," says Geiger, "and the fact is their careers are not stopped, if that means that they have many opportunities open to them. People on Select Time can either say, 'I'm comfortable here. Leave me alone,' or they can say, 'This shouldn't stop me at all.' If someone wants to take a senior job with a great deal of management responsibility there will be a lot of talk about whether they can do it. But the door will not be closed. We had a Select Timer take a major management job last year. We had a lot of discussion about it, but she's so good, and she has such leadership ability that it just seemed like a natural step. And we can call her at home if we need to. Those things just have to be worked out individually."

The attention that NCNB gives to the Select Time program and Geiger's vigilant monitoring offer a powerful refutation to the "mommy track" concept. Where many companies offer workers a hard choice—career or family—NCNB recognizes such rigidity as a harmful carryover from another era, and understands that time for family may be important at certain points in the careers of even the most ambitious fast-trackers. If the Select Time program continues to thrive, if workers can advance in their careers while in the program and can move back to full-time positions as their personal needs change, NCNB's innovations will offer a model for companies everywhere.

"I think the best thing about NCNB's response is that we offer so many choices," says Geiger. "We have some senior women with children who aren't on Select Time but they're working from eight-thirty to five and being very rigid about their schedules. They don't want to cut back from that because they're hard-driving people and they just enjoy the work. But they also want to be home by five-thirty to pick up their kids. Other people have decided they want to work less. And others have decided to keep working extra hours and get a nanny. That's what we wanted. We wanted to have all kinds of options. But we all have to be careful not to judge people by the options they've chosen."

# SAS Institute Inc.

SAS Campus Drive
Cary, NC 27513                                            919-677-8000

**Nature of business:** Software developer.
**Number of employees:** 1,400.
**Female employees:** 56 percent (49 percent of managers).
**Child care:** On-site centers for up to 328 children, aged six weeks to five years; subsidy program pays most child-care costs.
**Elder care:** No formal program.
**Family leave:** Paid disability leave for childbirth, plus up to one year unpaid parental leave; paid sick time may be used for care of ill dependents.
**Flexible work options:** Alternative working hours arranged individually.
**Other benefits:** On-site health-care center; recreation and fitness center; subsidized cafeteria with low-cost take-home meals; 100-acre campus with 6-acre lake for fishing, swimming, and boating.

Subsidized child care as part of an employer's support system.

*"We learned over the years, paying close attention to reports in the trade press, that turnover is very expensive for companies. And for a company of our size in 1981, major blocks of turnover among our young female workers would have been devastating. The company had a major investment in these women. So child care seemed like a sensible option."*

DAVID RUSSO
Director of Human Resources

SAS Institute Inc., developers of the SAS System, one of the world's most popular data-processing software systems, lies hidden from the busy highways that border its headquarters on two sides. Its entrance is marked only by a low, inconspicuous sign. Beyond the guardhouse, which is located so as to be invisible from the road, a dense forest screen opens up to reveal a collection of inviting-looking cream-colored buildings surrounded by several acres of carefully maintained parkland—

a landscape that could easily be taken for the campus of a well-endowed small college. The smallest buildings—the first SAS Institute built here—stand beside a six-acre lake, complete with dock and rowboats. Shady paths lead from the lake to a pair of larger, newer office buildings, and to the company's health-care center, its recreation and fitness center, and its two child-care centers.

The academic look here is no accident. The company began near North Carolina State University, where Jim Goodnight and three colleagues created a statistical analysis program, which they named the SAS System, to help graduate students track agricultural data. In the early 1970s, the group refined the program and occasionally sold copies to others who found it helpful in analyzing a wide variety of research data. In 1976, when government funding for their agricultural research ran out, the group decided to incorporate and give the software a bigger marketing push. Four years later the firm outgrew its first office in Raleigh and broke ground for a new facility on a wooded 100-acre tract in Cary, designing the grounds and building as an attraction for promising young engineers from graduate schools all over the country. The software industry in the 1970s was booming; the owners knew that if the business were to continue to thrive it would have to compete creatively for fresh talent.

In addition to planning an appealing physical environment, the company designed innovative policies intended to attract new workers and to keep and motivate those already aboard. Dr. Goodnight had worked for General Electric; all of the founders had worked in a university setting. At the Institute, they deliberately chose to create a less bureaucratic environment, where people could act on their own ideas with flexibility, and where individuals could feel assured of their importance to the organization. Jane Helwig, one of the founders, explains: "At SAS the feeling has always been that if you treat employees as though they make a difference to the company, they *will* make a difference to the company. An appreciation for the individual has always been a very strong part of SAS's philosophy."

> *This is the first company I've worked for that I really care about. I've cared about jobs that I've worked on before, and I've felt a loyalty to my immediate department, but that never extended to the company until I came to SAS. I think that has to do both with the department I work in—this is an excellent group and a very professional division—and with the philosophy of the company. SAS really believes in treating its employees well. We also have a really good product, and an amazing collection of people*

> who really care a lot about what they do. This is the hard-
> est-working company I've ever worked for.

At the time the company moved to Cary, in 1980, SAS Institute began planning a particularly dramatic gesture of appreciation for its employees—subsidized on-site child care. Because
she was a vice president, Jane Helwig's efforts to balance moth-
erhood and career were especially visible to the other founders
during the company's early years. "I wanted to be a good mother
to my baby," she remembers, "but SAS presented me with an
exciting opportunity, which I didn't want to miss out on. I was
fortunate to be able to find a baby-sitter ten minutes from the
office, and I would go and visit my baby at lunchtime because
I was breast-feeding. Jim Goodnight noticed that I was having
to spend all this time driving back and forth to the baby-sitter.
When I became pregnant with my third child in 1980, he started
talking about the idea of a day-care center."

David Russo, the company's director of human resources,
explains how SAS Institute came to see child care as both a
personal need for people like Helwig, and a matter of concern
for the company. "We became aware that we had a lot of women
who were in a typical career-family bind. A common profile
would be a young woman, educated in computer science or applied mathematics, who was several years into a career at a time
when the business was expanding rapidly, even exploding. And
she would come to a point where she and her husband would
decide that they'd like to have a child. Well, these young women
faced a tremendous dilemma. They knew that if they had a child
and quit work and stayed out with that child for two or three
years, the technology would have left them behind by the time
they came back. It would be beyond them. They would have to
go back to school to get back up to speed. From the company's
perspective, that personal dilemma translated into a serious business issue. A large proportion of our technical workers are
women, and in this business it can take two or three years before
people become truly productive. So the company ran the risk of
losing people who had finally become important contributors.
We learned over the years, paying close attention to reports in
the trade press, that turnover is very expensive for companies.
And for a company of our size in 1981, major blocks of turnover
among our young female workers would have been devastating.
The company had a major investment in these women. So child
care seemed like a sensible option."

In an effort to reduce exposure to liability, many companies
try to distance themselves from the child-care operations by
contracting with outside vendors. Jim Goodnight decided instead

to involve the business with the center as much as possible in order to insure that it would meet the company's standards and be accountable to those it served—the parents, the children, and SAS Institute. He chose to establish the center as a department of the company, its staff hired by the Institute, in space on the first floor of the company's new office building then under construction in Cary. Russo explains the company's approach: "If you're providing quality child care, if you hire a quality staff, liability is not a major issue. We have an umbrella liability policy and the risks to the company from an accident at the child-care center are no greater than our risks from a visitor falling down the steps in an office building. A lot of businesses look for all the reasons not to get involved with child care. Jim Goodnight looked at why we *should* get involved."

Many companies planning on-site child care also try to minimize the cost to the corporation by creating a self-sufficient venture supported by parent fees. SAS Institute took another route, deciding from the start to offer child care as a fully paid benefit of employment. At the time the center started, this was a relatively small commitment—with fewer than one hundred employees, the company didn't expect more than a handful of children to enroll. But as the company has grown, that initiative to provide free child care has become a far more significant financial obligation.

> *I came back after eight weeks with this baby; he's my third. I didn't really feel the need to stay home longer than that because I get to see him here during the day. I can continue to nurse him. My second one I nursed until he was eleven months old. And he's very well taken care of.*

> *Just knowing that she's here, and not having to dash out the door at four-forty-five to get across town to pick her up, is a big thing. That's saved me time. I can stay here until five-fifteen. That's only another half hour, but sometimes in a crunch that can make a difference. You don't feel you have to have one eye on the clock the whole afternoon.*

Another early decision has also had a profound impact on the evolution of the center. The person assigned to work out the details of getting the center going, a technical writer in Helwig's department, had her child in a Montessori preschool. When it came time to hire the center's director, she felt that her child's teacher was the natural choice. And so Montessori came to SAS Institute.

The center opened in 1981 with an enrollment of 6 children. Nine years later, in 1990, SAS Institute had grown to over 1,400 employees, sales had shot up from $10 million to over $200 million, and a new building for infants and toddlers expanded the child-care center's capacity to 328 children. By many measures still a small company, SAS Institute has built one of the largest child-care operations in the country.

The infant and toddler center, which has the capacity to care for 176 children under the age of three, stretches out in the shape of a giant "L," with covered drop-off areas that match the scale of those at many urban airports. Ten infant rooms line the sides of one corridor, each with a low carpeted "staircase" for climbing that extends over almost a quarter of the room. Each room also opens onto a grassy area, with low windows that allow even a crawling infant to peer out. The other wing of the building houses thirteen toddler rooms for children up to the age of three.

In the building for older children the Montessori teaching method prevails. Here, in rooms full of three-, four-, and five-year-olds, we watched the orderly play characteristic of Montessori schools. No toys lay loose around the room. Everything was in its place. The only playthings or materials out on tables or on the floor were those that children were using, either in small groups or by themselves. When a child was finished with a project, she put it away on the open shelves, showed the teacher what she'd like to do next, and listened as the teacher explained how the material was to be used.

Here, as in most Montessori schools, the materials were beautiful—blocks of lacquered wood in geometric shapes, sand trays in which children traced numbers or letters, jars of colored water, laminated cards with reproductions of great paintings or illustrations of reptiles and amphibians, templates and punches for making maps, and an array of mathematical and alphabet toys. Circles of children here gathered not just for the usual stories and songs, but for French lessons, which are part of the curriculum for children as young as three.

"We try to instill a strong sense of order in the child," explains Susanne Yellig, the preschool administrator. "Things are set out for a reason. Without clutter, the child can see more clearly. The materials on the shelves are changed regularly, so the children are constantly discovering something new."

In order to ensure a quality program, the SAS child-care centers have adopted teacher-child ratios much better than the state allows. For example, SAS Institute provides one care giver to every three infants, while the state allows one care giver for up to seven infants. SAS child-care workers also earn salaries that are considerably higher than those offered at other centers in the area. Several years ago David Russo showed Dr. Goodnight a chart of the market wage rates for some of the Institute's lower-paid jobs. Goodnight took his pen and drew a line along the 12,000-dollar level, telling Russo that no worker at the company would ever earn less than that figure. In an area where child-care workers generally start at minimum wage, that pen line has meant a significant income boost. In addition, as SAS employees, the teachers receive all of SAS's benefits.

As one result of SAS's policies, the company has an extremely low employee-turnover rate for both child-care personnel and company employees as a whole. Turnover at the entire company from 1984 through 1988 averaged just under 8 percent, compared with an industry average of 25 percent. "That by itself makes me feel good," says Russo. "But it makes me feel even better to realize that that figure includes jobs with some of the highest turnover in the country. We hire our own security force; we have our own housekeepers, groundskeeping staff, maintenance crew; we run our own cafeteria; and we run our own child-care centers."

> *When I was teaching in Raleigh, my daughter was in a family day-care situation. At the time, that's all we could afford. They gave no discount to workers at the center. So working here has made a big difference. Both my daughters are right here. If you have to work it's nice to have them where you can see them. I can see my four-year-old all day. I peek in her classroom all day. If she gets hurt she always comes and looks for me, for a little hug. And I can stop by and see my baby at lunch or go over when she needs me. It's like I'm not really leaving them. And the pay is much better than what I was getting before. When I started at SAS I just could not believe what they pay their day-care workers.*

> *I have twin boys at the child-care center. They're four now and they've been going since they were three months old. I had a lot of conflicting emotions at first, about getting back to work versus being at home. I think with two small babies anyone would feel that. But it worked out well. The fact that I could go and visit them during the day helped my transition back into work. I didn't worry about them during the day, but I missed them. So I would drop in at least once a day, and I would spend all or most of my lunch hour there.*
> *When they got to be a little older, I could tell that they*

*loved it over there, and that made me feel even better. As
we would drive up to the center their little legs would start
pumping and they would start laughing. They were so excited to see their teachers.*

*Now they're both very interested in the work that they
do in their classes. Sammy's on his third map. He pin-
punched out all the continents and pasted those onto a
map so he had two globes. We were amazed when he came
home talking about Australia and Europe and Asia. And
then he punched out a map of North America and he came
home talking about Guatemala and Panama. Now he's
working on the United States. Marty is much more active,
and also very verbal. And he just loves working with what
they call the movable alphabet. He's learning to spell
words, and that's become one of his favorite games at
home, spelling. They both really enjoy it. And they love
the other children as well, and their teachers.*

Although Dr. Goodnight may have originally decided to bring
services like maintenance, security, child care, and food service
in-house in order to ensure that their performance met company
standards, the decision to keep these workers on the same payroll
as computer scientists and salespeople has also broadened the
group that thinks of itself as SAS Institute, and ensures that the
company's respect for individual workers is not limited to an
elite core. At the Institute, kitchen workers as well as executives
are identified by nameplates on their doors.

Since the child-care center opened in 1981, the company has
continued to add benefits and facilities to improve the quality
of work life of its employees. From a crude running trail through
the woods in Cary, the company has gradually built up some of
the best exercise facilities in corporate America. At lunchtime
on the day we visited, several games were in progress on the
outdoor tennis and indoor racquetball courts, and an aerobics
class was in session in the aerobics exercise room, while basketball players enjoyed a game in the gymnasium. Upstairs a
dozen employees worked out in a well-equipped Nautilus room,
while others played pool and table tennis in a casual recreation
area.

An on-site health-care center, staffed by family nurse prac-
titioners and visited by a doctor, provides free care to employees
and their families. Parents can bring their children in for ear
checks and immunizations, athletes can stop by to have injuries
examined after a rough game of basketball, and routine physical
examinations can be scheduled to require a minimum of time
away from work.

The cafeteria is perhaps the most striking facility on the SAS campus. It opens into a spacious atrium with skylights, the octagonal space surrounded by a balcony with additional tables. The menu ranges from gourmet to basic fare, all at extremely low prices, and all with calories and fat content identified on the menu. Diners are serenaded by live piano music during the lunch hour, and any leftovers are packaged and sold as even less expensive take-home meals at the end of the day. The Institute has deliberately built no executive dining room, and Jim Goodnight, often with his wife and children, eats his meals there along with everyone else. The only reserved seating is for customers attending SAS software classes, and downstairs, where a section of low tables is reserved for children from the preschool.

> I take full advantage of the gym. It's not directly a family benefit, but because I can go there at lunch, it really is. If I didn't have a place to exercise at lunch, I couldn't do it at all. When you have young children, you're on a tight schedule. At my last job I had to drive to a health center, and it cut so deeply into my schedule that I just couldn't do it on a regular basis. Here, I go to an aerobics class three times a week, I walk or jog with a friend on this floor a couple times a week, and I'll probably take an introductory Nautilus course next month.

> I eat at the café every day, but I also take home leftovers for dinner. Since our daughter was born, the take-home meals have become a real help. I wouldn't have any time in the evening without them. And the prices are very reasonable. My husband and I both are addicted to the convenience, and it's certainly a healthy alternative to fast food.

> I use the medical clinic a lot. My four-year-old had a lot of ear infections, and it was so convenient just to take her up there and let them give her a prescription. Before, I'd have to leave work, take her to the doctor, and then pay a thirty-dollar doctor's fee for them to tell me she had an ear infection. So we use the health-care center a lot. We get their shots up there. And one shot can cost you thirty dollars at the doctor's office. So that helps out a lot.

The child-care center here was designed primarily as an aid to SAS employees, rather than as a lure in recruiting new workers, and that emphasis has been strengthened over time. In its early years, any employee could enroll their children at the center. Today it is open only to employees with at least a year of service. The policy change was one way of dealing with waiting lists when demand first outstripped supply at the center, but it also sends a strong message about the center's purpose at the company, which is to help employees who are committed to working at SAS Institute.

Managers are under strict instructions not to mention child care as a benefit at recruiting interviews. "It's easy not to boast about it, not to use it as bait, when you have a waiting list," Russo explains. "What's difficult is to make new employees understand that it's not an automatic benefit. We try to make it clear that if they're coming to SAS Institute for child care, they're making a terrible mistake. They'd better be coming here for the work. Child care is part of the benefit package that is offered, and it may be a help to them eventually, but it's not a guarantee."

Nonetheless, the child-care center does impress job applicants who visit the campus, and several employees we spoke to admitted that the center was at least part of the reason they came to SAS Institute. David Russo recalled talking to one new employee who was single and had no immediate prospects for marriage or children, who said he'd joined the Institute because he wanted to work for a company that cared so much about its employees that it would provide a health-care center and child care as benefits.

For the employees who do have the chance to enroll their children, the center has obviously proved to be a tremendous benefit. The financial savings are obvious, as is the convenience. But what struck us most in our conversations with parents was their repeated emphasis on the peace of mind the center offered, how it had freed them from a great deal of distraction and worry at work.

> *I was working at another company when I had my first child. I looked at eight or ten day-care centers and decided on one that I thought was best, based on ratios and environment, physical building, and the people that I talked with. I visited twice during my maternity leave just to touch base and gauge how long it took me to get there, those kinds of things. But the morning I went back to work, the first day I left him there, I just had a terrible, terrible feeling that what I was doing was wrong.*
>
> *There were two care givers in the room and I think twelve cribs. When I had visited I had not been there in the morning to see what it was like at the drop-off time. And there were babies crying and only so many arms. It*

hit me as I left that morning that my son was just another child to them. He was our entire life, but to them he wasn't anything special.

I felt awful all morning. I thought, What is it that you feel is wrong? Is it working and having a child? I had always planned on working with a family. I had always worked. I worked my way through school. I enjoy working. I just couldn't imagine staying at home. But I think I underestimated my feelings, and I just didn't feel good about the center. At lunchtime my husband called, and he was feeling pretty bad too. And while I was talking to him the day care called on my other line saying our son had a fever of 104. Well, that was it. I went in and told my boss that our baby had a fever, that I was leaving and I would not be returning. I had four years in. But I walked away and I never looked back.

The first year at home with him was wonderful, but by eighteen months I was feeling I'd go crazy if I didn't get out of the house. Our son needed other kids to play with and I was really missing the work. So I found a job at a medical clinic and we found a day-care home for our son. It seemed like a very loving home environment and I felt pretty good about it. Then, after he'd been there a couple of weeks, the woman informed me that most of her eighteen-month-olds were potty-trained. He had shown no signs of being ready, but she wanted us to potty-train him right away.

I was terribly upset. I didn't know what I was going to do. I was talking about it with a patient at the clinic during her therapy—saying that I didn't want to stay home but that day care was very hard—and she told me about SAS.

That makes it sound like I came to SAS for the day care, which is not entirely true. But I did come out to SAS and was immediately impressed with the physical campus. It seemed very laid-back, and there was a small group of kids from the center walking around with their teacher. The kids were stopping to pick up pine cones. And I thought, This is really neat.

I interviewed and was hired and came to work here. And it was an entirely different world. Not just being able to work and not worry about day care, but the whole program that SAS had. That was seven years ago. We have a second child now, a daughter who's two and a half, and when I compare my experiences with her to what it was like to go back to work nine years ago with my son, it's just amazing. This time around there was no guilt. I didn't

> *feel that I was tugging and weighing which was more im-*
> *portant, the work or the child. It was so easy. Day care is*
> *not even a concern for me now. Not once during the day*
> *does it even cross my mind, to wonder if she is doing okay,*
> *or if she's happy, or stimulated, or if she got a hug when*
> *she fell down. Because I know it's all here.*

In order to be fair to employees at other sites, the Institute offers an equivalent child-care benefit to its field employees. With the help of a consultant, the company identifies quality child-care centers in each employment area, and when employees enroll their children, the centers bill the company directly for the care.

All employees, whether at Cary or other sites, are covered by the company's leave policy, which allows up to a year of leave for personal reasons, including child care. "Our personal-leave policy says that it can be used for any legitimate reason," says Russo. "It doesn't have to be a tragedy. It doesn't have to be a catastrophe. It just has to be a good reason. And parenting, either for a father or a mother, is a good enough reason for us." So far just one father has taken a paternity leave, and that for just two weeks, but the door is apparently open. Another employee used a monthlong leave to move an elderly parent.

All employees are also covered by the company's sick-leave policy. The company has three categories of sick time, all fully paid and all accepted by managers as reasonable reasons to be out of work. Personal illness is the first, family illness the second, and disability—for longer-term absences—the third. "Kids are going to get sick," says Russo. "And we want our people to be honest with us. So we're open about it and say that time off to care for a sick child is a legitimate reason to take time off. We think that some companies are making a ludicrous mistake when they don't accept that."

Russo bristles about some of the comments he hears about the company's many employee-supportive policies. People commend him on the Institute's social consciousness, or wonder if the organization has become so much like a country club that people no longer concentrate on their work. "There are a lot of people out there who don't see that there is a good, solid business logic to doing these things," he says. "It just makes sense to think about ways to make your employees better able to concentrate on their work, ways to reduce stress in their lives, and ways to help them address problems they may not be able to address themselves. That's where Jim Goodnight has had a leg up on a lot of businessmen. Sure, he wants to be successful. And sure, he wants the company to make money. But he's always felt that good, committed employees are the basis for any business growth and profits. He sees his employees as this company's major assets. So he puts a great deal of money into both research and development and into these benefit programs, and feels that both investments pay off in the long run. The benefits we have allow employees to concentrate on their work; they help retain valued employees; and they help to make all of our people feel more a part of the organization."

# The Stride Rite Corporation

Five Cambridge Center
Cambridge, MA 02142                        617-491-8800

**Nature of business:** Manufacturer and marketer of children's and adults' shoes, sold under the brand names Stride Rite, Keds, and Sperry Topsider.
**Number of employees:** 3,600.
**Female employees:** 65 percent (35 percent of managers).
**Child care:** On-site centers in Cambridge and Roxbury, Massachusetts, for 110 children, aged fifteen months to six years (Cambridge center includes adult day-care wing and intergenerational activities); income-based subsidies; nationwide resource-and-referral service planned for 1991.
**Elder care:** On-site adult day-care center in Cambridge, Massachusetts, with capacity for twenty-four elders (center includes child-care wing and intergenerational activities); income-based subsidies.
**Family leave:** Paid disability leave for childbirth, plus up to eighteen weeks unpaid family leave; paid time off may be used for short-term care of ill dependents.
**Flexible work options:** Flexible schedules arranged individually; some part-time work.
**Other benefits:** Lunchtime seminars on family issues; on-site fitness center at headquarters.

Meeting employees' and the community's needs; a tradition of innovation.

*"We don't live in a vacuum. We live in a community. And that community has needs. It is people from the commu-*

*nity who buy our products and support our business. It doesn't seem so farfetched to have an interest in the well-being of that community. We're just broadening the definition of our self-interest."*

ARNOLD HIATT
Chairman

On a Tuesday morning at the Stride Rite Corporation's headquarters in Cambridge, Massachusetts, an unusual scene is unfolding. Two elderly women, Eva DaRosa and Margaret Donovan, are ferrying preschoolers, two at a time, from their classroom on the fourth floor of the company's office tower to a common area where a group of elders and teachers helps the children make a hand-print mural. The children are enjoying the hand-print project, but the real fun of the day has turned out to be the ride in Donovan's wheelchair. Each pair of children takes turns riding in Donovan's lap and pushing the chair with the help of DaRosa. One child gets to ride on the way out, the other on the way back to their classroom. The women are enjoying the event almost as much, and after a dozen runs have dubbed themselves the pony express.

This is Stride Rite's intergenerational day-care center, the first such center in American business, one of the first centers in the country to pair the care of children and the elderly.

Stride Rite has a long history of leadership in family-care issues. The company started its first child-care center in 1971, in Roxbury, Massachusetts, at a time when such initiatives were few and far between. That facility is still going strong, one of a select handful of employer-supported child-care centers with such a long track record. The company added a second child-care center for its Cambridge employees in 1983, and expanded that into the current intergenerational center in 1990.

The idea for Stride Rite's first child-care effort belongs to the company's chairman, Arnold Hiatt. He joined the business in 1968, when Stride Rite bought the small children's shoe company he had started, and he became president of the larger business two years later. One of his first acts as president was to propose a dramatic change in the company's practice of charitable giving. "The company had had a charitable foundation for some time," Hiatt explains, "but it had limited itself to the traditional kinds of gifts—to hospitals, universities, and other very visible community organizations—and had played a relatively passive check-writing role. I felt it was time for us to do something in a more targeted way, time to play a more active role in our community. At the time our offices and our plant were located in Roxbury, and I thought we ought to do something right there."

Since Stride Rite's primary business is children's shoes (though Keds and Sperry Topsider now contribute a substantial portion of the company's sales), the foundation has always concentrated its giving on initiatives that benefit children. As its first strong community initiative, Hiatt proposed that the foundation help to start a day-care center.

The board of directors took some convincing—they were uncomfortable at first about entangling the company in an endeavor so unrelated to its main business—but they eventually came around and allowed Hiatt to move ahead with his plan. As his primary model, Hiatt looked to the Head Start program, which by 1970 had proven its success as a means of giving underprivileged children a boost in their educations. Studies had shown that young Head Start graduates performed better in school, and most analysts foresaw long-term societal benefits as well: lower dropout rates for those who built on that early advantage, and lower unemployment and crime rates later on. As his first director, Hiatt hired Miriam Kurtzman, who had been running a Head Start program in East Boston.

The center was built in a space on the ground floor of the company's Roxbury factory, with a playground across the street in what had been a vacant lot, and it opened its doors in the spring of 1971. At some early stage, either during renovations or soon after it opened, the center's focus shifted slightly to include care for the children of employees.

"We're given credit for being a pioneer in employer-supported day care," says Hiatt, "but our aim was to provide child care for the community, for children of welfare families and single-parent households. Shortly after we started, however, one of our workers approached me and said, 'You're willing to do this for the children in the neighborhood. Why not do the same for our children?' And I said fine. And from that day forward we tried to maintain a balance at the center between children from the community and the children of our employees."

Stride Rite's Roxbury child-care center is still going strong, though changes at the company have led to changes in its population of children. The business moved its headquarters to Cambridge, and added a second child-care center there in 1983. The company has also changed the function of the Roxbury plant from a production facility to a warehouse and distribution center. The two moves have led to a drop in employment at the site, from about 1,500 when the child-care center opened in 1971 to approximately 150 today. The center still cares for the same number of children, but a higher proportion of them are from the community.

> *Having this child-care center here makes all the difference in the world to us. My daughter had been in family day care prior to coming to the center, and her care giver was warm and loving and wonderful, but she was very unreliable. She took a lot of time off and caused me a lot of stress. I had to use up my vacation and sick time with no notice. Now I can plan vacations with my family. She was also an hour away from where I worked, so I felt bad that I couldn't see her during the day. I hated that. Now my daughter is in the same building, and it's stress-free for me. She's getting the best care. The teachers are dedicated and sensitive; they're right on target with the children's developmental needs. I feel total confidence in the center. I can just go downstairs and see her. I get reports during the day from people who have seen her. Just knowing that I could go down there at any time is very soothing. And she knows that I'm in the building. She understands. She knows that when we come in she goes to the fourth floor and I go to the seventh.*

> *My son is three and a half and just started at the day care in July. It has taken so much stress out of our lives, because I can just bring him in to work with me, and the hours match my schedule. Where he was before, we had to pick him up at four o'clock. My husband, who is a police officer, could usually get off work in time to pick him up, but sometimes he had to work later and we would have to find someone else to pick him up. It was too early for us. And the earliest we could drop him off in the morning was at eight o'clock. I was always coming in late to work, because it was up to me to bring him in in the morning. It was very hard. Now I can just bring him with me when I come in to work, and take him home when I leave. It's no problem, And my husband is very happy too.*

Karen Leibold joined the company in 1983 as director of Stride Rite's new Cambridge child-care center. She headed the program for five years until moving into the broader role of director of work/family programs, and in her tenure with the business has overseen the relocation and expansion of the center, and the creation of an accompanying elder day-care center.

With the child-care programs well established and in the competent hands of Kurtzman and Leibold, Arnold Hiatt began to turn his attention to other ways of effecting positive change in the community with Stride Rite's charitable money. He established a fund of $300,000 for students and graduates of the law schools at Harvard and Northeastern University who participate in public-service activities, as a way of encouraging new lawyers to consider public-service careers. In the early 1980s, he also began to think about what the company could do to help the elderly in the community. "I began thinking about the enormous waste of energy that was building among the retired community," Hiatt says, "people who didn't have anywhere to channel their energy. I was aware of the opportunities that children provide as a focus, and their needs, now that so many don't have extended families or grandparents nearby. It seemed to me that these two groups had something to give each other."

That thinking began to gel when he read a *Wall Street Journal* article in 1986 that described the stresses faced by families with both child-care and elder-care responsibilities. He clipped the story and sent it to Karen Leibold with a note attached asking if it didn't make sense to offer services for both generations in the same place. That might have been the end of it, but Leibold picked up on the idea and began to think seriously about what the company could do.

"An on-site elder day-care center just seemed like a logical next step," says Leibold. "We had been looking to relocate the child-care center in Cambridge, and we had the opportunity to add this into the plans." Elder care was just beginning to surface as an employment issue. The Travelers surveyed its employees in 1985 and found that one in five had some responsibility for the care of an elderly relative, and surveys at other companies began to confirm that elder care was a concern for huge numbers of workers. But Stride Rite could find no models for the sort of intergenerational approach it had in mind. Companies were beginning to think about the issue, but very few had acted.

"We did a lot of reading that first year," says Leibold. "We did a lot of traveling. We did a lot of research to find out what was out there, what other employers were doing. We found some companies that were thinking about elder care, but very few that had reached the point of actually offering their employees any direct services. The field had just not yet been defined or even explored to any great extent. We found some intergenerational centers at nursing homes, where the businesses had started child-care centers as an employee benefit. But in those, the two services were kept separate, so the children and the elders had virtually no contact with each other. We found community service centers that provided child care or ran a Head Start program in one section, and a senior center down the hall, and the two groups would occasionally get together to celebrate holidays. There were beginnings all over, but at the end of that first year we realized that if we were going to do this, we would have to create the model ourselves, both in the intergenerational aspect and in the employer response to the whole elder-care issue."

The company made two connections early on that would guide its actions and help determine the form of the eventual program. Somerville-Cambridge Elder Services, a community agency, approached Stride Rite about providing care for the children of the agency's employees, and in the course of the discussions agreed to join forces with the company in an advising role as it created the elder-care program. The company made an academic link as well, bringing in Wheelock College as an additional partner in the venture to help shape the program and then to study its effects on the elders, the children, the workers, and the company. All along, the Stride Rite Charitable Foundation provided the basic funding for the project. The elder services agency and the college provided staff time and expertise.

> *My son, who is five, calls the elders in the center "the olderlies," which is something he made up. I've never heard anyone else call them that. He enjoys projects with "the olderlies." I know he feels very special about them. He's very quiet, and they may not know who he is, but he knows all of them. He knows their last names. They read stories together. They cook together. They made pizzelles one time. They make crafts together. Last Friday we had a magician in the center, and the children and the elders were dancing around together and singing and clapping hands. It was really very touching to see.*
>
> *The only other older people he has much contact with are his grandparents, whom we see every other week. And I see him interacting with them much more easily now. I don't know if he was frightened of older people before or not. But it seems as though this has made his relationship with older people a lot more open.*

As a first step, Stride Rite and its collaborators surveyed employees to determine the level of elder-care need, and the community to find out about the level of elder day-care supply. They found that 25 percent of Stride Rite's employees had some sort of elder-care responsibilities, and that another 13 percent expected to take on care-giving responsibilities within the next five years, figures in line with what other companies were discovering. And they found two elder day-care centers in the community, both of which were operating near capacity.

"We felt the need was there," says Leibold, "and growing. We decided that even if the center didn't fill immediately, we will eventually have enough of a population who will need it that it will offer an important benefit."

As the company moved forward with its plans for a new child-care center, it set aside space for an adjacent elder-care wing, and common areas for intergenerational activities. The staff at the center worked with experts at Wheelock and Somerville-Cambridge Elder Services to design the space to meet the needs of both elders and children, and to create an intergenerational curriculum.

The Stride Rite Intergenerational Day Care Center opened in February 1990, with space for fifty-five children and twenty-four elders. Both are housed on the fourth floor of the company's office tower, in a facility with three distinct areas. In each, efforts have been made to soften the effect of the office environment. From the elevator bank, the entrance to the center opens into the common area, with tables and chairs of all heights, a kitchen, and a low cooking counter with adjustable-height chairs. The hallway to the child-care center leads off to the left, broken up with zigs and zags to make rooms with corners and nooks, and to make the approach into the space less sterile. Brightly colored sections of wall, indoor climbing structures, pets on tables, and shelves filled with toys all tend to disguise the fact that the center is housed in a glass-and-steel tower. Only the huge windows, looking down four stories to the street below, offer a reminder of the corporate location. To the other side of the common space is the elders' area, with dark wooden furniture, wicker chairs, magazine racks, and plants. Double-hung windows here give a homelike environment to the inside space.

The center opened with just two elders, but through the spring and summer enrollment gradually swelled, until, by the fall of 1990, it took in eleven elders each week. Since the center is open only to elders with a narrow range of needs—they must be too healthy to need nursing-home care, yet frail enough to need some sort of help—the center is not a universal benefit. Not every elderly relative is a suitable candidate. As we went to press, the elder wing of the center remained largely a community rather than a company benefit; just one attendee, the grandmother of an employee, had any connection to Stride Rite.

After just a few months of operation, the intergenerational aspects were already proving to be a great success for those on both sides of the center. "The relationship between the children and the elders has really exceeded our expectations," says Leibold. "We thought we'd need to bring them together very slowly, with a lot of staff direction and with specific projects to do. What we've found is that they're like magnets with each other. They just come together. They enjoy each other's company. Sometimes it can be for five minutes at the beginning or the end of the day, when they meet in the entryway. Sometimes it's waving across the lunchroom at each other. Sometimes it can be an extended period of time, reading books together, or cooking, or making things with blocks or Play-Doh."

The elders sometimes wander down to play with the children in their rooms. The children don't have the same freedom, but they can ask permission to go visit the elder wing, and, if the timing is right, a teacher will take one or two children over, just to sit on the elders' laps, to talk, or to read a book. The elders can invite the children over for cooking projects, or to share something they have cooked, and both groups participate in regular combined activities.

> *My grandmother is in the center, my father's mother. She's seventy-three years old, widowed for thirteen years, and living alone for the last three years. She's too healthy and active to be in a nursing home, yet too proud to move in with another family member. She's very independent. So we found a retirement home for her, with a variety of levels of care, but over the past year, she was becoming depressed as some of her friends' health deteriorated. I didn't like going over to visit her after a while, because the conversation just focused on health.*
>
> *Since she's started coming in with me she's had much more exciting things to talk about, and she looks forward to it. This is a healthier group of people. They talk about current events. They go for walks in Boston, daily walking trips, to museums or plays. This provides her with stimulation for a good chunk of her day. And the children do wonderful things for the elders.*
>
> *Since she moved into the retirement home she hadn't done any cooking. They didn't have the facilities, and the residents weren't allowed to cook. Well, that was her passion before. And here she can cook, and she has an appreciative audience. I brought in her pizzelle iron—like a waffle iron—one day, for making the old Italian cookies that she used to make all the time. And she and the other elders rehashed the old recipe and got the children involved sprinkling powdered sugar on the cookies when they were finished. It was just a wonderful feeling for me to see her doing what she used to love to do.*

> *I think this has revived her. The center has given life back to her. She feels like she is coming here and giving while she is here. She's helping the children tie shoelaces. She's working with the children when they have art projects. My grandmother isn't able to read a book to them, but the other elders do that. She just enjoys what goes on there.*

Though the elder day care did not turn out to be a widely used employee benefit in its first year, employees with children in the center seem pleased with the center's broadened scope, with the chance their children now have to make contact with older people. For Arnold Hiatt, the fact that few employees have taken advantage of the elder day-care option is almost incidental. The important thing seems to be to try it out, to provide a service that benefits the community. If it can be a help to the company's employees eventually, so much the better. While many managers look at family programs in terms of their direct bottom-line effects—in reduced turnover, lower recruitment costs, and higher productivity—Hiatt seems to look at his company's interests from a different vantage point. "We don't live in a vacuum," he observes. "We live in a community. And that community has needs. It is people from the community who buy our products and support our business. It doesn't seem so farfetched to have an interest in the well-being of that community. We're just broadening the definition of our self-interest."

Leibold and Hiatt are proud to have created a model for other companies to study. Theirs may not be the one ultimately adopted by many businesses, but they have created an option. As they sort through the program and find out what works and what doesn't, they will undoubtedly provide a long-term service that goes far beyond the small number of people they directly serve.

> *At the end of the day, either I will take my grandmother home and spend an hour with her in the evening, or my father will come in and spend the last hour with her here. When I take her home, we'll often have dinner on the way home or go to a movie. It's a big change for me to visit her or take her out to dinner. She used to be depressing. Now she just bubbles over with stories of what's gone on that day. I feel like I'm the lucky one of all her nine grandchildren, because I get to see her every day. We all benefit from her stories and her new enthusiasm, but I get the benefit every day.*

# United States Hosiery Corporation

P.O. Box 160
Lincolnton, NC 28093                                        704-735-3041

**Nature of business:** Manufacturer of socks.
**Number of employees:** 282.
**Female employees:** 76 percent (75 percent of managers).
**Child care:** Near-site consortium center for 125 children, aged six weeks to twelve years, founded in cooperation with Cochrane Furniture Co.; center is open to serve both first- and second-shift workers, and provides care for mildly ill children at no extra charge to company employees; child-care subsidies offered at company's production facility in Hickory, North Carolina.
**Elder care:** No formal program, but land has been set aside for an elder day-care center.
**Family leave:** Unpaid leave must be applied for in six-week increments; no disability coverage for childbirth.
**Flexible work hours:** Flextime in most office and certain production jobs.
**Other benefits:** Tuition reimbursement; scholarship fund.

Quality child care as a long-term business issue—a consortium approach.

*"We have a problem in this country, and that is our educational system. People talk about it, but nobody in power wants to do anything about it. I feel that if you want to do something about education you have to start with day care, with one- and two-year-olds. You have to teach these youngsters the pleasures of knowledge, the importance of knowledge. And then try to carry it through in the school system."*

DANIEL L. BRIER
Chairperson

*Our son is adopted, and we got him when he was a year old. My husband is the dye-house manager, and I'm the data-processing manager, so neither one of us could afford to be out for a day. So when our son got sick we would split. My husband normally has to be here in the morning*

> to check things that happened on second shift. So he would come in in the morning, work until two or three, and go home. I would then come in in the afternoon and work until late in the night, trying to get things done. They've always been pretty flexible here. I could come in on Saturdays. I could come in on Sundays, they don't care. If it has to get done, it gets done, and if it wasn't real important anyway we'd just push it back a little bit. I didn't match hour for hour when I took time off. If I took a day off, I could sometimes make up that work in four hours on a Saturday, when people weren't telephoning.

Daniel Brier, president of United States Hosiery, began thinking about child care as an issue for his business in 1981, when a key married couple on his payroll adopted a child and the smooth flow of work at the company began to be disrupted by the necessities of parenting. Every childhood illness took one of the two managers out of work. Breakdowns in their baby-sitting arrangements meant lost time on the job. And because the two were in critical positions at the plant—both managed departments—their absences were particularly visible. The work always was done, but it often meant that one parent had to come back at night or on Saturday to take care of an important project. The couple has since had two more children, and their experiences have made Brier more aware of the problems faced by other working parents throughout the business.

Noticing those lost workdays and the odd hours parents sometimes worked to make up for them brought home the importance of child care as a business issue. Brier also felt the inflexibility of his workers' day-care arrangements as a business constraint. "We'd be in the middle of a meeting," he remembers, "and someone would pop up and say, 'It's four o'clock. I've got to go pick up my kid.' I'd sit there and wonder about that. Why couldn't they leave the kid for an extra hour? What was the big deal? And then I found out that it cost them fifteen dollars for that extra hour."

When the plant had to run overtime or on Saturdays, many parents couldn't work, and those that did, Brier discovered, often ended up paying out their extra earnings to child-care providers who charged punitive rates for care beyond their standard hours. The unreliability of some workers' day-care arrangements also led to absenteeism, and in a plant where time off was generally without pay, Brier not only felt those lost days on his own bottom line but felt for employees who were losing wages unnecessarily.

A tight labor market also began to make a center more attractive as a recruitment tool. In the middle and late 1980s, unemployment in the area hovered at less than 2 percent. At lunch on the day we visited, talk centered on how to recruit some of the workers from a neighboring factory that was shutting down. United States Hosiery's business expanded through the 1980s, and as it became increasingly hard to find good workers, a child-care center began to seem like a logical option.

> *I work overtime here sometimes. It's not usually a case of "have to." I do it when I want to. Where the children were before, she wanted them picked up as soon after five o'clock as possible, so I didn't usually get a chance to work over. Now I just call and tell them I'll be working late that day, and they usually say that's fine. I don't have to arrange it in advance. I just call that afternoon.*

Recruitment, a desire to reduce absenteeism, and the need to help employees balance work and family schedules might seem like reasons enough for taking action on child care. But when Brier talks, those issues come across as almost secondary concerns. Perhaps he is so used to couching his pitch for the center in those terms for other businessmen that he accepts them as a given, as something the listener should already understand and accept. What seems to have nudged him over the edge from thinking to acting are two other concerns: that he treat his employees as human beings, listening to their concerns and answering their needs where possible; and a deep belief in the importance of education to our country's future economic health.

"A company is never going to be good without good employees," Brier explains, "and one way to make good employees is to treat them like human beings, to listen to them and to respond to their concerns. One thing that happens when you start to listen is that you find out they know more about their jobs than any manager ever could, and they have ideas that can help the business. I also feel that when you listen to people you should listen to everything about them, including their problems with their spouses, with their health, with their kids. And it's not just to be nice. It makes good business sense. If you can help one of your workers with a personal problem, that worker is going to feel better about himself, better about the company, and is going to do a better job.

"Over the years I watched as employees had problems with child care, and I heard some of the stories, and after a while it just got to me. Here we were busting our chops trying to give them what they need, and we were ignoring the most important piece. If an employee has a legal problem, we have our lawyer take care of it. If someone has a financial problem, we sit down and try to work it out. If they have a divorce, we try to help them. If somebody dies in the family or there's a fire, whatever it might be, we're there. But on the most important issue, kids, we weren't there."

Brier's concern here was not just for the welfare of the parents at his company. He has strong feelings about the importance of education, and of quality child care to get younger children started on the right foot in life. And he was aware that quality child care was a scarce commodity in the area. North Carolina has a two-tier licensing system, with fairly low standards for the basic "A" license—for example, allowing teacher-child ratios for infants and three- and four-year-olds that would be illegal in forty-six of the fifty states—and higher standards for an "AA" license. There were no "AA"-licensed centers in Lincoln County, and even the poorer-quality care was in short supply.

> The day care where I had my daughter before came highly recommended to me, but I never got attached to it. She was in the infant room, and they all had little-bitty beds, and the room was maybe ten feet by twelve, and they had twelve of them. It was real cramped together. They would play in the hall area. There was one teacher for them, and then the director's office was right outside the room and she would come in if the other teacher needed help. It was hard to leave my daughter there. I remember the first day I took her there I was an hour late for work and I cried until lunchtime because it was so heartbreaking to leave her there.
>
> Before they started the center here, I had my son in another day care. He still talks about it. The day care that I had him in was something that I had to do. It was the only place there was that I could take him that early in the morning. I have to get in here at six-thirty. I hated leaving him there, but I didn't have a choice. I couldn't leave him at home by himself in the mornings, and there was nowhere else to take him.
>
> I guess the place took about forty kids, and they had two adults to watch them. There would be days when I'd just hate to come in to work. I went to get him one day and he had a brand-new shirt pocket ripped off. The next day a pants pocket was ripped off. He had bite marks all over him. Now these are kids that go to school. He's not perfect or anything, but I knew there had to be something better than that. Better supervision. Even now he'll ask me,

*"Mama, why did you make me go to that day care?" And I say, "Son, I had no choice. It's all I had."*

In the spring of 1988, Brier decided to stop thinking about the issue and do something. He did some basic research on what it would take to build a child-care center, and realized that his business was probably too small to support a facility of the quality and size that he envisioned. So he organized a meeting of business and government leaders to discuss his plan for a center that would serve employees of a number of area businesses. He proposed a center that would offer low-cost, high-quality care, one that would provide sick care and after-school care, and one that would attract qualified teachers by paying better-than-average wages. He offered a tract of land for the center at a below-market price and asked that sponsoring companies agree to contribute money for construction so that the costs would not be passed along to parents in the form of fees. In return he promised "a fantastic recruiting tool and a tool to reduce turnover." The reaction at that first meeting was generally positive, but it was clear that much more planning and discussion would be necessary before many businesses would make a commitment.

While area companies were a little slow to react to the idea, the local day-care community was not. Many child-care providers felt threatened by the proposal. Brier was, after all, planning a center that would be big enough to put a dent in their enrollment, and his talk about quality implied that their own facilities were inadequate. They responded by organizing a public relations campaign of their own. "We are meeting the needs," said one provider to a local reporter soon after that first meeting. "We meet all state requirements. We want the public aware of the impact on taxes this would have on both city and county." (The center, in fact, has never received any public money or tax benefits not available to all area child-care facilities.)

One local child-care professional reacted in a more positive way. Kim Kohut Heath, who had started and run five child-care centers in the Lincolnton and Charlotte areas, heard about the meeting and wrote Brier to offer her services. "I had to find out early if they were committed to a quality program," she recalls, "because if they weren't I wasn't interested in them." "Her goals matched mine," says Brier. "Her bottom line is kids." He hired her as the center's director at their first meeting.

*Our kids were in a small licensed day care near here before, with about twenty kids in two rooms. The babies on up to the three-year-olds were in one, with one teacher*

*there, and the older kids were in the other room with an-*
*other teacher. We live a thirty-minute drive away, and we*
*wanted them closer by so we could get to them quicker if*
*they were sick. But even though they were close before, we*
*never felt we could go see them during the day the way we*
*can here. Every Thursday now we take our middle son—*
*he's five—out to lunch. That's his day during the week and*
*he looks forward to it. I never took him to lunch at the*
*other place because I figured it was disrupting. Nobody*
*said anything, but they were small and they had a set*
*routine. If I took him to lunch and brought him back and*
*the other kids were sleeping, well, he was going to wake*
*them up. The place was so small that the kids were sleeping*
*on the mats where you had to walk in the door.*

As plans for the center continued to firm through the summer
and fall of 1988, the pool of interested businesses gradually dwin-
dled. The issue of liability scared off many prospects. Others
cited the need to be fair to employees at scattered work sites.
Still others claimed that their people didn't need day care. "That
was a good one," says Heath. "They'd go into their plants and
say, 'Okay, people we're looking at day care. Do you want to
put your kids in this center?' They wouldn't give any information about it, because they didn't want to get people excited if
the company chose not to participate. So their workers would
say, 'Gee, without knowing anything about the people or the
program, we're not so sure.' And the management would come
back to us and tell us their people didn't need it."

Swiss Knits, a small contract knitting company, signed on
during the summer for a few spaces at the center, and a few
weeks later Cochrane Furniture Co., an 800-employee manufacturer, agreed to support ten spaces. Cochrane had considered
opening its own child-care center two years earlier, but had set
the plans aside after investigating the costs. Three other large
employers opted out in the last weeks, leaving United States
Hosiery with the lion's share of commitment. Brier didn't back
down on the size of the center—it was planned and eventually
built to serve 125 children—nor did he cut out the plans for a
room for mildly ill children or for second-shift child-care facilities. "What do you do?" he asks. "You've just got to go forward
and try to prove them wrong."

*When I had my son I found out that I've got a muscle*
*disease and that he's got it too. He's sixteen months old*
*and not walking yet. His muscle tone isn't that good. We*
*took him to a neurologist, and he said that if we treat it,*

> it wouldn't make any difference, that if he was active he
> could outgrow it. And this center has a physical therapist
> that works with him. And it's free. So that makes me feel
> better, that he's getting help. One week we were out and
> she came to the house. You wouldn't get that at another
> center. And it's open here from six o'clock in the morning
> until six o'clock at night, and if we have to work Saturdays
> they're there. And the sickroom helps. They had pink eye
> one time, four or five out of the class at one time. I would
> have lost a day without the sickroom. Lost a day's pay.
> That hurts.

The three companies organized the center under two separate corporations, for tax and liability reasons. Workforce Park, Inc., which operates the center, is a nonprofit corporation. Its board is composed of parents, and the company's only assets are the center's two vans. It leases the building, furniture, and equipment, at cost, from a "C" corporation called Corporate Children's Services. The two corporations create a liability buffer between the center and the sponsoring manufacturers.

Groundbreaking took place in November 1988 and the center opened in December 1989. When we visited, in the spring of 1990, the center was fully enrolled for first-shift care—second shift started up in May of that year—and the center presented a lively contrast to United States Hosiery's main plant, just across the street.

The realities of sock manufacture dictate a quite different environment from that found in the child-care center. On the day we visited, rain and humidity outside had overwhelmed the newly installed ventilation system in the plant's dyehouse, and a light mist whipped through the air around the dyeing operation. A half-dozen workers filled huge computer-controlled dye vats with socks while others emptied the colored loads into spinning machines and then fed them into a massive drier. The floor in that section of the plant was wet with dye and wash water that dripped from carts wheeling between the stations. As the socks came out of the drier and went into the main plant, other workers hung them individually on aluminum forms that then passed through a pressing operation. Thousands of dangling socks snaked around the room to the final packaging workers, who folded, banded, bagged, and boxed them for shipping.

Across the street at the child-care center, floor-to-ceiling windows not only provide lots of natural light but allow babies to peer out at the trucks that roll up to the factory's loading docks. A great deal of attention has been given to some innovative details here. Two-year-olds play at specially built miniature wooden kitchen fixtures, with real faucets and nonworking burners. "I'd never seen kitchen play sets built to the right height for two-year-olds," says Heath. "They're all too big. So we had these made." A sand table across the room is filled with rice, a more manageable medium for indoor digs. In the three-year-olds' room, one corner looks like a large shower stall. "Even the most energetic teachers tend to avoid messy activities like painting sometimes," Heath explains, "so we installed this to make painting and cleanup as easy as possible. The children can paint right on the Formica walls or paper taped up on easels, and when they're done we just hose it down." Pets scurry around in their cages in each room—a hamster on one counter, a cage of finches on another. The furniture stands out as well. One of Cochrane Furniture's contributions was a full stock of fine oak furniture in all sizes, from tiny toddler tables to elegant sofas and Queen Anne wing chairs for the offices and lobby.

The teachers, whose pictures line the lobby with their education and background spelled out in brief captions, are among the most professional and caring that we met in our travels. Lincolnton has the advantage of being near a college with an early-childhood-education degree program, and Workforce Park's above-the-norm wages and professional approach seem to have brought it an exceptional crop of graduates. Younger children get plenty of hugs, lap time, and encouragement in their efforts, while the older children are provided with a large and varied menu of activities. The children clearly enjoy being there, and parents we talked to often mentioned the teachers as the reason they were so happy with the center. Some even said they'd picked up subtle parenting techniques from watching how the teachers worked with their children.

> It just seems like the people at Workforce Park are more up, or happy, and the kids just seem to come home in a better mood. They sing songs on the way home. My son used to be wild on the way home. They take them outside more during the day, which gets rid of that energy. We used to think he was hyper. I can see a big difference in him since he's been over there, just since the first of the year.
>
> To me this is more child development, without pushing it. The place we had them before was baby-sitting. You can just tell by the projects they bring home that they do a lot more with them over here. They brought home projects at the other place, but nothing like this, the paintings and what-not. In my daughter's room they make paint prints on the walls in that shower area.

*I don't worry now. I don't worry if he's happy. I don't worry if he's taken care of or if he's made to behave. Some kids, the longer you let them go the worse they get. And with him being over there I know he's not going to get by with murder without being corrected. One day a boy called another little boy "stupid." And instead of saying "Hey! You don't do that!" the teacher just walked up and said "Now that wasn't nice. You wouldn't like it if he called you stupid, would you?" And the little boy just dropped his head and said "No." I was amazed, because most places would say "You get over there!" and "Don't you ever say that again!" She just was so calm about it. And I'm sure it did him more good than her just raking him out.*

The back and side of the building look out on what may be the center's second-finest feature: a three-acre playground that arcs around in sections divided by age, and that curves down over a slope to offer an array of play spaces. The youngest children can toddle or crawl out to a small, level area designed just for them, with a playhouse, tunnels, swings set high enough that toddlers can walk under without fear of being kicked in the head, a low bridge and a small hill for climbing, and a raised playpen— set about three and a half feet off the ground—so that babies can watch the action from a new vantage point. The two- and three-year-olds have their own wooden climbing structures and playhouse, a gently graded hillside area for running and rolling, small boulders for climbing, an amphitheater for outdoor stories and songs, a raised waterfall trough, outdoor easels, and a tricycle path. The older children have perhaps the most unusual area, which takes in the steepest section of the hillside. Terraced steps, three feet deep and almost as high, offer jumping platforms, the landing softened by gravel on the top step, then sand, then bark chips. A "cave" carved into the hillside provides an inviting space for pretend play. The tricycle/bicycle path in this section snakes up and down some small hills, over a bridge with hiding space below, past a toy gas pump with realistic features, and past a garage next to a larger wooden climbing structure and a cluster of exercise bars.

The "Get Well Room," just off the front lobby, also sets this center apart as an innovative institution. Many companies realize that the days parents take off to care for mildly ill children cost them money, but few have come up with a solution that seems so widely appreciated by employees. Some businesses contract with hospitals to provide care, by reserving space and offering employee discounts for the care, but many parents are wary of bringing a mildly sick child to a hospital, and young children are often anxious about being left in an unfamiliar environment. Another option, a service that sends a provider to the home, is expensive, and though a parent interview with the care giver is always required, the child often has little chance to become familiar and comfortable with the person who will nurse her through an illness. The care giver who supervises the sickroom at Workforce Park teaches wellness programs throughout the center when the room is empty, so the children all know her.

"Children don't go to bed when they're a little bit sick," explains Heath, "they just play differently." The sickroom is stocked with the types of toys that encourage quiet, restful play: puzzles, books, dolls, blocks, doctor kits, and art supplies. The furnishings, too, are comforting. A soft couch, area rugs, low bookshelves, and a soothing neutral-color wallpaper combine to create an inviting space. For health reasons—and to meet licensing requirements—the room has its own kitchen and bathroom, a bathtub, a separate ventilation and heating system, and a separate entrance so that sick children don't go in and out through the main door with the other children. When it first opened, the center charged parents an additional dollar per hour for sickroom care, but it soon became apparent that the extra fee was deterring parents from using the service. A change of policy made it a free benefit, with the costs absorbed by the sponsoring companies. By April, when we visited, the room was being used regularly by batches of children with eye infections, low-grade fevers, diarrhea, and other mild conditions, subject to a lengthy schedule of criteria for admission and exclusion. Children with contagious diseases, for example, are only allowed in the room with others suffering from the same illness. Many of the parents we interviewed spoke with appreciation of work days the center had saved them. At both Cochrane Furniture Co. and United States Hosiery, most workers are paid by the hour and lose a day's wages when they stay out with a sick child.

> The sickroom is a big help, because my daughter seems to have earaches all the time. They go through that where they always have a cold or something. Before this opened up I would have to miss work. And now I don't have to do that. If it's too serious, you wouldn't want them there anyway, and then you stay home with them. But when they just have a slight fever or a runny nose or they're cutting teeth and have a fever they can go in the sickroom. She keeps a real close eye on them. And I can go check on her, or I'll just work half a day and then go get her. At other nurseries, if they just have the slightest temperature you

*have to go get them, and here they call you and then just put them in the sickroom. There's been many days here that I've worked that I wouldn't have been able to before.*

Another important component of the center is care for school-age children, both before and after school and during school vacations. Workforce Park actually began with a summer-camp program before the center opened, in the summer of 1989, which operated òut of a modular office structure owned by United States Hosiery. Twenty-eight children attended that first summer, and by all accounts they had a memorable time, with weekly swimming trips and almost daily field trips to area parks and to such spots as a television station, the county airport, a zoo, and a local hospital. In 1990, the summer camp operated out of the school-age classroom in the center, with an enrollment of fifty-eight children aged six to twelve.

The center's 6:00 A.M. to 6:00 P.M. schedule was also expanded in the early summer of 1990 to include second-shift care. It now stays open until midnight on weekdays, and, if three or more children need care, until midnight on Saturday as well. The center was built with beds and bathtubs for evening care, but it took some time before enough parents signed on to start the extended program. "It was one of those Catch-22's," says Heath. "We had to have children to open it, and we couldn't get children without it being open. Parents wanted to see what it was like before they'd commit themselves."

*If I didn't work here I'd still take my children over there. My son was in the program last summer and they learned something every day. Even if it was just something small, it was something that they learned. At the end of the summer they made them a book. And for everything that happened during the summer, every day, there was a page. A little something. And he still gets that book down and looks, and says, "This is when we went to see so and so, and we did this." At vacation, if it came down to choosing Workforce Park or vacation, well, he wanted Workforce. The thought of being out and having to miss something just killed him. So during school vacations he goes over there.*

When we visited Lincolnton, in the spring of 1990, Workforce Park was fully enrolled, but at some cost to United States Hosiery. The owner of Swiss Knits had sold his business, and the new owners pulled their support from the venture. While the true cost for the center totaled about $85 a week for each child, forty children of nonemployees were getting a bargain at $65. By the fall, when we went to press, Cochrane Furniture Co. had raised its commitment to thirty employee children from an initial ten, but United States Hosiery was still supporting what Daniel Brier had envisioned as a center for all the area's employers. The loss for the first year of the center's operation was projected at $150,000, a cost divided among the sponsoring companies based on their level of participation. That subsidy was expected to drop to $50,000 in 1991, once the start-up costs had been absorbed. "I may be setting our company up for a tumble with this," Brier admits, "where the cost is so much greater than we had anticipated that we'll have to say we can't afford it. But my attitude right now is that we *will* afford it. It is a necessary thing. And it will prove out." His early plans for additional wings to the center for elder care and for developmentally delayed children, to be run in cooperation with the county, have been set on the back burner as long-term goals. The land is available, but he realizes the time is not yet right.

While Brier was disappointed by the lack of commitment from other businesses in Lincolnton, he met with an even bleaker response to a similar proposal to serve employees in the area of the company's knitting plant in Hickory, about forty-five minutes away. "We were asked to talk in front of the Hickory Chamber of Commerce," he says. "And we had all kinds of people interested. But the main people who stepped forward were the real estate people who wanted to sell or lease us a building at too high a price. I guess the bottom line is that if you try to bring independent businesses together in a joint venture, which is the way I believe day care should go, it really requires people with good spirit, people who are not out to make money on the project. And there aren't too many people like that."

One Hickory business that came close to joining in to build a center opted instead for a voucher system, and this is what United States Hosiery eventually offered its own workers in Hickory when it became clear that a center would not be built. Workers there get the same $40-per-week subsidy that parents at Workforce Park receive through their discounted fees. Brier is not happy with that answer. "The voucher system is very simple," he explains, "but it doesn't, in my opinion, meet the long-term need we have in this country. We have a problem in this country, and that is our educational system. People talk about it, but nobody in power wants to do anything about it. I feel that if you want to do something about education you have to start with day care, with one- and two-year-olds. You have to teach these youngsters the pleasures of knowledge, the importance of knowledge. And then try to carry it through in the school system. Otherwise this country is going to go down the tubes. A lot of businesses are getting involved in these 'Adopt a School' programs, pouring money into a hole called a school. In my opinion it's too late. The kids are lost by the time they leave the preschool."

As Brier talks, it becomes clear that the issues of productivity, recruitment, and retention, while important to him as a business owner, are less vital than a larger issue: the need for quality child care at an affordable price in order to ensure an educated work force for the future. "The educational value of the center was a major concern for me. That was the reason we built it the way we did. If we had just wanted a day-care center we could have gone out and bought one of the local ones. They were offered to us. We could have bought a local day-care center for seventy-five thousand dollars instead of spending six hundred thousand dollars to start this. We could have done that and operated something that would satisfy the needs of our employees. If the regular rate was thirty-five dollars, we could have lowered it to twenty-five dollars and maybe made money. But that was not of any interest to me. From the beginning I wanted to do the job for the kids."

If Brier's enthusiasm wasn't enough to pull as many businesses into the partnership as he would have liked, it has rubbed off on the officials at Cochrane Furniture Co. Neal Rhyne, the company's liaison with Workforce Park during the planning stages, explains, "We wanted something for our employees that would be more than just a day care. We wanted it to be a learning center that would teach the children while they were there. After all, the children would spend more waking hours at the center than they would with their parents. It was very important to us to know what these children were exposed to, to try to help them learn while they're there. And that's the way it was designed and why we really support it." When asked what benefit the company gets out of its investment in the center he talks about the educational value for the children. T. E. Cochrane, president of the company, is just as full of admiration for what Brier and Heath have done. "At that first meeting when he presented his proposal I thought to myself, 'Well, if he can do this, I'll sure be surprised.' But that guy is a bulldog. If he wants to do something he's going to do it. We'd thought about doing something like this by ourselves, but never went ahead with it. So this was sort of a godsend to us, somebody to spearhead it, to put it all together. I think the value to us comes both in reduced turnover and in the mental attitude of our employees who have children over there. The children love it, they look forward to going, so the employees just don't have to worry. I think about the future, twenty years from now. If all children could have something like this, think what it would mean for the country and for the world."

Adds Brier, "I have a very simple way to get pleasure now," he explains. "I look over there at that playground. Now that's a playground. You can see the kids light up when they're out there. And what more pleasure is there in life? If you get too high in the ivory tower you lose touch with what the real world is all about. Business can become impersonal. I've been there. I've been a big shot in the real estate business. I've been president of a Wall Street house. And there's no need for it. It doesn't have to be that way."

> *I came to work here because a friend referred me to the company. She told me about the day care, that they were starting to build a center. They had just started clearing the land and when I interviewed they told me quite a bit about it. And that's what pulled me on in instead of trying other places as well. My daughter was three months old when I came in for the interview, and when they told me about the day care I wanted to work here instead of the other places. And now that she's in the center, it would take a lot for another company to lure me away from here. Because my daughter just loves it over there so much that I can't imagine taking her away. I tell them, "I'm going to be here until she's in kindergarten so you might as well move me on up or do something with me." That's what I used to tell them when I was on the switchboard—and they have moved me up to customer service. Where else would I get the learning atmosphere for her? I'd have to pay somebody that was well educated, pay them a small fortune to come to my home. It would take a whole lot to make me take her away.*

# AMERICA'S OTHER WORK-AND-FAMILY LEADERS

Thumbnail portraits of their policies and programs

# Acxiom

301 Industrial Boulevard
Conway, AR 72032                                    501-329-6836

**Nature of business:** Direct marketing.
**Number of employees:** 1,400.
**Female employees:** 65 percent (37 percent of managers).
**Child care:** Near-site center for 115 children, aged six weeks to five years; plans for after-school and summer programs; resource-and-referral service; pretax salary set-aside (DCAP).
**Elder Care:** Pretax salary set-aside (DCAP).
**Family leave:** Paid disability leave for childbirth, plus unpaid parental leave to a total of six months; part-time phase-in for returning mothers; ten paid sick days may be used to care for ill family members.
**Flexible work options:** Some part-time work.
**Other benefits:** On-site fitness center; lunchtime seminars on family issues.

Acxiom has a young employee population—the average age in 1990 was twenty-eight—and in the late 1980s it began to experience something of a baby boom. The response was a company-owned child-care center, opened in the fall of 1990. While the center was initially created to provide care for preschool children, the company has plans to expand it to accommodate school-age children, with both summer and before- and after-school programs.

While the bulk of Acxiom's employees work in Arkansas, and will have access to the center, more than three hundred work at offices in Pennsylvania and New Jersey. In a gesture toward fairness, the company has established a child-care resource-and-referral service at those sites. All workers can take advantage of the company's generous leave policy: up to six months off with a same-job guarantee (though employees must pay their own health insurance once the disability period expires). Mothers coming back from leave can arrange to work part-time with full benefits for a few weeks while they adjust to their new responsibilities.

# Aetna Life and Casualty

151 Farmington Avenue
Hartford, CT 06156                                    203-273-1619

*Nature of business:* Insurance.
*Number of employees:* 45,000.
*Female employees:* 69 percent (21 percent of managers).
*Child care:* Nationwide resource-and-referral service; funding to increase community supply of child care; arrangement with independent center near headquarters, with 38 spaces reserved for employees; pretax salary set-aside (DCAP).
*Elder care:* Nationwide consultation-and-referral service; long-term care insurance an option in flexible benefit package; support groups; pretax salary set-aside (DCAP).
*Family leave:* Paid disability leave for childbirth, plus unpaid family leave for six months or longer, subject to supervisor's approval; paid time off for short-term care of ill family members.
*Flexible work options:* Flextime and staggered hours common throughout company, with two-hour window at start and end of day; part-time workers and job sharers also common; some work-at-home options.
*Other benefits:* Worktime seminars on family issues, both at headquarters and at field offices; family-resource library at headquarters; support groups for parents; savings program with employer match; stock-ownership plan; adoption aid up to $2,000.

After Aetna's new leave policy and referral services were put in place in 1988, the number of women leaving the firm after maternity leave fell from 23 percent to 12 percent. Parents who want to come back to part-time schedules also have the comfort of full health-care coverage, as long as they work a minimum of fifteen hours each week. In 1990, 950 of the company's employees were part-timers.

Aetna is not directing its efforts solely at parents of young children. It sponsors support groups for single parents, seminars for parents of teenagers, and was one of the first companies in the country to offer a nationwide elder-care referral service.

# Joseph Alfandre & Co., Inc.

1355 Piccard Drive, Suite 450
Rockville, MD 20850                                301-670-0343

*Nature of business:* Developer of mixed residential and commercial communities.
*Number of employees:* 70.
*Female employees:* 39 percent (35 percent of managers).
*Child care:* Subsidy program; pretax salary set-aside (DCAP).
*Elder care:* Pretax salary set-aside (DCAP).
*Family leave:* Paid disability leave for childbirth, plus up to three months unpaid parental leave; nine paid sick days may be used to care for ill family members.
*Flexible work options:* Flexible work hours arranged individually; some part-time work.
*Other benefits:* Tuition reimbursement; profit-sharing plan.

One single mother at Joseph Alfandre & Co. works an odd schedule. Every morning she arrives at the office by seven o'clock. One day every week she works late, and on the other four she leaves in time to be home when her children arrive from school. That flexibility is unusual even at this unusual company, but it is a good example of how the business is working to meet the needs of working parents.

Joseph Alfandre & Co. creates communities reminiscent of neighborhoods of the 1920s and 1930s. Houses of different sizes draw people of different incomes. Walking paths and sidewalks, shops and office space within the community, even child-care centers are included in the developments to help to break down the normal divisions between residential and commercial areas, and to lessen people's need to use the car for every errand.

Just as the company is rethinking residential development to better match human needs, so it is rethinking the recent tradition of compartmentalizing and separating work and family. Joseph Alfandre & Co. is very much involved in helping employees with their child-care needs, and funds a subsidy program that pays between 25 and 50 percent of all employees' child-care costs (the maximum granted to those with family incomes of less than $18,000). The company has included a child-care center in one of its developments, and has reserved space for future centers in two others. The company hopes in the future to move its offices into one of those communities and to negotiate a discount for employees with the child-care provider.

## Allstate Insurance Co.

Allstate Plaza
Northbrook, IL 60062                                708-402-6234

**Nature of business:** Insurance and financial services.
**Number of employees:** 55,000.
**Female employees:** 53 percent (10 percent of officers).
**Child care:** Nationwide resource-and-referral service; pretax salary set-aside (DCAP).
**Elder care:** Pretax salary set-aside (DCAP).
**Family leave:** Paid disability leave for childbirth, plus up to two years unpaid family leave (with comparable-job guarantee restricted to leaves of six months or less); five paid days may be used to care for ill family members.
**Flexible work options:** Flexible schedules arranged individually; some compressed work weeks; some part-time professional jobs; some job sharing; some work-at-home.
**Other benefits:** Free infant car seats for new babies; employee-assistance program; lunchtime seminars on family issues; relocation school-match program; dependent life insurance; wellness program; healthy-pregnancy program; scholarship program; tuition reimbursement; 401(k) plan with employer contribution; dental insurance.

"You're in good hands with Allstate," says the slogan, and the company is working hard to apply that motto to its own workers who have family responsibilities. A 1988 survey showed that 42 percent of Allstate's younger workers (those under age forty-five) had children under thirteen, and another 19 percent planned to start families within the next three years. That translated into a clear business issue when the same survey found that almost half of those with children had missed work in the previous three months because of problems with child care—and had been out an average of five days.

Allstate has had a child-care resource-and-referral service for its employees since 1986. In response to the survey it lengthened its family-leave policy, began to allow paid time off for care of ill family members, and made it a formal policy to allow part-time professional employment.

Look for continued innovation from Allstate. According to compensation and benefits director Michael A. Snipes, the company intends to become a "premier employer" for people with family responsibilities. Its long-term strategy is to adapt policies and practices so that the organization will attract, retain, and empower a changing and diverse work force.

Allstate is currently assessing its employees' child-care needs, and researching the possibility of on-site child care. Areas under consideration include Chicago; Dallas; Long Island, New York; St. Petersburg, Florida; and Southern California.

## America West Airlines

4000 E. Sky Harbor Boulevard
Phoenix, AZ 85034                                          602-894-0800

*Nature of business:* Airline.
*Number of employees:* 12,500.
*Female employees:* 51 percent (35 percent of managers).
*Child care:* Near-site center in Phoenix provides twenty-four-hour care; additional centers planned in Phoenix and Las Vegas; network of home-based providers and centers in Phoenix and Las Vegas, monitored by a staff of child-care experts at the company, provides additional care for over 500 children; income-based subsidies; pretax salary set-aside (DCAP).
*Elder care:* Pretax salary set-aside (DCAP).
*Family leave:* Fully paid disability leave for childbirth, plus up to three months unpaid parental leave; paid time off for short-term care of ill family members.
*Flexible work options:* Flextime in some positions; many part-time options; some job sharing.
*Other benefits:* Employee-assistance program; on-site medical clinics in Phoenix and Las Vegas for employees and families.

Founded in 1983 with fewer than 300 employees, America West Airlines has grown up without some of the labor traditions of the older airlines. Women here work at jobs that are usually reserved for men, such as baggage handling and maintenance. In the spring of 1990, by chance, the airline ran its first flight with an all-female crew—from captain to flight attendants. Not only has it broken ground by opening jobs to women, America West has supported its working parents with an innovative child-care system that combines company-owned centers with a network of family day-care homes. The airline is one of a handful of American companies that offers parents such a choice.

All customer-service workers are cross-trained to work as flight attendants, ticket agents, reservations clerks, and ramp attendants, a costly program that not only gives the company a versatile work force but gives employees a host of options when family circumstances change their work requirements. While flight attendants must work full-time, the other customer-service functions can be handled by part-timers. And since part-timers receive the full travel-pass benefit and can buy family medical coverage for a small additional fee (about $25 more per month than the cost for full-timers), part-time work here is an attractive option.

## Arthur Andersen & Co.

69 W. Washington Street
Chicago, IL 60602                                   312-580-0069

**Nature of business:** Accounting and management consulting services.
**Number of employees:** 28,370.
**Female employees:** 44 percent (24 percent of practice managers; 4 percent of partners).
**Child care:** Nationwide resource-and-referral service; Saturday child care at some offices during tax season; pretax salary set-asides.
**Elder care:** Nationwide consultation-and-referral service; pretax salary set-aside (DCAP).
**Family leave:** Paid disability leave for childbirth, plus up to a year unpaid leave; two paid personal days for support staff.
**Flexible work options:** Managers may return from maternity leave to a part-time schedule, which can last to three years from the date of the child's birth or adoption.
**Other benefits:** Employee-assistance program; adoption aid up to $2,500; profit-sharing plan; 401(k) plan.

Twenty years ago, the accounting profession was largely a male domain, and talk of child-care assistance and part-time work would have seemed farfetched. But more and more women have entered the field, and more men in the field now have wives who work. A few farsighted companies, like Arthur Andersen & Co., have responded with family support systems and with greater flexibility. The numbers at Andersen show just how significant the changes have been. In 1981, just 8 percent of the practice managers (in audit, tax, and consulting) were women, and of the firm's 450 partners, just 2 were women. By 1990, women accounted for 24 percent of the practice managers, and the number of women partners had grown to 58.

In 1987 Andersen surveyed its employees to find out what they thought of the firm's employment policies and benefit programs. The results showed that people valued Andersen as a place to work, but many criticized its flexibility in bending to family needs, and many asked for the company's help in dealing with child-care issues. The firm responded the next year with nationwide resource-and-referral services for both child care and elder care, a flexible work program for managers, and with a longer leave policy.

Since then, a number of offices have established small Saturday child-care centers to help out during the busy audit and tax season. The largest of these, the facility in Chicago, can accommodate thirty children and remains open from January to April.

# Apple Computer

20525 Mariani Avenue
Cupertino, CA 95014                                    408-996-1010

*Nature of business:* Computer manufacturer.
*Number of employees:* 8,900.
*Female employees:* 45 percent (6 percent of upper management).
*Child care:* Near-site center for 73 children, aged six weeks to six years; nationwide resource-and-referral service; pretax salary set-aside (DCAP).
*Elder care:* Pretax salary set-aside (DCAP).
*Family leave:* Paid disability leave for childbirth, plus up to six months unpaid personal leave (not job-protected for all employees).
*Flexible work options:* Flexible schedules common; some part-time work; some job sharing.
*Other benefits:* On-site fitness center; employee-assistance program; six-week sabbatical after five years; adoption aid

up to $3,000; $500 gift to new babies and adopted children; profit-sharing plan; stock options available to most employees; savings plan with employer contribution.

For those fortunate parents who can use it, the Apple Computer Child Care Center offers a model program, with low child-teacher ratios, highly trained staff, and a roomy facility in an old school building a short walk from a park. It remains open from 7:00 A.M. to 7:00 P.M., allowing parents to put in a little extra work at the start or the end of the day. And, thanks to substantial support from Apple, the weekly fees are about the same as those charged by other centers in the area which offer more limited programs.

The only real drawback is that the center isn't large enough to accommodate all of the children of Apple's employees. It maintains a waiting list of approximately 200 names, leaving many parents to make their own child-care arrangements. Apple has come up with a fairer-than-usual way of dealing with the waiting list, however. Names are selected from it at random, a system that gives new employees at least as good a chance as anyone else of getting their children enrolled. The company also offers all employees, at Cupertino and at other sites throughout the country, help in finding child care through its resource-and-referral service. With cash gifts for new babies, a generous adoption-assistance policy, and a widely flexible workplace—as much as 80 percent of Apple's work force takes advantage of some sort of flexible schedule—the company will find its way onto any short list of good companies for working parents.

# Atlantic Richfield Company (ARCO)

515 S. Flower Street
Los Angeles, CA 90071                    213-486-3511

**Nature of business:** Oil, gas, chemicals, and coal.
**Number of employees:** 22,900.
**Female employees:** 27 percent (14 percent of managers).
**Child care:** Resource-and-referral service in many locations; support for after-school programs in Anchorage, Alaska; and Long Beach, California; pretax salary set-aside (DCAP).

*Elder care:* Consultation-and-referral service in California; pretax salary set-aside (DCAP).

*Family leave:* Paid disability leave for childbirth, plus up to six months unpaid family leave; in addition to personal sick days, six days per year may be used for care of ill dependents, and five for urgent personal business; paid time off for participation in community activities.

*Flexible work options:* Flextime at most facilities; some part-time work; some job sharing.

*Other benefits:* Lunchtime seminars on family issues; employee-assistance program; parenting and elder-care support groups; tuition reimbursement for job-related courses or degree programs; scholarships for employees' children; spouse relocation assistance; 401(k) plan with employer contribution.

When ARCO determined that latchkey children were a concern among its Anchorage, Alaska, employees, the company spearheaded an after-school program in the community. ARCO planned the program, and presented the idea to the local government with a promise of funding. The company is at work on a similar after-school program in Long Beach, California, where parents at another major facility face many of the same problems.

In an industry where the percentage of women workers remains low—below those found even in such professions as accounting and law—ARCO stands out as a company that recognizes family concerns. It has taken a positive stand with its policies of paid time off for family illness. It gives a same-job guarantee for ninety days to those on family-care leave, and a similar-job guarantee to those who choose to stay out longer. It extends the company's benefit package to part-time workers.

While flexible schedules were a common practice at the company by 1990 (outside of production facilities and refineries), part-time work was a less frequent choice. Just sixty employees worked part-time, among them a husband-and-wife engineering team who shared a single job in Alaska. We should note that many of the policies listed above, such as leaves and flexible work options, apply only to salaried, nonrepresented employees. Union contracts hold the company to different rules at many facilities.

# B&B Associates

31 Edwin Road
S. Windsor, CT 06074                    203-289-3426

*Nature of business:* Printer.
*Number of employees:* 220.
*Female employees:* 20 percent (15 percent of managers).
*Child-care:* On-site center for 24 children, aged four weeks to five years.
*Elder care:* No formal program.
*Family leave:* Paid disability leave for childbirth, plus up to six weeks unpaid parental leave.
*Flexible work options:* Flextime in some positions; some part-time work.
*Other benefits:* Profit sharing; tuition reimbursement.

Barbara Barbour started this business in her basement in 1978 after sensing a need for a quick-turnaround printer of grocery-store fliers. Her company not only has its own plant now, it has its own child-care center, run since 1985 as a department within the business. According to the tenets of conventional wisdom, Barbour should never have started this center. She has a small company, and one that employs a high proportion of male workers; and her center, with only twenty-four children, is well below what most experts consider an economical size. But the same informed hunch that sent her into business has led Barbour into supporting the child-care center, and by all accounts it has turned out to be a success.

Nine or ten of the center's spaces are generally filled by employees' children, the rest by children from the community. The company pays 20 percent of the fee for its own employees and tries to run the center on a break-even basis beyond that subsidy. Creative use of resources helps make that possible, including an innovative program that brings senior volunteers into that center for several hours every week.

The company is not as flexible as some that have a higher proportion of office workers, but the payroll does include a number of part-timers, and all of them are eligible for the full company benefit package, including medical insurance and access to the child-care center.

## Baptist Hospital of Miami

8900 N. Kendall Drive
Miami, FL 33176                                    305-596-1960

*Nature of business:* Hospital.
*Number of employees:* 2,830.
*Female employees:* 80 percent (7.5 percent of supervisors and managers).
*Child care:* On-site center for 183 children, aged six weeks to six years; on-site kindergarten to open in 1991, to expand to first and second grade in 1992 and 1993; summer camp for 100 school-age children; pretax salary set-aside (DCAP).
*Elder care:* Pretax salary set-aside (DCAP); elder day-care center for parents of employees planned, to open in 1992.
*Family leave:* Six months unpaid maternity leave, plus up to eight weeks of accrued sick leave and vacation time.
*Flexible work options:* A variety of schedules are offered, including eight-, ten-, and twelve-hour shifts, twenty-four-hour weekend shifts, and a range of part-time options.
*Other benefits:* Employee-assistance program; tuition reimbursement.

Baptist Hospital opened its child-care center in 1964, when it needed a special feature to attract workers to its out-of-the-way location. Access to the hospital then was by dirt road; today the approach is a six-lane highway. Rates at the center are reasonable, thanks to a substantial subsidy from the hospital, and the teacher-child ratios are fixed below those allowed by state law. Better-than-average pay and hospital benefits also keep the center teachers around: three have been on the staff for more than five years, one for twenty-five years.

The hospital staff, too, tends to stay. Turnover here is well below the national average, in part because of policies like primary nursing that give workers more control over their jobs, and in part because so many work options are offered. More than 400 employees work part-time or alternative schedules, and part-timers who work at least twenty hours per week receive the full benefit package, including health insurance. The hospital's flexibility with scheduling is not an altruistic gesture, explained Frank Stump, Human Resources Director at the hospital. "Part-timers and people with odd schedules fill a need for us, too. It helps both ways."

# Barnett Banks Inc.

P.O. Box 40789, 50 N. Laura Street
Jacksonville, FL 32202                              904-791-5394

**Nature of business:** Banking and financial services.
**Number of employees:** 17,500.
**Female employees:** 77 percent.
**Child care:** On-site center in Jacksonville for approximately 180 children, aged six weeks to five years; resource-and-referral service in Palm Beach; pretax salary set-aside (DCAP).
**Elder care:** Pretax salary set-aside (DCAP).
**Family leave:** Paid disability leave for childbirth; additional unpaid family leave negotiable; paid sick days may be used for care of ill family members.
**Flexible work options:** Flexible work hours arranged individually; part-time work common.
**Other benefits:** Employee-assistance program.

With its high percentage of women workers, Barnett Banks has known for some time that many of its employees face work-and-family conflicts. In 1989, it took a big step toward easing some of those conflicts by opening a child-care center at the bank's new office park in Jacksonville. Barnett Banks built the building and equipped it, then turned it over to La Petite Academy—a company which operates a national chain of for-profit child-care centers—to staff and manage the center. A task force made up of parents from the different subsidiaries in Jacksonville examined two national chains and one local provider before making the final selection. In return for free rent, La Petite Academy has agreed to give Barnett Banks employees a 17.5 percent discount from the regular rates, to maintain better teacher/child ratios than those allowed under state law, to keep the center open twelve hours a day, and to allocate a portion of the center to infant and toddler care.

The center serves a population of close to three thousand workers, and may eventually be expanded to increase its capacity. For employees at other sites, the company negotiated a discount at other La Petite Academy centers. In Palm Beach, it has also contracted to provide a child-care resource-and-referral service.

In a separate initiative, Barnett Banks of Jacksonville has

joined with several local agencies to sponsor a program that trains and equips welfare recipients to become family day-care providers. The bank provides the money for each participant to make necessary home repairs and to buy beds, toys, supplies, and the first year of liability insurance. By 1990, thirty individuals had set themselves up as providers through the program.

# Bayfront Medical Center

701 6th Street, S.
St. Petersburg, FL 33701                    813-823-1234

*Nature of business:* Hospital.
*Number of employees:* 1,900
*Female employees:* 78 percent.
*Child care:* On-site center for 124 children, aged eight weeks to twelve years; care for mildly ill children in hospital facility.
*Elder care:* No formal program.
*Family leave:* Paid disability leave for childbirth, plus up to three months unpaid parental leave.
*Flexible work options:* Some shift variety; some part-time work.
*Other benefits:* On-site fitness center; employee-assistance program.

Bayfront Medical Center opened its child-care center in 1989, the first licensed facility in St. Petersburg to offer infant care. Open from 6:00 A.M. to 7:30 P.M., the center also includes a school-age program for older children on certain holidays and during school vacations. Bayfront has had a unit in the hospital to care for employees' mildly ill children since 1988. During its second year of operation, Honeywell was invited to participate, and now both Honeywell's and the hospital's employees may use the service at a cost of $12 per day.

The hospital doesn't offer as wide an array of shifts as some, but eight-, ten-, and twelve-hour shifts are available in certain departments. Part-time positions can be found throughout the hospital.

# Berkshire Life

700 South Street
Pittsfield, MA 01202                                                413-499-4321

*Nature of business:* Life insurance.
*Number of employees:* 350
*Female employees:* 65 percent (45 percent of managers).
*Child care:* On-site center for 18 children, aged eight weeks to five years; pretax salary set-aside (DCAP).
*Elder care:* Pretax salary set-aside (DCAP).
*Family leave:* Paid disability leave for childbirth, plus up to three months unpaid personal leave; three paid days off allocated for care of ill family members.
*Flexible work options:* Flextime in most positions; some part-time work; some job sharing.
*Other benefits:* Lunchtime seminars on family issues; employee-assistance program.

Berkshire Life has created a small child-care center in what was once a caretaker's cottage at its headquarters site. In 1985, the company renovated the building, then turned the center's operation over to the local Girls Club. In all, it spent about $30,000 to get the center started, and has continued to provide maintenance, utilities, and food at no charge, and to subsidize employees' fees at a rate of $25 per week.

Lunchtime seminars here deal with elder-care issues, with managing adolescents, and with a range of other family issues. Sometimes they stray beyond those limits. The most popular to date was a lecture on groundskeeping given by the gardener who tends the plants around the company's offices.

# Beth Israel Hospital of Boston

330 Brookline Avenue
Boston, MA 02215                                                617-735-2000

*Nature of business:* Hospital.
*Number of employees:* 4,650.
*Female employees:* 70 percent (62 percent of officers and managers).
*Child care:* On-site center for 120 children, aged three

months to five years, to open in 1991; twelve spaces available at near-site consortium center; local resource-and-referral service; pretax salary set-aside (DCAP).

*Elder care:* Local consultation-and-referral service; pretax salary set-aside (DCAP).

*Family leave:* Twelve-week job-protected parental leave, with accumulated sick days, holidays, and vacation days applied for pay; longer leaves, up to a year, can be taken under special circumstances; paid time off may be used for short-term care of ill family members.

*Flexible work options:* Flexible work hours in some positions; wide variety of shift schedules; part-time work common; some job sharing; pilot work-at-home program.

*Other benefits:* Breast-feeding support program; in-house training program; lunchtime seminars on family issues.

Beth Israel Hospital may be one of the most flexible employers in the country. While many hospital managers wring their hands and say that rigidity is built into a hospital's system, Beth Israel has found ways to make all kinds of schedules work. It has part-time nurses on every shift, job sharers in almost every department, and an array of full-time shift schedules to choose from. Some people work their weeks in four ten-hour days, some in three twelve-hour days, and some in two weekend days.

Backing up that flexibility, the hospital will soon have its own child-care center, to open in the spring of 1991. To ensure a quality program at affordable rates, the hospital plans to support the center with substantial subsidies, including direct assistance to bring the rates down for lower-income employees.

"Probably at the core of our family-oriented policies," says Laura Avakian, vice president of human resources, "is our attitude that says it's okay to talk with us about family issues, about how to make it work so you can be both a parent and a good employee. We encourage people to make suggestions about how we as an institution can help them do that. And a lot of the ideas have come from the employees themselves. The alternative schedules have come from their proposals, worked out with supervisors so they fit the hospital's needs. The breast-feeding support program, which provides not only a private room with breast pumps and a refrigerator, but access to expert advice, grew from the suggestion of two employees. And the day-care center really grew out of discussions with employees."

As important as any of its family benefits is the hospital's system of worker empowerment, which has become a fundamental element of its nursing program. Nurses here are assigned primary responsibility for a set of patients during their shift, and are given broad power to make decisions about those patients' care. The result of all of the hospital's policies and systems is an unusually satisfied work force. Turnover here stood at 19 percent in 1990, the lowest in the area and well below the national average of 30 percent for hospitals.

# Blodgett Memorial Medical Center

1840 Wealthy Street
Grand Rapids, MI 49506            616-774-7444

*Nature of business:* Hospital.
*Number of employees:* 2,200.
*Female employees:* 80 percent (4 percent of managers).
*Child care:* On-site center for 120 children, aged six weeks to six years, open from 6:00 A.M. to midnight; on-site facility for care of mildly ill children.
*Elder care:* No formal program.
*Family leave:* Accrued sick time may be applied toward childbirth disability leave; unpaid parental leave negotiable; five paid days off may be used to care for ill family members.
*Flexible work options:* Variety of shift options; part-time work common.
*Other benefits:* Employee-assistance program.

Blodgett Memorial Medical Center planned its child-care center as a twenty-four-hour facility when it opened at the hospital in 1988, but by 1990, demand had not been strong enough to justify staffing the center between midnight and 6:00 A.M.. With two-shift operation, the center cares for almost 200 children. Another handful are served by the "Rainy Day" program, which cares for employees' mildly ill children.

Employees can choose between eight-, ten-, or twelve-hour shifts in different departments, or can opt for part-time assignments. The hospital extends full health and dental benefits to part-timers who work at least twenty hours each week.

# Bowles Corporation

RR 1, Box 735
N. Ferrisburg, VT 05473                    802-425-3447

*Nature of business:* Engineering, design, and fabrication.
*Number of employees:* 12.
*Female employees:* 6 (1 of 2 managers).
*Child care:* On-site center for 8 children, aged six weeks to twelve years.
*Elder care:* No formal program.
*Family leave:* Paid disability leave for childbirth, plus additional unpaid leave; paid time off may be used for short-term care of ill family members.
*Flexible work options:* Flextime standard; some part-time work.

The leave policy at Bowles Corporation is deliberately left as an undefined benefit, and how it works gives a good indication of this company's relationship to its employees. "We are very small and we are very flexible," explains Carol Bowles, co-owner of Bowles Corporation. "We're willing to work with a person to make their life easier. If that means a person needs six months off, their job will be there when they come back. We'll work it out." While owners of many small companies equate parental leave with financial ruin, Bowles feels it would ruin her business *not* to meet her workers' personal needs. Three of the company's twelve workers are on part-time schedules so that they can be home when their children come home from school, and again Bowles feels the company has made no sacrifice in allowing that flexibility. "If the work can get done, we'll work anything out," she says. "Frankly, I don't understand why companies are so set on the forty-hour week. I see it as a disadvantage. Companies could attract many good people if they'd bend their schedules a little."

Bowles Corporation also attracts and keeps workers with an on-site child-care center, a miraculous benefit for a twelve-person business to offer. The center began with two babies in a room in the office and is now based in a remodeled trailer nearby.

# The Bureau of National Affairs, Inc.

1231 25th Street, N.W.
Washington, DC 20037                  202-452-4200

*Nature of business:* Publisher of information on business and public issues, in print or electronic form, including material on work-and-family matters.
*Number of employees:* 1,450.
*Female employees:* 58 percent (45 percent of managers).
*Child care:* Resource-and-referral service in metropolitan Washington, D.C.; funding and other support for community child-care resources; pretax salary set-aside (DCAP).
*Elder care:* Pretax salary set-aside (DCAP).
*Family leave:* Accrued sick leave for childbirth, or five paid sick days for new fathers and adoptive parents, plus up to six months unpaid family leave; longer unpaid leaves negotiable; paid sick days may be used for care of sick children.
*Flexible work options:* Flexible work hours arranged individually; some part-time work; some job sharing; some work-at-home.
*Other benefits:* Adoption aid up to $1,000; employee-assistance program; lunchtime seminars on family issues, including elder care; family-resource library; one annual college scholarship for employees' children.

The Bureau of National Affairs is one of the leading sources of information on business initiatives relating to work-and-family issues, so it is fitting that the company has come up with a progressive set of policies and programs for its own workers. In 1982, the company initiated the formation of the Child Care Network, in the Metropolitan Washington Council of Governments, a public/private partnership that brings together area employers and agencies that are interested in child-care issues. In 1987, the company contracted with two local agencies to provide its employees with a child-care resource-and-referral service. BNA also contributes to efforts to recruit and train new family day-care providers.

While it has no formal policies on flexible work options, the company encourages managers to consider all reasonable requests. In one section several people work compressed four-day weeks; in another a husband and wife share a single editorial job. Several women returning from maternity leave have eased back into work with part-time schedules. Two marketing employees with young children work part of their week from terminals at home.

With its sick-leave allowance, BNA has become one of the few companies in the country to offer paid paternity and adoptive leave. All new parents are offered up to six months of unpaid leave, during which health insurance and other benefits continue.

# Leo Burnett Company, Inc.

35 W. Wacker Drive
Chicago, IL 60601                                    312-220-5959

**Nature of business:** Advertising agency.
**Number of employees:** 2,180.
**Female employees:** 55 percent (39 percent of officials and managers).
**Child care:** Resource-and-referral service; funding to increase community supply of child care; 80 percent reimbursement for care of mildly ill children; pretax salary setaside (DCAP).
**Elder care:** Consultation-and-referral service; pretax salary set-aside (DCAP).
**Family leave:** Fully paid disability leave for childbirth; additional unpaid leave negotiable; paid emergency time may be used for care of ill family members.
**Flexible work options:** Some part-time work.
**Other benefits:** Worktime seminars on family issues, including child care and elder care; fitness center; adoption aid up to $3,000; employee-assistance program; medical insurance covers well-baby care; dental insurance covers orthodontia; profit-sharing plan; on-site mammography testing for employees and spouses.

Part-time professionals at Leo Burnett get the full company benefit package, including medical and dental insurance. About fifteen worked part-time in 1990, including account executives and supervisors. The company was one of the first to add an elder-care referral service to its benefit package, and is one of the few that help out with the costs of care for mildly ill children.

Leo Burnett is the largest U.S. advertising agency based outside of New York City, and as such it offers people in advertising an alternative to the rigors of parenting in Manhattan. Burnett has a small list of blue-chip clients. With accounts like Pillsbury and Kellogg, which go back twenty-five years or more, life here tends to be more stable than at some of the more volatile agencies. Another attraction is the company's profit-sharing plan, which has consistently made a 15 percent contribution on behalf of every participant in each of the last several years. Growth can be an attraction too. Burnett's billings topped $3 billion in 1989, a threefold increase over the figure ten years before.

# Business Office Supply Co., Inc. (Bosco)

106 E. Broadway, Louisville, KY 40202
502-589-5522

*Nature of business:* Retail and contract office supplies, contract office furniture.
*Number of employees:* 100.
*Female employees:* 50 percent (50 percent of managers).
*Child care:* On-site center for 36 children, aged six weeks to five years.
*Elder care:* No formal program.
*Family leave:* Paid disability leave for childbirth; additional unpaid leave negotiable; paid time off may be used for short-term care of ill family members.
*Flexible work options:* Some part-time work.
*Other benefits:* Fully paid family medical insurance.

Stephen Zinc, owner and manager of Bosco, started thinking about child care when his first child was born in 1984. That thinking finally led to an on-site center in 1989, which is open to both employees and the public. Bosco subsidizes a portion of the weekly fee for employees, but otherwise hopes to operate the center as a break-even venture. Store and business hours are from 8:00 A.M. to 5:00 P.M.. The center stays open from 7:00 A.M. to 6:00 P.M. to accommodate any workers who need to put in extra hours at the start or end of the day.

# Byrne Electrical Specialists, Inc.

725 Byrne Industrial Drive
Rockford, MI 49341                                    616-866-3461

*Nature of business:* Manufacturer of electrical harnesses for office partitions.
*Number of employees:* 120.
*Female employees:* 95 percent (80 percent of supervisors).
*Child care:* On-site center for 130 children, aged six weeks to twelve years; pretax salary set-aside (DCAP) applied to center fees; resource-and-referral service at second site.
*Elder care:* No formal program.
*Family leave:* Paid disability leave for childbirth, plus unpaid family-crisis leave to total of ninety days (or longer, depending on individual needs).
*Flexible work options:* Some flexible work hours; some part-time work.

B yrne Electrical Specialists must be the only manufacturing company in the country to have more children in its child-care center than workers in its factory. That center grew from an idea into a 130-child facility in less than a year.

Owners Norman and Rosemary Byrne had thought for years about doing something with child care. Employees had mentioned that it would be helpful, and the couple was aware that no centers in the area took children under the age of two. But it was watching their own daughter juggle work at the company with two young children that finally moved them to action. "I worked while our children were growing up," says Rosemary Byrne. "And I saw her reliving all the frustrations that I went through." Late in 1988, a new addition to the factory freed another building that had been used as a warehouse, and the company suddenly had space to work with for child care. In January 1989, about six weeks after the decision had been made to act, the company had opened a small child-care center for business, complete with an infant room and a van to bring school-age children to and from area schools. Ten months, two renovation projects, and one addition later, the center was equipped and licensed for 130 children.

In 1990, the center was caring for forty-five children of employees, with the rest of the spaces filled by children from the community. Parent fees were set at a level to cover the center's operating expenses. Outsiders paid the full rate, while Byrne employees enjoyed a 30 percent deduction, made up for in the center's budget by company subsidies. Though the center cost the company close to $250,000 to start and expand in its first year, the Byrnes have no regrets, pointing to increased morale, lower turnover, and lower absenteeism at the business, and to the contribution they have made to their community.

## Campbell Soup Company

Campbell Place
Camden, NJ 08103                                   609-342-4800

*Nature of business:* Makes canned soups, frozen dinners, and packaged foods.
*Number of employees:* 32,300.
*Female employees:* 45 percent (18 percent of managers).
*Child care:* On-site center for 110 children, aged six weeks to six years.
*Elder care:* No formal program.
*Family leave:* Paid disability leave for childbirth, plus up to three months unpaid family-care leave; paid time off may be used for short-term care of ill family members.
*Flexible work options:* Flextime at corporate offices; some part-time work; some job sharing.
*Other benefits:* Adoption aid up to $3,000; on-site fitness center at headquarters; tuition reimbursement; employee-assistance program; lunchtime seminars on family issues.

When the Campbell Soup Child Care Center opened in 1983, it was one of a select few employer-supported child-care centers in the country. In the ensuing years, as other companies have begun to jump on the child-care bandwagon, Campbell has expanded the center and reorganized it so that it better meets its original goals. Set up at first as a facility run by Kinder Care, Inc., the center is now managed by Resources for Child Care Management, an organization that gives parents and Campbell a greater say in important decisions that affect the quality of care. The center today has lower child/teacher ratios than when it opened, and has expanded to include additional classroom space. Company subsidies keep rates at affordable levels while maintaining a high standard of care.

The company can be very flexible, too, depending on where you work. Most of the headquarters employees, for example, work some sort of flexible schedule. Part-timers who work more than twenty hours receive full benefit coverage. But flexible work options at Campbell are largely limited to the 9,000 salaried workers. Most of the company's hourly workers are unionized and subject to labor agreements and restrictions of plant operations that generally leave them out of the moves toward greater workplace flexibility. The company's three-month family-care leave, for example, is not extended to hourly workers. For salaried workers, particularly those at headquarters, the company is certainly among the most supportive and flexible in the country.

## Carlson Craft

1750 Tower Boulevard
N. Mankato, MN 56001                                  507-625-2828

*Nature of business:* Printer, specializing in personalized and commercial stationery.
*Number of employees:* 2,000.
*Female employees:* 65 percent (35 percent of managers).
*Child care:* On-site center for 170 children, aged six weeks to six years.
*Elder care:* No formal program.
*Family leave:* Accrued sick time applied toward childbirth disability leave, plus unpaid parental leave to total of three months; paid sick time may be used for care of ill family members.
*Flexible work options:* Flexible work schedules arranged individually; part-time work common.
*Other benefits:* Profit sharing; 401(k) plan with employer contribution.

Part-time work and odd schedules are a way of life at Carlson Craft. The company's president, Glenn Taylor, began working at the company as a part-timer while a student at nearby Mankato State University in 1959. Students are still a key ingredient in the labor mix at the company, as are parents, who have been attracted to the business's scheduling flexibility. People work all kinds of schedules at Carlson Craft, including ten-, nine-, eight-, five-, and four-hour days, on shifts that start at any time from 4:30 A.M. to 6:00 P.M. All workers who average at least twenty hours a week qualify for the full benefit package, which includes medical and dental coverage, profit sharing, and a 401(k) savings plan.

Since 1980, the company has backed up that flexibility with a high-quality child-care center, accredited by the National Association for the Education of Young Children, and supported by a substantial company subsidy. The idea for the center, and the initial motivation to get it started, came from an employee who was having trouble finding reliable, affordable child care. But management picked up on the concept with enthusiasm, and the company has given its full support to making the center a place where employees can bring their children with absolute confidence.

Glenn Taylor took a break from the business in the late 1980s to serve as a state senator, where he actively supported legislation to encourage more public and employer support for child care. In 1990 he returned to the helm of Carlson Craft, but maintains a strong public presence as a child-care advocate.

# Champion International

One Champion Plaza
Stamford, CT 06921                      203-358-7000

*Nature of business:* Paper and wood products.
*Number of employees:* 21,300.
*Female employees:* 19 percent (8 percent of managers).
*Child care:* Near-site center in Stamford for 60 children, aged three months to five years; on-site center planned at Libby, Montana, plywood plant; program for mildly ill children in Hamilton, Ohio; pretax salary set-aside (DCAP).
*Elder care:* Publishes an elder-care handbook with information and resources; pretax salary set-aside (DCAP).
*Family leave:* Standard childbirth disability leave, plus up to six months unpaid parental leave.
*Flexible work options:* Flextime in some positions; some job sharing.
*Other benefits:* Employee-assistance program; lunchtime seminars on family issues; tuition reimbursement; on-site fitness centers.

"Business must make child care its business," wrote Champion International's chairman and CEO, Andrew S. Sigler, in a 1990 newspaper editorial. "Child care isn't just mommy's problem, it's society's problem. First, employees with small children—mothers and fathers alike—are stretched thin trying to cope with job and family. That has to affect their work. Second, their kids are our national future. If this society doesn't care enough about all our children to help them get the best possible start in life, this country will rapidly go downhill."

Champion is starting to put that thinking into action. Its Downtown Children's Center in Stamford, opened in 1988, received NAEYC accreditation in 1990, a solid stamp of quality approval. And the company is working to create child-care support systems that meet the needs of employees at its many manufacturing sites. A child-care center in Libby, Montana, is planned to serve shift workers who have difficulty finding night care. In Hamilton, Ohio, the company is planning a program to provide care for mildly ill children, and is working with the local school system to create an after-school program. Task forces are meeting to consider child-care options at the company's Canton, North Carolina, and Pensacola, Florida, paper mills, and at its Klickitat, Washington, timber operation.

## Collins Divisions, Rockwell International

400 Collins Road, N.E.
Cedar Rapids, IA 52498                           319-395-1000

*Nature of business:* Commercial and defense electronics.
*Number of employees:* 7,800.
*Female employees:* 38 percent.
*Child care:* On-site center for 250 children, aged six weeks to nine years; income-based subsidy program at center; summer program for children to age twelve.
*Elder care:* No formal program.
*Family leave:* Paid disability leave for childbirth, plus up to six months unpaid personal leave (longer under special circumstances).
*Flexible work options:* Some part-time work; some job sharing.
*Other benefits:* Employee-assistance program; lunchtime seminars on family issues, including elder care; tuition reimbursement; recreation center.

The Collins Divisions may not offer the most flexible work environment in the country—flextime is not an option, for example, and part-timers aren't eligible for health-insurance coverage—but its huge child-care center merits a close look by working parents. When the company decided to do something about its employees' child-care needs in 1986, it didn't want to offer a Band-Aid that would benefit a few parents and leave others to make their own arrangements. So it built a center large enough to accommodate all of its employees' children; included infant care in the program, as well as after-school care and summer care for older children; and chose to support its operations, both with a direct subsidy and with a sliding fee scale that gives reduced rates to lower-income parents.

Backing up the child-care benefit is a strong employee-assistance program with counselors on staff, seminars on family topics such as elder care and parenting, and a fully equipped recreation center that is available to employees and their families.

## Corning Inc.

Corning, NY 14831        607-974-9000

*Nature of business:* Manufacturer of glass and ceramic products.

*Number of employees:* 28,000.

*Female employees:* 25 percent (14 percent of managers).

*Child care:* Nationwide resource-and-referral service; pretax salary set-aside (DCAP); company foundation supports community-based center in Corning and a local resource-and-referral agency.

*Elder care:* Pretax salary set-aside (DCAP).

*Family leave:* Paid disability leave for childbirth, plus up to twenty weeks unpaid family-care leave; part-time return with full benefits an option during leave period.

*Flexible work options:* Flexible work hours arranged individually; some part-time work; some job sharing; some work-at-home.

*Other benefits:* Adoption aid up to $2,000; lunchtime seminars on family issues; management training to increase sensitivity to gender issues.

Corning has long considered itself one of the leaders in meeting the needs of working parents. Its foundation provided funding to open a child-care center in Corning in 1980, and the initiative received a great deal of media attention. So when a 1987 study showed that female and black professionals were leaving the corporation at twice the rate of white men, the company was shocked.

Since then, Corning has revised many of its recruiting and career-development practices and put its professional and management staff through training workshops that deal with gender and race issues in the workplace. To reduce turnover among women, the company also took a series of steps aimed at reducing work-and-family conflicts. A part-time work policy was developed and the family-leave policy extended, and both were communicated as important options in the management-training workshops. The company's foundation supported the creation of a local child-care resource-and-referral agency in 1988, and in 1990 Corning contracted with Work/Family Directions to offer a nationwide child-care referral service to all of the company's employees. In 1990 Corning was looking at company support for additional child-care centers, both in Corning and at other sites, and was considering an elder-care referral service.

The tough self-examination is an ongoing process at Corning, and the corporate culture that was at least partly to blame for the loss of women and minorities in the 1980s won't change overnight. But the company has made great strides and has made the commitment to continue that progress. Bonnie Milliman is one beneficiary of the moves. When her first child was born, she left the company rather than return to her full-time job as an engineering supervisor. In 1987, with two children, she came back to a part-time position at the same level, a position made possible by the company's increased emphasis on flexibility.

## Courier-Journal

525 W. Broadway
Louisville, KY 40202                                       502-582-4011

*Nature of business:* Newspaper.
*Number of employees:* 1,230.
*Female employees:* 37 percent (30 percent of managers).
*Child care:* Near-site center for 100 children, aged six weeks to six years; income-based subsidies at center; pretax salary set-aside (DCAP).

*Elder care:* No formal program.
*Family leave:* Paid disability leave for childbirth, plus up to one year unpaid parental leave.
*Flexible work options:* Some part-time work.
*Other benefits:* Employee-assistance program.

An employee survey in the early 1980s revealed a growing need for child care at the *Courier-Journal*, and its owners, the Bingham family, responded by opening a child-care center nearby. Open since 1985, the center is housed in a building owned by the newspaper, and managed by a local United Way agency.

The *Courier-Journal* is now a Gannett publication, but the parent company has done nothing to cut back on the paper's commitment to the child-care center (and in fact has used the center as a model for the public/private partnerships of its own child-care initiatives). Though the newspaper doesn't contribute directly to the center's operating budget, it does subsidize fees of lower-income employees.

# Digital Equipment Corporation

146 Main Street
Maynard, MA 01754                                   508-493-5111

*Nature of business:* Computer manufacturer.
*Number of U.S. employees:* 75,000.
*Female employees:* 38 percent (5 percent of upper management).
*Child care:* Nationwide resource-and-referral service; funding to increase community supply of child care; pretax salary set-aside (DCAP).
*Elder care:* Pretax salary set-aside (DCAP).
*Family leave:* Paid disability leave for childbirth, plus up to eight weeks unpaid parental leave.
*Flexible work options:* Flexible hours can be worked out with individual supervisors; some part-time work; some job sharing; some work-at-home arrangements.
*Other benefits:* Adoption aid up to $2,500; employee-assistance program; tuition reimbursement; lunchtime seminars on family issues.

In late 1989, a senior management committee approved a new child-care strategy for Digital, which encourages local sites to sponsor child-care programs based on employees' needs and local business requirements. The company points to a near-site center in Reading, England, opened in 1990, as a first step in this process. As we write, sites in Burlington, Vermont; Marlborough, Massachusetts; Nashua, New Hampshire; and Bellevue, Washington, are investigating local child-care solutions. While many large companies shy away from local initiatives that may distribute benefits unevenly, Digital appears ready to take the plunge and direct its efforts toward solving local child-care problems.

The company has no formal policy toward flexible work options, but alternative work arrangements are common. As more and more employees have worked out individual arrangements with their supervisors, they have created a visible set of examples for others to point to when they make their own cases. The head-count system was changed in 1990 to register part-timers as fractional employees, a shift that makes it easier for workers to sell part-time proposals to supervisors. (Managers have an allotted number of "heads" in each area. Two half-timers now count as one worker, a policy which allows managers to hire part-timers, while keeping full labor contingents in their departments.)

Digital has also come to recognize that work-and-family issues are not solely a woman's concern. When the parental leave policy was opened to men in 1989, the company was surprised at the number of applicants. Forty fathers took leaves that first year, a high number for a company of this size. We're not sure if the fact shows that Digital has adaptable supervisors, or merely that the company has an unusual number of courageous fathers, but it brought home the point to managers here that many men want to take more responsibility for child care.

The company is reviewing possible elder-care benefits, and is looking at its sick-time policy—currently, sick days can only be used when employees themselves are ill, and not for the care of family members. As Digital starts to act on the many proposals under consideration, the company should become an even more hospitable place for working parents.

# Dominion Bankshares Corporation

213 S. Jefferson Street
Roanoke, VA 24040                                   703-563-7000

*Nature of business:* Bank holding company with offices in
Maryland, Tennessee, Virginia, and Washington, D.C.
*Number of employees:* 6,500.
*Female employees:* 78 percent (9 of 87 senior vice presidents).
*Child care:* On-site center at headquarters for 70 children, aged six weeks to five years; pretax salary set-aside
(DCAP).
*Elder care:* Pretax salary set-aside (DCAP).
*Family leave:* Paid disability leave for childbirth, plus unpaid maternity leave to total of four months; two months
unpaid adoption and paternity leave; in addition to employees' own sick time, five paid days off may be used for
care of ill family members.
*Flexible work options:* Flextime in some areas; part-time
work common, with some part-time managers.
*Other benefits:* Lunchtime seminars on family issues at
headquarters, with videos circulated to other sites.

Dominion Bankshares was the second bank in the country
to offer on-site child care when its center opened in 1986,
and the first to offer infant care. The center continues to be a
leader in terms of quality: it is accredited by the National Association for the Education of Young Children, and subsidized
by the company at a rate of $100,000 per year. The center is run
as a company department, its director reporting directly to the
human-resources group.

Despite the costs, the company looks on the center as a business asset. Before building it, the bank conducted extensive surveys and determined that the parents among its headquarters
population faced particularly acute child-care problems. A
quarter of the mothers polled said they had considered quitting
because of child-care problems. "There are no altruistic motives," explained president Warner Dalhouse in a 1987 interview.
"We do everything we do with the objective of profit." David
Furman, vice president of human resources, told us, "We see the
payoff in reduced turnover and lower recruiting costs. And we
think the morale of parents and *all* employees is better because
they think Dominion has done a good thing here."

The biggest problem with the center seems to be the waiting list, which rarely drops below fifty names. An expansion is possible, but not planned for the immediate future. In the meantime, working parents here should take comfort in the fact that this is one of the few companies that offers paid days off specifically designated for the care of ill family members.

# Donnelly Corp.

414 E. 40th Street
Holland, MI 49423                                      616-394-2796

*Nature of business:* Manufacturer of automobile mirror, lighting, and window systems; and specialty coatings on glass.
*Number of employees:* 1,800.
*Female employees:* 49 percent (18.5 percent of managers).
*Child care:* Resource-and-referral service; emergency care using network of family day-care homes; pretax salary set-aside (DCAP).
*Elder care:* Pretax salary set-aside (DCAP).
*Family leave:* Paid disability leave for childbirth, plus unpaid family leave to total of three months.
*Flexible work options:* Job sharing in both factory and office jobs.
*Other benefits:* Lunchtime seminars on family issues.

Donnelly Corp. has taken some steps toward greater flexibility for those with family responsibilities. It offers job sharing in both office and production jobs. It offers up to three months of family leave, with benefits, to mothers, fathers, and adoptive parents. But the company's real work-family benefit innovations have come in child care. Donnelly and other area businesses have been able to offer employees a child-care resource-and-referral service since the early 1980s, thanks to the organizational efforts of the nonprofit Community Coordinated Child Care agency. In 1989, Donnelly expanded that support by creating an emergency child-care program, drawing on that agency's network of family day-care homes. The company agreed to purchase spaces in several homes, to be kept open until employees at either company needed them for emergency care when normal arrangements fell through. After six months as a pilot program, Donnelly invited another local business, Haworth, Inc., to join in the venture, and turned its administration over to the child-care agency. It now offers the emergency-care system as a regular benefit, and continues to reserve five spaces in two homes for its employees' emergency use.

# The Dow Chemical Company

Willard H. Dow Center,
Midland, MI 48674                                    517-636-1000

*Nature of business:* Chemicals, plastics, pharmaceuticals, and consumer products.
*Number of employees:* 30,364.
*Female employees:* 25 percent (11 percent of officials and managers).
*Child care:* Resource-and-referral service in Midland, Michigan; Houston, Texas; Licking County, Ohio; and at more than twenty sales-office sites; support for community-based child-care center in Plaquemine, Louisiana, and for before- and after-school programs in Midland, Michigan, and Lake Jackson, Texas; pilot sick-child-care program in Lake Jackson, Texas; pretax salary set-aside (DCAP).
*Elder care:* Pretax salary set-aside (DCAP); elder care-giver fairs and seminars.
*Family leave:* Fully paid disability leave for childbirth, plus up to twelve weeks unpaid parental or family-illness leave.
*Flexible work options:* Flextime with half-hour window at some sites; some part-time work; some job sharing.
*Other benefits:* Work-time seminars on family issues at some locations; employee-assistance program; dual-career assistance program; spouse relocation assistance.

Dow continues to chip away at the issue of work-and-family conflict, trying out a range of options at scattered locations. Its child-care resource-and-referral service, offered only to Midland employees at first, is now available in Houston; in Licking County, Ohio; and at the company's sales offices. Dow's support for child-care programs in Michigan, Louisiana, and Texas have proven to be successful, and the company is considering ways to extend that support to other locations. Flexible work options at Dow are more limited than at some companies—fewer than 500 employees worked part-time in 1990, for example—and the company is looking at ways to expand those programs. The low percentage of female workers here may be a sign that the company is starting with a handicap in its corporate culture; the hiring of a national family-issues coordinator, the establishment of family-issues contacts in all major divisions, and the scattered support programs already in place suggest that Dow is moving in the right direction.

# Du Pont

1007 Market Street
Wilmington, DE 19898                                        302-774-1000

*Nature of business:* Chemicals and energy.
*Number of employees:* 105,000.
*Female employees:* 24 percent (8 percent of managers).
*Child care:* Nationwide resource-and-referral service; substantial support for community-based resources; pretax salary set-aside (DCAP).
*Elder care:* Nationwide consultation-and-referral service; pretax salary set-aside (DCAP).
*Family leave:* Fully paid disability leave for childbirth, plus up to six months unpaid family-care leave; part-time phase-in an option during leave period.
*Flexible work options:* Flexible work hours in many departments, pilot compressed-work-week program. Some part-time work, limited job sharing; pilot work-at-home program.
*Other benefits:* Lunchtime seminars on family issues at many sites; training to sensitize managers to family issues; cultural-diversity and sexual-harassment workshops for all employees; free medical checkups; discounted wellness workshops and fitness programs; on-site fitness centers at some sites; tuition reimbursement; 401(k) plan with employer contribution.

Du Pont has a tradition of offering excellent employee benefits, and has long been considered one of the premier employers in the country. It established a pension plan in 1904, added paid vacations to the benefit package in 1934, company-paid health insurance in 1936, and a disability-pay plan in 1937. The company's disability policy remains one of the best in American business: it offers full pay from the first day of absence, and continues for up to six months. The company is now working energetically to bring its family-care benefits and policies into line with that tradition of leadership.

A 1984 survey showed that 70 percent of Du Pont's workers with young children used some form of child care outside the home—a figure that translated into 25 percent of the entire work force. Those numbers showed managers that child care was a mainstream issue, one affecting huge numbers of employees, and the company responded with some dramatic measures. It worked to start a statewide resource-and-referral service in Delaware, home to a quarter of its employees. In 1986 and 1987 it pumped nearly $2 million into initiatives to increase the supply of care in the area. It also worked to involve the government and other employers in the same effort.

Since 1988, the company has broadened its scope to include national initiatives and a wider range of work-and-family issues. It lengthened its leave policy to six months and opened it to fathers, adoptive parents, and employees with adult-care responsibilities. It helped to create a sick-child-care program in Wilmington, and has started to act on local child-care initiatives in other parts of the country. In 1990, it launched nationwide resource-and-referral services for both child care and elder care. It is now looking seriously at ways to offer greater flexibility, not just for professionals, but for the production and shift workers who often are left out of the formula.

Du Pont is also working to change its corporate culture, to convince managers that flexibility and family-support systems are important to the long-term health of the business. A 1988 survey showed that 70 percent of employees with children are members of dual-career families, and that 25 percent of its male employees and 50 percent of its female employees have considered leaving Du Pont for a company that might offer more job flexibility. The numbers are probably consistent with those at other large companies, but Du Pont took the unusual step of releasing them to the media. The company felt that it had news about the stresses employees—particularly men—were feeling from work-and-family conflicts, and wanted to share that information with others. The effect was a storm of publicity that caught the attention of the company's own managers in a way that no internal publication could have. The company has now started a program of management training on family issues, in order to ensure that the company's policies reach the employees for whom they were intended.

Look for continued action from Du Pont on local child-care initiatives around the country, moves toward increased flexibility and alternative career paths, and continued efforts to re-shape a traditionally conservative corporate culture.

# Eastman Kodak Co.

343 State Street
Rochester, NY 14650                                716-724-4000

*Nature of business:* Manufacturer of photographic products.
*Number of employees:* 73,275.
*Female employees:* 25 percent (9.5 percent of managers).
*Child care:* Nationwide resource-and-referral service; pilot summer camp program in Rochester, New York; pretax salary set-aside (DCAP).
*Elder care:* Pretax salary set-aside (DCAP).
*Family leave:* Fully paid disability leave for childbirth, plus up to seventeen weeks unpaid family leave (for birth, adoption, or placement of foster child, or for care of seriously ill family members).
*Flexible work options:* Flexible work hours arranged individually; some part-time work; some job sharing.
*Other benefits:* Summer jobs for college-enrolled children of employees; adoption aid up to $2,000; employee-assistance program; spouse-relocation assistance; lunchtime seminars on family issues; on-site fitness centers; stock-ownership plan; profit sharing.

Eastman Kodak has a hands-off policy when it comes to many of its family-care policies, leaving much to the discretion of individual managers. It doesn't monitor the use of flexible-work options, for example, but lets managers know that flexible schedules and part-time work are in keeping with the company's business goals. Regular articles in the company newspaper citing successful alternative work arrangements help bring the point home. The up side of that approach is that understanding managers are free to make flexible arrangements with individual workers.

Eastman Kodak's child-care referral service has been a big help to parents—almost 2,500 called during its first two years of operation, and it helped place over 3,000 children in care. Through the service the company has also made strides in increasing the supply of child care in its key employment communities, recruiting and training more than 700 family day-care providers between 1988 and 1990. The company also ran a pilot summer camp in Rochester, New York, for four weeks during the summer of 1990. As we went to press, it was considering expanding the program's length for 1991, and increasing the number of on-site drop-off and pickup points.

## Edmar Corporation

P.O. Box 149
Bound Brook, NJ 08805                              201-560-9222

**Nature of business:** Owns and manages industrial property.
**Number of employees:** 20.
**Female employees:** 15 (50 percent of officers and managers).
**Child care:** Subsidy program pays two-thirds of child-care costs.
**Elder care:** No formal program.
**Family leave:** Paid disability leave for childbirth; additional unpaid leave negotiable; paid time off for care of ill family members.
**Flexible work options:** Flexible work hours arranged individually; 5 of 20 employees work part-time.
**Other benefits:** Tuition reimbursement; employee-assistance program.

Marguerite Chandler was a single mother with two young children when she took over her father's business in 1979, so it has been easy for her to identify with the concerns of working parents at the company, and to see flexibility and child-care assistance as important business issues. Time off for the care of sick children has always been a given here, and people work out leave arrangements on an individual basis. "I think it's just good business," says Chandler. "When you spend as much money as any business does to find the right people, train them, and integrate them into the work force, then it's just crazy to let them walk out the door. And it builds long-term loyalty with people when you treat them decently, with dignity, and with respect for the fact that they do have lives outside of work."

An informal policy of helping out with child care has grown into what is perhaps the company's most dramatic family benefit. Since 1988, Edmar has paid two-thirds of its employees' child-care expenses. In 1990, four employees used the program to help defray the costs of after-school care for their children.

# First Atlanta

2 Peachtree Street
Atlanta, GA 30383                                          404-332-5000

**Nature of business:** Banking.
**Number of employees:** 4,900.
**Female employees:** 73 percent.
**Child care:** On-site center at headquarters for 30 children, aged six weeks to six years; membership in nearby consortium center with twenty additional spaces; resource-and-referral service; pretax salary set-aside (DCAP).
**Elder care:** Pretax salary set-aside (DCAP).
**Family leave:** Paid disability leave for childbirth, plus up to three months unpaid maternity leave; ten paid sick days per year may be used to care for ill family members.
**Flexible work options:** Flexible schedules worked out individually; part-time work common in many departments; some job sharing.
**Other benefits:** Lunchtime seminars on family issues; employee-assistance program; 401(k) plan with employer contribution; stock-purchase program; wellness program.

First Atlanta became the first bank in the country to open an on-site child-care center in 1983, and the facility is still going strong. The center is managed by Corporate Child Care Consultants, its budget subsidized by the bank in order to give employees quality care at competitive rates.

When it became clear that the thirty-child center couldn't fill all of its employees' child-care needs, the bank joined with Rich's Department Store (see separate entry) and several other Atlanta employers to create the Downtown Child Development Center. The bank no longer subsidizes the consortium center, but its employees still have priority access to twenty spaces there, and the center continues to operate as a model program. Its low teacher-child ratios and child-responsive curriculum helped it earn accreditation from the National Association for the Education of Young Children.

The bank claims that women have begun entering its upper ranks (though it wouldn't disclose any details to us), and parents seem to have plenty of flexibility on the way up. Part-time work is easy to come by here at the lower levels, and a growing number of professionals are taking advantage of the option. Among the job sharers in 1990 were a pair of attorneys.

# First Hawaiian, Inc.

P.O. Box 3200
Honolulu, HI 96847                    808-525-8765

*Nature of business:* Banking and financial services.
*Number of employees:* 2,300.
*Female employees:* 70 percent (37 percent of officers).
*Child care:* Resource-and-referral service; subsidy program;
fully paid care for mildly ill children; pretax salary set-aside
(DCAP).
*Elder care:* Subsidy program; pretax salary set-aside (DCAP).
*Family leave:* Fully paid disability leave for childbirth, plus
up to six months unpaid parental leave.
*Flexible work options:* Part-time work common.
*Other benefits:* Lunchtime seminars on family health is-
sues.


Low unemployment rates in Hawaii have driven a number
of the state's employers to look at ways of attracting and
keeping women workers. As part of its effort, First Hawaiian
surveyed its employees on their child-care needs and discovered
that two of the most pressing issues were affordability of day
care and the lack of care for sick children. The company has
since tried to answer both needs. Its subsidy program pays half
of employees' dependent care costs, up to a maximum of $200
per month, and it pays the whole bill for parents who bring
mildly ill children to a facility at a nearby hospital.

The disability policy at First Hawaiian pays mothers on maternity leave their full salary from the first day they are out.
When the disability period ends, they have the option of going
on unpaid leave, but must pay their own premiums in order to
continue health-insurance coverage.

# Fleetguard, Inc.

311 N. Park
Lake Mills, IA 50450                                   515-592-1300

*Nature of business:* Manufacturer of filters for medium to
heavy-duty engines.
*Number of employees:* 1,800.
*Female employees:* 60 percent (41 percent of supervisors
and managers).
*Child care:* Near-site center for 110 children, aged six weeks
to twelve years; summer program for school-age children.
*Elder care:* No formal program.
*Family leave:* Paid disability leave for childbirth, plus up to
one year unpaid family leave (also available for care of sick
children, spouses, or parents).
*Flexible work options:* No flextime; no part-time work.
*Other benefits:* Fitness center.

Fleetguard's was the only company-sponsored child-care
center in Iowa when it opened in 1984. From the six
children enrolled at the start, the center has grown into a widely
used benefit for the 600 workers at the site. More than 100
children are now enrolled, from infants and toddlers to school-
age children who participate in the before- and after-school and
summer programs. Rates are reasonable—$63 per week for infant
care, and about a dollar an hour for after-school care—in part
because the company provides the space at a minimal charge to
the nonprofit group that runs the program.

The company offers generous unpaid leaves, but has yet to
deal with the need for flexible work options. As of 1990, Fleetguard did not offer part-time or flexible work schedules.

# Fox, Rothschild, O'Brien & Frankel

2000 Market Street, 10th Floor
Philadelphia, PA 19103                                 215-299-2000

*Nature of business:* Law firm.
*Number of employees:* 320.
*Female employees:* 63 percent (50 percent of associates,
8 percent of partners).

*Child care:* Resource-and-referral service; pretax salary set-aside (DCAP).
*Elder care:* Consultation-and-referral service; pretax salary set-aside (DCAP).
*Family leave:* Eight weeks paid maternity leave for associates, ten weeks paid maternity leave for partners, plus up to six weeks unpaid parental leave for attorneys; up to three months unpaid maternity leave for staff; extensions granted in special circumstances.
*Flexible work options:* Flextime and part-time work for both attorneys and staff; limited staff job sharing; some work-at-home for attorneys.
*Other benefits:* Lunchtime seminars on family issues.

Fox, Rothschild, O'Brien & Frankel is one of Philadelphia's prestigious law firms, dating back to 1907. In the past decade it has also become one of the outstanding law firms to work at for people with family responsibilities. The firm is one of a handful that offer both child-care and elder-care referral services, and one of the few that extend family policies relatively evenly to attorneys and support staff. The flextime hours are specifically aimed at support staff, so that staff members have adequate time for both office and home responsibilities. Schedules are arranged around core hours between 10:00 A.M. and 4:00 P.M.; workers divide the hours at the beginning and end of the day so that the office is always staffed at an adequate level. Attorneys as well as staff work part-time schedules here, among them one partner.

# G. T. Water Products

5239 N. Commerce Avenue
Moorpark, CA 93201                                      805-529-2900

*Nature of business:* Manufacturer of drain-cleaning devices.
*Number of employees:* 32.
*Female employees:* 17 (3 of 4 top-level managers).
*Child care:* On-site one-room school for 10 children, grades K through 12; plans for on-site child-care for younger children.
*Elder care:* No formal program.
*Family leave:* Paid disability leave for childbirth, plus un-

paid leave to total of six months; sick days may be used to care for ill family members.
***Flexible work options:*** Flextime for all employees; some part-time work; job-sharing possible.
***Other benefits:*** Adoption aid up to $1,500; $500 gift to expectant mothers.

G. T. Water Products' thirty-two employees boast a total of thirty children, two of them the offspring of founder George Tash. Clearly, this is one company where working parents are in the mainstream.

Ten of those children attend the company's on-site primary school, started in 1987 when Tash hired a teacher to instruct his own children at the office. Unlike the employer-supported schools in Dade County, Florida, and those planned in New York City, this one receives no financial support from the local school department. The school is licensed by the state, and G. T. Water Products pays the teacher's salary and buys all of the equipment and supplies. The school's hours match those of the workers, with a before- and after-school program that gives the children a break from the nine-to-three routine. Students are free to go into the offices to see their parents, and children are frequently seen around the desks at lunch.

# Gannett

P.O. Box 7858
Washington, DC 20044                    703-284-6000

***Nature of business:*** Newspapers and broadcasting.
***Number of employees:*** 37,000.
***Female employees:*** 40 percent (32 percent of managers).
***Child care:*** Resource-and-referral service in metropolitan Washington, D.C.; pretax salary set-aside (DCAP); Gannett Foundation supports community-based initiatives.
***Elder care:*** Pretax salary set-aside (DCAP).
***Family leave:*** Paid disability leave for childbirth, plus up to one year unpaid personal leave.
***Flexible work options:*** Flextime; some part-time work; some job sharing; work-at-home possible on temporary basis.
***Other benefits:*** Lunchtime seminars on family issues;

family-resource library; adoption aid up to $2,500; 401(k) plan with employer contribution; employee-assistance program; wellness program.

Gannett owns eighty-three daily newspapers around the country (including *USA Today*), along with fifty-two nondaily papers, ten television stations, and sixteen radio stations. With workers in so many different organizations, not all of the company's family benefits and policies are available to all workers. The child-care resource-and-referral service, for example, serves the corporate staff based in Rosslyn, Virginia— 2,000 out of the company's 37,000 employees. In another local initiative, Gannett has worked with a developer to help create a child-care center in an office park near its headquarters site. The company's foundation has provided funding to help recruit family day-care providers in metropolitan Washington, D.C., and to start a community child-care center in Reston, Virginia.

While most of the corporate effort is directed at headquarters staff, some Gannett-owned companies have topped the parent corporation with their efforts, and the company encourages independent action on work-family issues. The *Courier-Journal*, for example, a Louisville, Kentucky, newspaper, opened its own near-site child-care center in 1985.

# Genentech, Inc.

460 Point San Bruno Boulevard
S. San Francisco, CA 94080          415-266-1000

*Nature of business:* Biotechnology.
*Number of employees:* 1,830.
*Female employees:* 43 percent.
*Child care:* Near-site center for 258 children, aged six weeks to six years; resource-and-referral service; pretax salary setaside (DCAP).
*Elder care:* Pretax salary set-aside (DCAP).
*Family leave:* Paid disability leave for childbirth, plus up to six months unpaid parental leave.
*Flexible work options:* Flextime; some part-time work; some job sharing.
*Other benefits:* Six-week paid sabbatical after six years;

stock options available to all employees (95 percent of workers are stockholders); gift of one share of stock to each new baby.

Some companies test the child-care waters with small pilot programs. When Genentech's surveys indicated that employees needed help with child care, the company plunged in with a 20,000-square-foot, thirteen-room center at a cost of nearly $500,000. It expects to continue to subsidize the center at a rate of $500,000 per year in order to achieve quality care at reasonable cost to its employees. Since the surveys showed a particular need for infant and toddler care, ninety spaces at the center are reserved for children under two. The polls also showed a critical need for affordable care among lower-paid and single workers, and the company has responded with tuition subsidies, picking up half of the center's fees for those whose annual family income falls below $30,000. "Investing in a corporate day-care center is well worth the return in greater employee peace of mind and productivity," says G. Kirk Raab, Genentech's president and chief operating officer. Buffer Fennie, whose son Willie attends the center, told a *USA Today* reporter, "I don't know how you can put a price on that peace of mind. Science takes a lot of concentration, and I have it now."

# Georgia Baptist Medical Center

300 Boulevard, N.E.
Atlanta, GA 30312                    404-653-4000

**Nature of business:** Hospital.
**Number of employees:** 2,500.
**Female employees:** 70 percent.
**Child care:** On-site center for 150 children, aged six weeks to six years.
**Elder care:** No formal program.
**Family leave:** Paid disability leave for childbirth, plus up to four weeks unpaid parental leave; paid time off may be used to care for ill family members, up to five occurrences.
**Flexible work options:** Variety of shift options; some part-time work.
**Other benefits:** On-site fitness center; employee-assistance program.

Georgia Baptist Medical Center has demonstrated as strong a commitment to employer-supported child care as any hospital in the country. It opened its on-site center in 1952—becoming one of just twenty-seven hospitals in the country to offer on-site child care that year—and it has expanded the center and improved its quality over the decades since. The hospital currently subsidizes approximately 40 percent of the center's budget in order to translate the true weekly costs of about $135 per child into affordable parent fees of under $70.

The hospital prides itself on the quality of the center, and to keep good teachers pays salaries that are well above the community norm. Before a recent expansion brought in a batch of new teachers, the average length of employment at the center was seven years. Two teachers have been there for more than twenty years.

# Green's Stationery

308 Washington Street
Wellesley, MA 02181                          617-237-9301

*Nature of business:* Stationery store.
*Number of employees:* 18.
*Female employees:* 13 (3 of 5 managers).
*Child care:* Subsidy program.
*Elder care:* No formal program.
*Family leave:* Unpaid leave negotiable.
*Flexible work options:* Several flexible and part-time schedules in place.
*Other benefits:* Profit-sharing plan.

Debra Green, who manages her family's stationery store, came up with the idea of child-care subsidies when a single woman who worked at the store became pregnant. Green wanted the employee to come back after her maternity leave, and offered the subsidy as both an inducement and as a way to make work economically feasible for the new mother. Since then several other employees have taken advantage of the program, which pays up to $60 per week for preschool child care. In 1990, two fathers and one mother were receiving subsidy payments.

Green has also tried to meet the varied scheduling needs of

her employees. She has arranged part-time schedules that allowed parents to be home at the end of the school day. Several mothers worked out schedules that allowed them to stay home during school vacations and over the summer; as their children have grown up, all have since come back to regular full-time schedules.

# Group 243 Incorporated

1410 Woodridge Avenue
Ann Arbor, MI 48105                                313-761-3354

**Nature of business:** Advertising agency.
**Number of employees:** 106.
**Female employees:** 73 percent (15 of 25 managers).
**Child care:** On-site center for 50 children, aged two weeks to five years; pretax salary set-aside (DCAP).
**Elder care:** Pretax salary set-aside (DCAP).
**Family leave:** Paid disability leave for childbirth, additional unpaid leave negotiable.
**Flexible work options:** Flexible hours arranged individually; only part-time work is in cafeteria and child-care center.
**Other benefits:** Fitness center; lunchtime seminars on family issues.

Group 243's largest client is Domino's Pizza, also headquartered in Ann Arbor, and it is that company's fitness center that is open to the agency's employees. The child-care center, however, is Group 243's own. When president Janet Muhleman became pregnant with her first child and noticed that two other executives were also expecting, she decided that it was time to do something about child care. The center opened in 1983 as a department of the advertising agency, and the company continues to support it with a sizable subsidy in order to keep the quality high. Teacher-child ratios for infants here are kept at one teacher for three infants, and similarly high standards are followed for other age groups.

# HBO

1100 Avenue of the Americas
New York, NY 10036                                    212-512-1000

*Nature of business:* Cable television, entertainment.
*Number of employees:* 1,728.
*Female employees:* 58 percent (48 percent of officials and managers).
*Child care:* Resource-and-referral service in New York and Los Angeles; emergency child-care program in New York; member of consortium center in Los Angeles; pretax salary set-aside (DCAP).
*Elder care:* Nationwide consultation-and-referral service; pretax salary set-aside (DCAP).
*Family leave:* Fully paid disability leave for childbirth, one week paid paternity and adoption leave, plus up to twelve weeks unpaid parental leave with same-job guarantee; paid time off for care of ill family members at manager's discretion.
*Flexible work options:* Flexible work hours arranged individually; part-time work for returning mothers; some job sharing; limited work-at-home.
*Other benefits:* Lunchtime seminars on family issues; elder-care and parent-support groups; family-resource library.

Several of the Time Warner companies offer progressive family policies, but two stand out: HBO and Time Inc. Magazine Company (see separate description). HBO has offered a child-care resource-and-referral service to its New York employees since 1983, and was among the businesses that joined together in that city to create the Emergency Child Care Service. The emergency service sends providers to employees' homes when their normal child-care arrangements break down or when their children are mildly ill. HBO pays the full bill when employees use the service, and has found it even more useful than anticipated—one worker was able to use the service for an elder-care emergency soon after the program's launch. The company is also one of a select handful that offers paid paternity and adoption leave.

Parents coming back from leave have been able to work out a wide range of schedules at HBO, including combinations of part-time work and work from home. Most phase in to full-time work over a period of months, but some keep the flexible hours indefinitely.

# Hallmark Cards

P.O. Box 419580
Kansas City, MO 64141                          816-274-5111

*Nature of business:* Greeting cards.
*Number of employees:* 16,800.
*Female employees:* 53 percent (22 percent of upper management).
*Child care:* Resource-and-referral service in metropolitan Kansas City; funding to increase community supply of child care; pretax salary set-aside (DCAP).
*Elder care:* Consultation-and-referral service through Kansas City agency; pretax salary set-aside (DCAP).
*Family leave:* Accrued illness pay for childbirth, plus unpaid parental leave to total of six months.
*Flexible work options:* Flexible work hours arranged individually; limited part-time opportunity for professional employees; close to 8,000 free-lance and hourly part-timers; limited job sharing.
*Other benefits:* Adoption aid up to $3,000; family-resource center; employee-assistance program.

Flexible work options at Hallmark are to be found mainly among the ranks of the free-lancers (who are paid by the job) and "on call" workers (who are paid by the hour). Fewer than 100 professional employees work part-time, and while they retain membership in the company's profit-sharing plan, they sacrifice their medical and dental insurance coverage. Free-lancers work on a per project basis, and can arrange whatever schedules they please, so long as the work gets done. Almost 7,000 work on a part-time basis. Another 850 on-call (or hourly) employees work less than full-time schedules.

The company is looking at expanding its job-sharing program. In 1990, about thirty employees worked as job sharers. When children are sick at Hallmark, parents must either use vacation time (two weeks per year for the first five years of service) or take unpaid family-leave time.

# John Hancock Mutual Life Insurance Co.

John Hancock Place, P.O. Box 111
Boston, MA 02117                                617-572-6000

**Nature of business:** Insurance and financial services.
**Number of employees:** 18,000.
**Female employees:** 62 percent (20 percent of senior officers).
**Child care:** Near-site child-care center for 200 children, aged eight weeks to five years (may be expanded to include kindergarten); programs for school-age children during certain school holidays and vacations; statewide resource-and-referral service; pretax salary set-aside (DCAP).
**Elder care:** Local consultation-and-referral service; pretax salary set-aside (DCAP).
**Family leave:** Paid disability leave for childbirth, plus up to one year unpaid leave (with same-job guarantee for first six months); three sick days may be used for care of ill family members.
**Flexible work options:** Flextime common; some part-time work; some work-at-home.
**Other benefits:** Reimbursement for family-care expenses incurred during travel not ordinarily part of employees' jobs; adoption aid up to $2,000; management training to increase sensitivity to family issues; employee-assistance program.

John Hancock won attention with its "Real life, real answers" advertising campaign, and the company invoked the slogan when it launched a new family-care benefits package in 1990, which included construction of the largest corporate child-care facility in downtown Boston. "The John Hancock is real life, real answers to its customers," says David D'Alessandro, president of the Corporate Sector at John Hancock. "If our employees have real family-care issues, it is important for us to recognize these needs and provide some real answers."

In one year, the company swept through its family benefits package, extending the leave to a year (with company-subsidized benefit coverage for the duration), allowing personal sick days for family illness, stretching the limits of an already flexible workday to allow a three-and-one-half-hour window at the beginning and end of the workday, and launching an activity program for school-age children during certain school vacations and holidays.

To create the child-care center, Hancock hired Resources for Child Care Management, of Berkeley Heights, New Jersey, as outside consultants (the organization that manages the centers for Campbell Soup and Johnson & Johnson), but retained full control over the planning stages. The John Hancock center opened in the fall of 1990, and is owned and run by Hancock.

# Hanna Andersson

1010 N.W. Flanders
Portland, OR 97209                                        503-242-0920

*Nature of business:* Mail-order and retail children's clothing.
*Number of employees:* 208.
*Female employees:* 75 percent (90 percent of managers).
*Child care:* Subsidy program.
*Elder care:* No formal program.
*Family leave:* Paid parental leave (two weeks with one year of service, four weeks with three years), plus unpaid personal leave (paid benefits continue for twelve weeks).
*Flexible work options:* Flexible work hours in many departments; part-time work common.
*Other benefits:* Company-paid parking or bus pass; on-site fitness equipment; 401(k) plan with employer contribution; employee-assistance program planned for 1991; wellness program planned for 1991.

When Karen Johnson thought about breaking the news at work that she was pregnant, she recalled the tense negotiating sessions over leaves that she had heard about at other companies she had worked for. But Hanna Andersson, her employer, is not an ordinary company, and Gund Denhart, founder and president of the company, is no ordinary boss. Denhart congratulated Johnson enthusiastically when she heard the news and recommended from a mother's point of view that she consider a six-month leave.

Hanna Andersson has no formal policy about the length of leaves allowed (though it adheres to Oregon law, which requires that it allow at least twelve weeks), and that looseness lets people work out arrangements to suit their needs. The average leave here is three months, but people occasionally stay out for six. The company is not only extraordinarily flexible about leaves, it is unusually fair. The first two to four weeks of the leave are paid, and that policy applies not only to new mothers, but to fathers and adoptive parents as well.

When parents come back to work the company pays half of their child-care expenses, and in 1991 it may add a child-care referral service to the benefit package. Those who want to work unusual hours to spend more time with their children will find plenty of opportunity here. The company's controller works a four-day week, the design director has arranged a thirty-hour schedule, and the customer-service department has a medley of part-time schedules, including people who work a 5:00 to 8:00 A.M. shift to field early calls from the East Coast. Even the warehouse is flexible by most standards: workers can choose from four starting times between 6:00 and 9:30 A.M., part-time schedules can be had on weekend shifts.

# Heart of the Valley Center

2700 N.W. Harrison
Corvallis, OR 97330                                  503-757-1763

*Nature of business:* Nursing home and residential-care facility.
*Number of employees:* 158
*Female employees:* 92 percent (81 percent of managers).
*Child care:* On-site center for 33 children, aged six weeks to six years.
*Elder care:* On-site adult day-care facility planned.
*Family leave:* Up to six months unpaid family-care leave; paid sick days may be used for care of ill family members.
*Flexible work options:* Flextime in some positions; some job sharing.
*Other benefits:* Nursing-school scholarship program.

Heart of the Valley center not only offers convenient on-site child care for its employees but pays for the care on an increasing scale linked to the child's tenure in the center. When employees first enroll their children in the center, the company pays half of the weekly fee. Then, for every year the child is enrolled in the program, the company picks up an additional 10 percent of the bill, so five-year-olds who began in the center as infants are entitled to free care.

Dennis Russell opened the center in 1987 as part of an effort to ease staffing problems at his nursing home. At around the same time, he established a nursing-school scholarship program that grants full tuition to employees who have been at the company for four years—with no requirement that they come back after their training. Turnover has dropped dramatically in the years since, and he finds that better candidates are applying for jobs. Three employees have taken advantage of the nursing scholarship program by 1990, and the first nurse who graduated came back to work at Heart of the Valley that year.

# Hechinger

3500 Pennsy Drive
Landover, MD 20785                    301-341-1000

*Nature of business:* Building-supply stores.
*Number of employees:* 15,000
*Female employees:* 47 percent (27 percent of officers).
*Child care:* Nationwide resource-and-referral service.
*Elder care:* No formal program.
*Family leave:* Up to one year unpaid family-care leave, with accumulated sick time applied to childbirth disability period; paid sick time may be used for care of ill family members.
*Flexible work options:* Flextime with two-hour window in most ofice jobs; part-time work common; some job sharing; some work-at-home.
*Other benefits:* Employee-assistance program; stock-purchase plan; profit-sharing plan; tuition reimbursement; thrift and savings plan with 50 percent employer match; scholarship programs; wellness programs; extra days off with pay for childbirth and employees' birthdays.

Hechinger bills itself as "the world's most unusual lumberyard," and it matches its innovative retailing style with an outstanding benefit package. It was the first retailer to offer a nationwide resource-and-referral service for child care. Its health-insurance program, which requires a small employee contribution ($5 per month for individual coverage, $30 for families in 1990), includes orthodonture and 100 percent hospitalization coverage. While it doesn't offer disability insurance that would provide salary replacement for childbirth, its paid-time-off policy offers the same benefit for people who stick with their jobs. Sick days begin to accumulate at the rate of ten days per year when an employee is first hired, then the rate accelerates: to twelve days after two years, twenty after ten years, forty per year after twenty years. All of that sick time may be used for the care of family members, and it can be supplemented by vacation time, which also accumulates from year to year.

Matching the benefits as an attraction here are the opportunities for advancement. Hechinger's sales doubled between 1985 and 1990 as the company added new stores to its chain. In 1990 it owned and operated eighty-seven building-supply stores in eleven states.

# Hemmings Motor News

P.O. Box 256
Bennington, VT 05201                                802-442-3101

*Nature of business:* Magazine publisher.
*Number of employees:* 75.
*Female employees:* 80 percent (60 percent of managers).
*Child care:* Subsidy program (DCAP); in-house referral service.
*Elder care:* Subsidy program (DCAP).
*Family leave:* Six-week parental leave at two-thirds pay (supplemented by disability insurance), plus unpaid leave to total of six months; six-month part-time phase-in period for parents returning from leave; eight paid sick days may be used for care of ill family members; formal policy for family leave of longer periods planned; paid time off for involvement in children's schools.
*Flexible work options:* Part-time work common; limited work-at-home.
*Other benefits:* Seminars on family issues at nearby church hall; tuition reimbursement; reimbursement for health and fitness activities; paid time off to vote or give blood; employee designated charitable donations of $250 annually per employee; fully paid health and dental plans; five free bushels of "pick your own" apples.

A publisher of magazines for automobile enthusiasts would seem an unlikely candidate for innovative work-and-family benefits, but Hemmings Motor News is a surprising company. New mothers *and* fathers here can take up to six weeks off at two-thirds pay to care for their babies, and all parents are eligible for up to $350 each month in tax-free dependent-care subsidies (up to a cap of $3,000 per year). Those policies alone would put the publisher on our list, but the company also offers part-time work with full benefits. A few part-timers are truly that; they work reduced schedules every week. But more than twenty workers here are on cyclical schedules that give them full-time work for the first two weeks of every month, then two weeks off. Such schedules don't mesh with those of the average child-care provider, and the company helps guide workers to child-care that accepts on-again off-again charges.

Hemmings Motor News is also one of the few American companies with a policy allowing employees paid time off for involvement in their children's schools. Studies have shown that parent involvement is a key determinant of school quality, and the owners here feel a responsibility to contribute to the community in this way. The business also allows employees paid time off to vote or give blood.

# Hewitt Associates

100 Half Day Road
Lincolnshire, IL 60069                                708-295-5000

*Nature of business:* Corporate benefits and compensation consultant.
*Number of employees:* 3,450 (worldwide).
*Female employees:* 60 percent (40 percent of managers).
*Child care:* Internally managed resource-and-referral service; support for community child-care initiatives, including community-based child-care centers; reimbursement for care for mildly ill children (up to five days per year); reimbursement for overnight child-care expenses related to out-of-town travel; pretax salary set-aside (DCAP).
*Elder care:* Internally managed consultation-and-referral service; reimbursement for care of ill dependents (up to five days per year); reimbursement for overnight elder-care expenses related to out-of-town travel; pretax salary set-aside (DCAP).
*Family leave:* Paid disability leave for childbirth, plus up to

two years unpaid parental leave; six paid days off may be used for personal and family needs; up to three additional personal/family days may be purchased.

**Flexible work options:** Limited flextime and part-time work.

**Other benefits:** Family-resource consultant and library at each regional employment site; mothers' rooms at some sites; work-time seminars on family, health, and wellness issues; adoption aid up to $2,500; employee-assistance program; tuition reimbursement; reimbursement for smoking-cessation treatment; cancer consulting services; wellness credits through flexible compensation program.

Hewitt Associates provides expert advice on compensation and benefits to its corporate clients, so it isn't surprising that the firm offers its own associates an up-to-date array of family-care benefits. When Peter E. Friedes, chief executive at Hewitt Associates, began to conduct internal focus groups with working mothers in 1984, he learned that many faced problems finding support services to match their schedules. One woman had developed child-care arrangements in three of the cities she traveled to on business—sometimes she would take her preschooler along on the plane.

The firm's first responses were to pay for special baby-sitting services required when employees traveled, and to hire a person as a "family-resource consultant" to help working parents find the services they needed. Hewitt Associates has since expanded its family-support package to include reimbursement for the costs of care for ill dependents, support for community child-care initiatives, the encouragement of more part-time work options, and the hiring of internal family-resource consultants at all of the firm's regional centers.

Friedes believes the firm is reaping dividends on its investment in work-and-family benefits. "The cost to recruit good people is enormous," he explains. "Providing these work-and-family programs is much cheaper than having to hire new people. The savings to get back mothers with experience, versus having to hire and train someone else, *is large.* I believe that getting back a knowledgeable person for 60 percent of their time is better than having a full-time new recruit."

# Hill, Holliday, Connors, Cosmopulos, Inc.

200 Clarendon Street
Boston, MA 02116                                   617-437-1600

**Nature of business:** Advertising agency.
**Number of employees:** 430.
**Female employees:** 68 percent (48 percent of managers).
**Child care:** Near-site center for 36 children, aged two months to six years, with sliding fee scale based on parent income and age of child; pretax salary set-aside (DCAP).
**Elder care:** Pretax salary set-aside (DCAP).
**Family leave:** Two months paid maternity leave, same for adoptive mothers; paid time off may be used for care of ill family members.
**Flexible work options:** Some part-time work.
**Other benefits:** On-site fitness center; short-term and long-term disability insurance; 401(k) plan with employer contribution; health, dental, and life insurance.

Jack Connors, president of Hill, Holliday, Connors, Cosmopulos, had been considering the idea of a child-care center for the agency's employees in the early 1980s. When two of his senior managers became pregnant in 1984, that idea firmed into a commitment. The result, eighteen months later, was a small child-care center based in a nearby church. Twelve children enrolled that first year. By 1990, the center served twice that number.

The agency will entertain any reasonable request for alternative work schedules, but in 1990 just four women worked part-time. Whether on full- or part-time schedules, parents at the agency have a terrific resource in the child-care center. For Margaret Boles Fitzgerald, a vice president at the agency, it eliminated the anxiety of planning for care when she decided to have a baby. In an interview shortly after the center opened she said, "For me and my husband, the day-care center's existence gave us the wonderful freedom to think about having a child." Her baby was born in 1986.

# Hoffmann-La Roche Inc.

340 Kingsland Street
Nutley, NJ 07110                               201-235-5000

*Nature of business:* Pharmaceuticals and medical products; diagnostic products and clinical laboratory services; one of the world's largest manufacturers of pure bulk vitamins.
*Number of employees:* 17,800.
*Female employees:* 54 percent (11 percent of officers).
*Child care:* Near-site center in Nutley, New Jersey, for 122 children, aged two and a half to twelve years; center offers regular, emergency, and drop-in care for preschoolers, and after-school and summer care for school-age children.
*Elder care:* Consultation-and-referral service.
*Family leave:* Fully paid disability leave for childbirth, plus up to twelve weeks unpaid parental leave; up to twelve weeks unpaid leave for care of seriously ill family members.
*Flexible work options:* Flextime, part-time work, job sharing, and work-at-home available in most divisions.
*Other benefits:* Adoption aid; employee-assistance program; tuition reimbursement; career-development courses; technical-training courses; investment savings plan.

The growing flurry of interest in employer-supported child care must seem a little amusing to the people at Hoffmann-La Roche. This company's child-care center opened in 1977 after three years of surveys and planning. While many companies think of options like emergency child care and latchkey programs as new inventions, they've both been a part of Hoffmann-La Roche's operation for years. The major child-care issue this company wrestled with in the late 1980s was the small size of its center and the growing waiting list that parents faced to get in. One woman is said to have called the center to get her name on the list as soon as she learned she was pregnant—before telling her husband the news. In 1990 the company took a big step toward alleviating that problem, doubling the center's capacity with a $1 million expansion.

In addition to the preschool program, the Roche Child Care Center offers a state-licensed kindergarten program, before- and after-school care for children up to age twelve, a full-time summer program, and emergency care for children whose normal child-care arrangements have fallen through. From its early days the center has also provided information and counseling on family issues, referrals to other sources of care, and information on preschools, primary schools, and secondary schools in the area.

The company became involved with child care as early as it did in part because of the efforts of the Concerned Women of Roche, the oldest industrial women's support group in America. Formed in 1971, the group targeted child care as one of the major concerns of women at the company, and its efforts led directly to the early surveys, and, ultimately, to the creation of the center itself. The group has also lobbied for policies and programs that promote equal opportunity for women, and the company has a better-than-average record of promoting women to important jobs. Twenty-one of the company's vice presidents are women, and in 1989, a woman was appointed president of Roche Diagnostic Systems, one of the company's key business divisions.

# Honfed Bank

188 Merchant Street
Honolulu, HI 96809                           808-526-2375

**Nature of business:** Banking and financial services.
**Number of employees:** 700.
**Female employees:** 70 percent (46 percent of officers).
**Child care:** Resource-and-referral service; pretax salary set-aside (DCAP); pretax dependent-care subsidy an option in cafeteria benefit plan.
**Elder care:** Pretax salary set-aside (DCAP); pretax dependent-care subsidy an option in cafeteria benefit plan.
**Family leave:** Paid disability leave for childbirth, plus up to three months unpaid parental leave; sick-leave days may be used to care for ill family members.
**Flexible work options:** Flexible start times; some part-time work.
**Other benefits:** "Keiki Kokua" information program for new parents.

Whenever Honfed Bank hears that an employee is expecting or about to adopt a child, it sends an information packet, along with a letter of congratulations and encouragement from the bank's chairman. This is their introduction to the "Keiki Kokua" program, which loosely translates to "helping children." In the packet is a directory of more than one hundred local resources for new parents, a number of helpful pamphlets, and an explanation of the bank's family-care benefits and programs. The chairman's letter encourages employees to talk to the bank about any conflicts between their work and family needs. He admits that the bank can't accommodate every alternative schedule, but writes that "it might be worth discussing before you make a decision about your employment with Honfed. We would like to help, if we can!"

The bank is small enough that policies like flextime and leaves are not entirely formalized; individual arrangements are left to be worked out between employee and supervisor. But one work policy has been established in the employees' favor: part-timers who work at least twenty hours a week receive the same medical, dental, and insurance benefits as full-timers. Part-time tellers can choose between a compensation package that includes vacation benefits or one with a higher hourly pay rate and no vacation time.

# Household International

2700 Sanders Road
Prospect Heights, IL 60070                                708-564-5000

*Nature of business:* Financial services.
*Number of employees:* 12,000.
*Female employees:* 64 percent (39 percent of managers).
*Child care:* Internal resource-and-referral-service in Chicago and Salinas, California; funding for community-based child-care initiatives; pretax salary set-aside (DCAP).
*Elder care:* Long-term-care insurance for employees, spouses, and parents at group rates.
*Family leave:* Paid disability leave for childbirth, plus unpaid family leave (generally up to ninety days); paid time off for care of ill family members at discretion of managers.
*Flexible work options:* Flextime in most departments; part-time work common; some job sharing.
*Other benefits:* Employee-assistance program; wellness program; short-term and long-term disability insurance; books on child care for new parents.

Household International may not be a familiar name to the public, but most people know its subsidiary, Household Finance Company, and the company runs the tenth-largest MasterCard and Visa operation in the country. Household International is also quietly working to become one of the better companies in the area of work-and-family benefits. Employees in most departments can arrange flexible schedules around the core hours of 9:00 A.M. to 3:00 P.M.; almost 1,500 employees work part-time schedules (those who put in more than twenty hours a week receive full benefit coverage); and the company is promoting the wider use of job sharing.

Paid time off for sick days is a discretionary policy at Household International, as is its extension to include care for ill family members. The company's in-house child-care referral service was, by 1990, available only to the 4,000 workers in the Chicago area and to another 1,000 in the Salinas, California, credit-card operation.

## Hunter Industries

1940 Diamond Street
San Marcos, CA 92069                    619-744-5240

*Nature of business:* Manufacturer of irrigation equipment.
*Number of employees:* 500.
*Female employees:* 40 percent (25 percent of managers).
*Child care:* Near-site consortium center for 90 children, aged two to five years, to open in 1991; resource-and-referral service.
*Elder care:* Consultation-and-referral service.
*Family leave:* Unpaid personal leave to total of four months; six paid personal days may be used for family or any other reasons.
*Flexible work options:* Flextime for office workers; staggered shifts for production workers; limited part-time work.
*Other benefits:* Lunchtime seminars on family issues; tuition reimbursement; English- and Spanish-language classes; contract rates at local health club.

Ann Hunter Welborn had two young children when she joined her father's new business in 1983, and her awareness of the issues faced by working parents has much to do with the company's current family-friendly policies and benefits. A 1988 survey showed a high number of people on the payroll with family responsibilities, and the business has responded in several ways. In 1989 it contracted with a local counseling agency to provide its workers with resource-and-referral services for both child care and elder care. In 1991 the company will expand that support with a near-site child-care center, created in a three-way partnership between Hunter Industries, Palomar Community College, and the office-park developer from which the business rents its space. Hunter Industries employees will have priority at the center, thanks to $90,000 in company funding for the project. Once the center is functioning, its supporters plan to expand it to include infant care.

While most manufacturers resist any moves toward flexible working hours in production jobs, this firm has come up with a novel arrangement. Different manufacturing operations start at slightly staggered times, offering workers a choice of three starting times for both the day and afternoon shifts. An early start on the day shift enables many parents to leave in time to pick their children up at school.

# International Transcript

P.O. Box 517
Lincoln, RI 02865                                    800-933-3131

*Nature of business:* Transcription service.
*Number of employees:* 30.
*Female employees:* 29 (100 percent of managers).
*Child care:* Subsidy program pays full fee at nearby center.
*Elder care:* No formal program.
*Family leave:* Unpaid parental leave as needed (generally two to four months).
*Flexible work options:* Flexible hours the norm; part-time work common.

The medical-transcription business requires a well-trained and experienced work force, and the nature of the work tends to draw women with family responsibilities who need a job with flexible hours. Recognizing those two business facts, International Transcript decided in 1984 to offer its workers free child care at a nearby YMCA center, hoping the added benefit would keep good workers on staff and bring in others. Over the years, the company has paid for the care of dozens of children, and generally supports four to six at any given time. In 1990, a new child-care center opened in the company's office park, and as we went to press, International Transcript was trying to decide on the level of subsidy to offer there.

## Kemper National Insurance Companies

Route 22
Long Grove, IL 60049                                708-540-2000

*Nature of business:* Property and casualty insurance.
*Number of employees:* 8,500.
*Female employees:* 65 percent (33 percent of managers).
*Child care:* Nationwide consultation-and-referral service; pretax salary set-aside (DCAP).
*Elder care:* Nationwide resource-and-referral service; pretax salary set-aside (DCAP).
*Family leave:* Paid disability leave for childbirth, plus up to six months unpaid family leave (with same- or similar-job guarantee).
*Flexible work options:* Flextime in most departments; some part-time work.
*Other benefits:* Employee-assistance program; lunchtime seminars of family issues; management training to increase sensitivity on family issues; preretirement counseling; financial-planning seminars; wellness activities.

Kemper is one of the few companies to offer its workers both child-care and elder-care referral services, and one of the few to back up its written policies with a system of management training on work-and-family issues. Only a small number of employees work part-time here—approximately 250 in 1990—but those who work more than twenty hours are eligible for full benefit coverage, and part-time work is available for employees of all levels.

# Kingston Warren

Route 85
Newfield, NH 03856                    603-772-3771

**Nature of business:** Manufacturer of automotive weather-seal systems.
**Number of employees:** 700.
**Female employees:** 40 percent (14 percent of managers).
**Child care:** On-site center for 42 children, aged six weeks to six years.
**Elder care:** No formal program.
**Family leave:** Paid disability leave for childbirth; salaried workers may take paid time off for care of ill family members.
**Flexible work options:** Compressed work week standard in factory; some part-time work.
**Other benefits:** Worktime seminars on family issues; tuition assistance.

Factory employees at Kingston Warren work a four-day compressed-week schedule, a policy developed ten years ago with extensive employee input. The same employee-responsive attitude that led managers to listen seriously to that request also led, in 1986, to an on-site child-care center. Employees expressed a need, the company formed a committee of workers from all job levels, and then it acted on their recommendations. The center remains one of the best in the area; workers claim they couldn't find comparable care on their own, and certainly not at the rates the center charges. To keep those rates competitive and the quality at the center high, the company makes a substantial contribution to its operating budget. The center did offer night care when it first opened, but because usage was low, has cut back to a twelve-hour day, and is now open from 5:30 A.M. to 5:30 P.M.

# Lancaster Laboratories

2425 New Holland Pike
Lancaster, PA 17601                                717-656-2301

*Nature of business:* Analytical laboratory.
*Number of employees:* 400.
*Female employees:* 60 percent (45 percent of managers).
*Child care:* On-site center for 112 children (including 40 children of employees), aged six weeks to twelve years, with discounted rates for employees; pretax salary set-aside (DCAP).
*Elder care:* Plans for elder day-care center (should community/employee assessment survey show need) to open in 1991; pretax salary set-aside (DCAP).
*Family leave:* Paid disability leave for childbirth, plus up to two months unpaid parental leave; one-month part-time phase-in an option for returning mothers; paid sick days may be used for short-term care of ill family members.
*Flexible work options:* Flexible schedules arranged individually; part-time work common; job-sharing possible; some work-at-home.
*Other benefits:* Adoption aid up to $3,000; employee-assistance program; profit sharing; 401(k) plan with employer contribution.

When human-resources manager Carol Miller began looking at the issue of child care for Lancaster Laboratories in 1985, the company had fewer than 200 employees. Most companies that small would have dropped on-site child care from their list of options, but Miller came to see a center as a necessity for the business. The work force was young and largely female, and a survey showed that a quarter of the company's employees planned on starting families within the next five years. The business simply could not afford to lose large numbers of experienced workers. As founder Earl Hess's daughter, Miller knew she had at least one sympathetic ear at the top of the company, but she also knew that she had to make a sensible business proposition. Her solution was to find an outside organization to run the center as a for-profit business, with the company providing the space and certain services in return for a discount to its employees. The center opened in 1986 with the company guaranteeing a minimum enrollment to the provider. It is currently run by Child Care Learning Centers.

The company measures the success of the center both in the satisfaction of its employees and in the business's low turnover rate. Between 1987 and 1990, just three new mothers out of forty chose to quit and stay home with their babies. Dr. Hess has become one of the center's biggest supporters. Not only can he see the positive effects on his business, he can watch his own grandchildren grow up there. In 1988 he testified before Congress on the center's dramatic recruitment and retention benefit. Now he wants to expand the family-centered approach to include an elder day-care center. "When I can drop into the child-care center," he says, "and find one employee's mother rocking another employee's baby to sleep, then my dream will be fully realized."

# Levi Strauss & Company

P.O. Box 7215
San Francisco, CA 94120                   415-544-6000

*Nature of business:* Clothing.
*Number of employees:* 24,000.
*Female employees:* 74 percent (41 percent of managers).
*Child care:* Local resource-and-referral service in San Francisco; Levi Strauss Foundation funds community child-care facilities; pretax salary set-aside (DCAP).
*Elder care:* Pretax salary set-aside (DCAP).
*Family leave:* Paid disability leave for childbirth, plus up to five months unpaid parental leave; paid sick leave may be used in hourly increments to care for ill family members.
*Flexible work options:* Flexible work hours arranged individually; some part-time work; some job sharing; pilot work-at-home program.
*Other benefits:* Lunchtime seminars on family issues; family-resource library in San Francisco; employee-assistance program.

Levi Strauss has concentrated its early efforts to reduce work-family conflicts on its headquarters population in San Francisco. Its child-care resource-and-referral service, run through 1990 as an in-house operation through the employee-assistance program, served only the staff in San Francisco. Flexible work options, widely used in San Francisco, have not been as readily available to employees at the many U.S. production facilities. The approach has the advantage of allowing headquarters managers to monitor the effects of the family benefits and of increased scheduling flexibility, because the activities were close at hand. When the company launched a pilot tele-commuting program in 1989, designed with working mothers in mind, it found that more than half of the applicants were men. The company's policies and benefits also produced a number of very visible success stories. Donna Goya took extended leaves of absence when her two children were born (a year for the first, six months for the second), then cut back to a three-day schedule when they were young. In 1986, back on a full-time schedule, she was promoted to senior vice president in charge of personnel.

In 1990, the company decided to look at ways of expanding its family programs to more workers around the country. By the time this book comes out, the company expects to have an-nounced a broadly based series of family-care initiatives.

# Lincoln National Corporation

1300 S. Clinton Street
Fort Wayne, IN 46801                                    219-427-2000

*Nature of business:* Insurance.
*Number of employees:* 16,500.
*Female employees:* 71 percent (17 percent of officers).
*Child care:* Local resource-and-referral service run by com-pany staff; service recruits and trains family day-care pro-viders; pretax salary set-aside (DCAP).
*Elder care:* Sponsors elder-care fairs to link employees to local service providers; monthly elder-care support-group meetings; regular seminars on elder-care issues; pretax sal-ary set-aside (DCAP); elder-care consultation-and-referral service planned.
*Family leave:* Paid disability leave for childbirth, plus up to three months unpaid parental leave; part-time phase-in an option for new mothers.
*Flexible work options:* Flextime; some part-time work; some job sharing.
*Other benefits:* Adoption aid up to $1,250; monthly support-group meetings for working parents.

When Madeleine Baker joined Lincoln National in 1984 to create an in-house child-care referral service, she could find just 6 "professional" family day-care providers with quality programs in Fort Wayne. By 1990, after six years of recruiting, training, monitoring, and support, she had managed to build that list up to 274 homes. Along the way she had helped more than 1,200 parents find care for their children. In 1990, a part-time assistant was hired to meet the increase in child-care demands.

Parents at Lincoln National not only get the benefit of Baker's child-care network and her referrals, but can also take advantage of her counseling service, monthly support-group meetings, parents' newsletter, and annual child-care fair which helps bring parents and care givers together. In 1990, the company began helping employees with their elder-care needs as well, inviting agencies and service providers to an expanded family-care fair, and sponsoring seminars and support-group meetings on elder-care issues.

While the referral service is available only to the 4,300 workers in Fort Wayne, managers at Lincoln National's affiliates around the country are encouraged to investigate their options and develop work-and-family programs that best meet their own needs. Eventually some of these may surpass the benefits offered at headquarters. In 1990, for example, Employers Health Insurance Co., in Green Bay, Wisconsin, announced plans to build its own on-site child-care center.

# Lomas Financial Group

1600 Viceroy
Dallas, TX 75235                                    214-879-4040

*Nature of business:* Mortgage banking and financial services.
*Number of employees:* 1,700.
*Female employees:* 62 percent (40 percent of managers).
*Child care:* On-site center for 120 children, aged six weeks to six years.
*Elder care:* No formal program.
*Family leave:* Paid disability leave for childbirth, plus additional unpaid family leave.
*Flexible work options:* Flexible hours and compressed work weeks common in some departments; some part-time work.
*Other benefits:* Parenting workshops; tuition assistance; transportation subsidies.

Lomas Financial pulled in its horns quite a bit in the late 1980s, selling off subsidiary operations in order to concentrate on its mortgage banking business, but not once in that tough period did the company pull back support from its on-site child-care center. Chief executive officer Jess Hay is as firmly behind the center today as he was while he and his wife guided it to its opening in 1984. Hay is a believer in the importance of quality early-childhood education, and, thanks in part to his support, the center has received substantial subsidies through the years. It was one of the first centers in the country to receive NAEYC accreditation, an important stamp of quality approval. The company sees other, more directly business-oriented, benefits in the center as well: its presence has led to lower turnover, lower recruitment costs, and an increase in productivity.

## Lotus Development Corp.

55 Cambridge Parkway
Cambridge, MA 02142                    617-577-8500

*Nature of business:* Computer software developer.
*Number of U.S. employees:* 2,600.
*Female employees:* 53 percent (13 percent of upper-level managers).
*Child care:* On-site center for 72 children, aged three months to five years; subsidy program; local resource-and-referral service; pretax salary set-aside (DCAP).
*Elder care:* Consultation-and-referral service; pretax salary set-aside (DCAP).
*Family leave:* One month paid parenting leave, supplemented by disability insurance for childbirth, plus up to four weeks unpaid leave or up to three months part-time work schedule; paid sick and personal time may be used for short-term care of ill family members.
*Flexible work options:* Flexible schedules arranged individually; some part-time work; some job sharing.
*Other benefits:* Lunchtime seminars on family issues; two fitness centers; parent support groups; employee-assistance program; stock options; profit sharing.

Lotus Development Corp.'s child-care center was four years in the works before it finally opened in the spring of 1990. That careful planning process has led not only to a high-quality center, one with substantial support from the company, but to some innovative solutions to meet the varied child-care needs of the company's employees. The center is run as a department within the company, its teachers entitled to full company benefits, as a way of both attracting good staff and ensuring control over the center's operation. To help those who can least afford to pay for care, the company has adopted a sliding fee scale at the center, essentially granting subsidies to those whose household income is below $50,000.

But the center was not designed to be the final answer to employees' child-care needs. Surveys show that employees at the Cambridge site have more than 300 children who could use the center, yet, because of space limitations, the center was only built with space for 72. Those who end up on the outside after the random selection process can use the company's referral service as an aid in finding other care, and the company uses the same subsidy scale applied at the center to help them pay for the care they select.

Lotus has also set up an innovative parental-leave system, granting a month of paid parenting leave to any parent who needs it, whether for the birth, adoption, or illness of a child. A number of fathers have taken the leave, as has a grandmother, who used the time to care for her grandchildren when her daughter required surgery.

Some of the parenting and informational seminars at Lotus are open to employees' families, including sessions on communicating with teenagers and on family financial planning.

# Marquette Electronics

8200 W. Tower Avenue
Milwaukee, WI 53223                              414-355-5000

*Nature of business:* Manufacturer of medical electronics equipment.
*Number of employees:* 1,380.
*Female employees:* 40 percent (11 percent of managers).
*Child care:* On-site center in Milwaukee for 140 children, aged six weeks to nine years; near-site center in Jupiter, Florida.
*Elder care:* No formal program.
*Family leave:* Paid disability leave for childbirth, plus up to five months unpaid personal leave.

*Flexible work options:* Flexible schedules arranged individually; some part-time work.
*Other benefits:* Tuition reimbursement.

Child care at Marquette Electronics is a full-service operation, taking in infants, preschoolers, and school-age children. The older children can attend both the before- and after-school programs and the company's summer camp. The center is run as a department of the company, with a substantial subsidy, and staff are entitled to company benefits. Out of a concern for fairness, Marquette opened a similar center to serve the 200 employees at its Jupiter, Florida, plant.

# Massachusetts Mutual Life Insurance Co. (MassMutual)

1295 State Street
Springfield, MA 01111                                413-788-8411

*Nature of business:* Life and health insurance; financial services.
*Number of employees:* 6,000.
*Female employees:* 70 percent (49 percent of managers).
*Child care:* Resource-and-referral service in Springfield, Massachusetts, area; corporate contributions to near-site center in return for priority access and discounted rates for employees; pretax salary set-aside (DCAP).
*Elder care:* Consultation-and-referral service; pretax salary set-aside (DCAP).
*Family leave:* Paid disability leave for childbirth, plus up to eight weeks unpaid personal leave (with five years' seniority); three paid sick days may be used for care of ill family members.
*Flexible work options:* Flextime common; some part-time work; limited job sharing; limited work-at-home.
*Other benefits:* Employee-assistance program; lunchtime workshops on family issues; parent support groups; on-site fitness center; on-site medical clinic; on-site dry-cleaning and shoe-repair services.

Employees at MassMutual's home office in Springfield, Massachusetts, can bring their dry cleaning to work, have their shoes repaired at the office, and even get a haircut in an office barber shop. Since 1983, some have also been able to bring their children to a nearby child-care center which the company helped start with a generous low-interest loan. The center earned a recognition of quality when it received NAEYC accreditation in 1990, and in 1991 it will be doubling in size, to accommodate ninety-four children, aged six weeks to five years. At the same time, MassMutual is increasing its support for and ties to the center. Another low-interest loan will fund the expansion, and the business will be subsidizing parents' fees, using a sliding scale based on family income. The greatest subsidy rate will be 40 percent, for those who earn less than $25,000; the lowest 10 percent, for employees earning more than $45,000. In return, the center is allocating all of its new spaces to company employees. The company backs up its support for the center with a child-care resource-and-referral service, which has been offered to employees through a local agency since 1980. More recently MassMutual has added an elder-care referral service to the list of supports.

# Maui Land & Pineapple Co.

P.O. Box 187
Kahului, HI 96732                                      808-877-3351

**Nature of business:** Resort operator, land developer, and world's largest private-label pineapple packer.
**Number of employees:** 2,000.
**Female employees:** 45 percent (25 percent of managers).
**Child care:** On-site center for 50 children, aged two to five years.
**Elder care:** No formal program.
**Family leave:** Paid disability leave for childbirth, plus unpaid maternity leave to total of six months; unpaid leave available for care of ill dependents.
**Flexible work options:** Limited flextime.

Maui Land & Pineapple opened its child-care center in 1982 in response to a high retirement rate and a need to attract new, and generally younger, employees. Since opening the center, the company has found it to be a powerful retention tool, made all the more valuable because of competition from hotels and service businesses for its pineapple workers. In part because it has been created as a recruitment and retention tool, the center offers a high-quality program, backed by a 60 percent subsidy from the company. While parent fees are comparable to those at other centers in the area, the center offers lower child/teacher ratios and very low turnover among its staff.

# Mechanics & Farmers Savings Bank

999 Broad Street
Bridgeport, CT 06601                                    203-382-6363

*Nature of business:* Bank.
*Number of employees:* 450.
*Female employees:* 77 percent (54 percent of managers).
*Child care:* Subsidy program; resource-and-referral service; pretax salary set-aside (DCAP).
*Elder care:* Lunchtime seminars on elder-care issues.
*Family leave:* Paid disability leave for childbirth, plus unpaid parental leave to total of thirteen weeks.
*Flexible work options:* Some part-time work.
*Other benefits:* Lunchtime seminars on family issues; tuition reimbursement; employee-assistance program.

Mechanics & Farmers Savings Bank pays half of its employees' child-care costs. The only restrictions are that employees must be either single parents or part of a dual-income couple (in other words, no payments are made to families with at-home spouses), and, since the bank pays the providers directly, the care givers must be operating legally and must report their income. The subsidies went into effect at the end of 1987, along with a more generous leave policy, and the company saw an immediate result. In 1987, 33 percent of the women who went out on maternity leave did not come back to work. By 1989, the rate had dropped to just 9 percent.

# Merck & Co., Inc.

P.O. Box 2000
Rahway, NJ 07065-0900                    201-594-4000

*Nature of business:* Pharmaceuticals.
*Number of U.S. employees:* 18,000.
*Female employees:* 38 percent (5.5 percent of upper management).
*Child care:* Nationwide resource-and-referral service; support for near-site centers in Rahway, New Jersey, and West Point, Pennsylvania; additional center planned for new headquarters site in Whitehouse Station, New Jersey; care for mildly ill children at local hospital a company-paid benefit in West Point.
*Elder care:* No formal program.
*Family leave:* Paid disability leave for childbirth, plus up to eighteen months unpaid parental leave.
*Flexible work options:* Flextime at many locations; some part-time work; limited work-at-home.
*Other benefits:* Lunchtime workshops on family issues; spouse-relocation assistance; management training to increase sensitivity to family issues; employee-assistance program.

Merck is one of the old-timers in the area of family benefits. Its maternity-leave policy dates back to the 1950s, and for more than two decades its generous length of eighteen months stood out as the best in American industry. (Only IBM's, extended to three years in 1989, now tops it.) Merck pays all health-insurance premiums for the duration of the leave, and employees continue to accrue benefits and pension credits as if they were physically on the job.

Merck also stepped up to the challenge of employer-supported child care long before it became a fashionable business issue, and the company has come up with some innovative solutions over the years. Its first effort was to support an employee-run center, which opened in 1980 near the company's headquarters in Rahway. Merck provided the start-up funding and has continued to provide legal and other advice to the center, and training for its teachers. The center has otherwise supported itself with parent fees and occasional fund-raising activities. When it became clear in the late 1980s that the seventy-five-child center did not meet the full employee demand for care, the company decided to build an entirely new facility with room for twice as many children.

In West Point, Pennsylvania, the company's other key employment site, Merck has funded the expansion of an existing for-profit center in return for preferential access for employees' children. In July 1990, the company also started offering employees in West Point care for their mildly ill children as a fully paid company benefit, at a facility managed by a local hospital.

Merck brought flexible scheduling to its various workplaces in 1980, and though implementation is still at the discretion of individual managers, it has become so common throughout the organization that managers who resist it unreasonably now stand out as bad examples. An ongoing management-training process continues to emphasize the importance of flexibility and understanding in managing a diverse work force.

The future holds even more family-supportive moves at Merck. An elder-care referral service is under consideration. When the company builds its new headquarters in Whitehouse Station, New Jersey, a 150-child day-care center will be included in the complex. And by opening the door to local child-care initiatives such as those in West Point, the company has agreed to consider reasonable proposals at other sites. A regular winner of *Fortune's* "Most Admired Corporations" polls, Merck also deserves recognition as one of the best companies in the country for working parents.

## Herman Miller

8500 Byron Road
Zeeland, MI 49464                     616-772-3300

*Nature of business:* Manufacturer of office furniture.
*Number of employees:* 3,500.
*Female employees:* 40 percent (25 percent of managers and work-team leaders).
*Child care:* Local resource-and-referral service; pretax salary set-aside (DCAP).
*Elder care:* Local consultation-and-referral service; pretax salary set-aside (DCAP).
*Family leave:* Paid disability leave for childbirth, additional unpaid leave negotiable.
*Flexible work options:* Flexible work hours arranged individually; some part-time work; some job sharing.

*Other benefits:* Adoption aid up to $2,500; gift of rocking chair or $100 savings bond to new babies; occasional lunchtime seminars on family issues; employee-assistance program; profit-sharing plan.

Herman Miller is well known for its participative management style, and for its concern for individual workers. That philosophy of caring and of worker empowerment has led to one of the more progressive benefit packages in the country, and the company has long been in the front ranks of those businesses addressing family issues. Herman Miller joined with several other companies to help start a local child-care referral service in 1983, one that is available to serve the public and which works to improve the quality and availability of care in the area. To help employees with their elder-care needs it has contracted with a home health service to provide individual counseling and advice. The service sends nurses or social workers, depending on the need, to the elders' homes in order to assess their needs and help determine what services might be helpful.

The company is also trying to be flexible. More than 200 employees worked part-time schedules in 1990, 23 of them salaried professionals. While the company has no blanket flextime policy, individual workers can and do arrange schedules to fit their family needs. Through the company's profit-sharing plan, virtually every worker at the company is also a stockholder. Every fiscal quarter the company pays out a bonus to employees with over a year of service. All company contributions are invested in Herman Miller stock. In recent years the distribution has averaged 3 percent of employees' annual wages.

# 3M

3M Center
St. Paul, MN 55144                                    612-733-1110

*Nature of business:* Manufacturer of over 40,000 products, including Scotch transparent tape and Post-it notepads.
*Number of employees:* 49,000.
*Female employees:* 33 percent (12 percent of officials and managers).
*Child care:* In-house information service; subsidized pro-

grams in Austin, Texas, and St. Paul for care of mildly ill children; support for YMCA-run summer day camp in St. Paul; foundation support for community resources; pretax salary set-aside (DCAP).

*Elder care:* Pretax salary set-aside (DCAP).

*Family leave:* Paid disability leave for childbirth, plus up to two months unpaid "special leave" for mothers, fathers, and adoptive parents; five paid family emergency days may be used for care of ill family members.

*Flexible work options:* Flextime common; some part-time work; some job sharing.

*Other benefits:* Employee-assistance program; lunchtime seminars on family issues; adoption aid up to $1,500; savings plan with employer contribution.

3M is working to meet the needs of the parents on its payroll in a wide variety of ways. Its in-house child-care information service has been offered to employees since 1981. Some sites also contract with community child-care referral agencies. The company has supported a YMCA-run summer camp in St. Paul, and employees receive a discounted rate there; 3M donates vans to assist with transportation to and from the camp, so that employees can drop off and pick up their children at a park site convenient to the workplace. A second summer option is the Summer Science Academy, a program of science enrichment courses at the Science Museum of Minnesota, open to preschool through teenage children of 3M employees. In the St. Paul area and in Austin, Texas, the company subsidizes the use of care-giver services that send providers to employees' homes when their children are mildly ill. Parenting courses and lunchtime seminars offer additional information and support.

Flexibility is another 3M attribute. A program called Personalized Work Schedules allows many employees to tailor their work hours to their individual needs. Some begin their days as early as 6:15 A.M.; others don't start until 9:00. The only requirement is that every schedule must include the core period between 9:00 A.M. and 3:00 P.M.

# J. P. Morgan & Co., Incorporated

60 Wall Street
New York, NY 10260                                    212-483-2323

**Nature of business:** Banking and financial services.
**Number of employees:** 8,500.
**Female employees:** 52 percent (36 percent of officers).
**Child care:** Resource-and-referral service in New York and Delaware.
**Elder care:** Consultation-and-referral service in New York.
**Family leave:** Paid disability leave for childbirth, plus up to four months unpaid child-care leave for parents of newborn and newly adopted children; up to two months unpaid personal leave for other family needs; five consecutive paid "illness at home" days may be used to care for ill family members.
**Flexible work options:** Flexible schedules arranged individually; some part-time work.
**Other benefits:** Lunchtime seminars on family issues; employee-assistance program; adoption aid up to $3,000; college scholarships for employees' children (five per year); free or reduced admission to museums and cultural events.

The image of J. P. Morgan may not square with concern for child care and elder care, but the house of Morgan has become one of the leaders in creating a hospitable work environment for employees with family responsibilities. Mothers who go on childbirth disability leave receive full pay for four weeks with one year of service, and for up to eight weeks with two years of service. The four months of unpaid child-care leave is available to mothers and fathers, including adoptive parents, and is considered an entitlement here, not a starting point for negotiation. Though part-time work is not common, those who can arrange their work to fit reduced schedules receive full medical and dental benefits, as long as they work at least twenty hours per week.

# Neuville Industries

P.O. Box 286
Hildebran, NC 28637                                        704-397-5566

*Nature of business:* Sock manufacturer.
*Number of employees:* 575.
*Female employees:* 80 percent (50 percent of managers).
*Child care:* On-site center for 75 children, aged six weeks to six years; child-care subsidy program for second- and third-shift workers.
*Elder care:* No formal program.
*Family leave:* Paid short-term disability leave for childbirth, plus up to six months unpaid maternity leave if medically necessary.
*Flexible work options:* Some job sharing.
*Other benefits:* Employee-assistance program planned.

Neuville Industries has had on-site child care for almost as long as it has had a factory. When Steve Neuville founded the business in 1979, he faced low unemployment in the area and a history of high turnover in the hosiery industry— 30 to 100 percent at most mills. He knew he needed workers and he wanted to keep them. So he decided to open a child-care center. He started out with just 5 children that year, and has built the center up to keep pace with his growing business. The center was licensed to care for 108 children in 1990, though Neuville keeps enrollment below that in order to offer better care.

Providing quality care as an employee benefit is an expensive proposition here. Parent fees cover about 50 percent of the center's budget of $200,000, and Neuville pays the balance. But in an area where good child care is hard to find, the center has proved to be a powerful employment tool. Turnover at the company was just 8 percent in 1981, and has remained well below the industry average in the years since. Steve Neuville calculates that his savings in recruitment and training more than offset his investment in the center, and he cites a host of other benefits as well, including better employee selection and improved morale.

# The New England

501 Boylston Street
Boston, MA 02117                                          617-578-2000

*Nature of business:* Insurance and financial services.
*Number of employees:* 2,800.
*Female employees:* 60 percent (42 percent of managers).
*Child care:* Local resource-and-referral service; pretax salary set-aside (DCAP).
*Elder care:* Local consultation-and-referral service; pretax salary set-aside (DCAP).
*Family leave:* Paid disability leave, plus unpaid maternity leave to a total of five months; up to three months unpaid paternity leave; paid time off may be used for short-term care of ill family members.
*Flexible work options:* Flextime common; some part-time work; some job sharing; limited work-at-home.
*Other benefits:* Workshops on family issues, including elder care; family-resource library; information fairs to link employees with service providers; subsidized cafeteria; take-home food service; "mothers' room" for nursing mothers; parent support group; on-site health services, including wellness program; college scholarships for employees' children; tuition reimbursement; 401(k) plan with employer contribution.

The New England has quietly become one of the most supportive companies in the country for people with family responsibilities. The company has shied away from some of the flashier solutions—it has ruled out on-site child care because of its urban location, for example, and it gives no dependent-care subsidies—but it offers employees just about everything else imaginable. Workers here can take home low-cost gourmet meals from the company's cafeteria, and nursing mothers can use a mothers' room complete with breast pump and refrigerator. The New England was one of the first companies in the Boston area to provide a formal child-care referral service when it contracted with a local agency in 1983, and it added elder-care referrals in 1990. Flextime is standard throughout the business, around core hours of 9:30 A.M. to 3:30 P.M. Some 110 employees work part-time schedules, and the company has installed computer links to some workers' homes. The company has allowed maternity leaves of up to five months since 1976, and benefit coverage continues while employees are out. The New England is not likely to make the evening news with its low-key approach, but for its comprehensive support system and tradition of flexibility it has few rivals.

# New London Trust

P.O. Box 158
New London, NH 03257                    603-526-2535

*Nature of business:* Bank.
*Number of employees:* 85.
*Female employees:* 75 percent (50 percent of officers).
*Child care:* On-site center for 15 children, aged six weeks to five years.
*Elder care:* No formal program.
*Family leave:* Paid disability leave for childbirth, plus up to six months unpaid parental leave.
*Flexible work options:* Flexible work hours arranged individually; some part-time work.
*Other benefits:* Lunchtime and after-work seminars on family issues, including child care.

New London Trust became involved with child care after several employees expressed concern over the lack of adequate care in the area. A small child-care center now sits next door, run as a department of the bank. Flexibility here extends throughout the organization. Among the part-timers are tellers, marketing people, customer-service representatives, and officers.

# Northern Trust Corporation

50 S. LaSalle Street
Chicago, IL 60675                    312-630-6000

*Nature of business:* Banking and financial services.
*Number of employees:* 5,600.
*Female employees:* 65 percent.
*Child care:* On-site center for 72 children, aged three months to five years.

*Elder care:* No formal program.

*Family leave:* Paid disability leave for childbirth; additional unpaid leave negotiable; two floating holidays may be used for any reason, including care of ill family members.

*Flexible work options:* Flexible work hours arranged individually; some part-time work; some job sharing.

*Other benefits:* Lunchtime seminars on work-and-family and wellness issues.

Northern Trust took a giant step toward becoming a family-friendly employer when it opened its own child-care center in the fall of 1990—the first corporate-supported center within Chicago's Loop. The company has planned it as a high-quality center, with the goal of NAEYC accreditation. The plans also call for parent fees to cover its direct operating costs.

In early 1991, the company also plans to make important policy decisions that will allow a reasonable amount of paid time off for the care of ill family members (through 1990, some managers allowed it, while others didn't), and that will set guidelines for unpaid family leaves.

## Numerica Financial Corp.

1155 Elm Street, P.O. Box 60
Manchester, NH 03105                    603-624-2424

*Nature of business:* Banking and financial services.

*Number of employees:* 502.

*Female employees:* 77 percent (54 percent of officers).

*Child care:* Resource-and-referral service; pretax salary set-aside (DCAP).

*Elder care:* Information and guidance through employee assistance plan; pretax salary set-aside (DCAP).

*Family leave:* Paid disability leave for childbirth.

*Flexible work options:* Flexible work hours arranged individually; some part-time work.

*Other benefits:* Lunchtime seminars on family issues; employee-assistance program with elder-care specialist.

Carole Treen, Numerica's training director, is a former day-care center director, and uses both her expertise and her network of contacts to advise employees on parenting issues and to help them find care for their children. The company helps out in much the same way with elder care, offering an employee-assistance program through an agency that keeps an elder-care expert on staff. Among the part-timers here are one officer and a number of peak-time tellers, some of whom choose that schedule for parenting reasons.

# Official Airline Guides

2000 Clearwater Drive, Oak Brook, IL 60521
708-574-6000

*Nature of business:* Publisher of travel information guides.
*Number of employees:* 750.
*Female employees:* 72 percent (54 percent of managers).
*Child care:* On-site center for 71 children, aged six weeks to five years.
*Elder care:* No formal program.
*Family leave:* Paid disability leave for childbirth, plus up to three months unpaid parental leave.
*Flexible work options:* Flextime; some part-time work.
*Other benefits:* Profit sharing; tuition reimbursement; subsidized cafeteria.

For more than sixty years, Official Airlines Guides has published tables of airline schedules and fares and is now the world's leader in providing travel information to the public and to the travel industry. The company has traditionally employed a high proportion of women, and has long been aware of the conflicting demands faced by working mothers.

Former president James Woodward came up with the idea of a company-run child-care center in 1979, as the business planned an addition to its Oak Brook offices. He knew that an on-site center would help relieve some of the pressures felt by the parents on his staff, and he hoped it would also provide a strong recruitment and retention tool. The center opened in January 1981, and quickly proved him right. Turnover dropped from an average of 44 percent in the three precenter years to 22 percent in the years just after its opening. The center is run as a department of the company, its staff paid by Official Airline Guides and entitled to all company benefits. Tuition covers most of the center's expenses, but the company continues to underwrite a portion of its budget, an expense that it feels is more than balanced by savings through reduced recruitment and training costs.

The company helps working parents in other ways too, with a generous leave policy, and with schedules flexible enough to accommodate most individual needs. About sixty people work less than a full week here, and most of them are entitled to the company's full benefit package. Flexible schedules are available to almost all of the company's workers, and close to two hundred work a 7:30 A.M. to 3:30 P.M. routine in order to be home when their children return from school.

# Ohio Bell (an Ameritech Company)

45 Erieview Plaza
Cleveland, OH 44114                                    216-822-3187

*Nature of business:* Telecommunications.
*Number of employees:* 13,000.
*Female employees:* 51 percent (41 percent of managers).
*Child care:* Statewide resource-and-referral service; pretax salary set-aside (DCAP).
*Elder care:* Statewide consultation-and-referral service; pretax salary set-aside (DCAP).
*Family leave:* Paid disability leave for childbirth; up to one year unpaid dependent-care leave (with company-paid benefits for six months); part-time phase-in during leave period; four paid personal days may be used in two-hour increments for school conferences, care of ill family members, or for any other reason.
*Flexible work options:* Flextime in most departments; compressed work week an option; limited part-time work; limited work-at-home.
*Other benefits:* Adoption aid up to $3,000; statewide "TeenLine" counseling for parents and teens; lunchtime seminars on family issues; family-resource library.

The telephone companies are among the leaders in reshaping the workplace to meet the needs of people with family responsibilities, and Ohio Bell has led the way within the Ameritech Company. Like most of the telephone companies, Ohio Bell offers generous leaves: up to a year, with a program that allows workers to phase back into work on a part-time basis (for a period of up to three months). It has set a high cap on its adoption-assistance benefit—$3,000—and in 1990 it became one of a handful of companies to offer both child- and elder-care referral services. With an older employee population (the average age is forty-three), Ohio Bell's elder-care support systems are meeting with a strong response. The elder-care referral service fielded forty-five calls in the first month of operation, and almost 600 employees attended a series of lunchtime seminars on the legal and financial dimensions of elder care.

## Oliver Wight

5 Oliver Wight Drive
Essex Junction, VT 05452                    802-878-8161

*Nature of business:* Telemarketing and consulting services.
*Number of employees:* 17.
*Female employees:* 12 (2 of 5 managers).
*Child care:* On-site center for 10 children, aged six weeks to six years; pretax salary set-aside (DCAP).
*Elder care:* Pretax salary set-aside (DCAP).
*Family leave:* Three weeks paid maternity leave, supplemented by disability insurance; one week paid paternity leave; up to twelve weeks unpaid family leave; paid personal days may be used to care for ill family members.
*Flexible work options:* Flextime in some positions; some part-time and job sharing.
*Other benefits:* 401(k) plan with employer contribution.

Oliver Wight has had its own child-care center since 1981. President Darryl Landvater had a young child of his own at the time, and when the business outgrew his home, he decided to add child care to the office amenities. For the first three years it was a free benefit; now parents pay a regular weekly fee and the company contributes a small operating subsidy. Not only is the company one of the smallest in the country to run its own child-care center, it is one of the few small companies to have set up a pretax spending account to give employees a tax savings on their child-care expenses.

Telephones have to be covered between 9:00 A.M. and 5:00 P.M. in this telemarketing business, but the company has found ways to be flexible within those restrictions. Part-timers work at opposite ends of the day to ensure full staffing. Five of the company's seventeen employees work less than full-time schedules.

# Overseas Adventure Travel

349 Broadway
Cambridge, MA 02139                                    617-876-0533

*Nature of business:* Travel agency.
*Number of employees:* 20.
*Female employees:* 15 (3 of 5 managers).
*Child care:* On-site family day care for 6 children, aged one to six years.
*Elder care:* No formal program.
*Family leave:* Two months parental leave, with one or both months paid depending on length of service; leave can be supplemented by accrued vacation and sick time; paid sick days may be used to care for ill family members.
*Flexible work options:* Some part-time work.
*Other benefits:* Profit sharing; some free travel.

Overseas Adventure Travel is no ordinary travel agency. It offers no package tours of Disney World or London, but concentrates instead on hiking treks in Nepal, bicycle trips in Ecuador, safaris to the mountain gorilla reserve in Tanzania, and camping trips to Machu Picchu. The uninitiated might expect a swashbuckling Richard Haliburton type at the helm of such an enterprise, and they may not be far off the mark. Owner and president Judy Wineland started this business because she enjoys adventure herself. But she is also a mother of two, and as her company has grown, she has found a number of working parents at the desks around her.

Just as the company approaches travel planning with an open mind and a sense of adventure, Wineland came to the issue of children and work with a fresh perspective and a clean slate. Her husband runs a related business, and when their first child was born, both cut back their schedules in order to share child-rearing responsibilities. When they decided that they needed some form of child care, Wineland looked into the idea of a center linked to her travel agency. What she came up with is a novelty in American business: a family day-care provider who lives and offers child care on a floor of the company's three-story Victorian building. For the first year, Overseas Adventure Travel provided free rent and a salary to the provider, then switched to an arrangement in which the care giver is an independent contractor, paying rent to the company and charging parents market-rate fees. In the fall of 1990, four employees had enrolled their children in the upstairs care, and two more babies were due to join the company family.

Business hours at the travel agency are fairly rigid—the doors open at 9:00 A.M. and close at 5:30 P.M.—so flextime in the normal sense is not a real possibility. The company does, however, make arrangements for people to work less than full-time schedules. Wineland cut her own work schedule back after the birth of each of her two children, and another mother has done the same.

## Pacific Gas & Electric Co.

215 Market Street
San Francisco, CA 94106                415-973-5385

*Nature of business:* Gas and electric utility.
*Number of employees:* 26,000.
*Female employees:* 21 percent (19 percent of management employees).
*Child care:* Enhanced resource-and-referral service; pretax salary set-aside (DCAP).
*Elder care:* Pretax salary set-aside (DCAP).
*Family leave:* Paid disability leave for childbirth, plus unpaid parental leave to total of twelve months (six months with same-job guarantee); three floating holidays may be used to care for ill family members.
*Flexible work options:* Flextime common; some part-time work; some job sharing.
*Other benefits:* Lunchtime seminars on family issues; employee-assistance program; dental care, vision care, and additional vacation time options in flexible benefit package.

Pacific Gas & Electric is one of a select few companies in American business that offers a same-job guarantee on leaves as long as six months, and though no job guarantee is extended to those taking the full twelve-month leave we're told that the company has been able to accommodate most leave takers so far. The one drawback here is that the utility pays its portion of employees' medical-benefit coverage for only the first three months of the leave (though dental and vision coverage continue for the full leave), so the option is available only to those who can afford to pay their own medical-insurance premiums or who are covered by a spouse's policy.

Flexibility is another highlight at Pacific Gas & Electric. The company actively encourages managers to work out flexible schedules with their employees, and both flextime and compressed work weeks are common throughout the organization. Family concerns aren't the only reason behind this policy; the company is almost as concerned about traffic problems on the roads.

# Pacific Presbyterian Medical Center

P.O. Box 7999
San Francisco, CA 94120                    415-923-3467

*Nature of business:* Hospital.
*Number of employees:* 3,000.
*Female employees:* 70 percent (5 of 11 vice presidents).
*Child care:* Near-site center for 180 children, aged two to five years; pretax salary set-aside (DCAP).
*Elder care:* Pretax salary set-aside (DCAP).
*Family leave:* Paid disability leave for childbirth; up to three months unpaid family leave; paid time off (combined vacation, holidays, and sick time) may be used for family reasons; leave-sharing policy allows employees to donate unused paid time off to other employees facing emergency absences, including absence for the extended illness of a relative.
*Flexible work options:* Variety of shifts available; part-time work common.
*Other benefits:* Employee-assistance program; medical, dental, vision, and life insurance.

Pacific Presbyterian does not offer quite the variety of shifts that some hospitals do (see descriptions of Beth Israel of Boston and St. Vincent's Hospital, in Birmingham, Alabama), but it is experimenting with greater shift flexibility, and it does offer a great deal of opportunity for part-timers. A full 40 percent of the hospital's staff work part-time schedules, and as long as they put in at least twenty hours each week, all are eligible for full medical-, dental-, vision-, and life-insurance coverage. Those who want more flexibility can hire on as "casual day workers" and work when needed or when available, with a pay premium in lieu of benefits.

The hospital's child-care center opened in September 1989 as a joint venture with nearby Sherith Israel Synagogue. The synagogue had the space and wanted to provide a center for its members. The hospital contributed $80,000 toward renovations and an additional $20,000 in interest-free loans to help with start-up costs, and in return receives priority access for its employees. By the summer of 1990 the center had about 120 children enrolled, about 25 each from the hospital and the synagogue, and the two institutions were discussing plans to expand the center's program to include infant care and care for mildly ill children.

## Pacific Stock Exchange

301 Pine Street
San Francisco, CA 94104                                        415-393-7990

*Nature of business:* Stock exchange.
*Number of employees:* 450.
*Female employees:* 48 percent (25 percent of managers).
*Child care:* Pretax salary set-aside (DCAP).
*Elder care:* Pretax salary set-aside (DCAP); informal counseling and referral program in 1990.
*Family leave:* Paid disability leave for childbirth, additional unpaid leave negotiable; paid sick time may be used for care of ill family members.
*Flexible work options:* Flextime in many positions; some part-time work; some job sharing; limited work-at-home.
*Other benefits:* Pension plan; medical, dental, and life insurance.

A stock exchange seems like an unlikely place for family-benefit innovations. The prevailing image is one of men yelling on the trading floor. But almost half of the Pacific Stock Exchange's workers are women, and a 1988 survey showed that sixty of the exchange's employees cared for eighty young children.

Since this is a California employer, state disability insurance covers workers who are out for childbirth. But that coverage rarely gives full salary replacement, and the exchange allows workers to use accumulated sick days in fractional portions to raise the coverage to their normal pay level. Though management discretion determines unpaid leave beyond the disability period, the exchange does have a firm policy of paying its portion of employees' insurance benefits during any unpaid leave allowed: workers with a year of service are covered for three months, those with five years of service for six months.

Workers here also have access to California's free child-care referral service, and the exchange has an information program to let parents know about the service. Flextime and job sharing have been accepted here for years, and part-timers get the full insurance benefit package if they work at least twenty-four hours each week. In response to the 1988 survey, the sick time policy was extended to include doctors' visits and care of dependents. The result? Sick-time usage has not gone up at all.

In 1990, the exchange was the fortunate beneficiary of a graduate-student investigation of the elder-care needs of its employees. Forty workers· were revealed to have some elder-care responsibility, and the student followed up with counseling and referrals. The study had not been completed as we went to press, but may lead to some additional or enhanced elder-care programs.

# Paramount Pictures Corp.

5555 Melrose Avenue
Los Angeles, CA 90038                     213-956-5000

**Nature of business:** Television and motion-picture production and distribution.
**Number of employees:** 1,500 (plus up to 2,500 additional workers on per-project basis).
**Female employees:** Figures not available.
**Child care:** On-site center for 43 children, aged six weeks to five years; enhanced resource-and-referral service; pretax salary set-aside (DCAP).
**Elder care:** Pretax salary set-aside (DCAP).
**Family leave:** Paid disability leave for childbirth, plus up to thirty days unpaid personal leave.

*Flexible work options:* Flexible schedules arranged individually; limited part-time work; no job sharing.
*Other benefits:* Lunchtime seminars on family issues.

P arents at Paramount Pictures have Gary David Goldberg, producer of "Family Ties," to thank for their on-site child-care center. In the early 1970s, long before he began his television career, Goldberg and his wife had operated a child-care center of their own, and though his income as a television producer has risen to the point where affordable quality child care is no longer a critical personal issue, he is well aware of the problems most employees face. When his contract came up for renewal in 1985, he made the creation of a center a key demand.

The center opened in 1986, and today stands out as one of the highest-quality centers in the Los Angeles area. Teacher-to-child ratios are kept at one teacher for two infants, and never go higher than one to seven for preschoolers. The extended hours—7:30 A.M. to 7:00 P.M.—accommodate almost all workers, allowing them some flexibility at either end of the day. And thanks to a company subsidy, the rates are kept at reasonable levels: $100 per week for infants, $90 for toddlers, $80 for older children.

# Polaroid Corporation

549 Technology Square
Cambridge, MA 02139                      617-577-2000

*Nature of business:* Photographic products.
*Number of employees:* 8,700.
*Female employees:* 28 percent (1 of 20 officers).
*Child care:* Resource-and-referral service; income-based subsidies; pretax salary set-aside (DCAP).
*Elder care:* Elder-care information program in New Bedford, Massachusetts; pretax salary set-aside (DCAP).
*Family leave:* Fully paid disability leave for childbirth, plus up to six months unpaid parental leave; vacation time may be used in one-hour increments.
*Flexible work options:* Flexible work hours arranged individually; some part-time work; some job sharing.
*Other benefits:* Employee-assistance program; profit sharing; employee stock-ownership plan.

Polaroid has one of the longest histories of involvement with child-care issues of any American business. Its child-care subsidy program, launched in 1970, predates even Stride Rite's child-care center by a year. Both Polaroid's and Stride Rite's early efforts reflected the antipoverty concerns of the time, and were aimed primarily at lower-income employees. Polaroid's subsidy, still in effect, pays a percentage of its employees' child-care bills, based on a formula that factors in both family income and the number of dependents. In 1990, all permanent employees with combined family incomes of $30,000 or less were eligible for the program, and subsidies ranged from 20 to 80 percent of child-care expenses.

Polaroid also became one of the first companies in the country to help its workers find child care when it began, in the early 1970s, to offer referrals informally and to fund the Child Care Resource Center in Cambridge. The company now has a contract with that agency, and with another in New Bedford, Massachusetts, to provide its workers with an enhanced referral service that advises parents on their child-care options and steers them to openings at centers or with in-home providers.

Polaroid's disability policy is one of the best in the country, providing full salary replacement for up to sixty-five days during the first year of employment (one day of disability pay for one day worked, up to sixty-five), and up to twelve months for workers with a year of seniority. For women who take time off for childbirth, that coverage can make a tremendous difference. Flexible work options at Polaroid are a bit less extensive than at some companies, but informal arrangements have been made in many areas to accommodate employees with family obligations.

# The Principal Financial Group

711 High Street
Des Moines, IA 50392                       515-247-5111

*Nature of business:* Financial services.
*Number of employees:* 11,800.
*Female employees:* 80 percent.
*Child care:* Resource-and-referral service in Des Moines; reimbursement for overnight child-care expenses when employees must travel; support for community-based child-care resources; pretax salary set-aside (DCAP).

***Elder care:*** Pretax salary set-aside (DCAP).

***Family leave:*** Paid disability leave for childbirth, plus up to ninety days unpaid personal leave; three paid sick days may be used for care of ill family members at managers' discretion (and can be used in one-hour increments).

***Flexible work options:*** Flextime in most positions; some part-time work; some work-at-home.

***Other benefits:*** Employee assistance program; lunchtime seminars on family issues; on-site fitness center; dental insurance; adoption aid up to $2,500; 401(k) plan with employer contribution.

W orking parents in Des Moines should be thankful that The Principal Financial Group and other businesses have devoted so much effort to building child-care resources in the area. Even those who don't work at those companies can take advantage of Polk County's child-care referral service, and all parents in the area benefit from that agency's expanded function of recruiting and training family day-care providers. That system is in place in large part because of the efforts of a group of area employers.

Those who work at The Principal Financial Group have access to the referral service, as well as a range of other family-supportive policies, including reimbursement for overnight baby-sitting services when traveling, and flexible work hours with a two-hour window at the start and end of the day. Between Memorial Day and Labor Day, workers get an even bigger dose of flexibility: the company reduces the workday by a half hour during the summer.

# Procter & Gamble

One Procter & Gamble Plaza
Cincinnati, OH 45202                    513-983-1100

***Nature of business:*** Manufacturer of soap and detergents, as well as other household and personal-care products.

***Number of employees:*** 44,000.

***Female employees:*** 31 percent (5 percent of upper management).

***Child care:*** Support for community-based resources, including start-up funding for two child-care centers and a resource-and-referral agency in Cincinnati, and for a near-site center in Perry, Florida; child-care subsidies an option in flexible benefit plan; pretax salary set-aside (DCAP).

**Elder care:** Reimbursement for certain in-home and day-care expenses for elderly relatives an option in flexible benefit plan; long-term-care insurance an option in flexible benefit plan.

**Family leave:** Eight weeks paid maternity leave, plus unpaid parental leave to total of one year; part-time phase-in an option during leave period; vacation time may be used in half-day increments for family needs.

**Flexible work options:** Flextime in some departments; limited part-time work.

**Other benefits:** Adoption aid up to $2,000 per child ($6,000 maximum); spouse-relocation assistance; profit-sharing plan; lunchtime seminars on family issues; employee-assistance program; tuition reimbursement.

Procter & Gamble has long been a leader in employee benefits. Its profit-sharing plan, begun in 1885, is the oldest in American business. In 1915 it became one of the first employers in the country to offer sickness, accident, and life insurance as employee benefits. In the late 1970s and early 1980s, the company again took a leadership role by offering a series of family-care benefits and policies. It introduced a six-month child-care leave in 1977 (and has since expanded it to a year); it started an adoption-assistance program in 1982 to help employees with the costs of adoption; and, in 1984, it funded the start-up of two child-care centers in Cincinnati and a local resource-and-referral agency. The centers and the referral service now operate without ongoing support from Procter & Gamble, but they continue to serve company employees as well as the community.

By 1990, the company had expanded those early efforts with two other child-care initiatives. In Perry, Florida, it helped to create a high-quality child-care center to serve employees at that site, and in Norwich, New York, a local division worked with a number of other businesses to launch a consortium center. By the time this book appears, Procter & Gamble may have added a nationwide child-care referral service, and may have started a program of management training on family issues—both were under serious consideration as we went to press.

# Paul Revere Insurance

18 Chestnut Street
Worcester, MA 01608                              508-792-6375

**Nature of business:** Insurance.
**Number of employees:** 3,200.
**Female employees:** 73 percent (47 percent of managers).
**Child care:** Local resource-and-referral service; member of consortium center with priority access for employees; pretax salary set-aside (DCAP).
**Elder care:** Pretax salary set-aside (DCAP).
**Family leave:** Paid disability leave for childbirth, plus additional maternity leave to total of eight weeks.
**Flexible work options:** Flextime in most positions; some part-time work; limited job sharing.
**Other benefits:** Lunchtime seminars and workshops on family issues, including summer-camp fair; family-resource library; management training to increase sensitivity to family issues; employee-assistance program.

Paul Revere Insurance has offered its 1,700 Worcester-area employees access to a child-care resource-and-referral service since 1986. It also contributed to the start of, and continues to support, a consortium center that serves employees of six downtown businesses. The center was created to help fill the need for infant and toddler care, but it is small, with only twenty-four spaces, five of them for Paul Revere's workers, and the company recognizes that it meets only a fraction of employees' child-care demand. The company has made arrangements with other local providers in order to gain priority access for additional employee children, and it is considering plans to expand the consortium center.

An additional benefit for parents of school-age children is the company's summer-camp fair, which gives employees a chance to learn about summer options in the area. A management-training program, which includes a segment on understanding work-and-family issues, helps ensure that the company's flexible policies are put into practice.

# Rich's Department Store

45 Broad Street
Atlanta, GA 30302                                    404-586-4636

**Nature of business:** Department stores.
**Number of employees:** 9,000.
**Female employees:** 60 percent (60 percent of managers).
**Child care:** On-site consortium center in Atlanta; internal resource-and-referral service in Atlanta.
**Elder care:** No formal program.
**Family leave:** Accrued sick time applied toward childbirth disability leave, plus additional unpaid parental leave (generally not more than sixty days).
**Flexible work options:** Variety of part-time schedules available.

R ich's Department Store prides itself on its long history of community involvement. During the Depression, when the Atlanta school board issued scrip to the city's teachers, the store cashed the paper and held it until the city was able to make good on the payments. The company has built swimming pools at eight community centers, donated a wing at Georgia Baptist Medical Center, and founded an educational radio station. So it isn't surprising that when Rich's decided to do something about child care for its Atlanta employees, the company turned it into a community project. In 1985, Rich's provided the space in its downtown store and agreed to fund a portion of a consortium center to be used by several downtown employers. In addition to Rich's, First Atlanta, the Federal Reserve Bank, the *Atlanta Journal-Constitution,* and Georgia Pacific each contributed to the start-up cost in return for twenty employee spaces. Twenty additional spaces were reserved for the public.

Twenty Rich's employees still use the center, which has one of the lowest teacher/child ratios in the state, and is one of the few centers in Georgia to be accredited by the National Association for the Education of Young Children. While the other member companies have gradually eliminated their subsidies, according to a planned formula, Rich's still provides the space free of charge.

The company has yet to offer any comparable benefit to workers who can't take advantage of the center (twenty child-care spaces for 9,000 employees is, after all, but a drop in the bucket), but the company does offer some attractive flexible work options. There is plenty of part-time work available, and part-timers who work at least eighteen hours get the full benefit package, including partially paid health insurance.

# Riverside Methodist Hospital

3535 Olentangy River Road
Columbus, OH 43214                    614-261-5000

*Nature of business:* Hospital.
*Number of employees:* 5,700.
*Female employees:* 80 percent.
*Child care:* On-site center for 180 children, aged six weeks to five years; on-site program for mildly ill children; staffed pickup and drop-off space for children attending nearby summer camp; resource-and-referral service.
*Elder care:* Adult day-care discount for employees' families.
*Family leave:* Paid disability leave for childbirth, plus up to a year unpaid family leave; paid time off may be used for short-term care of ill family members.
*Flexible work options:* Variety of shift options; flextime in some positions; some part-time work; some job sharing.
*Other benefits:* Employee-assistance program; employee convenience center, which offers grocery-shopping, video rental, and dry-cleaning services.

Riverside Methodist Hospital provided shuttle transportation to a nearby child-care center for ten years before it opened its own center in 1989. That transportation service, along with the child-care referral service the hospital offered, gave managers constant reminders of their employees' child-care needs. When the hospital finally did act, it moved on a large scale, building a center large enough for 180 children and planning it with a built-in subsidy to ensure high-quality care. An additional "Get Better" center for the care of mildly ill children, staffed by hospital employees, offers a backup service for children up to age twelve, at a cost to parents of just a dollar an hour. In its first year of operation, the hospital calculates that the "Get Better" center saved it $21,000 in replacement labor costs for staff who would otherwise have stayed home.

The hospital continues to provide a child-care resource-and-referral service for parents who choose not to use the center, or who can't enroll their children because of the waiting list. It also provides a novel service for school-age children: a pickup and drop-off area for children attending a local YMCA summer camp. The area is staffed for two hours every morning to accommodate parents who must start work before the camp bus arrives.

In the summer of 1990, the hospital added yet another novel benefit: a convenience center that will do employees' grocery shopping while they work, order and pick up rental videos, and drop off clothes for dry cleaning. The center has turned out to be a popular timesaver, particularly among employees whose schedules are squeezed by family responsibilities.

## The Rolscreen Co.

102 Main Street
Pella, IA 50219                                            515-628-1000

*Nature of business:* Manufacturer of Pella windows, doors, sun rooms, and skylights.
*Number of employees:* 3,000.
*Female employees:* 45 percent (20 percent of managers).
*Child care:* Support for community-based resources.
*Elder care:* No formal program.
*Family leave:* Paid disability leave for childbirth; additional unpaid leave available.
*Flexible work options:* Job sharing in both factory and office positions.
*Other benefits:* Dental insurance; 401(k) plan with employer contribution.

In 1985, fifty-five teams of job sharers worked throughout The Rolscreen Company, in offices and on the factory floor. By 1990, the number had dropped to twenty-seven teams, but the company still considers it an important work option for those who use it. The program began in 1975, when a woman asked to share a job with her sister-in-law so that both could spend more time with their families. Participants today also include older men and women who want to spend more time on personal pursuits. Job sharers receive full health- and dental-insurance coverage.

# St. Paul Fire and Marine Insurance Company

385 Washington Street
St. Paul, MN 55102                    612-221-7911

*Nature of business:* Property and liability insurance (largest member company of The St. Paul Companies, Inc.).
*Number of employees:* 7,000.
*Female employees:* 69 percent (20 percent of officers).
*Child care:* On-site center for 100 children at new headquarters site, to open in 1991; support for community-based resources; pretax salary set-aside (DCAP).
*Elder care:* Pretax salary set-aside (DCAP).
*Family leave:* Paid disability leave for childbirth, plus up to six months unpaid parental leave; up to ten paid "essential leave" days per year may be used for personal illness, for care of ill family members, or for paternity and adoption leave (at discretion of supervisors).
*Flexible work options:* Flextime in most positions; some part-time work; limited work-at-home.
*Other benefits:* Lunchtime seminars on family issues; family-resource library; employee-assistance program; employee stock-ownership plan.

About half of St. Paul Fire and Marine's employees work on nonstandard schedules, varying their days around the set core hours of 9:00 A.M. to 3:00 P.M. Almost 100 work part-time schedules, and about 30 have made arrangements to work part of the week at home.

By 1990, the company hadn't yet taken the step of offering employees a child-care resource-and-referral service, but it was thinking about child care. An on-site child-care center was in the works at the headquarters site, planned for a 1991 opening. The company has also given substantial amounts of money to community child-care resources, including a grant of $35,000 in 1989 to the local child-care resource-and-referral agency, several other grants to help start or expand child-care centers in the Minneapolis–St. Paul area, and a grant of $10,000 in 1990 to a community effort to review and expand child-care resources. It is probably only a matter of time before employees here begin to benefit from a more formal internal support system, one that will extend some help to the thousands of workers outside of Minnesota.

## St. Vincent's Hospital

2701 9th Court S.
Birmingham, AL 35205                                    205-939-7000

*Nature of business:* Hospital.
*Number of employees:* 1,550.
*Female employees:* 75 percent (60 percent of managers and supervisors).
*Child care:* On-site center for 86 children, aged six weeks to five years; subsidized program for care of mildly ill children.
*Elder care:* No formal program.
*Family leave:* Paid disability for childbirth (for some workers), plus up to one year unpaid maternity leave; six months unpaid personal leave; five family sick days can be used for care of ill family members.
*Flexible work options:* Variety of full-time shifts offered (twelve-, ten-, and eight-hour shifts, twenty-four-hour weekend shifts, etc.); part-time work common; job sharing.
*Other benefits:* Employee-assistance program.

Many hospitals claim that flexible work hours are impossible for nurses and other medical workers, given the requirements of patient care. Institutions like St. Vincent's prove them wrong by running a kaleidoscope of shifts in different areas, effectively giving workers a choice of hours to meet their individual needs.

In 1989, St. Vincent's went a step farther and opened its own child-care center, and it did it in a way that demonstrates the hospital's commitment to working parents. The center is owned and run by the hospital. The teachers, all of whom have degrees in early childhood education, are hospital employees. Teacher-child ratios are kept well below state-mandated levels. And the rates for employees are reduced through a substantial subsidy. Betty Williams, vice president of human resources at the hospital, explains the thinking behind some of those decisions: "Our hospital is known as a quality institution. We have a reputation in this community, and we felt we didn't want to have child care that wasn't up to the quality of our patient care. Aside from that we recognized that child care could be a real recruiting tool for us. And because other hospitals in the area were beginning to offer child care, we felt we had to offer better care. Otherwise we'd just be keeping up."

St. Vincent's has also created an innovative program for the care of sick children. While some hospitals offer such programs as a way to generate money from otherwise empty beds, here the emphasis is on creating a valuable service for the employees. The hospital has contracted with a temporary health-care agency to provide in-home care givers to employees who call. The agency bills the hospital, and the hospital deducts two hours from the employee's bank of sick time. Employees who use the service save most of a day of sick time, and the hospital saves the cost of replacement labor.

## Seattle Times Company

Fairview Avenue N. and John Street
Seattle, WA 98111 206-464-2398

*Nature of business:* Newspaper publisher.
*Number of employees:* 2,000.
*Female employees:* 31 percent (31 percent of officials and managers).
*Child care:* Near-site center for 62 children, aged six weeks to six years; subsidy program; subsidy for care of mildly ill children; resource-and-referral service through employee-assistance program; pretax salary set-aside (DCAP).
*Elder care:* Consultation-and-referral service through local agency; pretax salary set-aside (DCAP).
*Family leave:* Paid disability leave for childbirth, plus up to six months unpaid maternity leave; up to six months personal leave for those with five years of service (may be combined with maternity leave); paid sick time may be used for short-term care of ill family members.
*Flexible work options:* Some part-time; some job sharing.
*Other benefits:* Employee-assistance program; lunchtime seminars on family issues.

An employee committee at the *Seattle Times* has guided the company into some novel solutions to family-care issues. In 1988, the company helped start a nearby child-care center, spending $200,000 to renovate a building it owned, and offering the space to the center for a dollar a year. The newspaper does not manage the center, and is not otherwise involved in its operation, but it continues to subsidize the fees of its needier employees in an innovative arrangement with the Consumer Credit Council. The council reviews employees' budgets and recommends subsidies to the employee committee. Subsidies are then paid in such a way that the recipients remain anonymous to the newspaper.

Some equally novel part-time arrangements have been made here, including one in which three employees share two jobs— each works for four months and takes two months off. More common are two- and three-day weeks, and part-timers who work half days.

## Standard Insurance Co.

1100 S.W. 6th Avenue
Portland, OR 97204                              503-248-2700

*Nature of business:* Insurance.
*Number of employees:* 1,500.
*Female employees:* 66 percent (19 percent of upper-level managers).
*Child care:* Resource-and-referral service; subsidy program; pretax salary set-aside (DCAP).
*Elder care:* Pretax salary set-aside (DCAP).
*Family leave:* Paid disability leave for childbirth, plus up to six months unpaid parental leave; paid sick days may be used for care of ill family members.
*Flexible work options:* Flexible work hours; some part-time work; some job sharing.
*Other benefits:* Seminars and video workshops on family issues.

Standard Insurance not only helps employees find child care through its resource-and-referral service, it helps them pay for the care they find. The company reimburses employees for a portion of their child-care expenses, using an income-based scale. The highest percentage, 35 percent, is paid to those whose household income falls below $13,200. The minimum 5 percent subsidy goes to those who earn more than

$50,000. By state law, the company must give at least twelve weeks of parental leave; it extends that to six months whenever business needs allow.

# Steelcase

901 44th Street, S.E.
Grand Rapids, MI 49508                                    616-247-2710

**Nature of business:** Office furniture manufacturer.
**Number of employees:** 14,200.
**Female employees:** 22 percent (11 percent of managers).
**Child care:** In-house resource-and-referral service; pretax salary set-aside (DCAP), with company contribution an option in flexible benefit package.
**Elder care:** No formal program.
**Family leave:** Paid medical leave for childbirth, plus unpaid personal leave (generally one to three months) with same-job guarantee.
**Flexible work options:** Flextime in some departments; job sharing in production and office positions; other part-time work possible.
**Other benefits:** Adoption reimbursement up to $2,400; on-site fitness center; on-site medical center; lunchtime parenting workshops; family-resource library; cafeteria offers take-home dinners and party platters.

Steelcase broke new ground when it established its in-house child-care referral service in 1979, and it has continued to be a leader in work-and-family benefits. The company introduced flextime in 1980 and launched a job-sharing program in 1982. Both were originally limited to office workers, and flextime remains an option only for salaried employees, but the job-sharing program has since been expanded to production jobs. Ninety-four workers shared forty-seven jobs at Steelcase in 1990. Three of the jobs were salaried professional positions (district sales manager, senior employment representative, and dealer services representative), eleven were hourly production jobs, and the balance clerical and administrative jobs. Another forty-five employees worked regular part-time jobs, twelve of them in the factory.

Steelcase's child-care referral service has grown over the

years, and now—in cooperation with a local child-care agency— maintains a list of almost four hundred family day-care providers. Each year it helps about four hundred employees place more than five hundred children in day care. The company has also added an emergency-care feature to the service. When normal child-care arrangements break down unexpectedly, Steelcase parents can call the referral service to find the names of providers willing to take children on a short-term basis with little or no notice. The referral service staff carry beepers and respond to calls at any hour.

Even the cafeteria here is run as a family benefit. Parents can order take-home dinners at cost from the gourmet lunchtime menu—a tremendous convenience appreciated by many working parents, and a healthy alternative to fast food. Every Steelcase employee is offered a free meal on her birthday, and if she orders ahead she can have a competitively priced personalized cake for dessert. Parents can use the same decorative cake service for their children's birthdays.

# Syntex

3401 Hillview Avenue
Palo Alto, CA 94304                415-855-5050

*Nature of business:* Human and animal pharmaceuticals and medical diagnostic systems.
*Number of U.S. employees:* 5,550.
*Female employees:* 49 percent (31 percent of managers).
*Child care:* Near-site center for 150 children, aged six weeks to six years; pretax salary set-aside (DCAP) for those who use center; income-based subsidies to help with center fees.
*Elder care:* No formal program.
*Family leave:* Fully paid disability leave for childbirth, plus up to two months unpaid personal leave; eight hours of paid personal time may be used to care for ill family members.
*Flexible work options:* Flexible work hours arranged individually; some part-time work; some job sharing.
*Other benefits:* Adoption aid up to $2,000; lunchtime and evening seminars on family issues, including elder care; employee-assistance program; college scholarships for employees' children; on-site fitness center; subsidized cafeteria; profit sharing.

Syntex is a hard-working company where long hours are the norm. As a result, such scheduling options as part-time work and flexible hours are not widely used here, though they are certainly available on a case-by-case basis. For parents who want a satisfying career with a company that makes beneficial products—Syntex was involved with the development of the birth-control pill and makes Naprosyn, the best-selling prescription drug for arthritis in the U.S.—the company helps out in other ways. It offers a fully paid disability leave for childbirth, and a same-job guarantee for leaves as long as four months.

In 1984, Syntex helped start a child-care center for its employees, renovating space in a nearby high school and contracting with an independent entity to govern and operate the facility. The company has since paid for expansion of the center, and has occasionally made up for operating deficits. Tuition is within the market rate for the area, ranging from $670 per month for infants to $455 per month for three- and four-year-olds in 1990. For some, those rates are lowered by company scholarships, which are based on family size and income.

## The Time Inc. Magazine Company

Rockefeller Center
New York, NY 10020                    212-522-1212

*Nature of business:* Magazine publishing.
*Number of employees:* 3,250.
*Female employees:* 54 percent (6 of 23 officers).
*Child care:* Nationwide resource-and-referral service; emergency child-care service in metropolitan New York area; pretax salary set-aside (DCAP).
*Elder care:* Nationwide consultation-and-referral service; pretax salary set-aside (DCAP).
*Family leave:* Paid disability leave for childbirth, plus unpaid parental leave to a total of one year; part-time phase-in for returning mothers possible.
*Flexible work options:* Some part-time work; some job sharing; some work-at-home.
*Other benefits:* Adoption aid up to $2,100; lunchtime seminars on family issues, including elder care; support groups for single parents, parents with children of various ages, and employees with aging relatives; developed "Work & Family Booklet" to help sensitize managers to work-and-family issues; profit sharing; employee stock-ownership plan.

The Time Inc. Magazine Company is one of the many companies under the corporate umbrella now called Time Warner Inc., and several of that group's businesses have taken progressive steps in their family policies. Almost all, for example, offer child-care and elder-care referral services. Little, Brown and Company offers an emergency child-care service to employees in the Boston area, and gives one-hundred-dollar savings bonds to new babies of employees. Warner Brothers Studio joined a consortium to establish the Horace Mann Child Care Center in Los Angeles, and in 1990 built its own center with a capacity for 108 children. But of all the efforts, those at the magazine company and at HBO stand out, and those two companies are the ones we have chosen to focus on in this book. (See separate description of HBO.)

The Time Inc. Magazine Company, which long had a reputation as a stronghold for WASP males, has been changing. Women hold some key positions now, particularly on the business side of the operation, and in the past few years the company has taken some innovative steps to assist those on its staff who have family responsibilities. The company's leave policy is the most generous in the corporate group. The company spearheaded the creation of an emergency child-care service in New York, which brings providers to employees' homes when children are mildly sick or when normal child-care arrangements break down. And both the child-care and elder-care referral services came to the organization through the magazine company. Other, less formal, programs also make the magazine company a receptive place for working parents. Seminars on family issues are a regular institution here, and several parent and elder-care giver support groups meet monthly.

# Trammell Crow Company

2001 Ross Avenue
Dallas, TX 75201                                    214-979-5100

*Nature of business:* Commercial real estate developer.
*Number of employees:* 3,000.
*Female employees:* 44 percent.
*Child care:* Near-site center for 60 children, aged six weeks to five years.
*Elder care:* No formal program.
*Family leave:* Paid disability leave for childbirth, plus up to six months unpaid personal leave; four weeks paid adoption

leave (with three years of service); paid sick days may be used for care of ill family members.

*Flexible work options:* Some part-time work.

*Other benefits:* Profit sharing; employee-assistance program.

Since 1982, employees in Trammell Crow's downtown Dallas office buildings have been able to drop their children off at the Trammell Crow Early Learning center, three blocks away. The firm's partners subsidize approximately a third of the center's budget. While the benefit is available only to employees in downtown Dallas, the company's leave and sick-time policies are effective throughout the organization, including paid time off for adoptive parents.

## The Travelers Companies

One Tower Square
Hartford, CT 06183-7151                                    203-277-0111

*Nature of business:* Insurance and financial services.

*Number of employees:* 38,000.

*Female employees:* 67 percent (19 percent of managers).

*Child care:* Nationwide resource-and-referral service; subsidies based on employee's annual pay; pretax salary set-aside (DCAP).

*Elder care:* Nationwide consultation-and-referral service; subsidies based on employee's annual pay; pretax salary set-aside (DCAP).

*Family leave:* Paid disability leave for childbirth, plus up to twelve months unpaid family-care leave (with no job guarantee after six months); three paid days off to care for ill family members.

*Flexible work options:* Flextime in many departments; compressed work weeks; some part-time work; some job sharing; some work-at-home.

*Other benefits:* Lunchtime seminars on family issues, including elder care; family-resource library; employee-assistance program; management training on work-force diversity and family issues; employee stock-ownership plan; 401(k) plan with employer contribution; free financial and insurance advice.

When The Travelers surveyed its employees on their family responsibilities in 1985, it discovered that one in four had children under the age of thirteen, and that one in five was responsible for the care of an older relative. With almost half of its work force made up of women in their childbearing years, the company decided to take a hard look at its benefits and employment practices.

The company had helped to found an employer-supported child-care referral service in Connecticut in 1982, and for some time had had a four-week maternity-leave policy, but in light of the statistics, both measures were deemed inadequate. In the fall of 1989, The Travelers announced a series of sweeping changes that moved the company into a strong leadership position in the area of work-and-family benefits. It extended its leave to a year, and opened it to fathers, adoptive parents, and people with elder-care needs (while the leave offers no job guarantee beyond six months, the company continues benefit coverage for the duration). It contracted with Work/Family Directions to offer a child-care resource-and-referral service to all of its employees around the country, and added elder-care referrals as an additional service. And it became the first major company in the country to offer subsidies to help employees pay for both child care and elder care. Some companies take shots at pieces of the work-and-family dilemma. The Travelers stormed the fort.

## US Sprint

8140 Ward Parkway
Kansas City, MO                                    816-276-6000

**Nature of business:** Telecommunications.
**Number of employees:** 17,000.
**Female employees:** 49 percent (34 percent of managers).
**Child care:** Nationwide resource-and-referral service; pretax salary set-aside (DCAP).
**Elder care:** Nationwide consultation-and-referral service; pretax salary set-aside (DCAP).
**Family leave:** Paid disability leave for childbirth, plus up to a year unpaid family-care leave; one paid floating holiday may be used in one-hour increments for family emergencies.
**Flexible work options:** Flexible work hours and compressed work weeks common; some part-time work; some job sharing.

> ***Other benefits:*** Working-partner relocation assistance; adoption aid up to $1,000; employee-assistance program; training to sensitize managers to family issues.

For several weeks in 1989, when US Sprint was in the midst of launching its child-care and elder-care referral services and expanding its "Workplace Flexibility" program, managers were required to wear buttons that read, "Family-Care—Ask Me, I Know." It might have seemed silly to some, but it indicates the company's commitment to making its work-and-family programs succeed throughout the organization.

While the company was always reasonably flexible, its new "FamilyCare" initiative, launched in the summer of 1989, has pushed it into the front ranks of family-responsive businesses. Sprint's leave policy—up to a year off with full benefits and a job guarantee—is one of the best in the country. One indication of the culture here is that men seem to feel comfortable taking the leaves: in the first year of the new policy, 20 percent of the leaves were granted to men. Flexible work arrangements really do seem to be taking hold here too, thanks to support from the top of the company and to an ongoing system of management training on the issue. About a third of US Sprint's employees worked on some sort of flexible schedule in 1990. Another 20 percent opted for compressed work weeks, and 5 percent worked at part-time jobs—including a fair number of professionals and managers.

Many companies have relocation-assistance programs. Sprint focuses more clearly than most on the special needs of working couples. It offers personalized career counseling for spouses of relocated employees, assistance in résumé preparation, help in locating jobs, and reimbursement both for job-hunting trips and for income loss related to the move—up to $2,000 per month for two months.

# U S WEST

7800 E. Orchard Road
Englewood, CO 80111                                    303-793-6500

*Nature of business:* Communication services.
*Number of employees:* 64,500.
*Female employees:* 56 percent (10 percent of officers).
*Child care:* Nationwide resource-and-referral service; company foundation funds early childhood education initiatives; pretax set-aside (DCAP).
*Elder care:* Nationwide consultation-and-referral service; pretax salary set-aside (DCAP).
*Family leave:* Paid disability leave for childbirth, plus up to a year unpaid family-care leave, or up to two years "enhanced" leave.
*Flexible work options:* Flextime and compressed work week available in most departments; some part-time work; some job sharing; some work-at-home.
*Other benefits:* Lunchtime seminars on family issues; employee-assistance program; 401(k) plan with employer contribution; employee stock-ownership plan; employer-paid defined-benefit pension plan.

The regional telephone companies are among the leaders when it comes to family benefits, and U S WEST stands out even in this group. The company's pilot two-year enhanced-leave policy is among the most generous in American business; it was one of the first companies to provide an elder-care referral service; and its foundation gives millions of dollars every year to early-childhood-education initiatives throughout the western states.

The foundation's educational efforts are a source of special pride at U S WEST, and though not a direct employee benefit, many of the initiatives have been an indirect aid, improving the quality and availability of child care in many communities. The foundation helped to create an enhanced child-care referral network in Polk County, Iowa; a before- and after-school program in Albuquerque, New Mexico; and a child-care center adjacent to the public high school in Sioux Falls, South Dakota. Says Jack MacAllister, chairman of U S WEST's board, "Our children are our future. Our choices are to invest our energy in educating them or to become a nation without skilled workers, a region unable to compete in the global economy, a people whose progress is hampered by social inequity."

# UNUM Life Insurance Company

2211 Congress Street
Portland, ME 04122                                      207-770-2211

*Nature of business:* Specialty disability and employee benefits insurance.
*Number of employees:* 5,000 (worldwide).
*Female employees:* 71 percent (56 percent of managers).
*Child care:* On-site center for 84 children, aged six weeks to six years; income-based subsidies; local resource-and-referral service; pretax salary set-aside (DCAP).
*Elder care:* Long-term-care insurance at group rates; pretax salary set-aside (DCAP).
*Family leave:* Paid disability leave for childbirth, plus up to three months unpaid parental leave; three paid personal days may be used for care of ill family members.
*Flexible work options:* Flextime in many departments; limited part-time work; limited job sharing; some work-at-home.
*Other benefits:* Lunchtime seminars on family issues; employee-assistance program; on-site fitness center; profit-sharing plan; 401(k) plan with employer contribution.

Terry Cohen, senior vice president of human resources at UNUM, likes to tell the story of how she was troubled several years ago by the habit the company's former chief executive officer had of calling early-morning meetings. With a young son at home, a husband who also worked, and a child-care arrangement that didn't accommodate odd schedules, Cohen was continually juggling work hours and scrambling for backup baby-sitters. She finally gathered the courage to raise the issue and still chuckles at the response. "It was no big deal. He wondered why I hadn't mentioned it sooner. He rarely scheduled another meeting outside the child-care hours, and always checked with me before he did."

The company has been aware of child-care issues for some time. In 1979 it worked with Kinder-Care to start a center for UNUM's employees in Portland, Maine. UNUM paid for the construction of a building and offered Kinder-Care a low rent in return for priority access and a 10 percent discount to the company's employees. In 1989, an employee survey showed that many parents still had serious problems with the cost of care and with the availability of infant care. UNUM responded with a child-care subsidy that pays $30 per week for one child, or $50 per week for two, to parents earning less than $25,000 annually. The company also changed contractors at the Portland center, turning the operation over to Koala Care, a local organization that owned and ran another center in the area. Parents now have a stronger voice in the center's operation, and, with an UNUM-funded renovation of the space, the number of slots reserved for infants and toddlers has more than doubled.

# Warner-Lambert Company

201 Tabor Road
Morris Plains, NJ 07950                    201-540-2000

*Nature of business:* Ethical pharmaceuticals, over-the-counter health-care and consumer products.
*Number of employees:* 11,000.
*Female employees:* 45 percent (18 percent of managers).
*Child care:* Nationwide resource-and-referral service; funding for community-based child-care initiatives; in-home care-giver program for mildly ill children; pretax salary set-aside (DCAP).
*Elder care:* Nationwide consultation-and-referral service; pretax salary set-aside (DCAP).
*Family leave:* Paid disability leave for childbirth, plus up to three months unpaid family-care leave; paid sick days may be used to care for ill family members.
*Flexible work options:* Flextime in most departments; part-time work and job sharing available in some areas; work-at-home possible.
*Other benefits:* Seminars on family issues; wellness programs; fitness center; tuition reimbursement; spouse-relocation assistance; SchoolMatch program to assist relocating families with school choices; employee-assistance program; management training scheduled for 1991 to increase sensitivity to family issues.

Many readers may not be familiar with the Warner-Lambert name, but most will recognize its brand-name products: Listerine mouthwash, Parke-Davis pharmaceuticals, Chiclets and Dentyne chewing gum, Junior Mints candy, and Schick razors, to name a few. It may be that the company's name finally gains some public recognition as a leader in the field of family benefits.

Between 1984 and 1990, the percentage of women in Warner-Lambert's work force jumped from 29 percent to 45 percent, and the company has responded to that trend—and the trend toward more dual-career families—with an array of family-supportive programs. The company offers both child-care and elder-care referral services to all of its U.S. employees. It has helped fund child-care centers near its major facilities, given marketing assistance to campaigns to recruit family day-care providers, and joined with other businesses in the area of its New Jersey headquarters to start a service that offers in-home care for mildly ill children.

# Wells Fargo Bank

420 Montgomery Street
San Francisco, CA 94163                           415-396-0213

*Nature of business:* Banking and financial services.
*Number of employees:* 25,000.
*Female employees:* 71 percent (64 percent of officers).
*Child care:* Nationwide resource-and-referral service; reimbursement for child-care expenses when employees must work late or travel; funding to increase community supply of child care; funding for California referral service; pretax salary set-aside (DCAP).
*Elder care:* Internal consultation-and-referral service through employee-assistance program; funding to increase community supply of elder day care; pretax salary set-aside (DCAP).
*Family leave:* Paid disability leave for childbirth, plus up to six months unpaid family leave; paid sick days may be used for care of ill family members.
*Flexible work options:* Flextime common; compressed work week in some departments; part-time work and job sharing common; some work-at-home.
*Other benefits:* Family-resource centers in San Francisco

and Los Angeles; management training to increase sensitivity to family needs; scholarships for employees' children; personal-growth leaves for employees with ten or more years of service; retiree temporary work-force program.

S everal hundred people job share at Wells Fargo, from clerical assistants to vice presidents. While the practice is often thought of as an opportunity for young mothers with husbands who work full-time, job sharers here include single mothers, husband-wife teams, and employees—men and women—who are phasing into retirement.

Wells Fargo has been involved with child-care and family issues since the 1970s. It was one of the first supporters of the California Child Care Initiative, a project to expand the supply and improve the quality of child care throughout the state; and it was one of the first to back the California Child Care Network, a statewide referral service and provider-support network. It is one of the few companies to reimburse workers for special overnight and evening child-care expenses when they must work late or travel. And its paid sick-time policy is one of the most generous and flexible around: paid time is earned at a rate of one day per month and can be used by employees for their own illnesses or when they need time off to care for family members. Unused time accumulates forever, and large banks of time can be a tremendous aid to long-term employees who need time off to care for adult dependents.

# White Flower Farm

Route 63
Litchfield, CT 06759                203-496-9624

*Nature of business:* Mail-order nursery.
*Number of employees:* 85, plus up to 125 additional seasonal employees.
*Female employees:* 60 percent (50 percent of managers).
*Child care:* Subsidy program; priority access at independent on-site center with room for 90 children, aged six weeks to five years.
*Elder care:* No formal program.
*Family leave:* Paid disability leave for childbirth, plus unpaid family leave to total of twelve weeks.

*Flexible work options:* Flextime in most positions; some part-time work; some job sharing.
*Other benefits:* Profit-sharing plan; 401(k) plan.

White Flower Farm once had its own child-care center, but, because of the cost, has turned it over to an independent operator. Though it is still called the White Flower Farm Day Care Center, the only remaining connection is that the farm's workers have priority over others on the center's waiting list. In place of its support for the center, the company now offers direct subsidies to help its employees with their child-care expenses. These are paid to employees as reimbursement for the cost of any licensed child care they select. The subsidies are limited to infant and preschool care, are available only to full-time employees, and range from $20–30 per week per child (depending on the child's age) to a maximum of $50 per week for each employee.

The flextime schedule here allows for starting times between 8:00 and 10:00 A.M., a policy that not only gives workers some maneuverability, but helps to keep the company staffed into the evening to field calls from western time zones. Job sharing took hold here in 1989, when two people took over the job of administrative assistant to the company's vice president.

# Wilton Connor Packaging

P.O. Box 7627
Charlotte, NC 28241-7627                    704-588-8522

*Nature of business:* Commercial packaging.
*Number of employees:* 77.
*Female employees:* 42 (46 percent of managers).
*Child care:* Resource-and-referral service; subsidy program; plans for on-site center.
*Elder care:* No formal program.
*Family leave:* Paid disability leave for childbirth, plus negotiable unpaid leave.
*Flexible work options:* No flextime, but hours arranged to meet needs of working parents.
*Other benefits:* On-site laundry service; door-to-door transportation including stops for child care; on-site English classes; children's clothing swap center.

Wilton Connor Packaging may be a small company, but it is one with big ideas, and many of its innovative programs could serve as models for companies many times its size. It is the only company we ran across with an on-site laundry facility, which was created to free employees' time after work, and to allow them to spend more time with their families. Workers can bring their laundry in with them in the morning, and the clothes are washed, dried, and folded during the day. They not only save time by using the service, they save money: the washing is offered at cost, with no company markup.

Wilton Connor Packaging is also one of the smallest companies we found that offers a child-care resource-and-referral service, and one of the few of any size that couples that service with child-care subsidies. The company pays $15 per week for every child in licensed care, or $10 for children in part-time and after-school care, making out the checks directly to the care givers. The subsidy program has allowed some parents to find better care than they could previously afford. When owners Catherine McDermott and Wilton Connor heard about the schedules and transportation routes of some of their employees—one woman took four buses and made two child-care stops before arriving at work at 7:00 A.M.—they launched a door-to-door transportation system. Workers drive city-supplied vans on two regular routes, carrying more than half of the company's workers to and from their jobs, with child-care stops along the way.

We visited the packaging business just as the van service and the child-care subsidies were beginning, and we talked to a number of employees who felt, some for the first time in their working lives, that they had a future with the business. Many of the jobs here are relatively unskilled, with pay comparable to that found in fast-food restaurants, but several workers had moved off the line into office jobs, and many held the first supervisory jobs of their careers. Every time we called to check back with the company it had new programs to announce—on-site English classes, credit-union membership, group disability insurance, a thrift-shop that recycles children's clothes and toys. While proud of each innovation, the company seemed to keep reaching for more. The ultimate goal here is on-site child care, and while this remained a long-term dream as we went to press, it may well have become a reality by the time the book comes out.

# Family-Friendly Options

## 1. Child-care support programs

A lingering ambivalence about whether mothers should work, a hesitancy about entering an area where businesses have little expertise, a fear of liability exposure, and the feeling that family problems are not business issues at one time kept most companies from providing any direct supports for child care. In the 1980s those barriers began to tumble as more and more companies took the step of providing direct services and as most of them met with positive results. Many of the employees we spoke with pointed to on-site centers or subsidies as reasons they came to work for or are staying at these more progressive companies.

While companies once thought of on-site centers as the only option, and many ruled them out as too expensive, today a much broader range of choices faces the manager who wants to do something to help employees find or pay for dependent care.

*Resource-and-referral service:* A service that helps employees decide what child-care options are right for them, teaches them how to look for quality care, refers them to providers in their area, and creates more care in the community by recruiting and training new providers.

- IBM, AT&T, Digital Equipment Corp., US Sprint, and about one hundred other large companies offer nationwide resource-and-referral services to their employees, through contracts with businesses like Work/Family Directions in Boston, Massachusetts, and The Partnership Group in Lansdale, Pennsylvania. Most of the large companies in the book offer this service.
- John Hancock Mutual Life Insurance Co., Polaroid Corporation, and many other businesses offer statewide or local resource-and-referral services by contracting directly with local agencies. About half of the mid-sized businesses in the book have chosen this option. Among the smaller companies to offer a resource-and-referral service in this way are Fox, Rothschild, O'Brien & Frankel (with 320 employees) and Byrne Electrical Specialties (with 120 employees).

- Hemmings Motor News, Hewitt Associates, Household International, Lincoln National, Rich's Department Store, and Steelcase manage their own resource-and-referral services for employees.

*Subsidies:* A direct aid to help employees pay for child care. Some companies offer a flat subsidy to all employees; others use a sliding scale that gives the greatest aid to lower-income employees. Subsidies can be paid directly to providers, or to employees as reimbursement for their expenses. Subsidies are sometimes used to balance child-care benefits offered at one site and not another.

- Polaroid has offered income-based subsidies since 1971. Among other companies to offer this option are Joseph Alfandre & Co., America West Airlines, Lost Arrow Corp., Lotus Development Corp., NCNB, Stride Rite, The Travelers Companies, and UNUM Life Insurance Company. While Polaroid, Joseph Alfandre & Co., and NCNB base their subsidies on total family income, The Travelers Companies measures only the employee's income.
- Alley's General Store and International Transcript offer employees full subsidies at nearby centers. SAS Institute Inc. offers its employees free tuition at its own on-site centers. Among the companies that offer partial child-care subsidies (either a set amount per week or a percentage of the employee's total child-care costs) are Edmar Corporation; First Hawaiian, Inc.; Green's Stationery; Hanna Andersson; Hemmings Motor News; Mechanics and Farmers Savings Bank; Dunning, Forman, Kirane & Terry; White Flower Farm; and Wilton Connor Packaging.
- United States Hosiery Corporation offers near-site child care at one production site, and, in a gesture of fairness, child-care subsidies at its second. Neuville Industries offers on-site child care to its day-shift workers and subsidies to those who work the second and third shifts.
- Honfed Bank, Procter & Gamble, and Steelcase offer child-care subsidies as an option in flexible benefit packages.

*Pretax salary set-aside (Dependent Care Assistance Program):* A provision in the U.S. tax code allows employees to establish spending accounts for dependent-care and medical expenses. Employees may set aside up to $5,000 in pretax income for these expenses. Any money not spent by year end, however, is forfeited, and the tax savings should be compared to the Child and

Dependent Care Credit available to all workers, since the employee must choose between the two measures.

- Most of the companies listed in this book offer this option. The smallest of them is Oliver Wight, with seventeen employees.

*Support for community initiatives:* Many companies have worked in partnership with public agencies or with other community facilities to create services, expand child-care facilities, and improve the quality of available care.

- IBM and AT&T have launched major initiatives to expand the supply and improve the quality of child care at key sites around the country. Du Pont has directed a similar effort at improving the child-care delivery system in Delaware, contributing money to start a child-care resource-and-referral service and supporting a number of ongoing care-giver recruitment and training programs.
- NCNB has offered low-interest loans in South Carolina to new or expanding child-care centers.
- Atlantic Richfield Company and The Dow Chemical Company have supported community after-school programs.
- The Bureau of National Affairs, Hallmark Cards, The Principal Financial Group, Procter & Gamble, The Rolscreen Company, and Warner-Lambert have all contributed funds or expertise to community-based child-care initiatives.
- Corning, Gannett, and Levi Strauss & Company have contributed to community-based child-care services through their foundations.

*Consortium efforts:* Companies often combine their efforts to create services and facilities.

- First Atlanta, Grieco Bros., Hunter Industries, Paul Revere Insurance, Rich's Department Store, and United States Hosiery Corporation each participated in the creation of child-care centers that serve a number of employers. Procter & Gamble is a sponsor of a new consortium child-care center in Norwich, New York.
- HBO and The Time Inc. Magazine Company joined with other New York City businesses to create an emergency child-care service.

*Family day-care networks:* A few companies have, either by themselves or through local resource-and-referral agencies, created networks of family day-care homes that offer priority access to employees.

- America West Airlines has created such networks in Phoenix and Las Vegas. Donnelly Corp., Lincoln National, and Lost Arrow Corp. have all organized similar networks of family day-care homes, which they support with ongoing recruitment and training programs. Steelcase and Donnelly Corp. reserve spaces in family day-care homes for employees to use when their normal child-care arrangements break down.

*On-site or near-site centers:* More and more companies are creating and supporting their own child-care facilities in order to ensure convenient, high-quality care to their employees. A center can be established as a department within a company, as a separate corporation with a mechanism for parent involvement, or it can be created through an arms-length relationship with a management company, a not-for-profit agency, or a for-profit provider. Operating money comes from a combination of parent fees and company subsidies.

- Lost Arrow Corp., Bowles Corporation (with just twelve employees), and St. Vincent's Hospital operate centers as departments within their companies, as does SAS Institute, which provides care for more than 300 children as a fully paid benefit of employment.
- S. C. Johnson & Son, Inc., established its center as a separate nonprofit corporation, and contributes an annual operating subsidy. The center is NAEYC accredited, as are the centers at Carlson Craft, Champion International, Dominion Bankshares, and Lomas Financial Group.
- Barnett Banks made an arrangement with La Petite Academy, a business which operates a chain of for-profit centers, to start and run an on-site center.
- BE&K created a movable child-care center near a construction site in Georgia, designed to be dismantled when the project is finished and rebuilt near another work site.
- Overseas Adventure Travel offers family day care in an apartment above its offices.
- Aetna Life and Casualty, Massachusetts Mutual Life Insurance Co., Merck & Co., Pacific Presbyterian Medical Center, and White Flower Farm have all made arrangements with providers to give their employees priority access at nearby centers.
- Merck & Co. and Procter & Gamble provided start-up fund-

ing for parent-run child-care centers, without committing themselves to long-term involvement.

*Care for school-age children:* Some child-care centers include before- and after-school care. Some companies offer special care during school vacations. Others have established or made arrangements with camps for summer care. A few offer on-site classrooms.

- Lost Arrow Corp., Byrne Electrical Specialists, Fleetguard, Inc., Hoffmann-La Roche, Marquette Electronics, and United States Hosiery Corporation offer before- and after-school care at their on- or near-site centers.
- Baptist Hospital of Miami, the Collins Divisions of Rockwell International, Fel-Pro, United States Hosiery Corporation, and S. C. Johnson & Son, Inc., run summer camps in addition to their regular child-care programs.
- 3M contributes to and operates a van service to and from a summer camp. Riverside Methodist Hospital of Columbus, Ohio, offers a staffed waiting area where children can wait for a bus to a nearby YMCA camp. Eastman Kodak Co. provides pickup and drop-off stations for a bus to a nearby summer camp.
- John Hancock Mutual Insurance Company contracts with a local agency to provide care during certain school holidays and vacations.
- Atlantic Richfield and The Dow Chemical Company have worked with local communities to create public before- and after-school programs.

*Emergency child care and care for mildly ill children:* Some on-site or near-site centers include facilities for the care of mildly ill children. Companies can also arrange priority access for employees' children at local centers or hospitals with sick-child facilities. They can also make arrangements with services that offer in-home providers when children are mildly sick or when normal care arrangements break down. A few companies offer on-site child care as a backup for days when normal care arrangements break down.

- United States Hosiery Corp.'s near-site consortium center includes a room for mildly ill children. Johnson & Johnson's on-site center has three rooms for the care of mildly ill children.
- Bayfront Medical Center, Blodgett Memorial Medical Center, and Riverside Methodist Hospital in Columbus, Ohio,

offer on-site care of mildly ill children in hospital facilities at rates discounted for employees.

- A number of companies have made arrangements with outside providers for care for employees' children when they are mildly ill or when normal arrangements break down, and have agreed to subsidize all or a portion of the fees. Among these are Leo Burnett Company, Fel-Pro, The Dow Chemical Company, First Hawaiian, HBO, Hewitt Associates, Merck & Co., 3M, Seattle Times Company, The Time Inc. Magazine Company, and Warner-Lambert. St. Vincent's Hospital has contracted with an in-home care-giving service, and charges employees two hours of sick time for each day they use the service.
- Steelcase and Donnelly Corp. reserve spaces in the homes of family day-care providers for occasions when employees' normal child-care arrangements break down.
- Arthur Andersen & Co. provides on-site child care on Saturdays during the tax season.
- Hoffmann-La Roche and S. C. Johnson & Son, Inc., offer emergency and drop-in care at their child-care centers.

*Reimbursement for child-care expenses when employees must travel:* Travel can be the bane of a working parent's existence, and it can be expensive to provide after-hours or overnight care. A few companies have recognized the problem and offer reimbursement for extraordinary child-care costs.

- John Hancock Mutual Life Insurance Co., Hewitt Associates, The Principal Financial Group, and Wells Fargo Bank all offer reimbursement for extra child-care costs necessitated by travel. Hewitt Associates extends its policy to elder care. Wells Fargo Bank will pay for child care when employees must work late.

## 2. Elder-care support programs

Elder care is a quieter matter than child care, and co-workers often don't realize they have similar care-giving responsibilities until company programs bring them together in information sessions or support programs. By the year 2000, demographic projections show that more employees will have elder-care than child-care responsibilities. Companies are responding with a range of support programs.

*Consultation-and-referral service:* A service that helps employees determine what their elder-care needs are, and helps direct them to available support systems and services. A key component of such a service is counseling to help employees cope with the stress of elder-care crises. A growing number of large companies offer nationwide referrals through such companies as Work/Family Elder Directions in Boston, Massachusetts, and The Partnership Group in Lansdale, Pennsylvania. Smaller companies are more likely to offer a similar service through a local agency or vendor.

- IBM offered the first nationwide elder-care consultation-and-referral service. Several other companies now offer much the same service. Those listed in this book are AT&T, Aetna Life and Casualty, Arthur Andersen & Co., Du Pont, Johnson & Johnson, Kemper National Insurance Companies, The Travelers Companies, US Sprint, U S WEST, and Warner-Lambert.
- A number of other companies offer local referral services, among them Atlantic Richfield Company; Beth Israel Hospital of Boston; Leo Burnett Company; Fel-Pro; Fox, Rothschild, O'Brien & Frankel; Hallmark Cards; John Hancock Mutual Life Insurance Co.; Hoffmann-La Roche; Hunter Industries; Lost Arrow Corp.; Lotus Development Corp.; Massachusetts Mutual Life Insurance Co.; Herman Miller; J. P. Morgan & Co.; The New England; Ohio Bell; Polaroid Corporation; Seattle Times Company; and The Time Inc. Magazine Company.
- Hewitt Associates and Wells Fargo Bank operate internal consultation-and-referral services.

*Subsidies:* While public funding is available for some elder-care expenses, many other expenses must be borne by individuals. A few companies offer subsidies to help with these costs.

- First Hawaiian, Inc.; Hemmings Motor News; and The Travelers Companies offer direct employee subsidies for certain elder-care expenses.
- Honfed Bank and Procter & Gamble offer elder-care subsidies as an option in their flexible benefit packages.

*Support for community resources:* A few companies have given support to community initiatives in an effort to expand the supply and improve the quality of elder care around the country or in areas where employees are finding particular difficulties.

- AT&T and IBM have made significant contributions to community elder-care initiatives around the country. Wells Fargo Bank has given support to efforts in California.

*Pretax salary set-aside (Dependent Care Assistance Program):* The same pretax salary set-aside system that can be used for child-care expenses may also be used for certain elder-care expenses, but is restricted to cases where the adult dependent lives in the employee's home, and to care during working hours.

Most of the companies in this book offer pretax salary set-asides as a limited elder-care benefit.

*Care-giver fairs and information sessions:* Some companies sponsor care-giver fairs in order to help link employees with elder-care service providers. Others offer informational seminars that can help employees determine their own needs and options.

- The Dow Chemical Co. and Lincoln National sponsor care-giver fairs.
- Ohio Bell, Fel-Pro, and many other companies offer seminars and workshops on family issues, including sessions on elder care.

*Long-term-care insurance at group rates:* A growing number of companies are offering employees a chance to buy long-term-care insurance at group rates for themselves, their spouses, and their parents. The insurance can help defray the cost of long-term nursing-home care.

- Aetna Life and Casualty, Household International, IBM, Procter & Gamble, and UNUM Life Insurance Company offer this option.

*On-site elder day care:* Some elders need care during the day, but are otherwise healthy enough to remain in their homes. Elder day-care centers meet their needs and the needs of employees who provide their care, and this is an option that some companies are exploring.

- Stride Rite has created an intergenerational center, with one wing given over to child care and another to elder care.
- On-site elder day care is planned at Baptist Hospital of Miami, Heart of the Valley Center, Lancaster Laboratories, and United States Hosiery Corporation.

*Emergency in-home care:* Elders occasionally need emergency care in their homes or in employees' homes, either because of illness or accident, or because of some other disruption to their schedules. A few companies offer employees help in finding and paying for emergency in-home care.

- Fel-Pro and Hewitt Associates offer subsidized emergency home care.

### 3. Time off for family matters

Companies that view work and family as separate realms in life, as commitments that ought not to interfere with each other, often have trouble accepting the fact that parents and workers with adult-care responsibilities sometimes need to take time off from work to deal with family matters. The states and the federal government have been equally hesitant to respond with mandates for employers. In 1990, the United States remained the only industrialized country with no national family-leave guarantees, and just fifteen states had tried to plug that gap on their own, some of those with measures limited to state employees. Time and again in our research we talked to people who had left jobs at unresponsive companies because they were not given enough time off for the birth or adoption of a baby, or because they were not allowed time off when their children or elderly relatives were sick and needed care. All of America's businesses are suffering from the failure of our educational system, and almost all bear part of the responsibility: quality schools require parent involvement, yet few companies allow working parents that luxury. From the company's point of view, granting workers time off for family matters is certainly an inconvenience, and can lead to some disruption at work. But what is gained when companies avoid short-term inconvenience and lose valuable employees? And what is gained in the long term if we sacrifice the next generation of workers for the sake of a few more hours of labor today?

The answers here are simple. Companies can offer leaves of adequate length, with benefit continuation and job guarantees; they can offer paid maternity, paternity, and adoption leaves; they can encourage employee participation in our schools by allowing paid time off for involvement in school activities; and they can extend paid sick time to employees for the care of ill family members.

- Fifty of the companies listed in this book offer parental or family leaves of six months or more. IBM has a three-year parental-leave policy; Hewitt Associates and U S WEST offer two-year leaves; Joy Cone and Merck allow eighteen months off. Among the companies that allow yearlong leaves are AT&T, Arthur Andersen, the Courier-Journal, Fleetguard, Inc., Gannett, John Hancock Mutual Life Insurance Co., Hechinger, Johnson & Johnson, Ohio Bell, Pacific Gas & Electric Co., Procter & Gamble, Riverside Methodist Hospital, SAS Institute, St. Vincent's Hospital, The Time Inc. Magazine Company, and US Sprint. Of those, John Hancock Mutual Life Insurance Co. and Pacific Gas & Electric stand out by offering same-job guarantees for the first six months of the leave.

- Lotus Development Corp., NCNB, Oliver Wight, and Overseas Adventure Travel offer paid parental leaves in addition to childbirth disability leaves, available to mothers, fathers, and adoptive parents. Hill, Holliday, Connors, Cosmopulos, Inc., offers two months of paid maternity leave to both natural and adoptive mothers (but not to fathers). Trammell Crow Company offers four weeks of paid leave for adoption.

- Hemmings Motor News and NCNB Corp. offer paid time off for employee involvement in their children's schools. Atlantic Richfield Company provides paid time off for participation in community activities.

- Most of the companies in this book offer paid time off for short-term care of ill family members. The amount of time ranges from one day per year, in the case of Syntex and US Sprint, to companies like Warner-Lambert and Wells Fargo Bank that allow all of an employee's sick days to be used for the care of ill family members. Some companies, like St. Vincent's Hospital and Atlantic Richfield Company have allotted additional paid days specifically for family illness or urgent personal business.

- Pacific Presbyterian Medical Center offers a leave-sharing program that allows employees to donate unused paid time off to others facing emergency absences.

## 4. Flexibility

Companies have traditionally relied on a fixed eight-hour day, a forty-hour week, and on review processes that judge employees by the number of hours they put in rather than by how productive, creative, or useful they are. Hastily called afterhours meetings are common at many businesses, creating regular scheduling crises for those with rigid child-care arrangements. Workers at many companies keep their office lights on when they leave, so that associates will think they are still hard at work; parents who have to leave at 5:00 to pick up their children at day care have told us that they can almost feel the eyes burning holes in their backs.

In today's world those practices are unnecessary and counterproductive, an unthinking holdover from the days when workers had spouses at home to mind the family. In our interviews with employees, both at good companies and bad, lack of flexibility came up repeatedly as the most important source of conflict between work and family demands. In our interviews with employees who had left jobs for family reasons, scheduling rigidity was the primary problem. Men and women both now want the flexibility to arrange their schedules around their family needs.

Companies are responding with more opportunities for part-time work, with job-sharing arrangements, with computer links so that employees can do some of their work at home, and with greater flexibility for full-time workers.

*Flexible work hours:* Schedule variations for full-time workers are broadly called flexible work hours. In most arrangements, workers agree to a set schedule that fits their family needs and the requirements of the job, and are expected to hold to it. A compressed work week is one such option, in which employees work their forty hours in four long days. Flextime generally refers to policies that allow for day-to-day scheduling variations.

- Most of the companies in this book will work out alternative schedules for individual employees. John Hancock Mutual Insurance Company, 3M, IBM, and many others offer flextime arrangements that allow employees to vary their schedules day by day. Kingston Warren offers a compressed work week for its production employees. Du Pont is experimenting with compressed work weeks in a pilot program; Lomas Financial Group, Ohio Bell, and Wells Fargo Bank have shifted to the four-day schedule in selected departments.

*Part-time work:* Arrangements in which employees work less than the standard forty-hour week. Many of the companies listed in this book provide full benefits for part-timers who work at least twenty hours each week. A few have created special programs to allow parents returning from leave to phase back in to work on a part-time schedule, generally for a specified period and with full benefits.

- Most of the companies in this book will work out part-time arrangements with individual workers, NCNB has created a novel program to ensure that part-time professionals don't fall off the career track. Joy Cone is one of the few companies to offer many part-time production jobs.
- Arthur Andersen and IBM offer part-time phase-in for new parents for three years from the date of birth or adoption. The Time Inc. Magazine Company offers an open-ended phase-in. Several companies offer phase-ins on tighter schedules, among them Corning, Hemmings Motor News, Lan-

caster Laboratories, Lotus Development Corp., NCNB, Ohio Bell, and Procter & Gamble.

*Job sharing:* Part-time arrangements in which two or more employees are responsible for handling a single full-time job. Some alternate weeks, some split each day or each week. We heard of one arrangement where three workers shared two jobs and each took a month off after working for two.

- Steelcase, Donnelly Corp., and Rolscreen have had job-sharing programs for a number of years; participants include production workers and managers.

*Work-at-home:* Sometimes called telecommuting, work-at-home programs allow workers to do some of their work from home.

- Most companies allow some work-at-home on an informal basis. AT&T, Du Pont, IBM, and Levi Strauss & Company have experimented with more formal programs.

## 4. Additional family support systems

Companies are finding more and more ways to ease conflicts between work and family, from financial aid for adoption to help with such mundane tasks as laundry and transportation. Some of the programs are costly; some of the most creative are both simple and inexpensive.

- Spouse-relocation assistance has become an increasingly important benefit as more workers find their careers linked to those of their spouses. Atlantic Richfield Company, The Dow Chemical Company, Eastman Kodak, IBM, Merck & Co., Procter & Gamble, US Sprint, and Warner-Lambert will all help spouses find jobs. Many will give serious consideration to hiring them. US Sprint's policy extends to "working partners." Warner-Lambert's program includes help finding schools for children.
- Many companies now offer adoption assistance out of a sense of fairness to the parents who were sometimes left out of the first round of family benefits. Some companies specifically match adoption aid to the average cost of childbirth. Others recognize that the costs of adoption can go much higher. Thirty of the companies in this book offer adoption-assistance plans. The best of them, which reimburse a maximum of $3,000 per child, are offered by Apple Computer, Leo Burnett Company, Campbell Soup Company, Hallmark

Cards, Lancaster Laboratories, J. P. Morgan & Co., and Ohio Bell.

- Some companies offer gifts to new parents or new babies. Allstate gives out free infant car seats to new parents. Genentech offers one share of stock to new babies. Herman Miller makes a present of a rocking chair or a $100 savings bond. Apple Computer and G. T. Water Products give new parents $500. Fel-Pro tops them all with gifts of $1,000. The company also gives $100 to newlyweds and to employees' children who graduate from high school.

- Beth Israel Hospital, Hewitt Associates, and The New England provide "mothers' rooms" for breast-feeding mothers. Beth Israel's program includes advice on working and nursing.

- Ohio Bell provides a "Teen Line" counseling service, open to both parents and teens.

- Fel-Pro offers college scholarships to large numbers of employees' children. More than 1,000 have benefited from the program, and quite a few of those now work at the company. The Bureau of National Affairs, S. C. Johnson & Son, J. P. Morgan & Co., The New England, Syntex, and Wells Fargo Bank also offer scholarship programs.

- Lunchtime seminars on family issues can also be helpful to employees. These might range from discussions on financial planning for elders to talks on sleep problems of young children. Half of the companies in this book offer some program of family-related seminars. Some back them up by helping to organize support groups for those with similar family concerns.

- A number of companies maintain family-resource libraries, among them The Bureau of National Affairs, HBO, Hallmark Cards, Hewitt Associates, IBM, Levi Strauss & Company, The New England, Ohio Bell, Paul Revere Insurance, St. Paul Fire and Marine, Steelcase, The Travelers Companies, and Wells Fargo Bank.

- Hewitt Associates and Numerica Financial Corp. have family-resource consultants on staff.

- The New England, SAS Institute, and Steelcase offer take-home dinners from the companies' cafeterias. SAS institute's cafeteria will even sell personalized birthday cakes.

- An employee convenience center at Riverside Methodist Hospital in Columbus, Ohio, will do grocery shopping, rent videos, and drop off or pick up dry cleaning for employees while they work. Massachusetts Mutual Life Insurance Co. has on-site dry cleaning and shoe repair. Wilton Connor Packaging provides door-to-door transportation in employee-driven vans, a low-cost on-site laundry service, and a children's clothing swap center.

## 5. Management sensitivity to family issues

The best policies in the world don't mean a thing if managers don't understand and get behind them, or if there is no real support for them from the top levels of the company. At many companies, written policies say one thing while management's actions say another. Small companies can be extremely flexible and understanding without any written policies, if their managers are tuned in to employees' needs. At larger companies it can be more difficult to ensure cooperation from front-line managers. The better companies realize that if they want progressive policies to reach all of their workers, if they want to move beyond "the luck of the draw"—where some workers have understanding managers and others don't—they need to create training programs and systems to reinforce the company's family-responsive goals.

- IBM, NCNB, and Johnson & Johnson have instituted mandatory training programs for all of their managers. Corning puts all managers *and professionals* through a training program. Other companies with management training programs on family issues include Du Pont, John Hancock Mutual Life Insurance Co., Kemper National Insurance Companies, Merck & Co., The Travelers Companies, US Sprint, Warner-Lambert, and Wells Fargo Bank.

## 6. Alternative career paths

The most helpful and understanding company in the world will ultimately be a frustrating place to work if employees who take advantage of flexible work options find their career progress stopped. Many law firms, for example, have begun to allow some flexibility, but continue to consider anything but full-time commitment a step off the partnership track. The better companies are working to find ways to ensure career advancement to excellent workers who choose to work alternative schedules during periods of their lives for family reasons.

- NCNB has assigned a vice president to monitor the career progress of part-time professionals.

# Index by Company Size (number of U.S. employees)

Since the choice of family-care options is often influenced by company size, we have here grouped the companies mentioned in the book by the size of their employee populations. (Profiled "Medalist" companies are indicated by boldface type.)

FEWER THAN 100 EMPLOYEES:

Joseph Alfandre & Co., Inc. (70)

**Alley's General Store (25)**

Bowles Corporation (12)

**Dunning, Forman, Kirrane & Terry (21)**

Edmar Corporation (20)

G. T. Water Products (32)

Green's Stationery (18)

Hemmings Motor News (75)

International Transcript (30)

New London Trust (85)

Oliver Wight (17)

Overseas Adventure Travel (20)

White Flower Farm (85)

Wilton Connor Packaging (75)

100 TO 500 EMPLOYEES:

B&B Associates (220)

Berkshire Life (350)

Business Office Supply Co., Inc. (BOSCO) (100)

Byrne Electrical Specialists, Inc. (120)

Fox, Rothschild, O'Brien & Frankel (320)

Group 243 Incorporated (106)

Hanna Andersson (208)

Heart of the Valley Center (158)

Hill, Holliday, Connors, Cosmopulos, Inc. (430)

Hunter Industries (500)

**Joy Cone Co. (300)**

Lancaster Laboratories (400)

Mechanics & Farmers Savings Bank (450)

Numerica Financial Corp. (500)

Pacific Stock Exchange (450)

**United States Hosiery Corporation (282)**

501 TO 2,000 EMPLOYEES:

Acxiom (1,400)

Bayfront Medical Center (1,900)

The Bureau of National Affairs, Inc. (1,450)

Carlson Craft (2,000)

Courier-Journal (1,230)

Donnelly Corp. (1,800)

Fleetguard, Inc. (1,800)

Genentech, Inc. (1,830)

**Grieco Bros., Inc. (750)**

HBO (1,728)

Honfed Bank (700)

Kingston Warren (700)

**The Little Tikes Company (1,450)**

Lomas Financial Group
(1,700)
**Lost Arrow Corp./Patagonia,
Inc. (520)**
Marquette Electronics
(1,380)
Maui Land & Pineapple Co.
(2,000)
Neuville Industries (575)
Official Airline Guides (750)
Paramount Pictures Corp.
(1,500)
**SAS Institute Inc. (1,400)**
St. Vincent's Hospital (1,550)
Seattle Times Company
(2,000)
Standard Insurance Co.
(1,500)

2,001 TO 3,500
EMPLOYEES:
Baptist Hospital of Miami
(2,830)
Blodgett Memorial Medical
Center (2,200)
Leo Burnett Company, Inc.
(2,180)
**Fel-Pro Incorporated (2,100)**
First Hawaiian, Inc. (2,300)
Georgia Baptist Medical Center (2,500)
Hewitt Associates (3,450)
**S. C. Johnson & Son, Inc.
(3,400)**
Lotus Development Corp.
(2,600)
Herman Miller (3,500)
The New England (2,800)
Pacific Presbyterian Medical
Center (3,000)
Paul Revere Insurance
(3,200)
The Rolscreen Co. (3,000)
The Time Inc. Magazine
Company (3,250)

Trammell Crow Company
(3,000)

3,501 TO 10,000
EMPLOYEES:
Apple Computer (8,900)
Beth Israel Hospital of Boston
(4,650)
Collins Divisions, Rockwell
International (7,800)
Dominion Bankshares Corporation (6,500)
First Atlanta (4,900)
Kemper National Insurance
Companies (8,500)
Massachusetts Mutual Life
Insurance Co. (MassMutual)
(6,000)
J. P. Morgan & Co., Incorporated (8,500)
Northern Trust Corporation
(5,600)
Polaroid Corporation (8,700)
Rich's Department Store
(9,000)
Riverside Methodist Hospital
(5,700)
St. Paul Fire and Marine Insurance Company (7,000)
**The Stride Rite Corporation
(3,800)**
Syntex (5,500)
UNUM Life Insurance Company (5,000)

10,001 TO 25,000
EMPLOYEES:
America West Airlines
(12,500)
Atlantic Richfield Company
(ARCO) (22,900)
Barnett Banks Inc. (17,500)
**BE&K, Inc. (12,000)**
Champion International
(21,300)
Hallmark Cards (16,800)

John Hancock Mutual Life Insurance Co. (18,000)
Hechinger (15,000)
Hoffmann-La Roche Inc. (17,800)
Household International (12,000)
Levi Strauss & Company (24,000)
Lincoln National Corporation (16,500)
Merck & Co., Inc. (18,000)
**NCNB Corporation (25,000)**
Ohio Bell (an Ameritech Company) (13,000)
The Principal Financial Group (11,800)
Steelcase (14,200)
US Sprint (17,000)
Warner-Lambert Company (11,000)
Wells Fargo Bank (25,000)

OVER 25,000 EMPLOYEES:
**AT&T (260,000)**
Aetna Life and Casualty (45,000)

Allstate Insurance Co. (56,000)
Arthur Andersen & Co. (25,850)
Campbell Soup Company (32,300)
Corning Inc. (28,000)
Digital Equipment Corporation (75,000)
The Dow Chemical Company (30,300)
Du Pont (105,000)
Eastman Kodak Co. (73,275)
Gannett (37,000)
**International Business Machines Corporation (IBM) (210,000)**
**Johnson & Johnson (30,000)**
3M (49,000)
Pacific Gas & Electric Co. (26,000)
Procter & Gamble (44,000)
The Travelers Companies (38,000)
U S WEST (64,500)

# Index by State

(Boldface indicates profiled "Medalist" companies. Italic indicates important employment sites outside of the headquarters state for multistate businesses. We have limited these additional references to sites at which the companies' primary family-care benefits are offered.)

*Digital Equipment Corporation*

*The Dow Chemical Company*

*Du Pont*

*Eastman Kodak Co.*

Genentech, Inc.

G. T. Water Products

*HBO*

*Household International*

Hunter Industries

**International Business Machines Corporation (IBM)**

**Johnson & Johnson**

Levi Strauss & Company

**Lost Arrow Corp./Patagonia, Inc.**

*Merck & Co., Inc.*

*3M*

Pacific Gas & Electric Co.

Pacific Presbyterian Medical Center

Pacific Stock Exchange

Paramount Pictures Corp.

Syntex

*The Travelers Companies*

*US Sprint*

*U S WEST*

*Warner-Lambert Company*

Wells Fargo Bank

COLORADO
***AT&T***

*Aetna Life and Casualty*

*Allstate Insurance Co.*

*Arthur Andersen & Co.*

*Atlantic Richfield Company (ARCO)*

*The Dow Chemical Company*

*Du Pont*

*Eastman Kodak Co.*

**International Business Machines Corporation (IBM)**

*The Travelers Companies*

*US Sprint*

U S WEST

CONNECTICUT
***AT&T***

Aetna Life and Casualty

*Allstate Insurance Co.*

*Arthur Andersen & Co.*

B&B Associates

Champion International

*Digital Equipment Corporation*

*The Dow Chemical Company*

*Du Pont*

*Eastman Kodak Co.*

*Hechinger*

*Hewitt Associates*

**International Business Machines Corporation (IBM)**

Mechanics & Farmers Savings Bank

The Travelers Companies

*US Sprint*

*U S WEST*

*Warner-Lambert Company*

White Flower Farm

DELAWARE
***AT&T***

*Aetna Life and Casualty*

*Allstate Insurance Co.*

*Du Pont*

*Eastman Kodak Co.*

*Hechinger*

**International Business Machines Corporation (IBM)**

*J. P. Morgan & Co., Incorporated*

*The Travelers Companies*

*US Sprint*

DISTRICT OF COLUMBIA
***AT&T***

*Aetna Life and Casualty*

*Allstate Insurance Co.*

*Arthur Andersen & Co.*

The Bureau of National Affairs, Inc.

Dominion Bankshares Corporation
The Dow Chemical Company
Eastman Kodak Co.
Gannett
Hechinger
International Business Machines Corporation (IBM)
The Travelers Companies
US Sprint
U S WEST

FLORIDA
**AT&T**
Aetna Life and Casualty
Allstate Insurance Co.
Arthur Andersen & Co.
Baptist Hospital of Miami
Barnett Banks Inc.
Bayfront Medical Center
Champion International
The Dow Chemical Company
Du Pont
Eastman Kodak Co.
**International Business Machines Corporation (IBM)**
Johnson & Johnson
Marquette Electronics
NCNB Corporation
Procter & Gamble
The Travelers Companies
US Sprint

GEORGIA
**AT&T**
Aetna Life and Casualty
Allstate Insurance Co.
Arthur Andersen & Co.
**BE&K, Inc.**
Barnett Banks Inc.
The Dow Chemical Company
Du Pont
Eastman Kodak Co.
First Atlanta
Georgia Baptist Medical Center

Hewitt Associates
**International Business Machines Corporation (IBM)**
NCNB Corporation
Rich's Department Store
The Travelers Companies
US Sprint

HAWAII
**AT&T**
Aetna Life and Casualty
Allstate Insurance Co.
Arthur Andersen & Co.
The Dow Chemical Company
Eastman Kodak Co.
First Hawaiian, Inc.
Honfed Bank
**International Business Machines Corporation (IBM)**
Maui Land & Pineapple Co.
The Travelers Companies
US Sprint

IDAHO
**AT&T**
Aetna Life and Casualty
Allstate Insurance Co.
Arthur Andersen & Co.
Eastman Kodak Co.
**International Business Machines Corporation (IBM)**
US Sprint
U S WEST

ILLINOIS
**AT&T**
Aetna Life and Casualty
Allstate Insurance Co.
Arthur Andersen & Co.
Leo Burnett Company, Inc.
The Dow Chemical Company
Du Pont
Eastman Kodak Co.
**Fel-Pro Incorporated**
Hewitt Associates
Household International

**International Business Machines Corporation (IBM)**
Kemper National Insurance Companies
3M
Northern Trust Corporation
Official Airline Guides
*The Travelers Companies*
*US Sprint*
*Warner-Lambert Company*

INDIANA
**AT&T**
*Aetna Life and Casualty*
*Allstate Insurance Co.*
*Arthur Andersen & Co.*
*The Dow Chemical Company*
*Du Pont*
*Eastman Kodak Co.*
**International Business Machines Corporation (IBM)**
Lincoln National Corporation
*The Travelers Companies*
*US Sprint*

IOWA
**AT&T**
*Aetna Life and Casualty*
*Allstate Insurance Co.*
Collins Divisions, Rockwell International
*The Dow Chemical Company*
*Du Pont*
*Eastman Kodak Co.*
Fleetguard, Inc.
**International Business Machines Corporation (IBM)**
3M
The Principal Financial Group
The Rolscreen Co.
*The Travelers Companies*
*US Sprint*
*U S WEST*

KANSAS
**AT&T**
*Aetna Life and Casualty*
*Allstate Insurance Co.*
*Atlantic Richfield Company (ARCO)*
*The Dow Chemical Company*
*Eastman Kodak Co.*
**International Business Machines Corporation (IBM)**
*The Travelers Companies*
*US Sprint*
*U S WEST*

KENTUCKY
**AT&T**
*Aetna Life and Casualty*
*Allstate Insurance Co.*
*Arthur Andersen & Co.*
Business Office Supply Co., Inc. (BOSCO)
Courier Journal
*Du Pont*
*Eastman Kodak Co.*
**International Business Machines Corporation (IBM)**
*The Travelers Companies*
*US Sprint*

LOUISIANA
**AT&T**
*Aetna Life and Casualty*
*Allstate Insurance Co.*
*Arthur Andersen & Co.*
*The Dow Chemical Company*
*Du Pont*
*Eastman Kodak Co.*
**International Business Machines Corporation (IBM)**
*The Travelers Companies*
*US Sprint*
*U S WEST*

MAINE
**AT&T**
*Aetna Life and Casualty*

Allstate Insurance Co.
Digital Equipment Corporation
**International Business Machines Corporation (IBM)**
The Travelers Companies
US Sprint
UNUM Life Insurance Company

MARYLAND
***AT&T***
Aetna Life and Casualty
Joseph Alfandre & Co., Inc.
Allstate Insurance Co.
Arthur Andersen & Co.
Dominion Bankshares Corporation
Eastman Kodak Co.
Hechinger
**International Business Machines Corporation (IBM)**
**NCNB Corporation**
The Travelers Companies
US Sprint
U S WEST

MASSACHUSETTS
***AT&T***
Aetna Life and Casualty
**Alley's General Store**
Arthur Andersen & Co.
Berkshire Life
Beth Israel Hospital of Boston
Digital Equipment Corporation
The Dow Chemical Company
Du Pont
**Dunning, Forman, Kirrane & Terry**
Eastman Kodak Co.
Green's Stationery
**Grieco Bros., Inc.**
John Hancock Mutual Life Insurance Co.

Hill, Holliday, Connors, Cosmopulos, Inc.
**International Business Machines Corporation (IBM)**
**Johnson & Johnson**
Lotus Development Corp.
Massachusetts Mutual Life Insurance Co. (MassMutual)
The New England
Overseas Adventure Travel
Polaroid Corporation
Paul Revere Insurance
**The Stride Rite Corporation**
The Travelers Companies
US Sprint
Warner-Lambert Company

MICHIGAN
***AT&T***
Aetna Life and Casualty
Allstate Insurance Co.
Arthur Andersen & Co.
Blodgett Memorial Medical Center
Leo Burnett Company, Inc.
Byrne Electrical Specialists, Inc.
Donnelly Corp.
The Dow Chemical Company
Du Pont
Eastman Kodak Co.
Group 243 Incorporated
**International Business Machines Corporation (IBM)**
Herman Miller
3M
Steelcase
The Travelers Companies
US Sprint
Warner-Lambert Company

MINNESOTA
***AT&T***
Aetna Life and Casualty
Allstate Insurance Co.
Arthur Andersen & Co.

Carlson Craft
*The Dow Chemical Company*
*Du Pont*
*Eastman Kodak Co.*
*International Business Machines Corporation (IBM)*
*3M*
St. Paul Fire and Marine Insurance Company
*The Travelers Companies*
*US Sprint*
*U S WEST*

MISSISSIPPI
**AT&T**
*Aetna Life and Casualty*
*Allstate Insurance Co.*
*Arthur Andersen & Co.*
*The Dow Chemical Company*
*Eastman Kodak Co.*
**International Business Machines Corporation (IBM)**
*The Travelers Companies*
*US Sprint*

MISSOURI
**AT&T**
*Aetna Life and Casualty*
*Allstate Insurance Co.*
*Arthur Andersen & Co.*
*The Dow Chemical Company*
*Du Pont*
*Eastman Kodak Co.*
Hallmark Cards
**International Business Machines Corporation (IBM)**
*The Travelers Companies*
US Sprint

MONTANA
**AT&T**
*Aetna Life and Casualty*
*Allstate Insurance Co.*
*Champion International*
*The Dow Chemical Company*

*International Business Machines Corporation (IBM)*
**Lost Arrow Corp./Patagonia, Inc.**
*The Travelers Companies*
*US Sprint*
*U S WEST*

NEBRASKA
**AT&T**
*Aetna Life and Casualty*
*Allstate Insurance Co.*
*Arthur Andersen & Co.*
*The Dow Chemical Company*
*Eastman Kodak Co.*
**International Business Machines Corporation (IBM)**
*The Travelers Companies*
*US Sprint*
*U S WEST*

NEVADA
**AT&T**
*Aetna Life and Casualty*
*Allstate Insurance Co.*
*America West Airlines*
*Arthur Andersen & Co.*
*Eastman Kodak Co.*
**International Business Machines Corporation (IBM)**
*The Travelers Companies*
*US Sprint*

NEW HAMPSHIRE
**AT&T**
*Aetna Life and Casualty*
*Allstate Insurance Co.*
*Arthur Andersen & Co.*
*Digital Equipment Corporation*
**International Business Machines Corporation (IBM)**
Kingston Warren
New London Trust
Numerica Financial Corp.

The Travelers Companies
US Sprint

NEW JERSEY
**AT&T**
Acxiom
Aetna Life and Casualty
Allstate Insurance Co.
Arthur Andersen & Co.
Campbell Soup Company
The Dow Chemical Company
Du Pont
Eastman Kodak Co.
Edmar Corporation
Hechinger
Hoffmann-La Roche Inc.
**International Business Machines Corporation (IBM)**
**Johnson & Johnson**
Merck & Co., Inc.
3M
The Travelers Companies
US Sprint
Warner-Lambert Company

NEW MEXICO
**AT&T**
Aetna Life and Casualty
Allstate Insurance Co.
Arthur Andersen & Co.
Eastman Kodak Co.
**International Business Machines Corporation (IBM)**
The Travelers Companies
US Sprint
U S WEST

NEW YORK
**AT&T**
Aetna Life and Casualty
Allstate Insurance Co.
Arthur Andersen & Co.
Corning Inc.
The Dow Chemical Company
Du Pont
Eastman Kodak Co.

HBO
Hewitt Associates
**International Business Machines Corporation (IBM)**
J. P. Morgan & Co., Incorporated
The Time Inc. Magazine Company
The Travelers Companies
US Sprint
U S WEST

NORTH CAROLINA
**AT&T**
Aetna Life and Casualty
Allstate Insurance Co.
Arthur Andersen & Co.
**BE&K, Inc.**
Champion International
The Dow Chemical Company
Du Pont
Eastman Kodak Co.
**International Business Machines Corporation (IBM)**
**NCNB Corporation**
Neuville Industries
**SAS Institute Inc.**
The Travelers Companies
US Sprint
**United States Hosiery Corporation**
Wilton Connor Packaging

NORTH DAKOTA
**AT&T**
Aetna Life and Casualty
Allstate Insurance Co.
**International Business Machines Corporation (IBM)**
US Sprint
U S WEST

OHIO
**AT&T**
Aetna Life and Casualty
Allstate Insurance Co.

Arthur Andersen & Co.
Champion International
The Dow Chemical Company
Du Pont
Eastman Kodak Co.
Hechinger
**International Business Machines Corporation (IBM)**
**Johnson & Johnson**
The Little Tikes Company
Ohio Bell (an Ameritech Company)
Procter & Gamble
Riverside Methodist Hospital
The Travelers Companies
US Sprint
U S WEST

OKLAHOMA
**AT&T**
Aetna Life and Casualty
Allstate Insurance Co.
Arthur Andersen & Co.
Du Pont
Eastman Kodak Co.
**International Business Machines Corporation (IBM)**
The Travelers Companies
US Sprint
U S WEST

OREGON
**AT&T**
Aetna Life and Casualty
Allstate Insurance Co.
Arthur Andersen & Co.
The Dow Chemical Company
Eastman Kodak Co.
Hanna Andersson
Heart of the Valley Center
**International Business Machines Corporation (IBM)**
Standard Insurance Co.
The Travelers Companies
US Sprint
U S WEST

PENNSYLVANIA
**AT&T**
Acxiom
Aetna Life and Casualty
Allstate Insurance Co.
Arthur Andersen & Co.
The Dow Chemical Company
Du Pont
Eastman Kodak Co.
Fox, Rothschild, O'Brien & Frankel
Hechinger
**International Business Machines Corporation (IBM)**
**Johnson & Johnson**
**Joy Cone Co.**
Lancaster Laboratories
Merck & Co., Inc.
3M
The Travelers Companies
US Sprint
Warner-Lambert Company

RHODE ISLAND
**AT&T**
Aetna Life and Casualty
Allstate Insurance Co.
Eastman Kodak Co.
**International Business Machines Corporation (IBM)**
International Transcript
The Travelers Companies
US Sprint

SOUTH CAROLINA
**AT&T**
Aetna Life and Casualty
Allstate Insurance Co.
Arthur Andersen & Co.
Digital Equipment Corporation
The Dow Chemical Company
Du Pont
Eastman Kodak Co.
Hechinger

**International Business Machines Corporation (IBM)**
NCNB Corporation
The Travelers Companies
US Sprint
U S WEST

SOUTH DAKOTA
**AT&T**
Allstate Insurance Co.
The Dow Chemical Company
Eastman Kodak Co.
**International Business Machines Corporation (IBM)**
3M
The Travelers Companies
US Sprint
U S WEST

TENNESSEE
**AT&T**
Aetna Life and Casualty
Allstate Insurance Co.
Arthur Andersen & Co.
Dominion Bankshares Corporation
The Dow Chemical Company
Du Pont
Eastman Kodak Co.
**International Business Machines Corporation (IBM)**
The Travelers Companies
US Sprint
U S WEST

TEXAS
**AT&T**
Aetna Life and Casualty
Allstate Insurance Co.
Apple Computer
Arthur Andersen & Co.
Atlantic Richfield Company (ARCO)
The Dow Chemical Company
Du Pont
Eastman Kodak Co.

Hewitt Associates
**International Business Machines Corporation (IBM)**
**Johnson & Johnson**
Lomas Financial Group
3M
NCNB Corporation
Trammell Crow Company
The Travelers Companies
US Sprint
U S WEST

UTAH
**AT&T**
Aetna Life and Casualty
Allstate Insurance Co.
Arthur Andersen & Co.
Eastman Kodak Co.
**International Business Machines Corporation (IBM)**
The Travelers Companies
US Sprint
U S WEST

VERMONT
**AT&T**
Aetna Life and Casualty
Allstate Insurance Co.
Bowles Corporation
Digital Equipment Corporation
Hemmings Motor News
**International Business Machines Corporation (IBM)**
Oliver Wight
The Travelers Companies
US Sprint

VIRGINIA
**AT&T**
Aetna Life and Casualty
Allstate Insurance Co.
Arthur Andersen & Co.
Dominion Bankshares Corporation
The Dow Chemical Company

Du Pont
Eastman Kodak Co.
Gannett
Hechinger
**International Business Machines Corporation (IBM)**
NCNB Corporation
The Travelers Companies
US Sprint

WASHINGTON
**AT&T**
Aetna Life and Casualty
Allstate Insurance Co.
Arthur Andersen & Co.
Champion International
Digital Equipment Corporation
The Dow Chemical Company
Eastman Kodak Co.
**International Business Machines Corporation (IBM)**
Seattle Times Company
The Travelers Companies
US Sprint
U S WEST

WEST VIRGINIA
**AT&T**

Aetna Life and Casualty
Allstate Insurance Co.
Du Pont
Eastman Kodak Co.
**International Business Machines Corporation (IBM)**
The Travelers Companies
US Sprint

WISCONSIN
**AT&T**
Aetna Life and Casualty
Allstate Insurance Co.
Arthur Andersen & Co.
The Dow Chemical Company
Eastman Kodak Co.
**International Business Machines Corporation (IBM)**
**S. C. Johnson & Son, Inc.**
Marquette Electronics
3M
The Travelers Companies
US Sprint

WYOMING
**AT&T**
Allstate Insurance Co.
US Sprint
U S WEST

# Index by Industry

(Profiled "Medalist" companies are indicated by boldface type.)

ADVERTISING:
Leo Burnett Company, Inc.
Group 243 Incorporated
Hill, Holliday, Connors, Cosmopulos, Inc.

AIRLINES:
America West Airlines

AUTOMOTIVE PRODUCTS:
Donnelly Corp.
**Fel-Pro Incorporated**
Fleetguard, Inc.
Kingston Warren

BANKING AND FINANCIAL
  SERVICES:
Barnett Banks Inc.
Dominion Bankshares Corporation
First Atlanta
First Hawaiian, Inc.
Honfed Bank
Household International
Lomas Financial Group
Mechanics & Farmers Savings
  Bank
J. P. Morgan & Co., Incorporated
**NCNB Corporation**
New London Trust
Northern Trust Corporation
Numerica Financial Corp.

The Principal Financial
  Group
Wells Fargo Bank

BIOTECHNOLOGY:
Genentech, Inc.

BUSINESS SERVICES:
Acxiom (direct marketing)
International Transcript (transcription)
Oliver Wight (telemarketing
  and consulting)

CLOTHING:
**Grieco Bros., Inc.**
Hanna Andersson
Levi Strauss & Company
**Lost Arrow Corp./Patagonia,
  Inc.**
Neuville Industries
**The Stride Rite Corporation**
**United States Hosiery Corporation**

COMPUTERS AND
  SOFTWARE:
Apple Computer
Digital Equipment Corporation
**International Business Machines (IBM)**
Lotus Development Corp.
**SAS Institute Inc.**

CONSTRUCTION:
**BE&K, Inc.**

CONSUMER PRODUCTS:
**The Little Tikes Company**
3M

ELECTRONICS
  MANUFACTURING:
Byrne Electrical Specialists,
  Inc.
Collins Divisions, Rockwell
  International
Marquette Electronics

ENGINEERING:
Bowles Corporation

ENTERTAINMENT,
  TELEVISION, FILMS:
HBO
Paramount Pictures Corp.

FOOD PROCESSING,
  PACKAGED FOODS:
Campbell Soup Company
**Joy Cone Co.**
Maui Land & Pineapple Co.

FURNITURE
  MANUFACTURING:
Herman Miller
Steelcase

GARDENING, NURSERIES:
White Flower Farm

GLASS AND CERAMICS:
Corning Inc.

HEALTH CARE, HOSPITALS:
Baptist Hospital of Miami
Bayfront Medical Center
Beth Israel Hospital of Boston
Blodgett Memorial Medical
  Center

Georgia Baptist Medical Center
Heart of the Valley Center
Pacific Presbyterian Medical
  Center
Riverside Methodist Hospital
St. Vincent's Hospital

HOUSEHOLD AND
  PERSONAL CARE
  PRODUCTS:
The Dow Chemical Company
Du Pont
**Johnson & Johnson**
**S. C. Johnson & Son, Inc.**
Procter & Gamble
Warner-Lambert Company

INSURANCE:
Aetna Life and Casualty
Allstate Insurance Co.
Berkshire Life
John Hancock Mutual Life In-
  surance Co.
Kemper National Insurance
  Companies
Lincoln National Corporation
Massachusetts Mutual Life
  Insurance Co. (MassMutual)
The New England
Paul Revere Insurance
St. Paul Fire and Marine In-
  surance Company
Standard Insurance Co.
The Travelers Companies
UNUM Life Insurance Com-
  pany

LABORATORY SERVICES:
Hoffmann-La Roche Inc.
Lancaster Laboratories

MANUFACTURING, MISC.
G. T. Water Products (drain-
  cleaning devices)

Hunter Industries (irrigation equipment)

The Rolscreen Co. (windows, doors, skylights)

Wilton Connor Packaging (packaging)

OIL AND GAS:
Atlantic Richfield Company (ARCO)

PAPER AND WOOD PRODUCTS:
Champion International

PHARMACEUTICALS:
The Dow Chemical Company
Du Pont
Hoffmann-La Roche Inc.
Merck & Co., Inc.
Syntex
Warner-Lambert Company

PHOTOGRAPHIC PRODUCTS:
Eastman Kodak Co.
Polaroid Corporation

PROFESSIONAL SERVICES:
Arthur Andersen & Co.
**Dunning, Forman, Kirrane & Terry**
Fox, Rothschild, O'Brien & Frankel
Hewitt Associates

PUBLISHING, PRINTING:
B&B Associates
The Bureau of National Affairs, Inc.

Carlson Craft
Courier-Journal
Gannett
Hallmark Cards
Hemmings Motor News
Official Airline Guides
Seattle Times Company
The Time Inc. Magazine Company

REAL ESTATE, MANAGEMENT AND DEVELOPMENT:
Joseph Alfandre & Co., Inc.
Edmar Corporation
Maui Land & Pineapple Co.
Trammell Crow Company

RETAILING:
**Alley's General Store**
Business Office Supply Co., Inc. (BOSCO)
Green's Stationery
Hechinger
Rich's Department Store

STOCK EXCHANGES:
Pacific Stock Exchange

TELECOMMUNICATIONS:
**AT&T**
Ohio Bell
US Sprint
U S WEST

TRAVEL SERVICES:
Overseas Adventure Travel

UTILITIES:
Pacific Gas & Electric Co.

# Request for Comments and Recommendations

We welcome your suggestions for employers to add to the next edition of *Companies That Care*. Please give us the company name and address; a telephone number and contact name if possible; and a short description of the company's policies regarding child care, elder care, leaves of absence, flexible work schedules, and any other benefits or characteristics you think are extraordinary.

We also welcome observations, positive or negative, from employees who have had personal experiences with the companies described in our book.

Send correspondence to:
Hal Morgan and Kerry Tucker
*Companies That Care*
c/o Fireside Books
1230 Avenue of the Americas
New York, NY 10020

Hal Morgan and Kerry Tucker, who are husband and wife, are the coauthors of *Rumor!* and *More Rumor!*, published by Penguin Books, and coeditors of *The Shower Songbook* and *The Kids' Bathtub Songbook*, published by Steam Press. Morgan's other books include *Symbols of America*, a history of American trademark art, published by Viking/Penguin. They have a three-year-old son, Wesley.

Tucker recently left the practice of law to write, an occupation she finds compatible with parenthood. She is the author of *Still Waters*, a novel published by Harper Collins.

Tucker and Morgan usually live in Watertown, Massachusetts, but currently live in Guilford, Connecticut, while Morgan pursues graduate study at the Yale School of Organization and Management.